Spike & Co

Spike & Co

Inside the House of Fun with
Milligan, Sykes, Galton & Simpson

GRAHAM McCANN

HODDER &
STOUGHTON

First published in Great Britain in 2006 by Hodder & Stoughton
A division of Hodder Headline

The right of Graham McCann to be identified as the Author of the Work has been
asserted by him in accordance with the Copyright, Designs and Patents Act 1988.

A Hodder & Stoughton Book

3

A CIP catalogue record for this title is available from the British Library

Hardback ISBN 978 0 340 89808 6
0 340 89808 9
Trade paperback ISBN 978 0 340 89809 7
0 340 89809 7

Typeset in Sabon by M Rules
Printed and bound by
Mackays of Chatham plc

Hodder Headline's policy is to use papers that are natural, renewable and recyclable
products and made from wood grown in sustainable forests. The logging and
manufacturing processes are expected to conform to the environmental regulations
of the country of origin.

Hodder & Stoughton Ltd
A division of Hodder Headline
338 Euston Road
London NW1 3BH

For
My Mother

Contents

Acknowledgements

This book only exists because Mic Cheetham, my agent, and Nick Davies, my editor at Hodder, had so much faith in what I wanted to write. Without people like them, very little nowadays, other than the most fleeting of commercial fashions, would reach the bookshops. I cannot thank them enough.

Among interviewees and advisors, I am particularly indebted to Beryl Vertue, Eric Sykes, Ray Galton, Alan Simpson and Brad Ashton, as well as to Barry Took and John Junkin (both of whom, sadly, have since passed away), and Norma Farnes and Tessa Le Bars. I am also grateful to the staff of the following institutions: the BBC Written Archives Centre; the National Archives; the London Metropolitan Archives; the British Library, Newspaper Library and Sound Archive; the Theatre Museum; the Margaret Herrick Library; the National Film and Sound Archive of Australia; the British Film Institute Library; and the University of Cambridge Library. I am pleased to acknowledge, in addition, the assistance of several other people at Hodder – Nicola Doherty; Eleni Fostiropoulos; Josine Meijer; and Hugo Wilkinson – as well as Ellie Jones, Bill Lyon-Shaw, Eddie Braben, Irene Melling, Sydney Rose, John Ammonds, Jeff Rawle, Steve Dobell and Christopher Potter.

Finally, my heartfelt thanks also go to Vera McCann, Silvana Dean and Dick Geary. Their kindness, and company, helped me see the project all the way through to its conclusion.

Picture Acknowledgements

© BBC Photo Library: 1, 8, 11, 12, 13, 17, 18, 20, 22, 24; Empics: 15, 30; Getty Images: 2, 4, 10, 14, 16, 19, 21, 26, 27, 29; Hartswood

Films: 28; Mirrorpix: 6, 19, 23; National Portrait Gallery London: 7; Popperfoto: 3, 5; TV Publications Ltd: 25;

Every effort has been made to contact all copyright holders of material reproduced in this book. If any have been inadvertently overlooked, the publishers will be pleased to make the necessary arrangement at the first opportunity.

1. The Front Door

It's a small world, but I wouldn't want to have to paint it.

BLOODNOK: Now Neddie, pull up a chair and sit down.
SEAGOON: I'd rather stand, if you don't mind.
BLOODNOK: Well, pull up a floor then.

They were all there, labouring away in the same place, conjuring up the kind of comedy that would make a whole country laugh. Just imagine it: a few bright minds buzzing, a few pens and pencils scratching and scribbling, a few battered typewriters tap-tap-tapping, and, summoned to life from a few piles of plain white paper, enough characters, contexts and catchphrases to engage and amuse and enchant a large and grateful nation.

Try to imagine some of the sights and scenes and sounds: an awesomely odd assortment of braggarts, buffoons, psychotics and simpletons from the far corner of a crazily familiar alternative universe, including the simple soul who likes walking around saying 'Hello dere!' to anyone who will listen – '*Hello dere!*'; a glum little man with big dreams but hopeless schemes from East Cheam – '*Stone me, what a life!*'; a stammering, fidgeting, gossiping, muttering misfit from over a garden wall – '*My flabber has never been so gasted!*; a pair of spectacularly non-identical identical twins from East Acton – '*Oooh, Eric!*'; some rags, some bones and a grown-up son stuck with his grown-out father in grimy old Oil Drum Lane – '*You dir-ty old man!*'; and a bald-headed, bad-tempered, big-mouthed bigot from Wapping – '*It stands to reason!*' Now picture all of them, and countless others as well, crammed within the same four little walls and beneath the same small roof. That is a house of·fun. That was, in fact, *the* house of fun.

This house of fun really did exist. It was the home of a quite unique writers' co-operative called Associated London Scripts – based in west London half-way up the Uxbridge Road on Shepherd's Bush Green – and, to begin with, it contained the following quartet of unparalleled comedy talents: Eric Sykes, Spike Milligan, Ray Galton and Alan Simpson. Packing those four together was like squeezing Plato, Galileo, Newton and Einstein into the same scruffy Ealing bed-sit, only with better sound effects and slightly fewer fights. This was one centre that really held: all kinds of wild, wise and wonderful comedy ideas – about sitcoms, about satire, about sketches and about love and death and life – flew out of every window and reached into every soul. The future of post-war British humour started to materialise in the combined out-trays of Spike, Eric, Ray and Alan.

As if providing a safe haven for this stellar comic quartet was not impressive enough in itself, the building would also come to serve as a home-from-home, meeting-place, rumpus room and/or occasional labour exchange to a truly extraordinary crowd of up-and-coming writers – including Johnny Speight, John Antrobus, Terry Nation, Dick Vosburgh, Eric Merriman, Dave Freeman, Barry Took and Marty Feldman. The scripts that went out of that house would help further the comedy careers of Frankie Howerd, Tony Hancock, Tommy Cooper, Peter Sellers, Arthur Haynes, Arthur Askey, Warren Mitchell, Dick Emery, Benny Hill, Bill Fraser, Harry Worth, June Whitfield, Kenneth Williams, Sid James, Ted Ray, Joan Sims, Charlie Drake, Clive Dunn, Terry Scott, Harry H. Corbett, Bruce Forsyth, Ronnie Barker, Hattie Jacques and Morecambe and Wise – to name but a few. They also helped shape and sustain such major series on radio and television as *The Goon Show, Educating Archie, Hancock's Half-Hour, Beyond Our Ken, Sykes And A . . ., Round the Horne, Steptoe and Son, Comedy Playhouse, The Army Game, Bootsie and Snudge, That Was The Week That Was* and *Till Death Us Do Part* (as well as generate such stage plays as *Son of Oblomov* and *The Bed-sitting Room*, and such movies as *The Rebel, The Wrong Arm of the Law, The Spy with a Cold Nose* and *The Plank*). In addition to all of this, the house gave birth to the Daleks for *Doctor Who*.

The influence of ALS, as the collective came to be known, would prove to be profound, and much of what was good and real and interesting about the popular culture that followed can probably be traced back to its address. The Beatles, for instance, grew up being inspired by The Goons as well as by Elvis Presley. Looking back from the mid-1970s, John Lennon would recall for readers of the *New York Times* how much he and the others benefited from having an 'honorary Goon', George Martin, as their producer, and how the band's 'studio sessions were full of the cries of Neddie Seagoon, etc., etc., as were most places in Britain': '*The Goon Show* was long before and more revolutionary than *Look Back in Anger* (it appealed to "eggheads" *and* "the people"). Hipper than the hippest and madder than *Mad*, a conspiracy against reality. A *coup d'état* of the mind!'[1] (When The Goons finally said goodbye, therefore, The Beatles were able to say: *Hello dere!*)

Something very similar had happened in the early 1950s at Radley College, where a prodigiously gifted young man called Peter Cook started coming over rather poorly every Friday evening just before *The Goon Show* was due to be heard on the sanatorium radio. Each broadcast was met by another pair of similarly attentive ears in a back-to-back in Leeds, where Alan Bennett was already getting quietly desperate, and at St Paul's School in London, where Jonathan Miller was still growing up, and on a housing estate in darkest Dagenham, where Dudley Moore was still waiting for any growing up to start. Together, when the four of them joined forces to form the Oxbridge team responsible for *Beyond the Fringe*, they drew on what they had heard back then to help bring modern satire to the masses ('Get up in a crate, Perkins, pop over to Bremen, take a shufti, don't come back').

It was also thanks in part to ALS that, at the start of the 1970s, prime-time American television suddenly started to grow up, because *All in the Family* – the first sitcom on that side of the Atlantic that dared to take on the censors – was adapted from *Till Death Us Do Part*. Sixty million people tuned in each week to find that there were now characters on US network television who sometimes fell ill, often resorted to bad language, knew all about sex, argued about politics, race and religion (and sex), and even used the lavatory. Everything that followed, right up to and beyond the arrival of Larry David's admirably audacious *Curb Your Enthusiasm* at the start of the next millennium, would benefit from the kind of realism, bravery and common sense that *All in the Family* first imported from ALS.

Other countries came to feel the benefit, too. Thanks to ALS's pioneering marketing of its writers' own formats, scripts and ideas, numerous communities outside of Britain and America – including Holland, Germany, Norway, Sweden and Portugal – would find a prominent place on their screens for a relationship like that of the Steptoes or a character like Anthony Hancock. Membership of the house of fun became the best kind of calling card to offer the entertainment world: ALS? That will do nicely. Class was recognised, and quality travelled.

The influence has gone on and on. Comedians as richly different in type and tone as Robin Williams, Ricky Gervais, Mike Myers, Steve Martin and Eddie Izzard; sitcoms as diverse as *Fawlty Towers, Frasier, Father Ted, The Office, I'm Alan Partridge, Only Fools and Horses, The Young Ones* and *The League of Gentlemen*; sketch-based and various other forms of 'broken comedy' shows including *Monty Python's Flying Circus, Not the Nine O'Clock News, The Fast Show* and *Little Britain*; satirical news and current affairs programmes such as *Spitting Image, The Day Today, Brass Eye* and *Have I Got News for You*; and surreal little sagas like *The Hitchhiker's Guide to the Galaxy*: they would all owe some kind of debt, whether they were aware of it or not, to the extraordinary legacy of ALS, and its comedy thread runs on all the way through to the current day.

This is why the original writers' collective deserves so thoroughly to be remembered, respected and celebrated. It only existed officially for about twelve years (stretching roughly from the end of rationing to the start of the devaluation of the pound), moved location on two occasions (first to Kensington, then on to Bayswater) and was shaken by the odd internal tension, but, while it lasted, it was always the one house in Britain that was committed to creating that most elusive but precious of commodities: pure and unadulterated fun. To those, then, who are curious to know where most of our favourite comedies came from, ALS represents the best site to start searching for answers, because ALS has the best claim to be the mother lode of modern British comedy.

The purpose of this book is to piece together the story of all that laughter, by providing a biography of this very special house: how it came to be built; who considered it to be a home; what went on within its walls; and what it sent out into the world. The story will take us from the early 1950s through to the late 1960s before returning us to the present day; it will involve some unrivalled writing talents, some unforgettable shows and characters and countless strange, colourful and richly revealing incidents. It is high time, therefore, that we went right back to the very beginning, knocked on the front door and ventured inside.

2. Reception

BLUEBOTTLE: Why do you not open the door?
ECCLES: How do you open the door?
BLUEBOTTLE: You turn the knob on your side.
ECCLES: I haven't got a knob on my side.

The Origins of Associated London Scripts

'Tis hard to mesmerize ourselves, to whip our own top;
but through sympathy we are capable of energy and
endurance. Concert fires people to a certain fury of
performance they can rarely reach alone.

Emerson

It all began one day close to the start of 1954, when Spike Milligan went to visit Eric Sykes. It was there, and then, that these two men had a bright idea.

These two men were always having bright ideas. Sykes, aged thirty, was the man who had already dreamed up countless wild and wonderful tall stories for the stand-up comedian Frankie Howerd (such as the one about him having to take a couple of elephants – yes, missus: two el-e-*phants!* – on the train from London all the way up to Crewe[1]), whereas Milligan, aged thirty-five, was the man who had dreamed up The Goons. Between them, they had been responsible for some of the freshest, most innovative and funniest material that had been heard on British radio since the end of the Second World War.

Sykes, at that time, was by some way the better-paid and more sought-after writer of the pair. Not only was he still (six years on from the start of his association with the celebrated stand-up comic) at Frankie Howerd's beck and call, but now he was also supplying the scripts for a hugely popular radio series called *Educating Archie* (which numbered the likes of Peter Brough, Julie Andrews, Tony Hancock, Hattie Jacques and Max Bygraves among its cast) as well as crafting a wide variety of bespoke comic lines, sketches and mono-logues for some of those international stars who were paying a flying visit to the London Palladium. Indeed, so highly did the BBC value his services that it had pulled some strings at the GPO to ensure that he was included among the first set of civilians in post-war London to receive a new private telephone (thus guaranteeing that he would be within reach whenever the call came from the Corporation).[2]

The idiosyncratic Milligan, on the other hand, continued to bemuse and unnerve more than a few of his BBC bosses, but not even they could doubt any longer how influential his brand of com-ical anarchism had become. Since graduating from writing rather erratically for a succession of mediocre acquaintances – such as the flat gag merchant Derek Roy – to writing quite brilliantly for himself and his like-minded friends – Peter Sellers and Harry Secombe – he had established himself as radio's inspirational free spirit, seeming as crucial to its *avant-garde* as Sykes seemed to its mainstream.

The two writers had known and liked each other since the summer of 1951, when Eric Sykes was in the Royal London Homeopathic Hospital recovering from mastoid surgery. He had written a letter of congratulation to Milligan and his co-writer of the time, Larry Stephens, a few days before, having heard and hugely enjoyed the first edition of their brand new radio show called *Crazy People*. He had been captivated, his letter enthused, by the 'joyful exuberance, the inventiveness, and the sheer disregard for any of the rules of broad-casting', and urged them to continue with everything except the show's name: 'Why should anything which did not conform be labelled crazy?'[3] Sykes was sitting in bed propped up by some pillows, his head swathed in bandages and his mind still groggy from the after-effects of the operation, when two excited-looking, pasty-faced young men poked their heads around his door: 'I'm Spike Milligan and this is Larry Stephens,' one of them announced with a broad and bright smile. 'Got your letter!'[4] A large but fast-moving matron shooed them away before anything more could be said, but the con-nection had been made, and, once Sykes was back in circulation, a warm and respectful friendship duly commenced.

Each one saw in the other a potential co-conspirator rather than a prospective comedy rival. Although they came from different back-grounds – Sykes (the son of an Oldham cotton mill overlooker) hailing from Lancashire's tightly-knit working class, and Milligan (whose father had been an Army NCO) from an odd Anglo-Irish strand of the tangled British Raj – and had different purposes for their prodigious comic gifts – Sykes was inclined to employ his to engage with the kind of people he considered his friends, whereas Milligan tended to use his mainly to confuse, confront and generally cut down to size anyone he considered the enemy of himself and his comrades – they were both hoping for, and fearing, the same sorts of things. Humour was their way of criticising what had come through war and encouraging what could now come through peace, and each one's comic style complemented the other as naturally as the left hand complements the right. 'Spike and I recognised a kindred spirit,' Sykes later remarked, 'and [from this point on] our careers would run on parallel lines.'[5]

The next couple of years saw them cheer each other on from a distance as they immersed themselves in their respective projects and made sure that the momentum was maintained. The odd drink was sometimes shared, and the occasional piece of advice passed from one to the other, but each man had his own deadlines, and so meaningful meetings proved few and far between. A collaboration almost happened in the autumn of 1953, when the BBC considered a proposal to help the two writers evolve as performers by commissioning a series of six to eight 'non-audience comedy shows of a humorous nature' for radio ('Both writers,' wrote Pat Dixon – a BBC producer – in a memo to some of his colleagues, 'are suffering from inhibitions in dealing with programmes with studio audiences and are desperate to get free from this embarrassment'), but the proposal came to naught.[6] Things would start to change, however, after that fateful day in 1954 when Milligan decided to pay Sykes a visit.

Sykes was working at that time in a set of offices situated five flights above a grubby-looking greengrocer's shop (formerly the site of a cramped little Victorian pub called The Olive Branch, but a place for fruit and veg since 1929) at 130 Uxbridge Road in Shepherd's Bush Green. He had been based there since February

1951, when Stanley 'Scruffy' Dale – the agent and manager whom Sykes shared with Frankie Howerd – persuaded his two successful clients to pool their resources and buy the lease on the entire set.

Setting up an unfurnished business five flights up from a green-grocer's shop was typical of Stanley Dale, whose thought processes were almost as disorganised as his wardrobe. Nicknamed 'Scruffy' because of his chronically unkempt appearance (it was not unusual for him to remain in bed, wearing a crumpled old pair of pyjamas flecked with cigarette ash, while conducting meetings with prospec-tive employers), Dale – whose own performing career had lasted no longer than a brief spell during wartime as MC of a 'Happy Show' in the Officers' Mess at RAF Station Lissett in East Yorkshire[7] – had been a booker for the Jack Payne Organisation before he persuaded Howerd and his full-time writer to place their careers under his sole control. Oscillating unpredictably between industriousness and indo-lence, he could be relied on to tick the correct boxes and cross out the right sub-clauses whenever the standard contracts turned up some-where or other on his bedspread, but, when it came to planning ahead and providing his clients with some pertinent and prudent profes-sional guidance, he was the kind of adviser who tended to come up with two or three extremely urgent-sounding suggestions and then curl up and drift off back to sleep (and the detail, more often than not, was lost in the dozing).

His suggestion about the offices at 130 Uxbridge Road had been that they would serve as a suitable place from which Howerd and Sykes – with Dale's 'expert' help – could co-ordinate their burgeon-ing professional affairs, and so a small cluster of companies were founded with the intention of doing precisely that: 'Frankie Howerd Limited' (set up – with Howerd, Dale and Howerd's mother, Edith, installed as its directors – to manage the comedian's earnings) was the first to be established, closely followed by 'Frankie Howerd Scripts Limited' (whose role – under the supervision of its own triumvirate of Howerd, Dale and Sykes – was to commission new material) and 'Eric Sykes Limited' (run by Dale and Sykes to manage all of the writer's various other freelance fees). As neither Howerd nor Sykes was particularly interested in monitoring monetary matters, the new

arrangement left Dale, by default, in sole control of all three companies' investments while the comedian fussed over his latest routine
and the writer laboured over his next script. The offices, as a consequence, remained curiously under-used, as Howerd was usually away
either working in the studios at the BBC or relaxing at his home
nearby, whereas Dale appeared disinclined to relocate his centre of
operations from the bed at his flat in the quiet Holland Villas Road to
his new chair and desk high above the noisy Shepherd's Bush Green.

When Milligan arrived to meet Sykes, therefore, he was rather
startled, after clambering over all of the crates of fruit, veg and surplus apostrophes that were blocking the entrance outside and then
climbing up the dark and dangerously rickety brown staircase, to
find that, five flights up, his celebrated friend was the only one who
was actually there. '[T]here were two floors of empty offices,'
Milligan would recall, '[with] Eric Sykes sitting in one of them wearing an overcoat that really looked like a *djellaba*, you know, those
things that go right down to the ground. It looked like a shroud, he
was so thin. I said to him – I had a mind to business – pity that all
these offices are empty. Why don't we form what is desperately
needed in this country, a writers' commune?'[8] The proposal did not
come out, in reality, quite as quickly or coherently as that,[9] but, as
Sykes had already started sketching out a similar sort of solution, it
did not take long, between the two of them, for the basic idea to grow
bolder and brighter and then really begin to beam. A place where
there could be a proper government of the writers, by the writers and
for the writers: it seemed like a dream that really deserved to come
true.

It was a dream, however, that had been dreamed, and dashed, once
before. Ted Kavanagh, the *doyen* of Britain's writers of radio comedy,
had first thought of the idea of creating some kind of special co-operative for the 'comfort and protection' of himself and his most
talented colleagues back in the early 1940s, when he was supplying
scripts on a weekly basis for Tommy Handley and the supporting cast
of an extremely popular show of the time called *ITMA* (an abbrevi-
ation of the phrase coined by the *Daily Express* to signal stories
about Adolf Hitler: *It's That Man Again*). Kavanagh wanted to

bestow a degree of dignity and prestige on a profession that was treated, in those days, as though it was destined to remain invisible: if, for example, the material was for a comedian appearing at a theatre, the humble writer was expected to sidle into the dressing-room, hand over a few foolscap pages of jokes in exchange for some kind of modest remuneration and then slip back out into the obscurity of a shadowy side-street; if, on the other hand, it was a script for a radio show, there would be a cheque in the post but no formal credit on the air. The result was that, as far as most of the public was concerned, scriptwriters did not exist – the comedians simply made it all up as they went along. This was what the creation of Kavanagh's co-operative was meant – by protecting each member's interests and promoting their public profile – to correct, but, due to a combination of discreet BBC opposition and freelance indecision, it never quite materialised. After trying in vain throughout the war years to realise his ambition, Kavanagh reluctantly lowered his sights and, in 1945, formed a far more conventional literary agency, Kavanagh Associates, and began doing what he could to foster the careers of such up-and-coming comedy scriptwriters as the solo Sid Colin and the brilliant partnership of Frank Muir and Denis Norden.

Milligan and Sykes, however, felt that, nine years later, the time was now ripe for them to go further and finally provide writers with a *bona fide* business all of their own. They already had the offices; now they just needed to find some partners.

The first two who came on board were Sykes's own current co-directors: Scruffy Dale and Frankie Howerd. Dale (as a budding entrepreneur) was eager to get his hands on a portion of the profits, whereas Howerd (who, as a chronically insecure and self-critical performer, was forever on the lookout for more comic material 'fresh from the quipperies') was eager to get his hands on some of the scripts, so neither of them wasted any time before agreeing to become involved (Howerd as, in effect, a sleeping partner, and Dale, when he was not asleep, as the manager).

The next pair to pool their resources were two of the most promising young writers around: Ray Galton and Alan Simpson. Galton, aged twenty-four, and Simpson, a few months short of twenty-five, had been writing together for radio since 1951, when Gale Pedrick, the BBC's script editor, arranged for them to supply some Bob Hope-style one-liners for Derek Roy. Both of them were working-class Londoners, and both displayed the kind of drive that came from the feeling of having to make up for lost time (they had spent the best part of three long years together in Milford Sanatorium, convalescing from tuberculosis, before commencing their shared career).

The reaction by others to their first professional wage packet underlined how novel, at the time, their chosen vocation was considered to be: 'We went to the Barclays Bank in Streatham Common when we got our first cheque,' Alan Simpson would recall. 'It was paid by the BBC and it was a Barclays cheque so we thought, "Well, we'll open an account at Barclays Bank – if it's good enough for the BBC, it must be good enough for us." So we went to Streatham Common Barclays, and the manager said, "Yes, what do you do for a living?" and we said, "We're scriptwriters," and he honestly thought we painted words on the front of shops – people had no idea what scriptwriting was, you see.'[10] They were just happy, however, to think that their written words were now being heard.

After working for Roy and the producer Dennis Main Wilson on a short-lived show known by the misleading title of *Happy-Go-Lucky* (it had actually been so miserable an experience as to have driven its previous producer to a nervous breakdown), they had taken over from the far more established team of Bob Monkhouse and Denis Goodwin as the scriptwriters of *Calling All Forces* – a popular BBC series (subsequently re-named *Forces All-Star Bill,* then *All-Star Bill* and finally *Star Bill*) aimed primarily at listeners in the armed services – and immediately impressed its two resident comedians, Charlie Chester and Tony Hancock, with the quality of their material.[11]

By 1954, Galton and Simpson were writing for Tony Hancock on a regular basis, and had started talking to Dennis Main Wilson about developing a new comedy show that, in contrast to the norm, would do without sketches, star guests and musical interruptions and concentrate instead on situation and character. They were working in their 'office' of the time – the cosy front room in Streatham that belonged to Alan Simpson's mother – when Spike Milligan called to inquire if they had an agent. Once they confirmed that they were not yet on anyone's books, Milligan proceeded to 'sell' them the idea of his and Sykes's forthcoming writers' co-operative. A meeting was arranged soon after upstairs at 130 Uxbridge Road, and, after a brief and friendly discussion, Galton and Simpson agreed to sign up. The date was 1 September 1954, and the nucleus of the organisation was now securely in place.

There was more than one internal view, however, as to what the co-operative could and should seek to achieve once it was properly up and running. Spike Milligan, for example, continued to find himself drawn (on a good day) to the heady dream – two measures of Karl Marx to one of Groucho – of being part of a community of free and equal artists working together in creative harmony and living out the old socialist dream of labouring, playing and criticising Hegel (or at least Derek Roy) after dinner, but inside a set of offices in Shepherd's Bush instead of out and about in some kind of continental commune;[12] both Galton and Simpson, on the other hand, set out from a rather more pragmatic sort of perspective, and were keen on cultivating a context within which there would at least be a greater degree of artistic – and commercial – autonomy for each individual and partnership, while everyone continued to engage with the existing marketplace; whereas Eric Sykes, more idealistically, was hopeful of fostering a unique kind of defiantly benign 'comedy conglomerate':

> I had great visions of what I was going to do with it. For instance, I wanted [the company] to have a big block of offices, and have the whole block full of writers. Because the thought process going through all of this building would be of comedy. Nothing but comedy. We would all do our own thing, but we would all subscribe to a fund that would be there when one of us hit a fallow period. We could go in to see each other and say, 'What do you think of this?' We could help each other. And we could find and help new writers, too. It would be a very special kind of conglomerate. I didn't want it to be about business. I wanted it to be about a profession. The profession of comedy.[13]

What drew complete agreement from all of the initial participants, however, was the conviction that the organisation ought to be, at its most basic, a proper non-profit-making co-operative that could be relied on to serve as 'a mutual protection society' for all of its hard-working writers.[14]

The board of six founding directors – Eric Sykes, Spike Milligan, Ray Galton, Alan Simpson, Frankie Howerd and Scruffy Dale – could and would have accommodated several more, but, as Alan Simpson would recall, the additional figures invited failed to commit themselves to the same essential vision:

> We tried to broaden it out a bit, and get Harry Secombe, Peter Sellers and Tony Hancock on board as part of it. Peter Sellers nearly did, but he didn't come in with us in the end because his financial adviser said it was unbalanced. The deal was that we all put in ten per cent of our income to run it, and Peter's agent pointed out that ten per cent of *his* income would have been vastly more than, for instance, Ray's and my income. So Peter said he'd join if it was a set fee – if we all put in, say, £5,000. But he wouldn't come in at ten per cent. And Spike, to his credit, said, 'Well, if these two lads aren't earning as much money at the moment, it's totally unfair to make them pay the same as the rest of us – so it's ten per cent or nothing.' So Peter withdrew. Then Harry Secombe passed because he was tied up at the time with [his manager] Jimmy Grafton. And Hancock didn't come in because he said it was nothing to do with artists – it was a writers' organisation. So it stayed as it was.[15]

It did not take long, however, for the six directors to realise that they were in urgent need of some help. Right from the very beginning, the offices were in an extraordinary mess, with ringing telephones going unanswered, papers being mislaid and cups of tea remaining unmade. A good and reliable secretary was needed – and quickly.

Spike Milligan found one quickly – but she was neither good nor reliable. Slow to act and prone to daydreams, she strained Milligan's patience more or less immediately by allowing him to dictate for several minutes before announcing matter-of-factly that she was just about ready to start. Ringing telephones continued to go unanswered and papers kept on being mislaid, but Milligan tried to console himself and his fellow directors with the thought that their secretary was at least capable of making drinkable tea on a relatively regular basis. One day, however, he went to the lavatory and was startled to find that the basin was stuffed full of tea leaves; summoning the secretary to the smallest room, he looked at her suspiciously, then stooped down, stared at the leaves, stood up straight again, narrowed his eyes and declared, 'You are going on a long journey.'[16] He only meant it as a joke – he was actually in quite a good mood that morning – but she took it as a heavy hint and shot straight out of the building. A good and reliable secretary was needed – and quickly.

Alan Simpson said that he knew someone – an old school friend of his from Mitcham County Grammar – whose skills, intelligence and personality would fit the bill very neatly indeed: a young woman by the name of Beryl Vertue. The only problem was that she had already told him three months before that she was not interested in changing jobs. She lived in Mitcham at the time with her husband, Clem (another one of Simpson's old school friends), and, as she had only recently recovered from an attack of tuberculosis of the lung, was working in a relatively undemanding post in an insurance office nearby. When Simpson called her again, therefore, her response was nothing more positive than coolly polite, but, as she had no wish to cause embarrassment to an old friend (who this time had more or less promised his fellow directors that he would get her to attend an interview), she agreed to take the trolley-bus to Shepherd's Bush and listen patiently to what was on offer. It would turn out to be a trip that would change her entire life.

She could not quite believe what she was seeing when, on the damp and chilly morning of 1 January 1955, she walked up the busy Uxbridge Road, saw the customers crowding around the crates of fresh pineapples and bananas outside the greengrocer's, and then pushed open the battered green door, made her way into the building and went all the way up to the fifth floor. Once inside, she came face to face with the decidedly unorthodox board of directors. Spike

Milligan, his dark eyes darting nervily from side to side, was sitting hunched up in his chair, looking tow-haired and crumpled in a scruffy white shirt with braces and a well-worn pair of woollen trousers; Eric Sykes, seeming pale and thin, was busy at his desk, searching through all of his papers with an urgency that suggested he had either mislaid a large pay cheque or was trying to find a stray sandwich; and Ray Galton and Alan Simpson were sitting together on the floor surrounded by what appeared to be piles of note papers and scripts. Vertue found a spare wooden chair and sat down nervously before them all, resting her handbag on her lap and trying hard not to look too uneasy.

Milligan then decided, unbidden and without any warning, to begin the interview and promptly took charge of how it was conducted, firing out disconnected questions in a rapid and scattershot fashion: Where do you live? Can you make cups of tea? Do you have any brothers? What kind of tea do you drink yourself? Do you have any sisters? What makes you laugh? How good are you at making cups of tea? What do you do with the tea leaves? On and on he went, allowing only the briefest of interjections from his fellow directors, eliciting plenty of laughs in the process but precious little information that Vertue considered pertinent. No one asked her about typing or dictation speeds, and no one inquired about references. The whole experience seemed to her like some kind of funny, silly dream, and so she decided to enjoy it until it was over, believing that she would then be allowed to get up, go back down the staircase and step back out again into reality. It did not prove, however, to be anything like as simple or straightforward as that.

After Vertue had responded to all of Milligan's questions, he fell silent for a moment, and then, quite suddenly, jumped up and declared excitedly: 'Well, I think you'll be perfect for us.'[17] Eric Sykes agreed, and so did Galton and Simpson. Vertue was shocked: she had almost forgotten that she had gone there to make it clear that she was not interested in changing jobs. Racking her brains for some means whereby she could try to make her escape, she came up with something that seemed like the smartest of strategies: 'I thought, well, I could price myself out of the job – that's the way to get out of it.'[18] Adding several more pounds to her current weekly wage, she proceeded to announce 'very grandly' that she would need to be earning at least ten pounds per week.[19] Watching the Mexican wave of raised eyebrows and puffed-out cheeks that this statement managed to provoke, she sensed that the strategy had almost certainly worked. '*How* much?' someone exclaimed. '*Ten* pounds? Ten pounds a *week*? We can't afford that!'[20] Vertue, feeling inwardly rather pleased with her crafty tactics, was already preparing to leave when one of the other writers was struck with a sudden insight: 'Hang on: if you divide it up between four, that would only be two pounds ten shillings a week each!' They all looked at each other and nodded: 'Of course!'[21] A stunned Beryl Vertue was then informed that she was hired. She had tricked herself into a new job.

Once the shock had subsided, however, Beryl Vertue began to enjoy being right at the heart of this unique comic hubbub:

> It was a bit like working in a little rabbit warren. The offices didn't really have a proper reception area; it wasn't as grand as that. The 'reception area' was my office. You opened the door to my office and then you were 'in'. My job involved, well, all kinds of things: I typed the scripts, dealt with all the fan mail, answered the telephone – they had a very antiquated switchboard that I had to operate to connect my phone to all of the other rooms – and I also had to deal with the greengrocer whenever he blocked up the entrance outside with his fruit and veg – which was often – and I bought the toilet rolls, did the plumbing, made the tea – I did everything really. The phrase was: 'Oh, Beryl'll do that.'[22]

Every day was different, every day was a challenge, every day brought some fresh kind of crisis and every day engendered plenty of new laughs. Vertue faced an intimidatingly steep learning curve, because she now found herself having to deal not only with an increasingly large and mercurial community of writers, but also with innumerable theatrical agents, lawyers and impresarios, an often pompous and obdurate BBC bureaucracy and, in due course, more than a few pushy movers and shakers from among British television's newly-established commercial companies.

Stanley Dale was around, and, officially at least, he was still the managing director, but, in practice, he proved to be of precious little help to the new recruit:

> He made me a bit nervous, to tell the truth. I could never quite work him out. He was a very small man – always, always, always smoking – and I used to go around to his house in Holland Villas Road and he would be in bed! There were bars on his window – because it was a lower basement – and there'd be a big dog – an Alsatian – peering out at you through these bars, and when you got inside you'd find that he was in bed, with all kinds of contracts and bits of paper scattered over his blankets. So I was always really nervous when I went round there. I was a very 'suburban' person in those days, so it seemed very odd to me to be going to see someone to talk about the office when they were in bed! He was called Scruffy Dale and he really was: scruffy. He was quite disorganised, too: I wouldn't be surprised if the odd important bit of paper ended up getting lost under his bed! He just wasn't the sort of person you expected to find working in that kind of business. Very odd.[23]

When it came to running the place on a daily basis, therefore, the principle seemed to be: 'Leave it to Beryl.' Right from the start, she was on her own. There was simply no time for her to stop and ask many questions, nor was there any handy 'user manual' for her to seek out and consult: there was nothing for it but to trust her own judgment, learn from any mistakes and hope that it would not be long before her early experiences started adding up to a reasonable degree of expertise.

One of her first tasks was to get all of the directors to agree on what their new co-operative should now be formally called. 'We actually wanted to be "Associated British Scripts",' she later revealed. This title, however, ended up being blocked by the powers that be: 'You had to apply to the local council to get a name, and they said we weren't big enough for "British", so we said, "Oh, all right, we'll be *London* then instead."[24] The name of the co-operative, therefore, was duly confirmed as 'Associated London Scripts' (or 'ALS' for short), and the company was formally launched. The dream had become a reality: there was a building, a set of offices, a group of writers, a secretary and an official name. There was even, as a security measure, a cheque for one million pounds framed and displayed on one of the walls: 'In case of bankruptcy,' bore the instructions underneath, 'break glass and cash cheque immediately.'[25] Now everyone involved with the co-operative could settle down and get to work. It was time for Associated London Scripts to start making its mark.

Each writer had his own distinctive space, habits and schedule. Spike Milligan, for example, was soon ensconced in an office at the top of the stairs above the reception. It was here, seated behind a medium-sized wooden desk upon which sat an old typewriter, a new paperweight, a small hole-puncher, an in-tray and an out-tray and a shiny black Bakelite telephone, that he began to bring some kind of order to an otherwise chaotic world – dividing up his possessions into various different categories and then surrendering them to the regiment of box files that were stationed all along one of his walls. One box was for unused, but still usable, ideas; another was for his children's notes and drawings; one contained correspondence with old war comrades; another one stored troublesome bills. Anyone who sent him something that caused any measure of distress was banished immediately to the box file labelled 'Bastards'; once that file was filled to the gills, any fresh pests were deposited in a second box labelled 'New Bastards'.

He was usually in the office by ten in the morning and back out of it again by seven in the evening, but what happened – or failed to happen – during the intervening hours depended as much on mood as it did on method. There would be times when he came rushing into the building, having come up with an inspirational idea on the journey in from Highgate to Shepherd's Bush, and other times when he shuffled through like a man on his way to the gallows. Once he had started work on a script he disliked ever having to stop; he wrote as he thought, and, if he came to a place where the right line failed to emerge, he would just jab a finger at one of the keys, type 'FUCK IT' or 'BOLLOCKS,' and then carry on regardless. The first draft would feature plenty of such expletives, but then, with each successive version, the expletives grew fewer and fewer, until, by around about the tenth draft, he had a complete, expletive-free, script ('It's done!' he would shout to no one in particular as he burst out of the office. 'I'm going home!').[26] Sometimes, when the pages stayed cold and blank, he would get up, move over to his window, and toot away on his trumpet, or pick up a baton and start 'conducting' a classical record, until something good crept into his head. Sometimes, when the four walls seemed to start closing in around him, he would sneak out and wander up and down Shepherd's Bush Green, poking his nose into the local antique shop (buying any peculiar curio that caught his eye) or getting up to mischief at William Nodes, the funeral parlour nearby (outside of which he liked to lie down and shout: 'Shop!'). On the odd bleak occasion, when the darkest kind of depression began to take a grip, he would hang a sign outside his door – 'DO NOT DISTURB. I'M DISTURBED ENOUGH ALREADY' – and lock himself away inside, sometimes staying there silent and alone for days.

Eric Sykes, on the other hand, would arrive bright and early each morning from his smart new house in Weybridge, having breakfasted on three eggs and a scattering of chips at the old-fashioned café a few doors down the road, and then, after joining the others for a quick cup of tea in Beryl Vertue's office, he would start planning his working day. He had a neat, sparsely furnished and orderly office, with a well-stocked drinks cabinet that most of his colleagues (and their guests) felt compelled to visit on a fairly regular basis. There would often be hours when he was away on the golf course, sorting through the ideas in his head and making mental edits as he moved from hole to hole, and then, eventually, he would reappear in his office and start writing like a man possessed. He preferred to use a pen rather than try to type, and, as his sight (like his hearing) was already beginning to fail, he put down each line in handwriting so large that each script ended up as a pile three times as high as the version Beryl Vertue would go on to type.

The mood, as a rule, was fairly businesslike, although sometimes, as Sykes would recall, the wit would evade the page and run instead in and out of the neighbouring offices:

> Here's an example. What happened, on one occasion, was this. Spike's office was just across the landing to me. And I was writing away, and there was a knock at the door: 'Come in.' It was the secretary that we shared. And I was handed a letter. It said: 'Dear Eric, What are you doing for lunch? Sincerely, Spike.' So I wrote: 'Dear Spike, I'm not doing anything special for lunch, but I'll be ready at about half-past one. Sincerely, Eric.' And I sent that off. Next thing: *Knock! Knock!* 'Come in.' Another letter. 'Dear Eric, Why half-past one? Sincerely, Spike.' So I wrote back again: 'Dear Spike, Because I am finishing something off which is rather important. Sincerely, Eric.' Into an envelope, lick the top, stick it down, off it goes. Then: *Knock! Knock!* It's Spike. He says: 'We've *got* to go now!' I said: 'Why?' He said: 'Because we're running out of paper!'[27]

Galton and Simpson, meanwhile, took to coming in each day and camping down on the floor of their own cosy office. Both men would stretch out their six-foot-plus frames across the threadbare carpet, position some drink and some cigarettes within easy reach, and then stare, and stare, and stare, until one or both of them came up with a serviceable idea (Simpson would usually be the one who got up and typed it, because Galton was never too keen on the noise). 'We could go two or three days without talking to each other,' Simpson would recall. 'We'd never say it was crap, we'd just grunt. If one said something and the other said nothing, then you knew you were wrong.'[28] There was no mess, no waste, with this pair: they were increasingly dapper men who produced increasingly dapper scripts, and when each one was done it was ready to be delivered. They were, as a consequence, the only writers during those early days who rarely took the opportunity to use Beryl Vertue as a sounding board: 'Spike would [come into my office and] read a script aloud, flinging his arms around doing all the voices,' she later recalled. 'Eric would *act* [his script] out, playing the various parts, [whereas] Alan and Ray would just hand me the script without a word.'[29]

Few people, other than Vertue, kept conventional office hours during the early days of ALS. Stanley Dale, predictably, was seldom in evidence on the premises, but Frankie Howerd was liable to come crashing in whenever he felt that a routine could do with a quick (and free) rewrite ('Ooh, would you mind? Could you possibly? Ah, er, ooh, if you could add, y'know, just a *touch* here and there, y'know, er, just a touch . . .'),[30] as well as when he fancied a soak in the unusually large bath that the co-operative had inherited from the previous owner ('This one's better for me bad back than the one I've got at home,' he used to mutter).[31] Thanks to the fact that ALS was relatively close to the BBC's Lime Grove studios (as well as to the newly-converted television theatre at the old Shepherd's Bush Empire), the offices would often be visited by a wide range of colourful characters on their way to or from a session in front of the cameras, including the eccentric comic actor Irene Handl (who always arrived with her two Pekinese – Gretzel and Pretzel – tucked under her arms) and the irascible small-screen personality Gilbert Harding (who was so asthmatic that his wheezing and panting could be heard long before he finally scaled all five flights of the infamous staircase). 'You never knew what, or who, was going to turn up,' Beryl Vertue recalled, 'but you just came to expect the unexpected.'[32]

The resident writers tended to toil away for most of the morning, until someone – usually Spike Milligan – suggested that it was probably time for lunch; within a couple of minutes of such an announcement, most or all of the directors and anyone else who happened to be visiting would move swiftly out through the front door, off down the street and straight into Bertorelli's restaurant, where, over a little pasta and a fair amount of wine, the first part of the afternoon would be allowed to pass. Whatever work still needed to be done, however, was done – even if it meant returning to the office and writing solidly all the way through to the end of the evening. Sometimes Milligan, for example, would finish so late in the day that, rather than endure the long ride on the last tube back to his home in Highgate, he preferred just to wrap himself up in a couple of old overcoats and curl up on the floor for what remained of the night.

Sometimes Eric Sykes, in contrast, would finish so early that there was still time for him to go off and play a few more holes of golf.

Sykes actually began collaborating with Milligan on certain scripts soon after the company was launched. The partnership seemed to make sense: whereas Milligan excelled at sparkling lines and comic riffs, Sykes was a brilliant storyteller who knew all about the value of structure, so the prospect of putting their talents together had always promised much. It turned out to be fun for both of them while it lasted, bouncing ideas back and forth across a desk and urging each other on, but the partnership ended abruptly after several productive months when a minor disagreement somehow managed to trigger an inexplicably dramatic clash. 'It was ludicrous,' Sykes would say of how such darkness intruded from out of the blue:

> [I]t was whether there should be 'the' or 'and'. I can't remember what the actual word was, or whether it should be 'in' or 'out' or whatever it was. By now our voices had increased in volume as if we were conversing with each other across the River Thames. Suddenly Spike picked up a heavy paperweight and threw it at me. Had I dodged, ducked, taken evasive action, it would probably have killed me. As it was, I stood rooted to the spot with shock and it missed me by a mile, crashing through the window, hurtling down onto the pavement of Shepherd's Bush.[33]

The sound of the shattering glass shook everyone who was hard at work elsewhere in the busy building. Inside Milligan's gloomy office, meanwhile, there were just two friends standing either side of a massive question mark:

> For a moment, we stared at each other in amazement. Then I went down to the street, brought back the guided missile which I plonked on Spike's desk, saying in a calm voice, 'Remember what date this was.' Pathetic and juvenile, Spike stared at me as if he'd just recited 'Humpty Dumpty,' his eyes darting all over the place as if he was trying to remember where he was. His shirt was open at the neck and I noticed red spots on his chest which hadn't been

there before. It was my first introduction to manic depression, an illness that was never more than an arm's length away throughout the rest of his life.[34]

The two men would continue, every now and again, to write for the same shows, but never again would they do so in the same office at the same time. Neither man wanted to risk ruining such a vital friendship for the sake of another contentious 'the', 'but' or 'and'.

In general, however, the atmosphere inside ALS – at least once the chipped and cracked paperweight was back in its proper place – could hardly have been any better. There was a genuine sense of camaraderie amongst the four writers, as well as a shared sense of pride in what their co-operative had begun to achieve. Not only were *The Goon Show, The Frankie Howerd Show* and *Educating Archie* still going strong, but ALS was also now responsible for *Hancock's Half-Hour* (which had launched at the start of November 1954), as well as various other shows, routines and series that were either on air or in the process of being developed. More and more producers took to calling on a regular basis, countless performers put in requests for tailor-made material and all kinds of new demands were placed on the celebrated comedy quartet. It came as no surprise, therefore, that, from 1955 onwards, ALS was on the look-out for talented new recruits.

The first additional writer to be enlisted was a 35-year-old East Ender by the name of Johnny Speight. The short, stocky, stammering but sharp-witted working-class son of a Canning Town docker, Speight had tried and failed to forge a full-time career as a drummer in a jazz band, and ended up settling instead for spells first as a milk-man and then an insurance salesman. Inspired by reading some of the most socially-engaged critics, novelists and dramatists of the modern age, he started writing as a hobby, attempting to create some overtly left-wing plays with a modern satirical edge about 'how awful it was living in Canning Town'.[35] It was his instinctive ability to come up with sharp little comic one-liners, however, that first brought him to the attention of the greatest patron of Britain's comedy writers of that time, Frankie Howerd, who read a sample script, purchased a joke and promised to pull some strings to help him turn his hobby into a profitable job.

Howerd sent Speight to Shepherd's Bush to meet the other ALS directors, but the budding writer almost fled before they had the chance to sign him up. On his first visit to the co-operative's offices, he climbed over a couple of unopened crates of oranges, puffed and wheezed his way up all five flights of stairs, and then took one look at the newly dandified figures of Ray Galton (his short beard neatly clipped, his handmade Turnbull & Asser silk shirt open at the neck, his drooping pipe emanating the sweetest of smoky smells) and Alan Simpson (resplendent in a maroon bespoke corduroy jacket and a fashionably bright and narrow silk tie) flat out on the floor facing each other and quickly decided that he would be well advised to execute a sharp exit back out of the building. 'We later discovered,' recalled Simpson, 'that he was convinced that we were homosexuals and that we were going to have our wicked ways with him!'[36]

Once Speight realised that he would be 'safe' on the ALS premises alongside his two eminently heterosexual new friends, and had then been assured that he had exceptional potential by Milligan as well as Sykes, he joined the organisation and commenced his professional career as a committed writer of comedy. Thanks to his association with such well-connected colleagues, he found work more or less immediately, starting early on in 1955 with his assumption of the sole scriptwriting responsibilities for a Sunday lunchtime series entitled *Mr Ross – and Mr Ray* (which was a loose little vehicle for the comedy-friendly musicians Edmundo Ross and Ray Ellington).

It was not long before he was paired up with someone who, at first glance, seemed an unlikely writing partner: John Antrobus, a 21-year-old pacifist from Aldershot fresh out of Sandhurst Military Academy. 'I left Sandhurst because I didn't want to kill people,' he later explained. 'I thought I'd be a famous comedian and writer. I spent two months sending scripts to Galton and Simpson and their new agency.'[37] As soon he arrived at ALS, Antrobus would say, it felt like home: 'I believe that the comedy that [ALS was] producing actually came out of the fragmentation of the war. Older writers, Spike Milligan and Eric Sykes, who'd been in the Army, they came through the absurdity of war; Ray and Alan got tuberculosis, so they were in a sanatorium that was full of, like, mad ex-servicemen as well. I mean, what an education for them. [. . .] We were both the survivors of the war and the children of the war.'[38] He did not quite know to whom, as a novice writer, he was suited, but he was certainly surprised by the decision made by his superiors: 'They partnered me with Speight, this gruff man from the East End. We were so different. Stalin was his hero. He would say "purge the bastards" and had a five-year plan for his career.'[39] Rather than resist, Antrobus chose to go with the flow, and started reading Camus and Sartre and Trotsky and Shaw, swapped his stiff-upper-lipped Sandhurst modulations for a 'newly invented Sarf London accent' and, just like Speight, spouted strong left-wing opinions on all of the latest key debates. The pair failed to do much to further the cause of the revolution, but they did write some good jokes for Frankie Howerd, so they were soon far too busy to contemplate storming the barricades.

They were talented people who now found themselves in the right place at the right time, and they knew it, so they were in no mood to abuse their good fortune. ALS was not a competitive environment in which to work, but it was, none the less, a community that was expanding at a remarkably rapid rate – so there was always another novice writer (or two) waiting in the wings if one allowed a new project to pass him by.

One of these other novice writers was John Junkin, who arrived after making contact directly with Spike Milligan:

> I was always mad about The Goons. So I wrote a Goon Show. And one day I was stuck in a day-watchman's job, and I realised I'd forgotten to take in a paper, so I picked up a telephone directory and I found Spike Milligan's number. I phoned it and I said, 'Do you buy scripts or do you buy ideas?' He said, 'I buy scripts. I've got a script agency. Why do you ask?' I said, 'I've written a script.' So he said, 'Well, I'll give you the address – post it to me.' And he gave me an address in Shepherd's Bush Green. I wasn't going to trust my 'treasure' to the post office, so one Saturday I travelled up there from Stratford East, which was where I lived at the time, and when I got

there I found that the address I'd been given was this greengrocer's shop. There was a green door next to it, with a small sign saying 'Associated London Scripts', and it was open so I went in. I went up the stairs and there was a reception office with nobody in it. Next to that were two rather smart little offices with nobody in them. So I went up the next stairs and there was a room that I think had been used previously for storing potatoes. So I went up to the next floor and heard a typewriter. I knocked on the door, a voice said, 'Come in,' so I did, and there was Spike. Which for me was a bit like walking in on God. He said, 'What do you want?' I told him. He said, 'I told you to post it!' I said, 'Yes, but I happened to be passing.' He gave me a very beady stare and said, 'Yes. Of course you did.' But, God bless him, he put the work that he was doing to one side and said, 'Give it to me.' And he read it from front to back. Marked it a bit like an exam paper. Then he gave it back to me and said, 'I can't buy it, but it's not bad. I think you can write and I think you should.'

So I began haunting the greengrocer's shop. At the time, there was only Spike, Eric, Galton and Simpson who had offices there. And I would go up, really, because I was stage struck. I mean, apart from those writers, there was Tony Hancock walking in, and Peter Sellers walking in – all my heroes! So just being around such people was quite a thrill. But, eventually, they phoned me at home one day and said, 'Would you like to write a radio script for Peter Sellers?' I said, 'Yes.' So they gave me the particulars, and I wrote it, and people liked it, so they then said, 'You'd better join the agency.' Which meant I signed a form and then carried on doing what I'd been doing before: haunting the place.[40]

Three more, similarly keen, scriptwriters joined at about the same time: Terry Nation, Dick Barry and Dave Freeman. Nation and Barry both hailed from Wales (Ray Galton would later claim that they turned up together fresh from the valleys, 'all hairy tweeds and walking sticks'),[41] whereas the 33-year-old Freeman (an ex-journalist, failed electrician and former detective with the Special Branch) was a Londoner born and bred. Terry Nation (born in Cardiff in 1930) had nursed an ambition to be a stand-up comedian until, after being told time and again at auditions, 'The jokes are very good; it's you who's not funny,'[42] he resolved to forge a career as a comedy writer instead; he met Spike Milligan in the summer of 1955 soon after moving down to London, showed him some Goon-influenced scripts, and then, like Junkin, ended up on the books at ALS. Dick Barry and Dave Freeman, meanwhile, were 'forwarded' to the co-operative by the BBC after both of them had bombarded the Corporation with countless samples of their scripts.

Nation and Barry were drawn, almost inevitably, straight into the orbit of Frankie Howerd, and contributed material (along with Speight and Antrobus) to the third series on radio of *The Frankie Howerd Show* (which started its run in October 1955). Nation then switched partnerships and started working with Junkin and Freeman on a range of new ideas while the three of them waited patiently for an offer (and office) to arrive. 'Eventually,' recalled Junkin, 'they sent us to see a man at the BBC called Alistair Scott-Johnson. This was obviously the great value of the agency: they had the contacts. We went to see him with an idea for a radio show about four men and came out with a contract to write a pilot script for Elsie and Doris Waters. Which we did. That became a series [a sitcom about a general store called *Floggit's*], and got us busy. And so they cleared the potato sacks out of the spare room and put in a table and three chairs, and Terry, Dave and I moved in there.'[43]

Being part of ALS in those days, recalled Junkin, felt more like being at the centre of an extended family rather than just being on the books of a thriving agency:

> We wrote some thirty-odd shows together out of that office, Dave, Terry and I, and it was wonderful, because it was like a club – they were all very friendly, very helpful. If you got stuck with an idea you could walk down and knock on Eric's door, and he'd say, 'What is it?' and we'd say, 'We've got so far with this, Eric, and now we're stuck – what'll we do?' And he'd help. They were all like that. Eric, Galton and Simpson, Spike – they were always very, very, helpful, and not in the least bit condescending to the new chaps. It was all very *family*. That's the best word I can use to describe it.[44]

Although more writers kept on arriving – Brad Ashton (an old class-mate of Harold Pinter's at Hackney Downs Grammar School); a New Jersey-born actor, voiceover artist and author named Dick Vosburgh; the ex-RAF entertainer Eric Merriman; the former journalist Maurice Wiltshire; and a Glaswegian taxi-driver turned gag man called Lew Schwartz were among them – the sense of mutual support endured. Everyone had a job, recalled Junkin, but there were no rigid rules as to how anyone should do that job:

> We'd all come in each morning, have a cup of tea in Beryl's office, and then everyone would go off to their own office and start work. You were left alone to apply your own rules, your own disciplines, depending on how you preferred to work and what you were working on. You'd go to lunch when you wanted, you'd go home when you wanted. You knew what you had to do, but how you did it was up to you. That was nice, that was always something you appreciated, but so was the fact that, if you *needed* advice, you knew that you only had to ask and you'd get it. The wonderful thing about the place was that there was always someone there to listen and lend a hand.[45]

'The freedom was good, too,' added Brad Ashton (who began at ALS by teaming up with Dick Vosburgh to supply scripts for a television series called *Alfred Marks Time*):

> There were days, for example, when some of us never got much work done before lunchtime, because we knew we had the time to ease into it. So in Terry Nation's office – which was quite a long office with a long strip of green carpet down the middle – we might play golf for about an hour or so, then we'd go into Lew Schwartz's office – he had a big dartboard on his wall – where we'd play darts for another hour, and then we'd go to lunch. After lunch, we'd all close our doors and get on with some work. It all got done, of course, but we also had a bit of fun along the way.[46]

The trust and the tolerance soon turned up trumps, because new and successful shows rolled out of the Uxbridge Road offices like a rapid succession of Bob Hope one-liners. There were series for Frankie Howerd, Peter Sellers, Bill Maynard and Terry Scott, Arthur Askey, Norman Evans, Bernard Braden, Jimmy Logan, Max Bygraves and Harry Secombe, as well as all kinds of stand-up spots, sketches and one-off specials for a wide range of well-known and up-and-coming performers. While it looked like some kind of 'fun factory' from the outside, it felt more like a uniquely benign and nurturing comedy college to those who were labouring away on the inside. There were times when some of the younger writers had the chance to acquire invaluable experience by working directly under the supervision of the current master craftsmen, such as the occasion when Sykes acted as script editor on various projects for Frankie Howerd, and the period in 1956 when Milligan and Sykes brought in the trio of Freeman, Junkin and Nation to assist them with the scripts for a five-episode Goon-like series for commercial television entitled *The Idiot Weekly, Price 2d*. There were also plenty of opportunities, of course, for the new recruits to push on ahead with their own personal projects, such as Dave Freeman's succession of technically imaginative series and specials for television (starting in 1957) starring his good friend Benny Hill. There was even the odd occasion when one or two of these young writers were also given the chance to perform, either by design (such as in television specials like *Closing Night*) or by chance (such as when John Junkin stood in for an ailing Eric Sykes in a sketch for *The Idiot Weekly, Price 2d*).[47]

Even the most 'old school' and monopolistically-minded executives at the BBC (who had feared initially not so much that the lunatics were going to take over the asylum, but rather that the lunatics would not know how to run their own asylum) stopped eyeing ALS with suspicion and started regarding (and respecting) it as a rich and very welcome (and cheap) incubator of highly reliable comedy material. They were also increasingly happy, as Beryl Vertue would later note, to treat ALS as a trustworthy trainer and manager of some of the most promising new writing talent:

It made sense from their point of view. It didn't take them too long to see that. The only other place for new young writers to go in those days was the BBC, and, after a while, the BBC didn't really know what to do with all of these people who were offering them scripts, so they started saying, 'Er, there's a group of people down in Shepherd's Bush who are interested in new writers – go down there.' So they did. And the really good thing about Eric, Spike and Alan and Ray was that, apart from being very successful them-selves, they also had quite an altruistic view of life, and they not only thought that there was likely to be a need for new writers now that television was expanding, but they also genuinely wanted to *help* them. So a lot of people who hadn't written professionally before came to Shepherd's Bush at this time and were helped by these four extremely successful writers.[48]

Producers over at the new commercial companies soon began doing the same, and, as a consequence, the business continued to boom and the co-operative was obliged to expand.

It was all but impossible for Beryl Vertue to take on any further administrative tasks, because, by this time, she was not only attend-ing to all of the secretarial needs of the writers but also acting as their agent:

That happened, like most things, sort of by accident. One day, Alan Simpson said that his and Ray's contract was coming to an end, and he asked me if I could deal with the next one for them and sort the money out. 'Oh,' I said, 'I don't know anything about that sort of thing – I wouldn't know what to do or what to say!' But he told me the kind of things that they wanted for their next contract, and I went ahead and got hold of this lady at the Copyright Department of the BBC, and said 'It's very difficult, you know, there are two of them, you see, and, oh, they're such good writers . . .' and so on and so on, and I ended up getting five guineas more for them than they'd had before. So, naturally, I was very pleased about that – it felt like a great little triumph. And then I started doing all of those sorts of things – not just for Alan and Ray but for the others, too – until, one day, someone said to me,

'How long have you been an agent?' Well, I know it probably sounds extraordinary now, but I hadn't realised that that was what I was! I'd just thought that I was a secretary who did a lot! So I became an agent very much by default, but turned out – I might say with some immodesty – to be a very good one. So it's funny how you can do well at something that had never even occurred to you.[49]

Additional secretarial help was therefore hired to assist Vertue with the day-to-day running of ALS. Pam Johnson, her sister, was the first to arrive – 'She worked particularly closely with Eric Sykes,' Beryl recalled; 'she used to look after him and his scripts and all of his mail'[50] – followed, at staggered stages over the next few years, by Joan Bandy, Coleen Caine, Josie Mills and Norma Farnes, along with other agents such as Roger Hancock and David Conyers, and the process of expansion duly progressed. More chairs and desks were ordered, more telephone extensions installed and more pigeonholes erected; the building could not have been busier.

It was not long, however, before the cramped and chaotic conditions proved intolerable, and so, soon after the start of 1957, Associated London Scripts left the rickety staircase and all of the crates of fruit and veg behind and headed east, a couple of miles across London, to a far smarter block of rented flats situated at 2, Cumberland House: a large and lavishly appointed red-brick mansion on Kensington High Street. It felt, as Beryl Vertue recalled, like a step in the right direction:

We thought we'd very much gone upmarket there, moving from Shepherd's Bush to Kensington. We were on the ground floor there. Some of the offices were nice and others weren't so good really; they were all quite large, but some of them were built around a well. I always remember Alan and Ray's office looked out on to this well, so it was always ever so dark, being on the ground floor as well. Mine was all right, though, because it was at the front; it had to be at the front because I was the first one people had to get to. So I did quite well there![51]

Whereas Galton and Simpson had to contend with the day-long gloom, both Sykes and Milligan managed to take possession of offices that looked out on to an intriguingly ambiguous post-war scene – the well-manicured and lushly elegant Kensington Gardens to one side of their windows, and the edge of a bleak and depressing bomb site (the future location of the Royal Garden Hotel) to the other – while the rest of the writers were scattered down and around the sides.

The directors took to lunching at a smart Chinese restaurant nearby named Fu Tong's – where each writer was given his own monogrammed chopsticks – and started to relish the ripening fruits of their labours, but fond memories of the earlier, simpler and cosier days remained. 'Shepherd's Bush was Upstairs Downstairs,' John Antrobus recalled, 'but in High Street Ken we were Ground Floor Sideways. There were no Upstairs People to shout Downstairs and no Downstairs People to come up with tea or more importantly con-tracts. We would shout sideways to each other and there were Further Down The Corridor And Round The Corner People.'[52] ALS was bigger, bolder and more businesslike now, as it needed to be, but, as a consequence, a little of the old charm had been left behind. 'It wasn't so nice,' reflected John Junkin of the era of Cumberland House. 'It was a grander premises, and there were grander offices, but a little of the personal touch had gone.'[53] John Antrobus agreed: 'We left our innocence there,' he said of the old Uxbridge Road enclave. 'We were beginning to sense our importance. We were going to kick the rest of the Fifties up the arse and start a New Decade.'[54]

So many projects were now bubbling away inside those four tall walls: Milligan was still writing *The Goon Show*, as well as develop-ing various new TV and movie productions; Sykes was still crafting scripts for the likes of Frankie Howerd, Max Bygraves, Tony Hancock and Peter Sellers while sometimes collaborating with Milligan, as well as performing in a number of his own television specials; Galton and Simpson were entertaining the nation with *Hancock's Half-Hour*; Johnny Speight was in the process of helping the comedian Arthur Haynes become one of the country's most popular television stars; Larry Stephens, Maurice Wiltshire and Lew Schwartz were contributing to Sid Colin's new military-themed TV sitcom, *The Army Game*; and every other writer seemed to be typing or scribbling something fresh and exciting for radio, television or the stage. The need to monitor and co-ordinate all of these multiple productions meant, as John Antrobus recalled, that ALS came to seem, for better or for worse, a more and more disciplined and regimented style of operation:

> In our new offices, opposite the entrance, there was a blackboard and upon it written in chalk were the writers' names and their current assignments, rather as if we were in an ops room of Bomber Command and Beryl Vertue, agent supremo, was pushing models around on a model table saying, 'Galton and Simpson returning from Pinewood Studios. Eric Sykes approaching ATV. John Antrobus and Johnny Speight stuck in The Goat and Boots . . .'[55]

'It was true,' Beryl Vertue confirmed:

> It still was all left to me, looking after the day-to-day running of ALS as a whole, and the blackboard was the only way I could think of to keep track of all of these very busy and successful writers. So I'd write their names on it and what each one was doing. That worked for a bit. But then one day it didn't seem such a good idea because, you know, someone would have a gap and someone else didn't, or someone had lots of things and someone else didn't have quite so many, and I didn't want to point *that* sort of thing out, so I scrapped that idea after a while!'[56]

Vertue's discreet surveillance skills were tested even further when yet another wave of young writers crashed through the doors of ALS, including the 28-year-old Barry Took (a struggling stand-up whose material had proved far stronger than his performance) and the 24-year-old Marty Feldman (another, less orthodox, comedian with a growing interest in shaping scripts), as well one or two of Frankie Howerd's additional 'quip-crafters'. No matter what sensible measures were taken, however, there was no way that a co-operative as peculiar as ALS was ever going to evolve into something as miserably run-of-the-mill as a 'proper' comedy business. 'I hated words like "business",' said Eric Sykes. 'We weren't ever in a "business" or a "job", as far as we were concerned, we were just trying to create laughter. So it didn't matter how we *arranged* things – there'd always be room for playfulness and mischief in our particular community.'[57] Dick Vosburgh, who was still working with Brad Ashton during this period on scripts for Alfred Marks, remembered one of the times when the old kind of mischief returned to make its mark:

> Brad and I had an office in Kensington High Street, and on one occasion I leaned over too far in my chair and my elbow went through a window and hit an artery, and blood spurted dramatically. And Spike Milligan heard my manful screams and rushed in and he applied an expert tourniquet. And then Brad Ashton drove me to Charing Cross Hospital, and the doctor looked at this wound, and kept looking at me very suspiciously, and said, 'How did you *say* you got this injury? This looks like a *knife* wound to me. Who applied this tourniquet?' And I said, 'Spike Milligan' – which *really* made him suspicious! And so I gave him Spike's phone number, and he phoned and said to Spike, 'There's a man here who *claims* that you applied a tourniquet, and his name is Vosburgh.' And Spike Milligan, characteristically, said: 'I've never heard of the man before in all my life!' And hung up.[58]

It was not only budding writers of comedy who were now attracted to the environs of Cumberland House. As Beryl Vertue recalled, one or two would-be writers of drama, beginning with a recent visitor from New South Wales named Peter Yeldham, started being added to the books: 'One day, an Australian got in touch – a lot of Australians at that time were pouring into London, and most of them seemed to be living in the Earl's Court area – and introduced me to a friend of his called Peter Yeldham. And Peter came to see me at the office and said that he wanted to write drama, amongst other things, and that's one of the reasons why I started moving into drama more, really, because I hadn't done that before. So it really was an interesting group of people, at that time, I must say.'[59]

The mass media of the time agreed, and, as a consequence, ALS started to acquire a higher public profile. Suddenly, writers, for the first time, were treated as though they were at least as interesting as – if not more than – the famous performers for whom they wrote. There were too many fascinating flights of fantasy, engrossing situations, witty observations and well-crafted turns of phrase coming out of the same place at more or less the same time for the most avid comedy fans not to notice, and, as a consequence, a growing sense of admiration soon began to spread among the listening nation: young people, especially, started wanting to write like Spike Milligan, Eric Sykes or Galton and Simpson as well as act like Peter Sellers or Tony Hancock. Funny words came to matter as much as funny deeds.

Several newspapers and magazines took note of the company's impact both within the industry and beyond in the broader culture, and dispatched photographers and reporters to 'High Street Ken' to find out what exactly was going on at Britain's so-called 'fun factory', and a number of colourful articles duly appeared cataloguing the relentlessly 'zany' and 'larger than life' characters who were responsible for creating so much bright and popular comedy. The likes of Milligan and Sykes were more than happy to play up to such outside expectations – it served to preserve them, perversely, a measure of privacy, while promoting a commercially serviceable myth – so readers were soon fed entertaining stories about, for example, Eric Sykes ('Britain's £20,000-a-year top TV scriptwriter') wandering to work in a striped ankle-length night-shirt ('My latest fashion, sir, for preventing a shine on one's trousers' seat') and then joining Spike Milligan ('wearing a Roman fringe and a toga') in an organ recital by tapping away on twin Olivetti typewriters.[60] It was much the same with the coverage of the other featured writers: the tone was kept upbeat and celebratory, and only a little light was allowed in upon the magic. This, after all, was a success story, and not just any old success story but rather one whose novelty and unorthodox charm struck a chord with a public that had grown weary of excessive convention, austerity and deference.

It seems that the burgeoning success of the co-operative also caused certain celebrity friends to seek to strengthen their ties with ALS, because the new company letterhead at Cumberland House listed not only Stanley Dale as 'Managing Director', Alan Simpson as 'Chairman' and Beryl Vertue as 'Secretary and General Manageress', but also, in addition to Dale, Frankie Howerd, Milligan, Sykes and Galton and Simpson, the names of Peter Sellers and Tony Hancock were included on the board of ALS directors.[61] The precise nature of the (relatively short-lived) role played by Sellers and Hancock remains something of a mystery – 'I can't even remember them ever being listed among the directors,' said Beryl Vertue, 'I'm really bemused by that'[62] – but the presence of their names on the company's notepaper certainly lent the organisation an extra layer of lustre.

The only person who seemed singularly unimpressed by the rise and rise of ALS was its new landlord. As Ray Galton recalled:

After we'd been there a little while, [the building] was bought by a property dealer called Jack Rose. When he looked at the list of tenants he found that we were an agency and we were only paying eight guineas a week. And he said, 'Right – I'm getting you out so you'd better start looking for new premises!' Well, we became quite friendly with him, because he used to come into our office quite often and say, 'Right! You're going, you know! You're not staying! Don't get too comfortable, 'cause you're not staying! You're all going! I'm not having this!' And one day he came into our office and said, 'Right: get your hats and coats on – I'm going to take you for a walk!'[63]

Rose took the slightly bemused directors round to the other side of Kensington Gardens, to Bayswater, where he stopped, rubbed his hands together and smiled smugly, and then announced that he would soon, at long last, be rid of the lot of them – because he had found them another home. Galton continued:

Right opposite Millionaires' Row is Orme Court. We walked down there to Number Nine. He said, 'That's the place.' He said, 'It's

£26,000 freehold.' And we said, 'Very nice. It's lovely. But where are we going to get £26,000?' He said, 'Oh, *God!* I'll get you a bloody mortgage as well if you like!' And that's how we moved in to Orme Court. And it was the best day's work we ever did.'[64]

Number Nine Orme Court was a subtly elegant red-bricked Edwardian house that, when the directors first ventured inside, had the shape and feel of a slightly sleepy little London club, with a narrow hallway, a small reception area, a cosy front office and a curved staircase leading up to the flights of larger rooms above. It was a quiet, capacious and self-contained place, and a wonderful refuge for writers. ALS moved in there at the start of January 1962, after a difficult couple of years dealing with the fall-out that followed the abrupt and acrimonious departure of a disgraced Scruffy Dale (whose own private business ventures – which included wrestling promotions and skiffle contests – had, his colleagues discovered eventually, been funded in part by some of the profits embezzled from Frankie Howerd, Eric Sykes and the rest of ALS).[65] Now managed solely by Beryl Vertue (with a reconstituted board of directors that included Milligan, Sykes, Galton and Simpson, Frankie Howerd, Beryl Vertue and another agent called Peter Rawley),[66] Associated London Scripts soon settled into Orme Court and embraced the new decade with relish.

The narrow street outside Number Nine now bulged with Bentleys, Rolls-Royces and Spike Milligan's belligerently-driven Mini. Inside the premises, each star writer kept on trying to push the standard ever higher. Milligan continued to explore all aspects of advanced goonery long after the demise of *The Goon Show*. Eric Sykes starred in his own prime-time television show. Galton and Simpson went from strength to strength with the groundbreaking sitcom *Steptoe and Son*, the varied and rich *Comedy Playhouse* and two technically inspired series of *Frankie Howerd*. Barry Took (following on from where he and Eric Merriman had left off with *Beyond Our Ken*) and Marty Feldman taught Middle England how to know, accept and even love such 'fantabulosa omipalones' as Julian and Sandy in radio's *Round the Horne*. Johnny Speight ridiculed every aspect of British bigotry in *Till Death Us Do Part*. Terry Nation dreamed up the Daleks for *Doctor Who*. Countless other ALS writers contributed sharp political satire each week to BBC TV's *That Was The Week That Was*. The comedic invention that came out of the co-operative illuminated the rest of the decade, inspiring a generation of programme-makers and delighting a grateful nation.

The output of each office at ALS was prodigious, the achievement of each individual remarkable. In the chapters that follow, we will open each door in turn, and witness some of the wonders that occurred within.

3. The Offices

Every gag fresh from the quipperies!

ROOM 1

Spike Milligan

We haven't got a plan so nothing can go wrong.

The first office in Associated London Scripts, beyond the area overseen by Beryl Vertue, was always the office that belonged to Spike Milligan. It was the first one at the top of the stairs at 130 Uxbridge Road, the first one past the reception at Cumberland House and the first one up the stairs on the left at Number Nine in Orme Court. The location suited his notoriously mercurial moods: easy to get into when the enthusiasm was full, and easy to get out of whenever the creative spirit fell sadly flat.

One never knew quite what to expect from Spike Milligan. Not even Spike Milligan knew quite what to expect from Spike Milligan. That was part of his appeal, and part of his problem. He could make you laugh, make you think, make you angry, make you sad and sometimes make you shake your head and wonder what on earth it could have been that he was trying to achieve. He could do much the same for himself.

He was a rootless sort of character: half-English, half-Irish, technically Indian and temporarily stateless. A British citizen born abroad, he was deprived of this status in 1960 when, thanks to a change to the letter of the law, he was informed that from this point on he would have to be known legally as a 'British subject without citizenship'. An offer to 'correct' the situation, so long as he agreed to pay the sum of £55 and swear allegiance to the Queen, was rejected on the grounds that, as he had spent the whole of the Second World War defending the British Monarchy and all of its subjects, it was an insult to now demand any further proof of patriotism. The upshot was that an angry and hurt Spike Milligan chose to take out Irish nationality – even though, at the age of forty-two, he had not yet actually set foot on Irish soil.

He was a mass of contradictions. Like Groucho Marx, whatever it was, he was against it – except when he was for it. Like Sigmund Freud, a cigar could symbolise just about anything he wanted it to symbolise – except when he wanted it to just be a cigar. An egalitarian elitist, an intolerant liberal, a sceptical Catholic, a republican royalist, a gregarious misanthrope, a gullible man full of cunning – that was Milligan in a nutshell, and Spike in a nutcase.

The first joke that he wrote, he claimed, was about the man who went to a psychiatrist, took off his hat and revealed that a duck was attached to the top of his head. 'When did this start?' asked the puzzled psychiatrist. 'Well,' answered the duck, 'I first noticed two little lumps on my feet . . .'[1] Comedically, Milligan never looked back after that: never imitating, always innovating, forever searching for the fresh laugh. 'I love breaking clichés,' he would say. 'People hang on to clichés. The cliché is the handrail of the crippled mind.'[2] He kept on writing because he had to write, because he kept on having ideas that he felt compelled to see written down. He was never sure where the ideas came from ('It's chemistry,' he said. 'It's like the shape of your nose, you're stuck with it'),[3] but there were times when he wished that they would come more often, and times when he wished that they would stop for a while and leave him alone and in peace.

He was brave and he was naïve. He wanted to be truthful and honest, but he also wanted to be loved. After tearing up the comedy rule book, he searched for humour by treading along the fine line between sense and nonsense without the security of a safety net. Eschewing familiarity in favour of the unexpected and the inexplicable, there were times, inevitably, when his comedy took off and soared and there were also times, equally inevitably, when it fell so hard and so flat as to register a wave on the Richter scale (such as the dark night early on at Coventry when, after the audience had sat silent and stony-faced through the first few minutes of his act, he walked forwards to the footlights, said, 'You *hate* me, don't you?' and then turned and trudged all the way back off the stage).[4] It was all or nothing, sunshine or storms, with Spike, but when it went right it was truly wonderful, and it enlightened the whole of the comedy world.

Born Terence Alan Milligan on 16 April 1918 in a military hospital in Ahmednagar, India, Spike was the first child of Leo Alphonso Milligan, an Irish-born Lance Bombardier in Britain's Royal Artillery, and Florence Winifred Kettlebrand, an enthusiastic amateur pianist and contralto singer from Leicestershire. According to his father, the baby Terence often wet the bed, was prone to temper tantrums and 'never stopped screaming' throughout a privileged but peripatetic childhood.[5] There was a brief period of hospital leave in England when Terence was just fourteen months old (due to feeding problems between him and his mother), followed back in India by spells at Kirkee, Poona (where, at the age of six, he was sent to a convent school for girls – the choice, he would say, of his 'over-protective' mother),[6] Belgaum and Hyderbad.

After spending several more years in Rangoon, in Burma, where a second baby Milligan – Desmond Patrick – was born in 1925 and Leo was promoted to the rank of Acting Sergeant Major, the family ended up in England, in 1933, in a rented two-room flat in Catford. The fifteen-year-old Terence – or rather 'Terry' as he now preferred to be called – stood by the rails of the ship that was steaming up the Thames and gained a sobering insight into what he and the rest of his family might soon be obliged to endure: 'I looked over the side of the ship, and there was a tugboat. I found a carnation and threw it into the tugboat, thinking a sailor might put it in his hat. He didn't. He crushed it with his heel. It was a lesson. England [seemed] much tougher, less sensitive; a land where you suppress your emotions.'[7]

The contrast between a secure and privileged little pocket of Imperial India and a Great Britain now in the grip of the Depression could hardly have seemed more stark to the teenaged Terry: exchanging white-hot blue skies for grey and brilliant sun for miserable rain, the Milligans moved from a cosseted existence on the subcontinent (where the family's supposed superiority to the native inhabitants was 'emphasised by every facet of our lives' – not least of which was the fact that they were waited on by several servants, a full-time cook and a gardener – and the children enjoyed an outdoor lifestyle that

included regular swims in tropical rivers, plenty of hours spent playing with pet dogs and ducks and even the odd tame monkey, and
muggy nights listening to the growls and groans of tigers that seemed
no more than a few yards away from the bedroom window)[8] to a
tough life in a grubby south-east London suburb (where the family
had to subsist on a miserly two pounds ten shillings a week, and
each day began with yesterday evening's left-overs reconstituted as
breakfast-time bubble-and-squeak).

'To begin with,' Spike would write, 'I couldn't believe it. I could-
n't get used to it. I think I was thrown into a state of shock from
which I never properly recovered.'[9] He was sent to resume his sketchy
education at a local technical college, the Greenwich and Woolwich
Continuation School, but his parents removed him again after just a
couple of terms; it seems that some of the other pupils had mocked
him for sounding odd, 'foreign' or 'posh', and most of the actual les-
sons had left him cold, uninspired and profoundly frustrated. There
would be no chance of further advancement, however, as far as his
schooling was concerned: with Leo's meagre funds now well on their
way to being exhausted, it was deemed time for the fifteen-year-old
Terry to start work and begin earning a regular wage. The belief
that he had failed to complete a 'proper' education would niggle
away at him, deep down, for the rest of his life: he would describe
himself many years later as being 'embarrassingly inadequate
educationally',[10] and, as the actual impoverishment grew ever more
exaggerated in his memory, he bemoaned the lack of any encouragement at home for him to read (sometimes alleging that there were no
books at all in the house, and sometimes complaining that there were
no books other than the Bible, *Robinson Crusoe* and *The Swiss
Family Robinson*) or advice on how to write ('I never saw an inkwell
or even a pen in my house,' he claimed. 'Writing was unheard of').[11]

One of the few things that brightened his life in Britain during his
last few teenage years – and bestowed some hope on his view of the
future – was popular modern music. 'I had shown a liking towards
music [back in India] and learnt to play the ukulele when I was about
seven,' he would recall. 'When we came to England I found I liked
jazz and bit by bit I learnt to play the guitar, then the double bass,

then the trumpet. I won a Bing Crosby crooning competition at the Lewisham Hippodrome.'[12] The trumpet came into his possession care (unwittingly) of one of his earliest full-time employers – a tobacco firm by the name of Speers and Ponds in Ludgate Circus – from whom he secreted a few 'spare' cigarettes each day and then sold them on at a modest profit. The manager discovered the scam and not only sacked the young man but also had the police charge him with theft; Milligan escaped from court with his freedom intact ('He is an artist, sir,' said his well-rehearsed father to the indulgent judge, 'and wanted only to enrich his life'),[13] and the budding artist soon-to-be-known-as 'Spike' went on to toot on his trumpet to his heart's content.

He flitted from job to job during the day and strutted from gig to gig during the night. There was a dreary spell toiling as a glorified tea-boy at a stationer's shop called Straker's in the West End of London, followed by a short-lived stint as an assistant storeman at Keith Prowse of Bond Street, and a similarly brief and unhappy period slaving away as a semi-skilled fitter at the Woolwich Arsenal, but there were also many wild and joyful evenings spent entertaining local audiences as part of a dance band called Tommy Brittell's New Ritz Revels and another jazz ensemble named the Harlem Club Band, as well as a confidence-boosting part-time night class in orchestral practice at Goldsmith's College in Lewisham Way.

The worse the day jobs became, the more precious the night gigs would get. He knew what he wanted to do with his life: he wanted to be himself, he wanted to play, he wanted to write and he wanted to perform. The need to express himself in such ways was, he would say, 'in my blood'.[14]

'There are several people who have influenced me,' Spike would recall of these formative years, 'and I suppose it started off with me taking a liking to Jesus. I thought that he sounded like a good guy, I liked the sound of him. I liked what he did and I think his Sermon on the Mount was one of the most beautiful pieces of delivery I have ever known – Caesarian mind you, but beautiful. Then I took a liking to a Captain Ball who was an air ace in World War 1. When he got dropped over the lines, the English would go up and say, "Please can we have our Ball back?"'[15] Milligan picked and mixed his role models as he matured, assimilating bits and pieces from a wide range of concepts and characters: 'I got into Marxism and Trotskyism and was very influenced by Lenin who seemed to have the right doctrine, but you can't run [a society] on that line unless you become like a glutinous jelly, so I left them behind and got into Louis Armstrong, Bing Crosby, Albert Schweitzer, Socrates and men like that.'[16]

It was, none the less, the character of Leo Milligan that cut the deepest. 'My father had a profound influence on me,' Spike would confirm; 'he was a lunatic!'[17] Although often away out on patrol during the years when the children were growing up, Leo could still be an exuberant presence in the home, trying to make up for the lost time by telling jokes, singing songs, doing silly little dances and dressing up in cowboy outfits in order to play games of 'let's pretend' with his two young boys. He was an odd mixture of the formal and informal, the important-looking soldier and the self-deprecating amateur entertainer, but it would be this nimbus of oddity that would come to fascinate his eldest son, reminding him of how much of 'ordinary' adulthood was really just an act. Leo, after all, was an Irishman who knew how to pass himself off as British, a poor man who was happy to be thought of as rather posh and a modest would-be vaudevillian who rather enjoyed being treated like a noble warrior. He was also, much to his son's secret amusement, a bald man who wanted the world to consider him hirsute: 'He went bald when he was very young, about seventeen, and so he used to wear a wig which in those days looked like shredded GPO directories.'[18] According to Spike, his father remained 'so incensed' about having been deserted by his hair that he prayed on a regular basis for it all to come back: 'I'm certain he went to a priest and confessed, "Dear Father forgive me, I have gone bald." "Go away, my son, buy three wigs and say one Hail Mary."'[19]

It was through listening to Leo reminisce (and embellish) that young Terry grew up feeling Irish and working-class. 'He told me about when he was a boy in Sligo,' Spike would recall. 'Very poor. The whole area was poverty-stricken. They'd go to church on a Sunday and the plate would go round and they'd give it to the priest,

Father McCartney. He'd say: "Jaysus! The number of buttons in this plate, it's a wonder your clothes aren't droppin' off!"'[20] It was also through listening to, and watching, his father act the clown that Terry came to feel keener than ever to do exactly the same.

Always a 'frustrated entertainer', Leo had once won an amateur talent contest at Collins Music Hall in Islington, and could sing, act, tap dance and attempt one or two topical impressions, but, although he had his bold and buoyant moments, he 'didn't have the courage' ever to test his talents as a professional. 'He used to live in a romantic world,' claimed Spike. 'He loved a drink, he was full of stories. He came to me one day and said, "I've never killed a tiger." I said, "Why are you telling me?" "Well I've got to tell somebody!" I thought all fathers were like this lunatic. He used to tell the kids all these stories, about shooting elephants, strangling giraffes by hand. I said, "What's all this, Dad? It's all lies isn't it?" He said, "Oh yes, all lies. But what would you rather have: a boring truth, or an exciting lie?"'[21]

Spike's mother, Flo, would remain another abiding influence, although the nature of her impact was rather more ambiguous. She set, and enforced, the rules of good behaviour ('Mum was a great one at disapproving of everyone who didn't conform,' her younger son, Desmond, would recall).[22] She also stressed the importance of being, and being seen to be, a good Roman Catholic (the house was always full of crucifixes, plaster saints, lighted candles and bowls of holy water, and prayers were said each night without exception). She loved both her sons, but she loved them more when they did precisely as she wished. 'She was a good mother,' Spike would say, but he admitted that her moods were unpredictable: 'She was always either hugging me close and loving me to death or hating me and screaming at me. I couldn't understand it. I didn't understand the extremes of temperament. I couldn't cope with it at all.'[23]

By far the greatest influence on Milligan's life, however, was not a person at all but rather a harrowing international event: the Second World War. This was his war, his generation's war, and it would shape and shake the rest of life.

He joined Britain's armed forces on 2 June 1940. Like his father and grandfather before him, he became a gunner, in D Battery of the

56th Heavy Regiment of the Royal Artillery, and was stationed in East Sussex at Bexhill-on-Sea. The next five years would see him acquire a new name ('I'd like to play the trumpet as well as Spike Hughes does,' he told the Battery pianist. 'Oh, I see,' came the sarcastic reply. 'We're going to have Spike Milligan next, are we?'),[24] a new sense of camaraderie and, as the time went by, a depressingly fresh set of fears and foes.

The period began rather well, for him, because he found a discreet niche for himself as one of the Army's in-house mischief-makers (mumbling sarcastic asides, sticking up irreverent notices on every available wall and door, and organising elaborate 'saluting traps' for the most rank-conscious of the officers – startling sequences in which a succession of soldiers would suddenly appear as if from nowhere and spring into a sober salute – along with a more public role as an entertaining musician in the company band ('The Boys of Battery D'). Thanks to the well-stocked library that he discovered while billeted at a local boarding school, he also began reading widely for the first time in his life (devouring all that he found by, among others, Charles Dickens and George Eliot), and started to think about what he himself might one day be able to write. All of this, however, happened before the full horrors of war were witnessed.

Things grew progressively more hard and harsh when the conflict intensified abroad. Soon after the start of 1943, Milligan, like ten thousand other anxious young men, was shipped off to North Africa, and then, in September of the same year, he was moved on to Salerno in southern Italy.

The great personal trauma of his war took place at the beginning of 1944. On 22 January, Milligan (struggling on in spite of suffering from bleeding piles and serious fatigue) was on the move in the small Italian town of Lauro with orders to deliver fresh batteries and a new transmitter set to the nearest British operation point. The noise of the infantry was close and constant, and countless enemy bombers buzzed overhead and fired into the trees and on to the rocks and walls nearby. Milligan, fearing that these could well be his last few moments on earth, took shelter in a small olive grove on the outskirts of the town, and, like so many other soldiers did in such harrowing situations, he rummaged through his pockets in search of something to smoke:

> I was counting out my Woodbines and reached five when this weird sound hit my ears. I can't describe it. It was like a razor blade being passed through my head. The next I remember, someone was giving me a cup of tea in a forward dressing station, but my hands were trembling so much I couldn't hold it.[25]

The man who had rescued him from all of the mortar fire was his friend and fellow gunner, Bob 'Dipper' Dye, who many years later recalled: 'My First Aid involved carrying Spike right away back to a safer area nearer to the River Garigliano, where there was a First Aid Post. Spike was unable to speak, in what I classed a coma.'[26]

Shrapnel had ripped a huge hole in his left leg. It had also more or less shattered the core of his nervous system. Injured and shell-shocked, he was pulled out from the front line and sent off to a reception centre for the wounded in Naples, but, after it was deemed that he had recovered enough to be sent back, it soon became clear that something inside was still not right. Every time that he heard the sound of a gun being fired he shook and spoke with a stutter. His nerves were shot.

An Army psychiatrist assessed him and concluded that he was unfit for further fighting, so Milligan was dispatched back to base camp – where he promptly had another breakdown. Coming from a military family, the feeling of having let the lineage down, of having folded and 'failed', proved hard for him to accept: 'I formed this terrible mental image of being a coward,' he would later reflect. 'The major demoted me at the time as unsuitable – of course I was unsuitable. I was ill!'[27] He spent the remainder of the war as an entertainer with the combined services' Central Pool of Artistes,[28] playing the trumpet and guitar in various dance bands and orchestras as well as becoming one of the founder members (alongside a violinist and double bassist) of a tight little jazz group called the Bill Hall Trio.[29]

These concert parties were the best form of therapy he could have found, exposing him as they did to an extraordinary range of like-minded misfits, gadflies and playful eccentrics. There was one comrade, for example, who would come on stage and launch into a succession of manic somersaults and back-flips before singing 'It's a Long Way to Tipperary', after which he allowed one of the people manning the fly bars to drop an egg straight on to his forehead; as the yolk trickled down towards his eyes and nose, he would smile triumphantly and declare, 'I've finished, I'll be bound!' and then he strolled back off the stage (during one night, however, his colleagues grew so bored with the act that they used a hard-boiled egg to trigger his finale, knocking him out cold as soon as it bounced off the top of his head).

Another misguided performer specialised in making xylophone noises with his mouth while an assistant pounded on different areas of his head with a ping-pong ball, and a couple more 'extemporised' musically with an old water tap, a metal bucket and a rusty bayonet. One of Milligan's favourites, for predictably perverse reasons, was a strange little man called 'The Great Zam':

His real name was Dick something, and he had an assistant who came on dressed in a kind of loin-cloth and his skin was covered in brown boot polish, it must have been, because you could smell it, and he had a black wig on. He was supposed to be a brown person. He started by beating a gong which was obviously a dust-bin lid painted gold, and it didn't ring, it just went thud when he hit it, then he would announce, 'From the mystic Far East, the Great Zam.' And the Great Zam would come on with this big turban made out of old putties on his head, and an old football jersey dyed black, football boots painted gold, and things like that, and he would say, 'I am the Great Zam, and I come from the middle of the Congo, and I cannot speak a word of English.' He did his act speaking like this, with a very strong Lancashire accent, and at the climax of his act he'd say, 'I will sit in yon chair, and be able to take ten thousand volts through my human body and survive it.' He had this chair with a lot of lights on it, he then sat in it and was strapped in, and suddenly there was a smell of burning hair and he started to shout, 'Get me out of the chair, switch it off, something has gone wrong,' and that was the end of the Great Zam![30]

The war-weary Milligan relished being part of such an odd but harmless bunch, and, as the shows kept on coming and going, he began to claw back a vital degree of self-confidence. He particularly enjoyed his role in the Bill Hall Trio, whose popularity filled him with pride. '[T]hat was the turning point for me as far as service entertainment was concerned,' he would say of his contribution to the Trio's success.[31] Gradually, Milligan stamped his signature on certain aspects of the act, helping to shape both its sound (which became increasingly reminiscent of the Hot Club de France) and its image (which went from being straightforward and soldierly to whimsical and bohemian, with old rags instead of uniforms and frenzied irreverence in place of old showbiz *politesse*): 'We put some props on stage,' Milligan would recall more than four decades later, 'a dustbin, a clothes line and stuff like that. We had trick trousers that fell down and we even did a chorus with a blown-up balloon and sometimes we spoke in foreign accents. The act absolutely brought the service audience to their feet. I've never known anything like it in my life since, quite exhilarating and exciting.'[32] The experience left him feeling, once again, like a talented entertainer.

The instinct to entertain, he would later claim, had been evident as early as infancy, and, thanks to his parents, his nature was actively nurtured:

> I grew up in the atmosphere of entertainment. The first chance I had was when I was about seven at the Convent of Jesus and Mary in Poona. [. . .] They asked me to play the part of a clown in a nativity play. I've been a clown ever since. The Mother Superior wanted to make me black but only had some dark blue paint, so they made me a blue clown with red lips. I remember getting laughs and liking it. The first thing I did was to jump up in the air and mouth the word 'Oh'. It got lots of laughs from the audience. Then the Mother Superior said I couldn't go near the crib where Jesus was, because it wouldn't be nice. This hurt me and I did go on despite that and I took my hat off and I remember them clapping.[33]

He also asserted, however, that this instinct had often been under-mined by his own lack of confidence in his abilities as a performer. His success on stage during the latter stages of the war, therefore, would prove crucial to the course of his subsequent career, because it bolstered his fragile self-belief just when the time arrived to contem-plate what he could and should seek to do next.

When the war was finally over and Milligan was due to be demobbed, the organisers at the Central Pool of Artistes (which was now known as Combined Services Entertainment, or 'CSE' for short) intervened to ask him, along with many of his fellow performers, to stay on in Italy and continue providing some pleasant distraction for what remained of the British troops. He agreed to do so, and duly took the next step forward as a fledgeling entertainer, appearing on the same bill as such well-established international stars as Gracie Fields. 'I'll book your act that I've seen tonight when you get back to London,' an impresario named A.C. Astor told the Bill Hall Trio after a Victory Night Concert in Rome, and he went on to keep his word, handing Milligan and his two fellow musicians their first pro-fessional dates in post-war Britain. They toured the country's old music-halls and new cabaret clubs, returned to Italy for another quick flit from gig to gig as support for a popular local outfit by the name of Angelini and his Orchestra, then went back to England, managing one fleeting appearance in front of the cameras at the BBC's Alexandra Palace, and a handful of decent and not-so-decent dates at the high-profile Moss Empires before, early in 1948, the Trio finally ran out of steam and disbanded (Bill Hall's parting words to Milligan – 'Yew'll nevah fahkin' work again' – suggest a somewhat acrimonious ending).[34]

Spike was ready for a solo career. The music had been delightful, but he had come to feel frustrated by his colleagues' reluctance to progress with the comedy as well as the jazz: '[T]he other lads wouldn't change the act or experiment,' he later complained, 'so I broke away from the trio and started an act on my own.'[35] He needed to start over-stepping the mark, flouting conventions and confounding expectations. He needed to make himself, as well as everyone else, laugh. Now that the war was over, Milligan simply found it impossible not to be comical. 'It seemed silly to go on being serious,' he said, 'after having had five very serious years. I suppose the idea was to get as far away as possible from what was normal. It was a reaction to the stringencies of war.'[36]

When people later came to ask him what contributed to the fruition of his own form of humour, he would claim that it lurked somewhere in the prosaic unreality of real life. 'I got my influences listening to the Members of Parliament making fools of themselves in the House of Commons,' he said, '[as well as from] listening to the bus conductor grumbling about the crowds and arguing with the man who tried to bring a dog kennel or a double-bass on to the bus. My influences were all around me, in real life.'[37]

He did draw inspiration from a number of other sources, however, including American vaudeville and movie comedians such as the Marx Brothers and W.C. Fields, as well as from the 'nonsense poet' Edward Lear, the British-born Canadian-based humorist Stephen Leacock and the English comic writer and journalist J.B. Morton. He marvelled at the Marx Brothers (and the brilliant writers who worked for them – a list that included S.J. Perelman, George S. Kaufman, Morrie Ryskind, Ben Hecht, Arthur Sheekman, Harry Ruby and Bert Kalmar) for their sharp, pacey, pun-laden and sardonic 'sideways' style of eliciting laughs (e.g.: WOMAN: 'You must leave my room – we must have regard for certain conventions!' GROUCHO: 'One guy isn't enough – she's gotta have a convention!'; GROUCHO: 'Either this man is dead or my watch has stopped!'; GROUCHO: 'Now here is a little peninsula, and here is a viaduct leading over to the mainland'. CHICO: 'Why a duck?').[38] He also adored W.C. Fields for his artfully devious verbosity ('Don't be a luddy duddy. Don't be a moon calf. Don't be a jabbernowl. You're not *those*, are you?'),[39] audacious acerbity ('There is not a man in America who has not had a secret ambition to boot an infant')[40] and sheer mischievousness (only Fields, for example, would have dared to enrage the censors by having his character knock back the drink at a place called the Black Pussy Café).

Edward Lear's richly surreal and comical poetry was another enduring source of fascination for Milligan, who began writing his own Lear-like limericks during the war. The first one (he claimed) was a dark little ditty he dreamed up to tease a somnambulant comrade:

> *There was a young man called Edser,*
> *When wanted was always in bed, sir.*
> *One day at one,*
> *They fired the gun,*
> *And Edser, in bed, sir, was dead, sir.*[41]

Besides empathising with the manic-depressive Lear's lifelong battle against what he called 'The Morbids' – those dark bouts of mental distortion that intruded so rudely on his moods – Milligan always revered Lear for his rare facility of verbal invention (a stuffed rhinoceros, for example, became a 'diaphanous doorscraper'; a 'blue Boss-Woss' was plopped into 'a perpendicular, spicular, orbicular, quadrangular, circular depth of soft mud'; and exotic creatures called 'Quangle-Wangles', 'Pobbles' and 'Jumblies' were allowed to inhabit the texts).

Milligan took from Stephen Leacock (who satirised, in such short story collections as *Sunshine Sketches of a Little Town* and *Arcadian Adventures with the Idle Rich*, the common insularities of modern life) an appreciation of the resonance of the odd but well-turned phrase (such as: 'Lord Ronald said nothing; he flung himself from the room, flung himself upon his horse and rode madly off in all directions'),[42] as well as a keen appetite for light-hearted parodies of well-known literary figures, devices and genres (echoes, for example, of Leacock's 1911 Sherlock Holmes spoof, 'Maddened by Mystery: or, The Defective Detective', would be evident in several of Milligan's own efforts during the 1950s[43]).

As for J.B. Morton (who, under the pseudonym of 'Beachcomber', contributed a humorous column called 'By the Way' to the *Daily Express* from 1924 to 1975), Milligan had been a fan of the writer's work since childhood, when he and his brother used to keep the cuttings in a scrapbook and act out and embellish some of the episodes. Captivated by such recurring comedic archetypes as the eccentric inventor Dr Strabismus of Utrecht, the con-artist Captain de Courcy Foulenough, the fiercely nationalistic British ambassador Great White Carstairs, the decadent headmaster Dr Smart-Allick and the crustily pedantic Mr Justice Cocklecarrot, Spike would go on, eventually, to create his own repertory of comedy characters (and, by his own admission,[44] would model one of them – *The Goon Show's* famously feckless Bloodnok – on Beachcomber's spectacularly shifty Foulenough).

In sum, Spike Milligan drew inspiration from clever, playful, non-conformist wits who would rather be true to what they felt was real and right than pander to what they felt was fashionable and popular. Each ingredient would make a difference to the final mix.

It took time, however, for these various strands to bind themselves together, and, as Milligan would acknowledge, there were several months after the demise of the Bill Hall Trio when the budding writer and performer 'just sort of wandered around' the well-known 'demob' haunts of London.[45] Among the regular places he frequented was Allen's Club in Soho (where, if one knew the right people, one could 'eat now and pay later') and the Lyon's Corner House in Coventry Street (which stayed open through the night and always accommodated a good number of ex-servicemen). Milligan did what every would-be entertainer of the era tried to do: pick up advice and gossip, make useful contacts and seek out opportunities to perform. It was a struggle, but he persisted.

He was eventually taken under the wing of Jimmy Grafton, the proprietor of a famously convivial London pub (situated at 2, Strutton Ground in Victoria) by the name of the Grafton Arms. Recently demobbed, Grafton had already re-established himself in civilian life not only as a full-time publican but also as a part-time comedy scriptwriter, and one of his regular customers, Derek Roy, had just been installed alongside Frankie Howerd as a resident comic on the BBC's hugely popular radio show *Variety Bandbox* (thus guaranteeing the publican a fortnightly writing commission). Impressed by Milligan's quick and distinctive wit around the bar, Grafton and his wife found a room for him in the attic and invited him to help craft some suitable material for Derek Roy.

The arrangement worked rather well: Milligan would dream up all kinds of unorthodox ideas in his cosy little garret while Grafton supervised the downstairs bar; after midnight, the two men would meet up, share a drink, and Milligan would dazzle Grafton with his brightly creative imagination, and Grafton would enlighten Milligan with his disciplined attention to structure, detail and the particular needs (and limitations) of the specific recipient of their comedy scripts.

Spike began, hesitantly, by trying to write very basic little gags with a slightly surreal edge, such as:

Q: 'Dear Sir, my wife has just made a pancake ten feet in circumference. Is this a record?'
A: 'I don't know, try playing it on the gramophone.'

Q: 'Dear Sir, when a girl goes out walking with two boys should she walk in the middle?'
A: 'No, the two boys should walk in the middle.'[46]

Some of the material worked, but much of it did not – at least not when delivered by conventional comedy performers. Milligan wanted to work and wanted to write, but, both technically and temperamentally, he was just not suited to producing rack after rack of *prêt-à-porter* gags for the nightly needs of passing stand-ups. It was like a cow trying to help make a sausage: unnatural, unwise and suicidally perverse. Only when Milligan started pursuing the true heart of his humour, instead of seeking meekly to turn a murmur of it into a cheap and superficial commodity, did he begin to fashion a real future.

He did not so much 'do an act' as perform a weird sort of whimsical puzzle. 'Normally,' he later explained, 'a comic comes on to a real fanfare of upbeat music. For me, there was nothing. Then, from the back of the stage, wearing a pair of zip-up slippers, I'd appear going "Der-dum, der-doh – der-doh, der-dum."' The audience that witnessed this would sit nervously in silence, waiting and wondering as to whether this wild-haired, dark-eyed, pencil-thin figure was building up to a recognisable punchline or was destined merely to fizzle out with an embarrassing failure. Milligan, holding his nerve, kept moving in his odd little quick-slow zig-zaggy way, waiting until he could hear some mumbles of confusion before heading up towards the centre of the stage. 'Eventually,' he recalled, 'I'd make it to the microphone and say, "I must be a big disappointment to you."'[47]

He was not the only comedian to depict the old model of the music-hall droll at its most dark and devious – the great Lancastrian performer Frank Randle (a veteran of the Northern halls), was, in many ways, just as dangerous, unpredictable and pigheadedly contrary, on stage, as Milligan ever was – but Spike was certainly by far the most intriguing and inventive young performer to attempt something so reckless in post-war London. He fascinated, he unnerved and he amused, and no one knew what next to expect.

A bid to win a residency at London's best-known home of nude revues, the Windmill Theatre off Piccadilly, came to naught after he angered the irascible manager, Vivian Van Damm ('V.D.' for short), by apologising for turning up fully clothed. On 10 March 1949, however, he did manage to get an audition before the BBC, and, as the following report card confirms, his performance elicited a relatively positive response:

SPIKE MILLIGAN. (Comedian.)

c/o Jimmy Grafton, Graftons, Strutton Ground, Victoria, SW1.
Tel. ABB 3266.

Tall, good looking young man
10 March, 1949. (Nuffield Centre Show.)
PERFORMANCE: Patter, burlesque impressions, vocal finish etc.
9 minutes.
EXPERIENCE: T.Vd as member of the Bill Hall Trio 1947 and broadcast in the *Hip-Hip-Hoo-Roy* series.
REMARKS: Talent, good looks and a pleasant singing voice make him a very good subject for T.V. but his material needs careful attention as he is inclined to overdo the 'crazy' parts. If the act is condensed and script vetted should prove suitable for Tele Variety.[48]

By the autumn of that same year, the BBC was using him not only as Jimmy Grafton's co-scriptwriter but also, for thirteen weeks, as a sidekick in a new radio show – designed as another brightly superficial showcase for the pallid but popular Derek Roy – called *Hip-Hip-Hoo-Roy*. It was a bitter-sweet experience for Spike Milligan: he was grateful – or at least relieved – to be given the nation-wide wireless exposure, but resentful of having to play such a modest role in what he regarded (in spite of his own contributions) as a thoroughly substandard star vehicle for a thoroughly substandard comedy star ('when he came to the punch line,' Milligan fumed of the many troublesome radio days that he spent in the shadow of Derek Roy, 'he put a funny wig on to get a laugh').[49] Even his admirers, he felt, seemed to be reigning him in rather than helping him run free.

There was some small degree of greater liberty to be had during the first half of the following year, when he toured the US Army and Air Force bases in East Anglia, lapping up the laughter at his anti-authoritarian attitude and cherishing the attention of a military audience whose likes and dislikes he knew unusually well. Back home in London, he treated Jimmy Grafton's pub as a strange kind of stale beer-smelling comedy laboratory, trying out new words and sounds and characters on his landlord's brand-new, bulky, reel-to-reel tape recorder. Friends, fans and a growing number of kindred spirits started chipping in with the odd silly voice or funny one-liner, and, in time, word-of-mouth ensured that a number of movers and shakers, including one or two at the BBC, began to prick-up their ears and listen.

In 1951, after five years of mounting frustration and misery working for Derek Roy (whom he ended up dubbing 'the world's unfunniest comedian'),[50] serving as a dresser to the comic actor Alfred Marks, touring on and off with CSE, trying out new routines and ideas on stage at the military-friendly Nuffield Centre and continually badgering the BBC, Spike Milligan finally got his chance to write what he wanted, and needed, to write: his own show – *The Goon Show*.

This show (which will be discussed in detail in Chapter 6) would go on to be the big thing, the great thing, the enduring thing in his life. It made his name, ruined his health and left him with the kind of comedic achievement that, in terms of sheer invention, impact and influence, would prove impossible for him (or anyone else) to match, let alone ever surpass.

Associated London Scripts, on the other hand, would outlast the nine-year run of *The Goon Show* and provide Milligan with a lasting sense of pride in what he, alongside his fellow founding directors, had done to find and foster a new generation of top quality writing talent. The company lent him a sense of security, but it also gave him a feeling of power, and he would always believe that he had used it unusually benignly and wisely. Behind the scenes, he gave his time and his encouragement to countless would-be comedy writers, making his own heavy schedule even more burdensome as a consequence. 'That's something that usually goes unmentioned and unappreciated about Spike,' remarked John Junkin. 'Yes, as we all know, at times he could be very difficult and very, very, temperamental, but he was also capable of being incredibly kind and thoughtful and supportive, especially to those who really needed encouragement, and many writers, myself included, owe him an awful lot for that.'[51]

Even ALS, however, came, in time, to cause him a measure of bitterness and regret. He always claimed that he had wanted it to be a deeply idealistic, genuinely caring and sharing, and positively politicised writers' co-operative, but, when the very first 'proper' in-house weekly meeting took place, he flounced off soon after it started in a palpably furious rage. As John Antrobus recalled:

> Johnny Speight asked something like, 'If all the ten per cents [paid into the company by each one of the writers] add up to more than the salaries, rent and the office charges, where does the excess money go?' Whereupon Spike stalked out and returned to his office, slamming the door, never to return. It was a comment of sorts, though I have not been able to decipher it. Was Spike on the side of The Workers but hopelessly compromised? Or did he want to grind us down into the dust until we arose with bloody

revolution in our hearts when he would have said, 'I did it for your own good, lads. You had to see for yourselves how corrupt the system is.' Or did he not enjoy discussing company policy with writers such as me and Johnny who had spent the previous hours in The Goat and Boots discussing Trotsky, spending our ill-gotten gains getting pissed again? One thing was for sure. The flag of Communism would not rise outside our premises. We were all on nice little earners as we fiercely debated Socialism.[52]

There would no more weekly meetings, and Milligan went on to try, somewhat grudgingly, to tolerate rather than teach. His morality and politics were big, bold, all-or-nothing affairs, more akin to Rorschach ink-blots than to rigorous philosophical systems, and it only needed someone to request one small clarification, rather than just embrace a bundle of decidedly woolly generalisations, to send him scurrying back inside his office, where he would toot on his trumpet, feed the pigeons that always gathered outside on the floor of his balcony ('Morning, lads') and shake his head at the state of society:

> *Pull the blinds on your emotions*
> *Switch off your face.*
> *Put your love into neutral*
> *This way to the human race.*[53]

'I love my fellow man,' he would grumble, 'but he's a two-faced bastard.'[54]

Women were another matter. He probably thought that most of them were two-faced bastards, too, but he found some of them far too fascinating to resist. He could be engagingly flirtatious, and certainly loved being around attractive and intelligent women, but he always found the routine wear and tear of long-term relationships hard to bear. There would be three marriages (the first, in 1952, to June Marlowe, with whom he had three children – Laura, Sean and Sile – ended in divorce nine years later in 1961; the second, in 1962, to the actor Patricia 'Paddy' Ridgeway, with whom he had a daughter, Jane, ended with Paddy's premature death in 1978; and finally, in

1983, to his former secretary, Shelagh Sinclair), and there would be innumerable affairs and casual flings (sometimes several of them carried out separately but simultaneously), but Milligan never stopped hoping for – and regretting the absence of – a genuinely happy, settled and secure domestic environment. 'The whole business of being responsible for a family somehow crushed me,' he would say of his first attempt to make marriage matter more than moments. 'I felt inadequate. I think I *was* inadequate. It wasn't June's fault. Poor girl, she couldn't cope with me and you couldn't blame her.'[55] He never gave up: he would just go on trying, and failing, and trying to fail better.

His personal relationships, even more so than his professional ones, would often be blighted by his irregular descents into clinical depression. 'It is like a light switch,' he would say of the start of each collapse. 'I feel suddenly turned off.'[56] The first nervous breakdown arrived at the end of 1952, a month after the birth of his first child (and the start of his wife's subsequent incapacitation due to a serious post-natal fever) and one month into the third gruelling series of *The Goon Show*. Weighed down by money worries, struggling against an insomnia that had been exacerbated by his noisy neighbour, Peter Sellers (who had a habit of playing his latest batch of records loudly in the middle of the night), and battling against all of those censorious bureaucrats (real and imagined) whom he took to be his enemies at the BBC, Milligan had been suffering for some time:

> The madness built up gradually. I found I was disliking more and more people. Then I got to hating them. Even my wife and baby. And then there were the noises. Ordinary noises were magnified in my brain until they sounded a hundred times as loud as they were, screaming and roaring in my head . . . [Finally] I thought, 'Nobody is on my side. They are letting me go insane. I must do something desperate so they will put me in hospital and cure me. I know what I'll do. I will kill Peter Sellers.'[57]

Picking up a potato knife that he found on the draining board by the kitchen sink, Milligan bolted out of his flat and across the hallway, and went straight through Peter Sellers's glass front door. He did not even know whether his old friend was actually in residence there at the time; he was on the floor and in a trance, covered in flecks of blood and shards of glass. His wife summoned a doctor, who decided to send him to a nearby psychiatric hospital – St Luke's – in Muswell Hill, where he was put in a strait-jacket and placed in an isolation ward.

He remained there in a dazed and sedated state for fourteen days, growing a long brown beard in the process as he slipped in and out of consciousness and battled against a succession of dark and terrible dreams. He suffered from what seemed like endless hallucinations, seeing a lion crouching in the cupboard, coat hangers dangling down like corpses from the ceiling and even a vivid little scene from the Crucifixion. He wrote a poem about it while he was there:

> *The pain is too much*
> *A thousand grim winters grow in my head.*
> *In my ears the sound of the coming dead*
> *All seasons*
> *All sane*
> *All living*
> *All pain.*
> *No opiate to lock still my senses*
> *Only left, the body locked tenses.*[58]

By February 1953, however, it was decided that he was well enough to return home, and, dreading the prospect of sinking any deeper into debt, he forced himself straight back into the 'slog of writing', and resumed performing at the start of the following month.

There was no sense of 'recovery', however, or of being 'better' or 'healthy'; there was just a hollow feeling that came from having been let back out, misunderstood and unresolved, into the same hard old world. He did not think that he was 'cured'; he just made an effort, for the sake of everyone else, to look and act as though he was cured.

The burgeoning success of ALS seemed to help him for a while. It

gave him a sense of purpose, and even a degree of paternal and professional pride, to preside over such a remarkable community of
comedy writers. The strain of writing *The Goon Show*, however,
soon dragged him down again into the depths of the old depression.

It did not help that he no longer had anyone with whom he could
collaborate on a regular basis. Jimmy Grafton, who acted as script
editor and sounding board for the first three series, had now left
Milligan to his own devices, as had, during the fourth series, his regular writing partner Larry Stephens. Eric Sykes was still around to
supply a script of his own, but, after Spike nearly beheaded him with
that flying paperweight, he was disinclined to co-write in the same
room. Some of the younger members of ALS, such as John Antrobus,
were certainly willing and able to assist, but the problem was that
Milligan's standards were becoming so high, and his style so distinctive, that delegating became practically impossible. It therefore came
to feel, on far too many occasions, as though it was down to him to
do it all – and do it better than ever before.

Obliged to continue churning out the scripts at a rate of twenty-six
per year, he kept on draining himself of every last drop of mental and
emotional energy, and then had to recharge his batteries and put
himself through the whole punishing process all over again. John
Antrobus later described Milligan's intensely manic method:

> Spike writing. The typewriter clicking maniacally. The waste paper
> basket over-spilling and balls of screwed up paper littered round
> his feet. Totally absorbed. The balls of paper rise. The room fills
> with cast off pages. Work. The typewriter clicks and rattles. Faster
> and faster as Spike submerges under the tide of revisions. Click-
> click-clickerty-click-click-rap-a-tap-tap machine gun fire writing
> take no prisoners Spike. Until he emerges out of his office clutch-
> ing the finished script, paper balls rolling on to the landing and
> shouts: 'It's done! I'm going home!'[59]

He was often wildly, eerily creative during this period, but at a terrible cost to the state of his nerves. 'The best scripts I wrote,' he would
later claim, 'were when I was ill':

[T]he ones that I wrote best were when I was ill – a mad desire to be better than anybody else at comedy, and if I couldn't do it in the given time of eight hours a day I used to work 12, 13 and 14. I was determined. There was a time when I was positively manic. I was four feet off the ground at times, talking twice as fast as normal people. Working on this with great fervour to write this stuff and to hear [the other *Goon Show* performers] do it every Sunday. I couldn't wait for them to do it, to hear how it sounded, because it would be acclaimed when it went out. 'I've done it, I've done it' – and then I had to go and start all over again, that was the awful part of it.[60]

As well as all of these scripts, there were also endless letters: Milligan was, and would remain, an almost obsessive sender of missives to the national newspapers, protesting to them about abortion, vivisection and factory farming; complaining about the noise made by car horns, radios and lawnmowers; demanding rapid and unilateral disarmament of nuclear weapons; urging Mao Zedong to stop encouraging the Chinese people to breed; and he also wrote to the then Prime Minister, Harold Wilson, about (and with) a leaky pen.

He was often a restless presence in ALS. His sartorial preferences could be as random and striking as his emotional states: one morning he might arrive attired in a well-cut jacket, a sober tie, a crisp white shirt, a pair of smartly pressed trousers and shiny black leather shoes, the next time he would turn up in trainers, scruffy black corduroy jeans, a thick shaggy sweater and a black woolly hat topped with a hairy pom-pom, and on another day he might wander in wearing what looked like a hastily customised Victorian nightshirt. Work was modulated largely by mood, but, when the brain started buzzing, there was no one more palpably busy than Milligan – although Beryl Vertue, as his most trusted amanuensis in those days, often found herself obliged (regardless of her countless other time-consuming concerns) to keep up with his breathless pace. Indeed, so needy could he be when climbing up to a creative peak that, in 1956, Milligan felt the need to write to the then Head of Television Light Entertainment at the BBC, Ronnie Waldman, to ask if the Corporation would help facilitate the urgent installation of a private telephone in Vertue's home – because she was away from the office at weekends: 'It is at the weekends that I find myself in a bit of a spot,' he explained, 'as I get a lot of ideas that I want taken down' (the amiable Waldman, acknowledging in his reply that 'the association of the BBC Television Service with your own Organisation, Associated London Scripts, is an important contribution to the flow of our programmes,' agreed to do what he could to assist).[61]

Always acutely sensitive to any noises from nearby (the door of his office, like the front door of his home, bore the notice: 'This door can be closed without slamming it. Try it and see how clever you are'),[62] he would sometimes be wound up into a tight little coil of frustrated rage by the sound of other typewriters tap-tap-tapping while his stayed terrifyingly silent. On one such occasion during a depressingly unproductive summer's afternoon, the endless metallic rhythms emanating from Galton and Simpson's office opposite drove Milligan to despair of ever being able to lose himself in his script, so he decided to remove all of his clothes, walk across the landing and up the stairs to the next floor, and enter the office of Eric Sykes (the one writer at work in the building that day who was quietly using a pen). 'I'm stuck on these last two lines of the sketch,' he announced abruptly, placing the pages on Sykes's desk. 'Tell me what you think, will you?' Sykes scanned the relevant sentences, then looked up at his stark naked friend and said matter-of-factly, 'They're very good,' and then resumed his silent scribbling. 'You bastard,' muttered Milligan. 'Well,' Sykes replied without raising his eyes, 'it *is* rather warm in the office today.'[63]

When the low mood dripped all the way down to as black as ink, however, the whole building seemed to brood. 'We'd all get very worried,' Beryl Vertue remembered:

> There was one time, for example, when Spike was *really* depressed and upset and tired and everything, and he'd shut himself up in his office for two or three days. If you banged on the door, which you didn't like to do, he'd just shout and say, 'Go away!' Well, anyway, one day – it was a really nice, sunny day – I thought, 'I've had

enough of this, I'll see what's going on.' So I knocked on the door and this feeble little voice said, 'Yes, who is it?' I said, 'It's me, Beryl . . . I just wanted to say that it's spring, and I've brought you something.' So he said, 'What is it?' And I said, 'Well, if you open the door I'll show you.' So eventually he did open the door and it's all dark inside – he had all of the blinds down and these joss-sticks burning – and he just looked all tired and unshaven and everything, and so I gave him this little bunch of primroses. And he seemed really touched, actually, and he said, 'Thank you,' and put them on the edge of the desk, and then he went to the window and lifted up a corner of the blind – just enough for the primroses to get some sunlight on them, but no more. And he said, 'That's lovely, thank you,' and then I left. It was so sad, but the next day he did buck up enough to leave the office. That's how he was.[64]

'The whole world is taken away,' he would say of these periods during which he locked the door and took to bed. 'There is this terrible emptiness. I just want to go away, disappear, cover myself up until it goes away.'[65] The terrible impenetrability of the condition drove Milligan down into an increasingly desperate state: 'It's invisible,' he said of the depression. 'There's no written diagrams. It's an abstract, it's a sensation, and if you ask people to paint it most depressives will draw black.'[66] Whenever he sensed that the pressure was starting to lift, he always reached out to a pen and some paper and a typewriter, and worked his way back into the world: 'Van Gogh was a manic depressive: he had to paint. I had to write. I really mean *had* to. Like it was easing, it was lubricating, my way out of this terrible *blackness*.'[67]

The bouts of blackness would never go away. There would be many more lock-ins and lock-outs, and many more objects kicked, thrown and smashed, and more telephone conversations ended by the telephone receiver being unscrewed, strangled and dumped in the rubbish bin next to his desk. Norma Farnes – who, in addition to being his agent and manager from the late 1960s onwards, would also become (in Eric Sykes's words) Milligan's 'psychologist, mother figure and his umbrella when it rained'[68] – grew used to all of the

angry signs and hastily scribbled notes that were stuck on the outside of his office door (saying things like, 'GO AWAY, CREEP!';
'*ILL!*'; 'I'VE HAD ENOUGH – JESUS HAD IT EASY!'; 'I'M VERY
VERY ILL'; 'I'M NOT IN'; and 'LEAVE ME ALONE!'), but, as she
would recall, there was one exceptionally harrowing occasion at
Orme Court when even she was shocked by how low his spirits had
sunk:

It was 1972 and he had been ill for two weeks. He had not emerged
once from his office and did not want anyone to see him. This was
one of those depressions when his face was distorted with great
dark pouches beneath his eyes. He rang soon after I arrived home
from the office and said he wanted to see me, so I drove back to
Number Nine. He had unlocked his door so I walked in. I can still
feel the heat that hit me, as if a furnace door had just been opened.
The atmosphere was suffocating, with the windows closed and
the blinds drawn. A small table lamp barely lit the room. Spike
announced that he had come to the conclusion that there was no
point in living, because if he did, inevitably, he would sink into
depression once again and he could not face that any more. He
went, as if in slow motion, to a grey filing cabinet and took out a
brown leather case. Out of it he pulled a revolver.

'It's loaded,' he said, and begged me to shoot him. Suicide was
out of the question. I was the only person that would do this for
him. It would be easy. He would turn his back and it would take no
more than a second.

The heat was unbearable and in that unreal atmosphere I
thought for one split second that I would do it. He was crying
silently, the tears running down his cheeks, pleading with me to
pull the trigger. But then I knew I could not do it.[69]

She would keep him alive in the years that followed by knowing when
to coax and cajole and when to stay calm and quiet and leave him to
suffer alone. There would be mornings, at two or three o'clock, when
her telephone would ring and it would be Spike, asking: 'Are you
awake?' 'No,' she would groan in the gloom, only to hear him say

cheerfully, 'Well, you are now. Tell me about yourself. Are you all right, Norm?' There would also be moments during days – it could be morning, noon or night – when, all of a sudden, he would burst out of his office and growl at her: 'I'm always being overwhelmed by time wasting and you're the biggest waster of my time!' She came up with a sage stock response: 'Get on with it.'[70] He did, and she would ensure that there was always something for him to get on with and write – in spite of his seemingly obsessive desire to alienate every one of his potential producers.

The BBC was always the employer that bore the main brunt of Milligan's mercurial moods. 'He thought that the BBC did the best programmes,' Farnes recalled. 'On the other hand, when they wouldn't do what *he* wanted to do, then he hated them.'[71] Unable to acknowledge or accept that the BBC was there to serve the public rather than Spike Milligan, he would continue to rant, rave and over-generalise about the Corporation on a depressingly regular basis.

No broadcaster's hand was ever bitten harder, or more often, by one of the performers it fed. Sometimes it was eminently understandable, and sometimes it was not, but, regardless of who was culpable and who was not, the dispute was rarely handled, on Milligan's side, with much sympathy or tact. It was never about a case of mere incompetence or indifference as far as Spike was concerned – it was always part of some kind of devious conspiracy to add yet another dark cloud to his sky.

Sometimes the issue was about a perceived reluctance to experiment sufficiently with sound: 'I was trying to shake the BBC out of its apathy,' Milligan later explained about his weekly battles with the men responsible for conjuring up his increasingly surreal audio effects. 'Sound effects [up until then] were "a knock on the door and tramps on gravel" – that was it and I tried to transform it. And I had to fight like mad, and people didn't like me for it.'[72] Sometimes, it was about a proposed change to the regular schedule – as was the case, for example, on 22 September 1955, when (after requesting and getting more time in which to rehearse) a distinctly rattled Milligan responded thus:

Anybody who comes to hear a show at 3.45 on a Sunday afternoon must be:

(a)   Without a home

(b)   Gormless

Psychologically it is a bad time to perform a comedy show. It is like doing *Rigoletto* in the middle of Bond Street, but apparently my opinion does not matter any more.

Go ahead, grind it out.[73]

Sometimes, as was the case in an emotional letter (headed 'Spike Milligan' in pencil and underlined in green ink) that he sent to the current Head of Variety, Jim Davidson, on 16 July 1958, it was about his nagging conviction that he was being routinely under-paid as well as chronically under-appreciated:

Dear Jim,

This is the last letter in this game of silly fellows that we are all playing. I have returned my contract to my London office unsigned. These are the reasons: I asked, that as The Goon Show was a senior show to *Hancock's* [*Half-Hour*], that I thought it fair to ask for a rise that would at least bring my fee level with the writers of that Half Hour. I am told that it was rejected and that your excuse was, 'Two people wrote Hancock's show therefore the fee is higher.' Pardon me for saying so but this is utter twaddle and bureaucratic Mumbo Jumbo. I write *The Goon Show* alone, does this mean that less work is done on the script? Do I not work twice as hard, alone, and the strain twice as great? [H]ave not Galton and Simpson the pleasure of each other's help? Are you paying script fees by the number of writers or by the popularity of the show? You are saying the former, I disagree, as a result if you cannot see it fit to pay me the equal of *Hancock's Half-Hour*, this terminates our alleged negotiations for *The Goon Show*. If I do not hear an answer within fourteen days from now, I will sign the contract that the [commercial broadcaster] ABC are offering me. This in my opinion is not a letter meant to bring about ill feeling, it's just that I stand for what I think is right, which in this case I could get the support of the Radio and TV Writers' Association in proving that my demands are not unfair.

Sincerely,

Spike.[74]

In fact, 1958 was a veritable *annus horribilis* for the BBC as far as diatribes by Spike Milligan were concerned. After telling the *Daily Mail* in March that he was 'always on the verge of getting the sack' from the Corporation, he had proceeded to complain about its many 'torpor-ridden' executives, its shameful lack of interest in 'ideas' and its lack of due respect for 'the most progressive comedy writer in the country' – namely, he let slip, one S. Milligan Esq.[75] A little more than a month later, when he was working on a show in Australia, he told reporters in Melbourne that the BBC was, among many unpleasant things, 'a small-minded bureaucracy' that was 'run by idiots for idiots'.[76] The offending quotes soon reached Kenneth Adam, the BBC's somewhat tetchy Controller of Television, via Reuters, and he promptly exploded with rage, telling his colleagues that, if Milligan had indeed said such brutally unkind and ungrateful things, he should be banned – officially and very publicly – from BBC radio and television for at least a year.[77] The ban never actually happened, but the grumbling rumbled on, and it was left to the producer Dennis Main Wilson, one of the BBC's many great and shrewd free spirits of that era, to put the long-running tensions into some kind of perspective when, in October 1959, he distributed a memo about Milligan that said: 'He has done and said some very stupid things. On the other hand, he *is* 10% genius,' and thus was well worth tolerating.[78]

Those who mattered most at the BBC seemed to agree, because Milligan (in addition to his various stage, movie and literary activities) would go on getting work there in the era that followed *The Goon Show* – including such radio projects as *The Omar Khayyam Show* in 1963–4; two series on BBC2, from 1968 to 1969, contributing to *The World of Beachcomber*; and, most notably, six series (from 1969 to 1982) of his own extraordinarily anti-formulaic sketch-comedy show (also on BBC2) called *Q*.

He was, indeed, well worth it. He was impossible, but he was also invaluable: a crucial service was being performed. 'I've always had to fight through the Benny Hills in the wilderness,' he once explained:

> They are the main bunch in the army, they know the obvious and what they think the audience wants – bums, knickers, tits, funny double-entendre jokes, things like that. But in the long term, to live on a diet of that becomes boring, so what I try to do is to do what the [army] patrols do, I try to go out into enemy territory where nothing has happened before, and, of course, you get shot at like mad out there, but I would rather be up there, trying to do something different than what is here already.[79]

A deeply flawed man, and sometimes a very ill, unreasonable and angry man, but, none the less, a great comedy writer who was supremely, stubbornly, brilliantly and beautifully *sui generis*. Spike Milligan could not help but be a comic revolutionary, because he was incapable of recognising comedy's rules. The philosopher Friedrich Nietzsche once made the infamous complaint: 'I fear we are not getting rid of God because we still believe in grammar.'[80] Milligan expunged all of the false gods from British comedy, because he refused to worship its syntax. After him, we would find it so much easier to see the sense in nonsense.

He helped to change it all – usually from inside that office at ALS. Everyone else who worked there, for all of their own great and special talents, could not help but be hugely impressed. 'We were very close,' his old friend Eric Sykes would confirm. 'It was a very small office.'[81]

ROOM 2

Eric Sykes

If you understand comedy, you understand life. Drama, tragedy – everybody has these. But with humour you've got all these and the antidote. You have found the answer.

Eric Sykes would sit at the desk in his office and write out in long-hand every word of every script. When, as the years went by, his sight began to fail, he merely moved his head closer to the paper and carried on writing as usual. When, eventually, his sight had all but gone, he felt where the page was, positioned his pen at the appropriate point, and carried on writing as usual. Even when, as happened on more than one occasion, his pen ran out of ink and filled the page with nothing but the faintest of indentations, he still carried on writing as usual. It was what he did. It was what he had to do. It was what he always did so well.

Eric Sykes was post-war Britain's pre-eminent solo comedy writer. In terms of versatility, consistency, precision and popularity, no one else came close. He seemed equally at home when writing for stand-ups, supplying sketches, scripting sitcoms or shaping whole shows. He was a master of the mainstream, but he also proved himself remarkably adept as a contributor to the *avant-garde*, crafting key material for The Goons as well as for the likes of Frankie Howerd. More than anyone else, he made the art of writing comedy seem like a stable, and admirable, profession.

He was born in the heart of the North of England – 'where all good comedians come from'[1] – at 238 Henshaw Street in Oldham, Lancashire, on 4 May 1923, the second son of Vernon Sykes, a cotton mill spinner, and Harriet (née Stacey), a home-maker. Tragedy struck before consciousness came, because Eric's mother – aged just twenty-two – died while giving him birth. Years later, as an adult, he would come to believe in the presence of his late mother as a kind of guardian angel, guiding him on to greater success ('I can tell when she's there,' he would say. 'I sense a touch on my shoulder'),[2] but, as an infant, he was left alone to discover her absence.

He was separated from his surviving family for the first two years of his childhood because, while his father was afforded time alone in which to grieve, his maternal grandmother could only find room for his older brother, Vernon Jnr, and so Eric was placed in the care of a nearby female friend. Upon being returned to his father's custody at the end of 1925, he discovered that he not only now had a step-mother, called Florrie, but also a new baby stepbrother, named John. Now considered too old to be cradled maternally, but still young enough to miss it, Eric received no parental help in overcoming his 'desperate yearning to belong, to be acknowledged,' although 'even a smile would have sufficed',[3] and felt 'like a lodger in my own house'.[1] His pragmatic response to this lack of familial warmth and intimacy would be to retreat inside 'the fantasy world in my head, which transcended the hopelessness of the surrounding poverty and deprivation'.[5]

Comics, movies and sport became his favoured forms of recreation and temporary escape. He could lose himself in the plot of a cartoon strip, cinema serial or football match, and then start imagining how else things could, or should, have gone, with what twists and turns transpiring along the way. His own little stories, dreamed up in the idle hours, would mix the North of England with exotic foreign elements drawn from glimpses of Hollywood and colourful periodicals. All that he saw of the real and bigger world beyond Oldham was limited to what he witnessed during Wakes Week, the annual holiday for workers and their families from Lancashire's cotton towns, when Vernon took his wife and children to one of the nearby seaside resorts, such as Fleetwood, Southport, Morecambe or, most memorably, Blackpool ('our Shangri-La').[6]

Academically, Sykes would later claim to have been an under-achiever in every subject except art (for which he always averaged about ninety-eight out of a hundred).[7] Always quite a sickly child (soon after he was born, the family doctor took one look at him, shook his head and said, 'You'll never rear him'),[8] he coped with the no-nonsense hustle and bustle of an over-crowded working-class school as well as he possibly could, taking care not to disturb the teachers so that they would not care to disturb him, and he left at the age of fourteen with a basic ability to 'read, write, add up, subtract and divide' (thus feeling, as he later put it, 'well equipped to take my place as a member of the working class').[9] There followed spells spent labouring as a woodworker, painter and greengrocer's assistant before bowing to his supposed destiny and joining his father inside the mill.

When war intervened, Sykes joined the RAF as a wireless operator, but was seconded to the Army (serving in Normandy, Brussels and, for the longest period, Schleswig-Holstein), earned a Sergeant's stripes, and began performing (under the pseudonym of 'Rick Allen') in a CSE touring revue called *Three Bags Full*. There was a fair amount of talent in this troupe – Denis Norden was one of the writers, and the budding comic actor Bill Fraser was the officer in charge – but there were also plenty of opportunities for the untried and untested, such as Sykes, to show what they had to offer. He started off by attempting a comedy drunk act ('it was simple but well beyond my capabilities'),[10] then talked his way into being part of a close harmony quartet (of which, contrary to his claims, he had no previous experience), before settling into the role of a contributor to humorous sketches. Then, at the start of 1946, just when his thoughts were drifting ahead to the imminent date of his demob, he was transferred 'inexplicably' to the Army Welfare Services (AWS) HQ at Winsen in Lower Saxony, where he was appointed compère of an extravagant new revue called *Strictly Off the Record*.

He ended his period of service, belatedly, in circumstances akin to a screwball farce. First, he was informed by the Army that, as he was still technically in the RAF, the AWS did not have the authority to release him, so he was put in a truck and dispatched to the nearest RAF base in Gütersloh – where a puzzled officer checked his files, found no trace of anyone called 'Eric Sykes' and so, passing the buck in the best bureaucratic fashion, sent him on to the next nearest base. He ended up being passed like an unaddressed parcel to three more local RAF camps until, out of a mixture of pity, embarrassment and exasperation, he was sent back home to Britain on compassionate leave. It was there, after much scratching of heads within Whitehall, that Geoffrey de Freitas, the new Labour Government's Under-Secretary of State for Air, decided to intervene, facilitating Sykes's demobilisation, six months late, at Padgate.

After spending Christmas at home in Oldham, he resolved to try his luck as a performer down in London. He felt that he looked the part – if, that is, the part called for someone tall, skinny and Buster Keaton-ish with sad, soulful eyes ('I've got one of the most miserable faces in the world')[11] rather than someone short, stubby and clown-like with a revolving bow-tie – but he knew that he still had much to do if he was ever to graduate from concert party comic to professional comedy actor, so there was no time now to be lost.

He arrived in the capital at the start of 1947 – and, with wretched luck, found himself stuck in a tiny rented room opposite Euston Station, alone and out of work, during what turned out to be one of the worst British winters on record (there were regular gales, floods and snowstorms, the temperature plummeted to $-2.7°C$ and some parts of the country registered their coldest months since 1740).[12] Spending most of each miserable day travelling on tube trains in search of some warmth, and subsisting on little more than the odd piece of bread or bowl of thin soup, he was soon suffering from serious malnutrition, sores were breaking out over his skin and his eyes were struggling to focus. If he had not encountered, quite by chance, his old concert party officer, Bill Fraser, in the middle of a thick fog on London's Embankment at the start of another bitterly cold night, his failing health might well have collapsed completely within a matter of a few more weeks.

Fraser, who was obviously (but discreetly) distressed to find an old friend looking so pathetically impoverished and unwell, invited Sykes to visit him backstage at the nearby Playhouse Theatre in Northumberland Avenue, where he was starring in a popular revue called *Between Ourselves*. The meeting was, Sykes would recall, a crucial turning point in his life as well as his career:

> We chatted for a bit, and then he looked at me and said, 'I feel a bit peckish. Can you nip round the corner to the delicatessen, Eric, and get me some smoked salmon sandwiches?' So he gave me some money, and I went off and got them – this big plate of them – brought them back and he said, 'Go on, help yourself.' So he carried on chatting as he applied his make-up, and I sat there in the warm and started eating these brown bread and smoked salmon sandwiches. Well, I was so hungry, I ended up eating the whole lot! And I saw him give me a furtive little glance and this very, very, faint little smile, and I realised that he hadn't wanted the sandwiches for himself at all. He was too busy getting himself made up for the show. But he'd seen me looking like death, and he'd fed me without embarrassing me. Then he said, 'How would you like to write for me, Eric?' Well, I wasn't a writer, but I only had a penny in my pocket, so I said, 'Yes.' So he handed me this lovely new, white, crisp five-pound note, and he employed me for the next three weeks – during which time he never asked me to write him a single word, but what he did do was to pay me five pounds a week, and give me advice about how to get an agent, how to apply for a job, all of those sorts of thing. So that man, Bill Fraser, saved my life, and helped start my theatrical career.[13]

Sykes returned to Oldham and, after spending the best part of a fortnight recuperating in bed, began looking for work on the stage. He found it as a member of a repertory company – first in Oldham, and then, still hoping to get back to London, at Warminster in Wiltshire.

Repertory in Oldham seemed eminently worthwhile – its company had a fairly prestigious reputation, and the range of roles was rewarding – but repertory in Warminster proved far less inspirational, and Sykes's spirits began to sag. He was still billing himself as 'Rick Allen', accompanied by the knowingly specious claim: 'You may have heard him on *Variety Bandbox*.' The misinformation was a sign of his frustration: *Variety Bandbox* was the BBC's pre-eminent prime-time Variety show, and its hugely popular star, Frankie Howerd, was Sykes's (and his father's) favourite comedian, but the Warminster regular had not yet been on radio, let alone brushed shoulders with the likes of Frankie Howerd on *Variety Bandbox*, and, by the autumn of 1947, the dream was looking doomed. It was at this point, however, that good fortune intervened in the form of none other than the famous Frankie Howerd.

Howerd had burst on to the scene at the end of the previous year, when he made his BBC Radio debut, fascinated audiences and broadcasters alike with his rambling tales and bravely unconventional style of delivery ('Ladies and Gentle-*men* – no . . . Ah, no . . . Now listen! No . . . No, don't laugh . . . Oh, no, um, no, come on now, please, *liss-en* . . .') and was installed more or less immediately as one of the two resident comedians on *Variety Bandbox*. By the start of 1947 he was well on his way to becoming a national household name, but the problem was that, unbeknownst to the listening audience, he was fast running out of material. Jokes, stories and routines that had served him well for several years in Army concert parties were now being used and then discarded in the space of an hour due to the voracious demands of the fortnightly show.

By the start of the spring of 1947, Howerd was relying on a single A4 sheet of about twenty or so one-liners that he bought each week from a jobbing gag-writer by the name of Dink Eldridge, which he duly studied, picked out the one that sounded the least as though it had been transcribed from short-wave radio, and then proceeded to stretch it out – via innumerable 'No . . . Eh? . . . Ooh, no . . . Yes . . . Where was I? . . . Er . . . Yes!' interjections – into a full-length comedy routine. It was clearly not an arrangement that could be allowed to continue indefinitely. With more and more air time to fill, increasingly high audience expectations to meet and a debut solo summer season in Clacton that still required to be scripted, it was obvious that he needed to hire a proper, full-time, comedy writer as soon as was humanly possible.

Howerd spent much of the rest of 1947 trying in vain to track the right man down for the job. Finally, at the end of November, shortly before he travelled up to Sheffield to star in a pantomime, he came up with a suitable candidate. Casting his mind back to his days touring Germany shortly after the end of the war, he recalled seeing – and admiring – a fellow young comedian who was appearing at the time in another CSE revue. It was Rick Allen – a.k.a. Eric Sykes.

After making a number of casual inquiries, Howerd found that he and Sykes had an old wartime friend in common: the seasoned comedian Gordon Horsewell, who was now performing under the stage name of Vic Gordon. When Gordon called Sykes to tell him how keen Howerd was for the two of them to meet up, Sykes could not have felt more thrilled: 'It was as if,' he recalled, 'the King had contacted me for a game of skittles at Buckingham Palace.'[14] He did not actually know what Howerd looked like – he only knew the sound of his extraordinary voice and the 'sheer brilliance' of his special brand of 'happy nonsense' – but Gordon provided him with a suitably vivid description and then advised him to arrange to visit the star as soon as possible.

A few days later, an excited Sykes travelled by train to Sheffield, and made his way to the Lyceum Theatre. There, in a dressing-room backstage, he set eyes on Frankie Howerd for the first time. He was more than slightly taken aback when Howerd started to explain how much he had admired the material Sykes had written during the war – because Sykes knew that he had not written any material during the war. The act that Howerd recalled so warmly had in fact been built from second-hand material culled from American shows, such as *Midnight in Munich* and *Duffle Bag*, heard on short-wave radio – just as Howerd's had. When Sykes pointed this out, he was rather surprised – and very pleased and relieved – to find that his hero still seemed interested in finding a way to use him on the show: 'He said, "Do you think that you *could* write for me?" Well, I'd never written anything for anyone in my life! So I said, "Well, er, no doubt: when do you want it?" And he said, "Eight days from now." So I said, "All right, hang on a minute, have you got a bit of paper?" And then he went out to do the matineé performance of the pantomime, and by the time he came back at the end I'd written his first script.'[15] A new comedy partnership had begun.

It proved, almost immediately, a near-perfect union. Both men had always gravitated towards the kind of comedy that came from character and context rather than gimmicks and gags; both of them had lived through the absurdities of war and then come to terms with the uncertainties of peace; both of them had an affinity for the routine experiences of ordinary working people; and both of them seized on any chance to cock a snook at pretension and pomposity.

Each man understood the other, and, while Sykes found in Howerd someone who cared enough to champion his talent and support his new career, Howerd found in Sykes someone who could provide him with precisely the kinds of words, rhythms and images – right down to the 'ums' and the 'oohs' and the 'aahs' – that suited his distinctive style of stand-up. 'He was brilliant,' Howerd would later say. 'I was able to help him, I think [in the beginning]. He had great ideas for lines and I knew something about construction.'[16] Sykes would make a similar point about the dynamics of their collaboration:

> When I was first writing for him, Frank would say, 'The only thing is, Eric, you've got to have a beginning, a middle, and then the end's got to come *up* instead of just fizzling out.' He'd give me very helpful little pieces of advice like that. But he was a gift to me. I mean, just to *listen* to him, he was almost writing the next script for me. Frank's *style* was his own, and I copied his style, but I did have my own flights of fancy in my head.[17]

What Sykes did was to use these flights of fancy to craft scripts that contained not jokes but *situations* in which Howerd's established comedy character could at last come fully to life. He did not just 'use' words: he made words work. He made them, via Howerd's captivating delivery, act as a catalyst on the imagination (e.g.: 'It was so quiet I could hear the light shining on me').[18] When one heard his words, one *saw*.

The effect was electric: never before, and arguably never again, would Frankie Howerd sound so sure, so bright, so right and so joyously alive. One of the first and most memorable of these routines concerned a surreal attempt to transport a couple of 'items' from London up to Crewe:

. . . And the boss came up and he said, 'Ah, good morning.' He said, 'I want you to collect some goods from the depot and deliver them from Crewe.' Ooooh, I thought! Ooooooh, good, y'see! No. 'Cos: *Crewe*! 'Cos, I've always wanted to go abroad. So. Yes. Anyway. Yes. Anyway. I went along to the depot, and I saw the foreman. I said, 'Look,' I said, 'I want to sign for these goods.' And he said, 'They're labelled and ready. Get 'em out of here, quick.' So I signed for them, y'see. I went along. They were labelled and ready all right. Two elephants! *Two elle-ee-phants!* I was a-*maaaazed*! I said, 'I shall never get these to Crewe!' He said, 'I don't care *where* you're getting 'em to, but get 'em out of *here*!' He said, 'The place has been in uproar. *In uproar the place has been!*' So I got a bit of string. And I, um, tied it round their necks, y'see, and I led 'em out into the street. Oooh, I did feel a ninny! I tried to look as if I wasn't with 'em! Anyway. Well. *No!* But the way people stared! The way people *stared!* You'd think they'd never seen two elephants going down the underground before! And I had a shocking – *Liss-en!* 'Ere! *Liss-en!* Yes! Ye may titter! *Titter ye may!* – I had a *shocking* time with 'em down this underground. No. What I had to do, y'see, I had to tie one to a slot machine, and push the other one on to the tube train. 'Cos they'd only let me take one on at a time. No. Well, it was rush hour. And, of course, the elephant was *furious*, because it had to stand! Yes! It played the devil! So, anyway, I got it to King's Cross station, and I parked it there, y'see, but then I came back for the other one that I'd left tied up. And when I got there, there it was: gone! So I said to a porter, I said, 'Look, I left an elephant here tied to a slot machine. It's gone!' He said, 'Yes – and so 'as our slot machine!' Anyway, I dashed into the street and looked for it, and I could soon see the way it had gone, because there were crowds of people lining the road – waiting for the rest of the procession. *What a silly thing to do!* I mean, you'd think they'd have more sense, wouldn't you? And, honestly, I've never seen such a silly crowd of people in all me life! None of you were in Tottenham Court Road, were you? No! I didn't think you were. No. Anyway. Um. Now where was I? . . .[19]

On and on the tall tale went, with its teller sounding like he was having the time of his life. '*Cease!*' he shrieked, as the audience's laughter grew louder and louder, '*Cease!*'

It was great stand-up, great writing and great radio. Freed by the inspired Sykes from the onerous chore of scraping together a script, Howerd was finally able to relax (at least by his own nervy standards) and invest all of his intellect, invention and energy into eliciting from his audience the greatest possible quantity of laughs. Delighted that his bold comedic ideal had at last, more or less, been realised – the original anti-patter act had completed its evolution into what he now termed a 'one-man situational comedy'[20] – his powers as a performer rose up to reach their peak.

The impact of these routines grew deeper and richer as each fortnight gave way to the next, because, as Eric Sykes would observe, the characterisation of the on-air 'Frankie Howerd' was edging closer and closer to perfection: 'It was continuous, and that was important. When I started writing for Frankie Howerd, I was only ever writing Frankie Howerd's next script. I wasn't ever writing *my* script, and hoping that Frankie Howerd would do it. I was continuing, from one script to the next, Frankie Howerd's persona. So there was a clarity of purpose about everything I wrote for Frank.'[21]

The Howerd and Sykes partnership made *Variety Bandbox* seem more like a special event than merely a routine radio show, regularly drawing in an audience estimated to be at least 42 per cent of the total adult population of the nation (a percentage which in those days amounted to 15,120,000 people – but, if both children and those adults still in military service had also been included, the figure would probably have been nearer to 21,000,000).[22] It also helped to confirm Frankie Howerd's reputation as one of the biggest stars on British radio.

The timing, for both, could not have been any better. Radio was a medium that was about to reach its peak: the number of radio licences would rise from 11,081,977 in 1948 to a record 11,819,190 in 1950 before commencing its sudden and inexorable decline during the rest of a decade that (thanks to the advent of television) saw listeners transmutate into viewers.[23]

No one felt more proud about this fact than Eric Sykes. Although he still hoped that the chance would eventually come when he could resume his fledgeling career as a performer, a recent sobering experience had reconciled him, in the short term, to his current role as a writer:

> I had actually said to Frank one day, 'Listen, Frank, I don't want to spend *all* my life writing for you. I am a comedian in my own right.' So he said, 'Well, write a script for the two of us.' And so I wrote a double act for us, and he paid for the recording studio in Bond Street, and we went and did it. And after it was over we listened to it back. And after about ten seconds I said, 'Turn it off! Turn it off, Frank!' He said, 'No. You are going to listen to this all the way through.' I was in agony, because Frank was, you know, Frankie Howerd, and I was, well, I was pathetic. As I sat there listening to it, I was sweating with embarrassment. And so, after it was over, he said something to me that was very sagacious – because he was a very perceptive, thinking, man – he said, 'Eric, you have a gift for writing. Because writing comes easy to you. You *suspect* it. You probably think, "Well, if I can do it, anybody else can do it." Well, it's not true. Now, you've heard that recording. Concentrate on your writing.' So I said, 'Yes, yes, Frank, you're quite right.' And I did. It would be about two or three more years before I again had any aspirations to be on the stage.[24]

In 1949, therefore, the knowledge that he had played some vital part in his hero's achievement was a good enough reward, for the moment, for Sykes:

> I lived in Oldham, and I went home one weekend – it was a nice, warm, Sunday evening – and I walked along this street, and every door was open (because they used to be in those days when it was a warm evening), and out of every door – *every door* – I could hear *Variety Bandbox*, and Frankie Howerd saying the lines that I'd written. And I had to hug myself – because I knew what the next line was![25]

In the space of little more than a year, Sykes had gone from being just another avid listener to a singularly artful writer, and now his words were being heard by almost half the nation.[26] Life was good, really good, and he knew it.

Howerd seemed to be everywhere in those days: touring the country in lavish theatrical extravaganzas, such as *Ta-Ra-Ra-Boom-De-Ay*, and visiting military bases overseas on behalf of CSE, as well as taking his own solo stand-up shows on the road up and down the nation; appearing in high-profile summer shows and pantomimes; attending several Royal Variety Performances and also a private concert at Buckingham Palace; making the odd novelty record; and starring in more and more radio shows. Howerd's increasingly busy schedule was also, of course, Eric Sykes's increasingly busy schedule. The more pressure that the comedian placed on himself, the more, as a consequence, he heaped on his heroically uncomplaining scriptwriter:

Whenever he was appearing somewhere, like, let's say, in Blackpool for a summer season, I'd write his act for that particular show, but then I would carry on with his radio material. I would write his usual opening spot with Billy Ternent [for the next edition of *Variety Bandbox*] and his own solo spot in my office in London, and then I used to get on the train and go up and see him in Blackpool or wherever he was, read out these two spots, and if he liked them, fine. Then we had to wait until Frank heard from the BBC who the next guest celebrity was going to be. When he knew, he would put me in a room in whatever villa he was hiring for the season, give me a bottle of Scotch and a typewriter, lock the door, and when I knocked on the door and asked to come out it meant that I'd finished writing the guest spot. And once I had read that out to him and he'd said that he liked it, I used to get the train back to London. It was done like that: straight up and straight back down. In fact, the train sometimes used to wait for me at Euston! I'd come rushing on to the platform and they'd say, 'Here he is,' and on the train they'd have a restaurant car with one particular table that always had three bottles of Double Diamond beer on it, and one glass, and that was for me! No one would bother me. I was a regular. It was a lovely time.[27]

Howerd, ever fearful of his career losing momentum (and with it his popularity), decided to leave *Variety Bandbox* in 1950 and launch his own radio show, *Fine Goings On*. Scripted, as usual, by Sykes, it went out on air the following year, and did well enough without quite reassuring Howerd that he had done the right thing in breaking away from a sure-fire prime-time success like *Bandbox*. A chronic worrier, he went back to basics in 1952, recording (with Sykes, as usual, in tow) a concert party tour of British military bases in the Middle East, and then returned home to make his debut series on television, *The Howerd Crowd*. The demand was still there, the ratings and reviews were still good, but Frankie Howerd was tired and dogged by self-doubt, and, slowly but surely, his career was losing its sense of direction.

Eric Sykes's own career, on the other hand, was now going from strength to strength. Besides continuing to write for Howerd, he was also (since June 1950) collaborating with his old RAF friend Sid Colin on a new radio series called *Educating Archie*, starring (as odd as it may now seem) the ventriloquist Peter Brough and his wooden doll, and featuring a supporting cast that included Julie Andrews as Archie's playmate, Hattie Jacques as the over-amorous Agatha Dinglebody, Max Bygraves as an odd-job man and (from 1951) Tony Hancock as a tetchy schoolmaster ('Flippin' kids!'). An instant hit – it managed to attract an audience of twelve million listeners, and won a national newspaper's 'Top Variety Show' award, during its very first year on air[28] – *Educating Archie* cemented Sykes's reputation as the most imaginative young comedy writer in British radio, and also showed that, if he so wished, he could now pursue a career that would be independent of Frankie Howerd's.

Although he did not appear inclined to abandon his famous patron, Sykes certainly appreciated the fact that, at long last, his talent was being more widely – and publicly – acknowledged:

Frank had always been fine. It had been other people that had kept my contribution a kind of secret. I'd said to the BBC, 'I would like a credit, as Frank's writer, because, you know, he's reading out what I write word for word in every show.' But they said, 'Ah, well, if we gave you a credit a lot of people would be disillusioned, because they, the public, think that he makes it up as he goes along. If they thought for one minute that it was all written for him, he'd lose a lot of fans.' And then they said to me, 'Would you *like* Frank to lose a lot of fans?' Well, naturally, I said, 'No,' and that was it. It was emotional blackmail.[29]

Howerd had sympathised with Sykes, and so the comedian was the first to applaud his writer's new achievements:

He was happy for me, because he felt that he'd helped to 'create' me in a way. And I agreed with that, because without Frank I would never have considered myself to be a writer. He had opened the door for me to enter this profession. He made me understand that I was a writer and had a special gift for it. I always felt in his debt, and so, if Frank ever wanted anything, he knew that he only had to pick up the phone and ring me and, no matter how busy I was, I would always give him precedence. I was so grateful to Frank.[30]

The formation of Associated London Scripts in 1954 further underlined the extent of Sykes's success. His shows were topping the ratings, his services were commanding an increasingly high price and he now had, in partnership with Milligan and Galton and Simpson, his own scriptwriting company – with all of the security, independence and influence that came with it. Arriving for work each day dressed smartly and conservatively in an expensive camel-hair overcoat (that usually had a script and a cigar tube or two poking out of its pockets) and a tailored suit or blazer, he would enter his office, say hello to the portrait of Harriet, his late mother, that he always had on his wall and then settle down to write. He loved his job, and it showed.

While he kept on doing what he had been doing before, he now also allowed himself the odd little experiment, such as his first ALS collaboration with Milligan, *Archie in Goonland* – a one-off 1954 radio special in which Peter Brough and Archie Andrews entered the world of The Goons via a Lewis Carroll-style magical mouse hole[31] – and made it known that he was open to novel offers. When Britain's first commercial television service was launched the following year, Sykes found himself in greater demand than ever, and his power increased accordingly. The BBC, anxious to hold on to such an asset, began allowing him, unprecedentedly, to devise, write, cast, appear in and direct his own television specials, such as the star-studded *Pantomania* in 1955 and, the next year, *Dress Rehearsal* and *Opening Night*.

Praise came in from all directions: from broadcasting executives, such as Ronnie Waldman, BBC TV's Head of Light Entertainment; from major programme-makers, such as Peter Eton, the producer of *The Goon Show*; from respected performers, such as Frankie Howerd, Max Bygraves, Billy Cotton, Terry-Thomas, Tony Hancock and Peter Sellers (with whom he would appear in several television specials);[32] and from a broad assortment of critics, columnists and many members of the general public. Even Spike Milligan – never the most generous of men when it came to acknowledging the full value of a collaborator – was happy to go on record to register the extent of his respect, describing his friend and colleague as a great writer, a wonderfully droll performer and, in general, 'a bit of gold in show business'.[33] Everyone, it seemed, had come to regard Eric Sykes as rather special.

It had something to do with his remarkable industry and consistency, which enabled him to supply top-class material to several shows and performers at any one time, but it also had to do with the extraordinary rapport he was able to strike up with whomever he happened to help. He was not just a writer; he was also part biographer and part psychologist. He seemed to possess the rare ability to see deep within a particular performer, appreciate their needs and tastes and values and habits, and then produce material that appeared to have emerged from them instead of from Eric Sykes. Other writers gave performers words; Eric Sykes also gave them thoughts and feelings. He refined them as personalities.

Frankie Howerd knew it earlier, and better, than anyone. Before Sykes, he had been obliged to take another performer's jokes and stories and hammer them into a suitable shape for his act, which was rather like a Michelin-starred chef trying to tenderise the coarsest bit of old beef. When Sykes started writing for him, he just had to say the lines to sound like himself: the material flowed out, with all of his natural rhythms and tics in their rightful place, and, equally impressively, the *meaning* was always effortlessly apposite (if Howerd *had* been obliged, say, to take two elephants all the way up to Crewe, one knew that he *would* have coped, or rather failed to cope, in the very same manner as his on-air *alter ego*).

Tony Hancock would come to feel much the same: Sykes was probably the first writer to bring out something of his real character, his authentic sounds, with an incredibly sensitive attention to detail. In one radio show, for example, the sound of marching soldiers was meant to be followed by Hancock remarking, 'All from Russia.' When the performer asked Sykes how he wanted the line to be said, the writer replied: 'As if you are tapping the ash off a cigarette.'[34] Hancock knew immediately, and precisely, what he meant – and it suited him down to the ground: Hancock suddenly started sounding more like Hancock. A Sykes script made a performer sound sure and sharp and real.

It was never an accident. It was always the result of a painstaking effort to craft something brilliantly bespoke. 'You have to get to know the [performer] as a friend,' he later explained, 'it can never be just a business arrangement. Then you start to study them technically, by watching them perform, until you know exactly what they can do and what they can't say. It's the little things you have to pick up – whether they get a laugh best with a line or just a hook.'[35]

This was one way in which Eric Sykes helped to enhance the art of comedy scriptwriting. Another way came through the discipline and rigour of his texts: each element slotted together in a structure that kept the story, sketch or sitcom engagingly coherent. Programme-makers knew that a script by Eric Sykes would arrive thoroughly edited and properly paced. John Browell, one of the most noteworthy producers of *The Goon Show*, would observe that, while Spike

Milligan's scripts were the most 'inventive and fantastic', the 'cleverest' ones were written by Eric Sykes – 'because he was an extremely intelligent writer and he could write in Goon idiom, but also bring a sensible storyline to bear and add a more logical conclusion.'[36]

The inspiration for his comedy came mainly from within. There were, it is true, a few literary influences: like Spike Milligan, for example, Sykes was a great fan of the humorist Stephen Leacock: 'He shows Man with his pants off. You can't be pompous with no pants on. When you strip off pomposity we are all idiots underneath.'[37] There were also one or two inspirational role models in movies – including Buster Keaton, Laurel and Hardy and Jacques Tati (all of whom he admired for their ability to make the most of their visual medium). His real comedy muse, none the less, would remain his own memory:

> [Your comedy] is all derived from a period in your life when you were absorbent like a sponge. You keep writing and rewriting that period and ring the changes but you don't change fundamentally. My period was bowler hats and watch chains and highly polished boots – the Sunday best of the 'thirties. In the week there'd be clogs going past from quarter to seven till five to seven when the mill opened, millions of clogs. They would all stop and then you'd get the odd one running like mad. At half past five the whistle would go and all the clogs would clatter back again. It was a funny period. Look at the way they posed for portraits or the way they dressed for motor cars or aeroplanes. They felt that they should be wearing different clothes for doing such interesting things, so they turned their caps back to front. [. . .] I love that period. [. . .] It's full of warmth and humour and it's very funny. I think we've lost a lot of humour because we've lost a lot of humanity.[38]

Sykes faced a serious challenge to his career when, with bitter irony, the man whose comedy confirmed such a sharp pair of ears and eyes began to suffer from problems with his hearing and sight. His hearing had started deteriorating early on in the 1950s, when he had an operation on his right ear (due to an infected mastoid) at the end of

1951, and he lost much of the hearing in his left ear ten years later following another serious piece of surgery (he would cope with the condition initially by using a conventional type of hearing-aid and then, when that proved inadequate, by wearing special lens-free bone-conduction spectacles, which captured sounds via hidden pads that vibrated just behind his ears). His sight began declining more slowly but significantly during the 1960s until, later in life, he was diagnosed as suffering from a degenerative condition known as 'dry macular disciform' (a severe and progressive loss of central vision) and could only read his own scripts with the aid of a special 'Aladdin' low-vision magnifying machine.[39] Not even these frustrating problems, however, would ever discourage him from his writing.

He had the emotional support of his wife, Edith Milbrandt (a Canadian-born nurse whom he met when he was recuperating from his first ear operation and married in 1952), and their four young children (three daughters – Kathy, Susan and Julie Louise – and one son – David), as well as his friends and colleagues at ALS, and he also took up golf to distract himself in between scripts, but there would still be discreet moments of darkness: 'I am only happy when I'm working,' he admitted once to an interviewer. 'If I'm not working I get screwed up because my time is going, my life is slipping by. Sometimes I get so miserable that I have to shut myself away from people and tell the children, "Kids, it's a bad day today," and I wander round the garden and get over it.'[40] Most of the time, however, he was fine, because he was keeping himself so busy.

Deadlines never seemed to be much of a problem, because he always organised his time so well. There were slots for his rounds of golf and slots for his regular meals of egg and chips ('take him anywhere,' Johnny Speight would say, 'to the most lavish gourmet restaurant, and he would order egg and chips'),[41] but there were also plenty of periods set aside for every aspect of the creative process. A great analyst, as well as a great writer, of comedy, he allowed himself enough hours and days to mull over an idea in depth, twisting it this way and that way and inside and out until, when he was satisfied that it made complete sense (or utter nonsense), he wrote it all down at a strikingly rapid pace. He was almost as disciplined in the studios, although he was too talented an actor ever to curb his own spontaneity entirely, and no rehearsal was ever wasted. When it came to appearing in front of the cameras, he had learnt a great deal early on in his career from working with some of the best programme-makers around, including the pioneering television director Bill Lyon-Shaw,[42] so his technique was acutely attuned to all of the blockings, close-ups and cuts. Sykes was, in sum, a consummate modern professional: bright, industrious, even-tempered and both willing and able to take on and master whatever new challenge arrived.

Performing, in particular, was certainly getting to be an increasingly regular option as time went by. He started making more frequent appearances on television during the latter part of the 1950s (contributing to shows fronted by the likes of Tony Hancock, Peter Sellers and Terry-Thomas, as well as hosting a number of specials for the commercial station ATV); he wrote and performed on stage in the very popular 1958 London Palladium revue *Large as Life*; and he also began to pop up in movies – first in minor roles, such as the brother-in-law in the 1956 comedy-musical *Charley Moon*, and then, early on in the next decade, as the lead in such cheap and cheerful efforts as *Village of Daughters* (released in 1962 as the first in a five-picture deal with Metro-Goldwyn-Mayer), before carving out a niche for himself as a valuable member of the supporting cast (striking up a particularly memorable rapport with Terry-Thomas in several movies, including one of the big-budget international success stories of 1965, *Those Magnificent Men in Their Flying Machines*).

As the 1950s came to an end, the BBC, having managed to insert an 'exclusivity clause' into Sykes's latest contract, was eager to make the most of his multiple talents. Besides keeping him busy with his various writing projects, plans were also being hatched to use him more often as an actor, a director and producer and even a quasi-executive.

Sykes had actually already been earmarked, along with Frank Muir and Denis Norden, to become one of the Corporation's brand new 'comedy consultants'. The idea was the brainchild of Eric Maschwitz, BBC TV's then Head of Light Entertainment, and his deputy, Tom Sloan: acknowledging the need to compete more assiduously with an increasingly aggressive and successful ITV, the two executives had come up with the imaginative response of recruiting an 'in-house' corps of relatively fresh writing talent groomed expressly for the future needs of the BBC. As Sykes, Muir and Norden were probably the three most experienced and respected writers of comedy at work in Britain at that time, Maschwitz and Sloan had no hesitation in identifying them as the 'dream triumvirate'.

A meeting was duly organised in Tom Sloan's office at the newly-built Television Centre in White City right at the start of 1959.[43] The two executives explained their vision to the three writers: they would have responsibility for finding and guiding new talent and novel projects, as well as greater freedom to develop their own favoured shows and formats. Each man would get the security of his own special four-year contract; a comfortable office alongside all of the grandees on the fourth floor of the new building (once, that is, it was ready: until then, it was admitted, they would have to make do with a caravan behind the scenery block in the car park); a generous amount of secretarial assistance; plenty of private writing time; and easy access to the legendary BBC Club bar. Muir and Norden decided that the timing was more or less right for them to accept the offer,[44] but Sykes declined on the grounds that, as a director of Associated London Scripts, he was still 'desperately hoping to find new writers' for his own organisation, so a conflict of interests seemed inevitable. Maschwitz and Sloan had to settle, reluctantly, for a duo instead of a trio.[45]

One of the first people to benefit from this new arrangement, however, was none other than Eric Sykes the performer. He and one of his ALS colleagues, Johnny Speight, had been bouncing ideas back and forth for some while about a possible sitcom for him and his good friend Hattie Jacques, and, when Speight came up with the pilot script and had it filmed by the BBC, Muir and Norden were the ones who not only commissioned a series but also recommended that a second be made straight after. First screened on 29 January 1960, *Sykes And A . . .* would go on to run for nine series over the course of the next seven years (or sixteen series in nineteen years if one counts the later shows – which were heavily reliant on the earlier scripts and stories – that were just called *Sykes*), establishing both of its stars as much-loved small-screen personalities.[46]

Sykes also starred in another new ALS sitcom, this time on BBC Radio, the following year: a gentle, Ealing-style police comedy, called *It's a Fair Cop* (featuring a supporting cast that included Deryck Guyler, Hattie Jacques, Leonard Williams and Dick Emery), that was written by John Junkin and Terry Nation. 'It did OK,' Junkin would recall, 'it got a nice, warm reaction, and pretty decent ratings, and I think we would probably have done more than one series had Eric's TV series not been such a big hit so quickly'.[47] As it was, Sykes spent much of his time during the first half of the 1960s writing for, and appearing on, peak-time television, before turning down several more small-screen offers – including an invitation to star in a new BBC sitcom called *Oh Brother!* (the role would end up going to Derek Nimmo)[48] – and seizing instead the long-awaited chance to make his very own movie.

The Plank, which was released in 1967, would be a dream come true for this most visually inclined of Britain's leading comedy writers ('a visual laugh,' he once said, 'is worth three pages of dialogue').[49] Scripted and directed by Sykes, and featuring Sykes himself at the head of a starry cast, this short movie – the first to be made (on this occasion in partnership with Bernard Delfont) by a new ancillary company of ALS named Associated London Films – was meant originally to co-star Peter Sellers until he became distracted by the offer of a much bigger, Hollywood-funded production (*Casino Royale*) and the gloriously droll Tommy Cooper was persuaded to take his place. The aim was to create a movie that did without all of the things that normally came between the viewer and the basic frame of the comedy action: so there were no camera tricks, no sudden cuts and zooms, no excess of extreme close-ups and, most strikingly, no words. Sykes wrote the script with the camera instead of a pen, capturing all of the comic trials and tribulations experienced by two hapless workmen (played by Sykes and Cooper) as they struggled to put one wooden plank in its rightful place.

The effect was simple, economical and extremely engaging (it was deemed by the critic of *The Times* to be enjoyable enough 'even for sceptics'),[50] and the movie's great and enduring success – stretching right across the usual range of ages and areas – would inspire Sykes to return to the genre on several more occasions, sometimes for the big screen (such as *It's Your Move* and *Rhubarb* in 1969) and sometimes for the small (such as his later series of shorts for Thames Television, which included a 1978 remake of *The Plank* and, in 1988, *Mr H is Late*). Partly a homage to the kinder, gentler, friendlier era of Laurel and Hardy, and partly a response to the increasing cliquishness of what now passed as mainstream humour, these productions would be among the most personally satisfying of Sykes's long career, even though some of them (particularly the efforts at Thames) lacked the overall polish of his previous achievements. Although, by this time, he could barely hear and scarcely see, he still relished mixing together what he considered to be the essential ingredients of good comedy: an engaging situation and a believable cast of characters, with plenty of action and perfect timing. It still mattered to him – not primarily for his own benefit, but rather for that of his broad and loyal audience.

'I was, and am, totally dedicated,' he would say, 'to a comedy that induces people to laugh, not chuckle or titter or, at worst, snigger, but to throw back their heads in a joyous burst of capitulation.'[51] No one would work harder, throughout and beyond the golden era of ALS, to keep achieving such an effect.

ROOM 3

Galton & Simpson

The first thing is that it's got to be funny.
That's not a cop-out, it's a starting-point.

There was Ray Galton and there was Alan Simpson: two men
stuck inside the same room, writing about two men stuck inside
the same room. First they wrote about Tony and Sid, and then they
wrote about Albert and Harold, but they always wrote about relationships in such a way as to make them seem real.

Galton and Simpson can lay claim to being the founding fathers of
the Great British Sitcom – not only because they were the first to
unite situation and comedy within a self-contained programme
format, but also because they went on to ensure that the connection
was funny and real and right. They did not just combine situation
with comedy; they also, and even more importantly, crafted believable characters locked together in proper relationships. They gave us
recognition sitcoms: when we heard or saw them, we turned to each
other and said, 'That's you,' or 'That's them' or 'That's us.'

Writers of comedy have always been under-appreciated – while
the best of their colleagues in drama are afforded their own lofty-
sounding title of 'playwright', they themselves are never referred to as
anything other than 'scriptwriters', and rarely receive serious con-
sideration for the most prestigious of the literary plaudits – but
Galton and Simpson were not just great writers of comedy: they
were great *writers*, full stop. They could capture all of the salient
social, economic, political and cultural dreams and schemes of
modern British life; they could reflect with real insight, compassion
and intelligence on love and loyalty and fears and fakes; they could

move you, surprise you, challenge you and make you think; and they could also make you laugh.

They spoke our language, they saw our sights. First on radio, and then on television, they provided us with beautifully crafted little stories about class and capital and virtue and vice that, in their own distinctive way, struck just as clear and true a chord – among as many, if not more, people – as anything that came out of the Royal Court. As Denis Norden, one of their few true peers, would observe: when the plays of Harold Pinter were added to the national school curriculum, the sitcoms of Galton and Simpson should have been included, too.[1]

They were the great writing partnership of the late 1950s, '60s and '70s – the pair that never let the standard drop. Not only in their two most celebrated sitcoms, *Hancock's Half-Hour* and *Steptoe and Son* (both of which will be discussed in depth in Chapter 8), but also in their own televised series of 'playhouses' (which saw, for the first time, comedy writers get their names above the title) and their other work for stand-ups, sketches, the theatre and movies, they underlined the value of comedy that had a brain in its head and blood in its veins. They became, in the process, celebrities in their own right, as well as inspirational role models for anyone within the working class who was nursing an ambition to write.

Their own partnership, however, was a positive that came from a negative. Before Galton and Simpson met, neither had been expected to survive beyond his teens.

Ray, the son of Herbert Galton, a bus conductor, and Christina Hemphill, was born on 17 July 1930 at 25 Enbrook Street in Paddington. Alan, the son of Frank Simpson, a milkman, and Lilian Ellwood, was born eight months earlier, on 27 November 1929 at 33 Concannon Road in Brixton. Unlike Milligan and Sykes, Galton and Simpson were too young to serve in the Second World War (nor would either of them be well enough to be conscripted into National Service), but, inevitably, their outlook was shaped by the suffering, deprivation and uncertainty of the period all the same.

Ray Galton, for example, grew up in a broken home in Morden – his father, who was away during wartime in the Navy, had separated from his mother – and, as he would later recall, his own future seemed fairly bleak:

> I left school in the last year of the war, when I was fourteen, to become a plaster's apprentice – don't ask me why. Then I worked at the Transport and General Workers' Union in Smith Square and that was almost as bad. I remember running up the steps of Morden tube station to queue for a bus home one night, and it was as if a light bulb came on in my head. I thought: 'I can't go on doing this for the rest of my life.'[2]

One year later, in January 1947 (during the same exceptionally cold winter that came close to seeing off Eric Sykes), a serious illness intervened: after suffering from a cluster of worrying symptoms (tiredness, night sweats, loss of appetite and an increasingly bad cough) for some time, Ray Galton's health collapsed dramatically. When his brother, Bert, came home on leave from the Merchant Navy, he recognised immediately (having seen the physical effects of the condition before) that Ray was probably suffering from tuberculosis.[3] He was sent straight off for an X-ray the following day and, when the result came back, he was informed that he did indeed have advanced tuberculosis of the lungs.

It was one of the cruellest domestic hazards of the time, and, for more than a century, the chief destroyer of young adult lives (about four hundred deaths were recorded in Britain each week during the 1940s).[4] Until 1953, when it became a matter of national policy to vaccinate all children aged between twelve and thirteen, it was not uncommon for school friends and teenagers to suddenly go missing from their local environment – and not just for weeks or months but often for three or four years – after falling victim to this distressingly widespread viral condition. Rates of infection in Britain had been rising for some time both before and during the war years (particularly among the overcrowded and poorly fed working-class communities), and, by the end of the 1940s, Britain was recording as many cases as fifty thousand per year. Galton was one of the many unfortunate young people whose life was to be disrupted.

Aged just sixteen, he was given no more than a few more weeks to live. Although there was usually, in those days, a waiting list of up to two years for a spare bed in a sanatorium, so precarious was Galton's condition that he was admitted within a mere ten days to Surrey's recently converted Milford Sanatorium at Tuesley Lane in Godalming.

It was there, for what was left of his teenage years, that his life was put on hold. Suddenly, he would recall, he found himself in an environment where the only thing that mattered was survival:

> The doctors were tough with me. The treatment was rest and I didn't get out of bed for over a year. There was some absolutely horrific surgery, where they took away your ribs and pressed the lung down. As long as the lung didn't work, the bacilli couldn't live. We all feared it; I think it was the worst operation known to man. In the end I had an artificial pneumothorax instead. They pumped air between the thorax wall and lung and compressed it. It had the same effect.[5]

There was no real routine, as such, unless one counted the various ways whereby the patients were obliged to wait until they got well:

> We lived in two-bedded cubicles stretching down a long ward. The place was full of blokes who'd come straight from the war; as I was only just seventeen, I was a kind of mascot for a while. There was a weird system of promotion: 'absolute bed rest' meant you were washed in bed, you couldn't even get up to pee; 'semi-absolute 1' meant you could use the lavatory in the morning; 'SA 2' meant you could go twice a day; 'bed' meant you could use the lavvy and put your clothes on to see the film show once a week. The word we dreaded most after our weekly examination was 'same'. I still can't bear to hear it. It meant no progress, you stayed where you were – for how long, nobody knew. The idea was to build you up, then see how much you could take before you broke down. Some really fit bloke would be out of bed and walking the rounds of the building, then he'd collapse and the TB would start

again. When that happened, the mood of the whole sanatorium would go down. We had our sputum tested each week and if you threw a positive – and I always did – you'd be demoted and back to where you started. When you're in that situation, you think there's a conspiracy to keep you in. Other times I got the 'black dog', as Churchill called it, when I'd turn my head to the wall and wouldn't talk to anyone.[6]

Alan Simpson, meanwhile, had left Mitcham Grammar School in 1945, aged sixteen ('I had the choice of staying on, but I hated it so much I couldn't wait to get away'),[7] still harbouring hopes of becoming either a professional footballer or, failing that, a professional sports reporter. When both of these ambitions were discouraged by his parents, who wanted him to find a job that promised a car or a decent pension, he looked for a tolerable alternative: 'I decided I wanted to go in the Navy and be a ship's writer. I fancied the uniform. In the end I got into shipping. I thought it was romantic. I was a postal clerk at thirty bob a week. I had about three jobs in two years, then I was taken ill.'[8]

One seemingly ordinary morning in 1947, while he was travelling on the bus across London to work, he cleared his throat and coughed up blood. After being rushed to St George's Hospital, near London Bridge, for an urgent examination, it was discovered that he, too, had contracted pulmonary tuberculosis. Things then went from bad to worse: he suffered a full-blown haemorrhage in bed the following night, but, as there was still such an acute shortage of places in the local sanatoria, he and his family had no choice but to wait for a space to become available. It was a desperately tragic week for the whole of the Simpson household, because Alan was taken ill on the Wednesday, and then his father, who had been stricken for some time with leukaemia, passed away the following day: 'In one swoop, my mother lost her husband, and her son was given the last rites.'[9]

Alan survived, but only just, and was admitted to a holding base while he waited for a bed at a sanatorium, for one reason or another, to be vacated. Thirteen months later, he finally arrived at Milford.

It was here, confined to his bed, that Simpson, like Galton, began an extraordinary new process of self-education. The only things available for battling the boredom were books, and so both men proceeded to devour far more of them, drawn from a far broader range, than they (or any other working-class children for that matter) had ever had the chance to sample at school. There were plenty of humorous works by the likes of Thorne Smith, P.G. Wodehouse, Damon Runyon, George and Weedon Grossmith, Robert Benchley, James Thurber, Mark Twain and Stephen Leacock, but there was also a seemingly endless supply of classical fiction, biographies, historical studies, travelogues, essays, political theories and social commentaries. 'I was reading three books a day,' Simpson recalled. 'I used to read one in the morning, one in the afternoon and one in the evening. I destroyed my eyesight in the process; I became short-sighted. But I must say I wasn't selective – my mother used to just bring books in and I used to read them: the rubbish, the good stuff, all of it.'[10] Although Simpson had yet to encounter Galton, the seeds of comedy's most cultured and well-read writing partnership were already being sown.

Given the relatively great size of the sanatorium, the actual meeting would not take place until the day when one of them was transferred to a bed much nearer the other. When that finally happened, Galton (now a well-established resident of Ward 14) first saw Simpson (a new arrival from Ward 2) through a glass darkly:

Behind the beds there were glass doors and a corridor, leading to the wash-houses, to be used by fittish people. So I'm lying there and it suddenly goes all dark across the windows. I looked round to see what was happening, and it was the biggest bloke I'd ever seen in my life – six-foot-four, and weighing God knows how much. Everyone in the sanatorium was supposed to be about three-stone-something-or-other. I said, 'Who's that?' And they said it was another patient. He was very late in getting up; they couldn't get him out of bed; he wouldn't be persuaded to get out of bed. In there, we all wanted to get out of bed; except Alan. He thought if he stayed in bed long enough, and ate, he'd get out of there. And it worked – he got out long before I did. So that's how we met – I just

saw this shadow go across a window. Spike Milligan always used to
call him He Who Blocks Out The Sun.[11]

It did not take long, Simpson would recall, for the two of them to
form a firm rapport:

> When we got talking we found we had identical likes in terms of
> entertainment. [. . .] We were both comedy fans. We were also film
> fans and had the same taste in music – in fact, it's amazing how
> close our thoughts [would become] regarding politics, culture,
> wine, food. More importantly, though, our sense of humour was
> almost identical, which meant that as soon as we started working
> together we became almost telepathic. We could finish off each
> other's sentences.[12]

Ray Galton's original next-bed neighbour, Tony Wallis, had turned
their cubicle into something that resembled a cramped engineering
workshop, with a big RAF 1155 radio receiver (a relic from a disused
Lancaster bomber) taking pride of place, so he and Simpson had
access to stations overseas, such as AFM Munich-Stuttgart (the
American Forces' network), and could listen to the great interna-
tional comedy programmes of the era – *The Jack Benny Show, The
Fred Allen Show, Duffy's Tavern, The Adventures of Ozzie &
Harriet, The Life of Riley, The Couple Next Door, Father Knows
Best, Fibber McGee & Molly, The Phil Harris & Alice Faye Show, Vic
& Sade, The Bickersons* and many others – and compare them to the
best of the domestic output, such as *ITMA, Much Binding in the
Marsh, In Town Tonight, The Bradens, Variety Bandbox* and the
newly-launched *Take It From Here*: 'We were very conversant with all
the American shows,' Galton would recall, 'and they were more
sitcom-oriented than [the ones on British radio] were, and, we
thought, very superior, too.'[13]

Thanks to the ailing engineers who were stuck inside the sanatorium, a primitive form of in-house entertainment, Radio Milford,
was set up – initially broadcasting for an hour each day from inside
a converted linen cupboard. As the station grew in popularity, its

broadcasting hours were extended and a Radio Committee was established to find and foster fresh programme ideas. Both Galton and Simpson were keen to play their part:

> Ray and I went on the Radio Committee, and we broadcast an hour a day. Mostly it was gramophone record request programmes – visitors requesting records for the patients; the female patients requesting records for the male patients (and for some of the female patients, too. It was quite a liberal sanatorium). So Ray and I said, 'Why don't we make it like a mini-BBC?' We started doing 'Seat in the Circle'; because every Wednesday in the canteen they used to show a film, and only those people who were allowed out of bed could see it. For the rest of them, there was 'Seat in the Circle'.[14]

They also covered the occasional tennis match between the doctors and the nurses (and would have reported on other sporting events had there actually been any taking place) as well as attempting their own version of the popular BBC panel game *Twenty Questions*. 'Anyway,' Simpson would recall, 'one day we said, "The only things we're not doing are drama and comedy." So the head of the Radio Committee said, "Right – do some." So we undertook to do six fifteen-minute sketches, pastiches on sanatorium life, called "Have You Ever Wondered?" The idea was: have you ever wondered what would happen if doctors became patients, [or if the BBC's *In Town Tonight* show came to Milford] and so on. Anyway, we dried up after four. And as far as we were concerned, that was our career finished.'[15]

Simpson left the sanatorium a few months prior to Galton, but, when members of his local church concert party (with which he had been associated since before the time of his incarceration) asked him if he would consider writing them some comedy material, he waited until his friend was released, called him over and resumed their fledgeling collaboration. It worked so well that, having been through so much together inside the sanatorium, they realised that they now felt more at home with each other than they did with anyone else. 'When we got out of [the sanatorium],' Galton would recall, 'we used to go to parties where we would look on people of the same age enjoying themselves in a way that we could never . . . we couldn't join in. We'd look across the room at each other and there was a knowing smile. We didn't have to say anything. We knew that we were both regarding the goings on with the same degree of amazement.'[16]

The pair decided to try their luck as full-time comedy writers. They had already corresponded with Frank Muir and Denis Norden, their favourite comedy writing partnership of the time ('They didn't believe in "dumbing down" to their audience,' said Alan Simpson. 'They gave their audience a bit of credit. Some of their stuff was really quite erudite. And we admired that'), seeking expert advice. 'We asked,' Simpson would recall, 'a) "How do you become comedy writers?" and b) "Can we work in your office to see how it is done?" And they wrote a very nice letter back to us putting us off because, as we ourselves subsequently found out, there is no way that you want two spotty-faced Herberts looking over your shoulder while you're working.'[17] What Muir and Norden did advise them to do was to send a sample of their material to the BBC's script editor, Gale Pedrick, who was always on the look-out for up-and-coming talents. It was the only cue that was needed.

Basing themselves in the cosy little lounge of Alan Simpson's mother's house at 6 Church Walk in Streatham Vale, they settled down to work (with Galton arriving each morning at nine and staying until just before eleven-thirty, when it was time for him to catch the last bus home). As Simpson, while a shipping clerk, had been obliged to learn how to type (albeit with one finger per hand), he sat at a desk, hovered over the typewriter and took responsibility for transcribing the lines while Galton (watched sleepily by Nigel, the family cat) stretched out on the floor and stared at the ceiling. Using Muir and Norden's *Take It From Here* (which was structured so as to accommodate three main sketch sequences, including one that was usually a playful pastiche of a popular novel, play or movie) as their template, they cobbled together a ten-minute, pun-laden piece about Captain Henry Morgan the pirate.[18] They duly sent it off to Gale Pedrick and then crossed their fingers and hoped for the best.

A week or so later, a letter – bearing the bold BBC initials on the envelope – landed on the mat at Alan Simpson's house. With his heart beating quickly, he opened it up and, much to his delight, discovered that it contained a positive response:

I remember getting on the bus and rushing over to Ray and shouting and waving the letter from Gale Pedrick. He wrote that the sketch was highly amusing and asked us to go to see him. We were knocked out. Even to get a letter from the BBC was fantastic. If it had said nothing else we would have been showing this letter to everybody saying, 'Of course, we know something about writing – did you see this . . . er . . . letter from the BBC? They say the stuff we sent them was quite amusing.' We would have lived on that for the next forty years.[19]

When Pedrick met them in his office at Broadcasting House, he applauded one joke that he had particularly enjoyed – it was about Morgan's crew playing 'Jane Russell pontoon', and, when someone asked what sort of pontoon was 'Jane Russell pontoon', the reply was: 'It's the same as ordinary pontoon only you need thirty-eight to bust!' – and said that he would circulate the script among the BBC's radio producers and let them know if anyone expressed an interest. They would not have long to wait.

The most prompt response came from the office of Roy Speer, who was currently labouring to lift Derek Roy's under-performing *Happy-Go-Lucky*, but it did not come from Speer himself but rather from his star, the struggling gag man Roy. After being invited to meet him at his home in Bryanston Street (just behind Marble Arch), a nervous Galton and Simpson were ushered through to Roy's study by his somewhat eccentric secretary (a tiny, incredibly sad-faced man named Johnny Vyvyan – who would later find fame of sorts himself as a lugubrious stooge for a succession of popular comics) and received an offer to supply him regularly with some funny one-liners. It was not a lucrative offer – Roy, like many stand-ups of his generation, had a deserved reputation for being 'careful' with his money ('"Stingy" is the word,' Ray Galton would put it. 'We used to get two-and-six a joke')[20] – but, for two budding writers eager for a break, it promised the chance to commence a professional career, so they agreed without hesitation.

The job was, Simpson would recall, quite an eye-opener:

> Ray and I used to go to the recordings, and it was obvious that the show was dying on its feet. It was awful. One day, Roy Speer had a nervous breakdown, he'd had enough of it, and he was carted off to a nursing home. So the head of the BBC [Variety Department] came down and said, 'We'll have to carry on somehow,' and brought in a new producer, Dennis Main Wilson. Well, the first thing that he did was sack all of the established writers. Then he came up to us and said, 'You two tall blokes – are you writers?' And we said, 'Yes,' so he said, 'All right, then, *you* write the show!' We said, 'Well, er, yes,' even though we didn't think, or at least we weren't too sure, that we could do it. Because we knew that if we had said no, we would have been finished. Our only saving grace was the fact that the show was so bad it couldn't have been any worse, so we were in a win-win situation.[21]

'We worked every hour that God sent,' Simpson added. 'Until three in the morning. Dennis [Main Wilson] was driving over with fish and chips just to sustain us.'[22] After slaving away for Roy until his unloved series had hobbled to a welcome close, they moved on to other, much bigger and better, radio shows, such as *Workers' Playtime* (writing, for the first time, for Tony Hancock), *Calling All Forces* and *All-Star Bill*, producing sketches and monologues for innumerable comedians and plenty of occasional guest celebrities. 'Each show had guest comics, guest actors and singers,' Alan Simpson would recall, 'and we had to adapt our writing for their different styles. This is how we learnt our craft, it was an invaluable apprenticeship.'[23]

1953 was the year that real progress was made. First, they started planning a new kind of radio comedy show – one that would do without the conventional structure of sketches, special guests and musical interludes – for Tony Hancock. Second, while those plans were taking shape, they were asked to take over from Eric Sykes (who at that time was otherwise engaged) as scriptwriters for the next high-profile radio series by the most popular stand-up star of the decade: Frankie Howerd. Although Howerd still asked Sykes to oversee their output as editor, the individual shows would be more or less their own, and the positive reaction that the series received – from listeners and critics alike – would greatly enhance the reputation of Galton and Simpson.

Running from November 1953 to March 1954, *The Frankie Howerd Show* was a genuine triumph. It was a finely crafted and wonderfully characterful comedy show that not only knew how to attract an exceptionally high calibre of celebrity guest, but also, more pointedly, knew what to do with them once it had them. Emulating the example of Eric Sykes writing for the comedian in *Variety Bandbox*, Galton and Simpson created the kind of playfully prickly routines that enabled Howerd to mock both the real and the supposed pretensions of such stars as Margaret Lockwood, Robert Newton, Cicely Courtneidge, Robert Beatty, Joan Collins, Dennis Price, Diana Dors, Robert Morley, Claire Bloom and, most memorable of all, Richard Burton (who found the show's attitude refreshingly down-to-earth).

'We'd have all of these big-name guest actors come on and say things to Frank like, "You're not very good, are you?"' Alan Simpson recalled. 'And, of course, Frank would then explode, "How *dare* you!" He would be outraged at the suggestion that he wasn't a brilliant actor. And much of the comedy would go on from there.'[24] Just as Eric Morecambe would do a decade or so later ('Don't look now – a drunk's just come on'), Howerd would often fail either to recognise a star, or recognise what particular talent had made the person a star. When Richard Burton came on, for example, Howerd instructed the actor to get on with it and start playing his trumpet. 'He would treat them like dirt,' Ray Galton reflected. 'Burton would say, "Well, what did you think of my performance?" And Frank would say, "Well, er, ah, um, it was, er, um, ah, yes, it was, um, ah – I like your socks!"'[25] The teasing went down well on both sides of the microphone. 'We had great fun writing the scripts for all these great names,' Simpson said. 'It was a marvellous opportunity and, for us, a wonderful break.'[26]

If 1953 had been encouraging, the following year would prove momentous. Apart from continuing with their work for Frankie Howerd, they also gained a decent degree of security within the BBC as well as a fair measure of independence as co-founders of their own co-operative – and then they had the pleasure of bringing their own programme project to fruition. The first occasion for celebration arrived on 20 March 1954, when the BBC offered Galton and Simpson a three-year contract that would guarantee the pair of them a wage of at least £3,685 and ten shillings per year.[27] Then, in September, they became co-directors of Associated London Scripts. Finally, on 2 November, the first edition of their brand-new series, *Hancock's Half-Hour*, reached the air. Galton and Simpson had well and truly arrived.

Running for 103 episodes and six series on radio, from 1954 to 1959, and then sixty-three episodes and seven series on television, from 1956 to 1961, *Hancock's Half-Hour* would secure the reputation of Galton and Simpson as a pair of truly great comedy writers. Muir and Norden had already introduced a kind of 'semi-sitcom', 'The Glums',[28] into the structure of *Take It From Here* in 1953, and the British-based American husband-and-wife team of Ben Lyon and Bebe Daniels had been starring in *Life with the Lyons* (a sort of 'soap-com') since 1950, but Galton and Simpson's *Hancock's Half-Hour* represented a giant step forward for British radio: a complete, self-contained comedy that relied on the development of its characters, rather than on a succession of quick-fire gags, to engage and amuse its audience.

Chronicling the development of Britain's own nascent brand of situation-comedy, one critic observed at the time that while Hancock, as the star of the show, deserved enormous credit for making the transition from comic to comic actor, Galton and Simpson deserved an equal amount of applause, if not more, for 'gearing their inventiveness to illuminating' his talent via a series of scripts that served 'massively to enlarge [his] personality'.[29] Those American reviewers who came across the show would largely agree, with one of them

noting not only that the 'enormously funny' performer had 'the particularly good fortune to have first-rate material,' but also that
'American situation comedy might not be hurt by a [similar] touch of
inventiveness and topical references.'[30]

Ensconced in a series of increasingly large and luxurious offices at
their base at ALS, they were now, in the second half of the 1950s, part
of a comedy writers' aristocracy. They started getting their suits tailored in Jermyn Street and Savile Row; dined at decent tables at The
Ivy and Le Caprice; became connoisseurs of good food and fine wine;
and seemed to see every major new play and movie, read every major
new novel, consider every topical ideology and track every major
fashion that, like their own work, was currently reinvigorating British
culture. Their younger, discreetly impressed ALS colleague John
Antrobus would describe the appearance of Galton at this time as
'suave, always well dressed in a superior, Edwardian, *Clockwork
Orange* fashion [with] an eye for the ladies,' while Simpson was 'tall,
dark and handsome [but] no Flash Harry. You could never tell how he
was playing his cards.'[31] The money and the fame failed to spoil
them – Simpson still referred to Galton as a 'right hairy big-headed
twit', and Galton still dubbed Simpson a 'genial hungryguts'[32] – but
it did lend them a certain public lustre. They were the beacons of a
new breed of star writers, an inspirational sign of what could now be
achieved with words and wit.

They called themselves 'week-day' writers, engaged in a proper
job, and they almost always took the weekends off. Although they did
once 'knock out' an episode in a mere four hours ('a land-speed
record for us'),[33] their more typical pace would see them shape one
half-hour script with due care and attention over the course of about
two-and-a-half to three weeks. Whatever editing was needed
occurred as and when one or the other of them spoke.

Galton still stretched himself out on the floor and stared at the
ceiling, and Simpson still sat at the desk and typed, just as they had
done in Lil Simpson's little lounge in Streatham, but now, at the end
of each working day, they went off to their elegant Surrey homes
and their attractive young wives (Galton married Tonia in 1956,
Simpson married Kathleen in 1958) in brightly-polished Rolls-Royces.

The great comic poets of quiet desperation and thwarted social ambitions had made it all the way up to the high life.

A profile of the duo published in *The Times* during this period underlined their unprecedented celebrity status: here was a couple of comedy writers, the kind of programme contributors who used to be neither seen nor heard, being lauded by the country's paper of record. Likening the dandified Galton to a 'du Maurier illustration of artist life, an illusion completed by a Sherlock Holmes-style meerschaum pipe', and Simpson to a taller, broader version of Tony Hancock, the profile went on to underline their special status in both radio and television, and reported with respect their opinions on the reasons for their success:

> We like to steer clear of pretension and parish-pump humour such as you find in many West End revues: perhaps one reason for the success of the Hancock shows is that they generally stay close to life as known by their audiences, finding humour in popular news-papers and double-feature film programmes, or putting Hancock in the sort of situation in which we all feel ineffectual. Even Hancock's supposed intellectualism is the sort of tatty intellectu-alism picked up by the ignorant: his quotations are always recherché and wrong, his allusions deliberately obscure as well as irrelevant: he may be able to take in himself and Sidney James, but all the other characters see through him at once.[34]

It may be quite commonplace nowadays, but, in the 1950s, the sight of comedy writers being accorded so much space, in the arts section of a broadsheet newspaper, was a phenomenon of which it was prac-tically unheard. Suddenly, Galton and Simpson, alongside Milligan and Sykes, were helping the profession of comedy writing to be taken seriously.

There would be numerous awards in the years that followed, including a Guild of Television and Directors' 'Scriptwriters of the Year' presentation in 1959; two tributes from the Screenwriters' Guild in 1962 and 1963; as well as a special John Logie Baird Award in 1964 for their 'Outstanding Contribution to Television'. There would also be frequent critical encomia, some spectacular audience ratings and plenty of praise from their professional peers (including one of their old heroes, Frank Muir, who praised them for showing real 'insight into human nature' and 'an understanding of the way people behave and pretend').[35]

Now the highest-paid writing partnership currently working in British radio and television, they were not only responsible for *Hancock's Half-Hour,* but also contributing material (both officially and, as a favour, unofficially) to various other shows and stand-ups – including BBC TV's 1957 sketch series *Early to Braden* – as well as teaming up occasionally with other ALS writers to supply scripts for the odd new television project, such as a one-off show in 1958 for Peter Sellers called *The April 8th Show (Seven Days early).* They also did their best to look after their favourite performers, such as Sid James, for whom – after he and Hancock had gone their separate ways in 1960 – they would craft a new star vehicle named *Citizen James* ('It was purely out of sympathy for [him] being ditched,' Galton later confessed).[36]

Apart from Tony Hancock, Frankie Howerd was the other performer who most often needed their help. In 1958, for example, his latest attempt to lift his flagging career, a strange sci-fi musical-comedy called *Mr Venus,* looked like falling flat before the end of rehearsals, so, as usual, he called on his co-directors at ALS for vital assistance. The original script, by the playwright Alan Melville, was dispatched to ALS for a series of increasingly urgent and substantial rewrites by Galton and Simpson (and then, after Simpson had departed on a long-awaited family vacation, by Galton and Johnny Speight). 'It had started in the usual way,' Galton would recall. 'Frank asked us to touch it up – "Y'know, just put a joke in here and there, yeah, y'know, just a few wheezes, nothing too fancy" – and then, of course, we got asked to do more and more and more.'[37] Eventually, the script became so blatantly 'Howerdised' (with the star now turning the show's many flaws into cues for additional comedy) that an outraged Alan Melville demanded that his name be taken off the credits. The result was in some ways a marked improvement (while the first-night critics disliked the play *per se*, they found its star 'very funny indeed whenever he leaves the plot to look after itself and becomes a gawky nursemaid, a nervous speaker on the television screen, a rogue elephant let loose in a television studio, or better still a prisoner conducting his own defence, cross-examining himself in the witness box and asking himself such a complicated question that he has to ask himself to be good enough to repeat it'),[38] but the troubled production ran for just a few days more than a fortnight, and Howerd's ailing reputation reeled from yet another low blow.

Helping Frankie Howerd to claw his way back up to his rightful place at the top of the show-business ladder became a kind of mission not just for Galton and Simpson but for all of the writers at ALS during the late 1950s and early 1960s. Time after time, either Eric Sykes or Galton and Simpson or, failing them, one of their colleagues would make time in their busy schedules to act as the unofficial script doctors on their old friend and patron's latest under-performing project. As Ray Galton recalled, it was rare for such rewrites to lead to remuneration:

> They tended to be looked on as favours. At least by Frank! Whenever Frank was in a hole, he'd call you and say: 'Ooh, would you mind? Could you possibly? Ah, er, ooh, if you could add, y'know, just a *touch* here and there, y'know, er, just a touch . . .' And, of course, the 'touch here and there' would nearly always end up as a complete rewrite, and I don't think he ever paid us for it. But you didn't mind. It was always a joy writing for him. We always got a lot of laughs out of it.[39]

They never gave up looking for a practicable way to help him. Teaming up with their ALS colleagues Johnny Speight and Barry Took, they wrote a one-off show for him in 1960 called *Ladies and Gentle-Men*. Then, in 1961, after their long collaboration with Tony Hancock had finally come to an end and Tom Sloan invited them to nominate their next project, they told him without hesitation that they wanted to team up next with Frankie Howerd. 'He looked at us as though we'd just said something astonishing,' Ray Galton recalled, 'and then he said, "*Frankie Howerd*? Oh, no, no, he's finished. You don't want to do a series with *him*"':

> So we said, 'Why not? We *like* him. We think he's great!' He said, 'No, he's finished on television – his last series for the BBC was an absolute disaster! Believe me, he's finished in the business!' So we said, 'Come on, Tom, don't be daft! Frank's a genius!' In the end, he buzzed his PA, Queenie [Lipyeat], and asked her to bring in this great tome with all of the charts and audience appreciation ratings and what have you for Frank's last series [*Frankly Howerd*], and then he said, 'Do you see? An absolute disaster! Terrible audience figures and even worse appreciation ratings. Look at the charts. Terrible! No, you don't want to do *that*.' What he suggested instead was that we fulfil a programme title he'd thought up: *Comedy Playhouse*. He said he'd got these ten half-hour slots, and that we could do anything we liked with them, so long as we used that title – which was a fantastic offer that was just far too good to turn down. And to be fair to him, he also told us, 'Look, if you want Frank to do one of those, then that's fine, absolutely fine, it's entirely up to you – do what you want.' So we started out with *Comedy Playhouse,* and number four in the series turned out to be *Steptoe and Son*.[40]

Later on, they would manage to write an episode expressly for Howerd – a seed of a potential new sitcom entitled *Have You Read This Notice?* – but, by the time that this particular edition eventually went out on air (as part of a second run of *Comedy Playhouse* in 1963), the success that they were enjoying with other projects (most notably, of course, *Steptoe and Son*) precluded them from pursuing it any further.

Steptoe and Son was, by this stage, well on its way to breaking through the ten million mark for its weekly viewing figures (with several more million still to come), and, in the process, it was winning its writers some of the best reviews of their already distinguished shared career (and its readiness to explore darker themes and emotions prompted Frank Muir to praise the 'terrible consciences' of

Galton and Simpson: 'They worry about the world; they care very deeply about things. It's the other face of comedy in a sense'),[41] but still they kept the door open for Frankie Howerd. They were involved, for example, when Howerd made what turned out to be his triumphant 'comeback' at Peter Cook's new satirical nightclub, The Establishment, in 1963 (straight after some ill-starred appearances there by America's most controversial comic of the time, Lenny Bruce). Coaxed by his new manager, Beryl Vertue, into adapting his act for a younger and less deferential generation, he went to the ALS offices at Orme Court and worked with Sykes, Speight and Galton and Simpson on a suitable new opening routine. What they came up with would work like a treat: 'And ladies and gentlemen,' the key part of the fresh preamble went, 'I must tell you this: I hope you haven't got the wrong impression, ladies and gentlemen, if you've come along here tonight expecting Lenny Bruce – I'm sorry, I'm no Lenny Bruce. And if you've come here expecting a lot of crudeness, and a lot of vulgarity, I'm sorry, but you won't get it from me – so you might just as well piss off now!'[42]

After this, and a similar routine on the late-night satirical show *That Was The Week That Was* (or *TW3* as it was often known), Galton and Simpson again collaborated with Howerd – who was now enjoying a hugely successful West End run as the star of *A Funny Thing Happened on the Way to the Forum* – on a major new, eponymously titled, BBC peak-time television series. It was hard work for Howerd (who had to appear on stage every Monday through to Saturday, learning Galton and Simpson's new scripts in between performances, and then rehearse and record the show in the studio every Sunday) but it was well worth it. Everything about *The Frankie Howerd Show*, from the classy direction from Duncan Wood to the composition of the supporting cast (which included such reliable character actors as Patrick Cargill, Frank Thornton, Hugh Paddick and Julian Orchard), underlined the exceptional quality at its heart: the best stand-up comedian in Britain at his most artful and self-confident, and the best pair of comedy writers in Britain at their most playful and slyly mischievous.

Running for six weeks, from 11 December 1964 to 15 January 1965,

Spike Milligan in 1957, ever ready to elbow any foolish consistency.

Another good day at the office: Eric Sykes relaxes after completing his latest script

'No, missus, *liss-en*!'
Frankie Howerd and
Eric Sykes in 1956.

Alan Simpson and Ray Galton: The masters of the Great British sitcom.

'I'm a grass': Johnny Speight typing another *Till Death*.

The regalia of success:
Speight and his Roller.

John Antrobus: 'God
is dead and satire is
King and bollocks to
the Establishment'.

Eric Merriman and Barry Took in 1959:
'We like: Chinese food. We dislike: each other'.

'How Bona to vada your dolly old eek!' Barry Took and Marty Feldman.

An early toast to the spirit of goonery: [l-r] Harry Secombe, Michael Bentine, Peter Sellers and Spike Milligan.

'My eyes aren't what they used to be. They used to be my ears'.
The Goons in 1956.

Sykes And An Identical Twin in 1962.

High quality mainstream comedy: Sykes, Richard Wattis and Deryck Guyler in a scene from *Sykes And A . . .*

'Did Magna Carta die in vain?' Tony Hancock shares his wisdom with his writers.

The wonderful Hancock: 'It's *him* that's at fault – he's a rotten writer!'

the series not only managed to strike a reasonably happy medium between stand-up and sketches (paving the way for all of Howerd's subsequent television appearances, including *Up Pompeii!*, by appearing to grant him the licence to step out of the situation at will, look straight at the camera and address the viewers directly), but it also seized the opportunity to take revenge on all of those old doubters within the BBC ('*Frankie Howerd?* He's finished!') by returning, again and again and again, to that comically shady executive presence, 'Thing' (a measure of Tom Sloan mixed with a dash or two of irascible radio producer). At the end of the opening episode, for example, Howerd asked the viewing audience to be sure to deliver a favourable verdict 'so that old "Thing" can have his extra six inches of carpet'.

Viewers, according to the BBC's own audience research reports, were 'delighted to welcome Frankie Howerd back to their screens', as 'far too little had been seen of this "engaging" comedian in recent years'. There was a particularly positive reaction to the way that his opening and closing monologues had dominated the show, and 'it was widely felt that his new scriptwriters – Galton and Simpson – had provided him with material that "suited him to a T".'[43] Even Howerd himself – who was an incorrigible self-critic – declared that the series had been 'superlative'.[44] Not many great writers of sitcoms had also proven themselves so adept at scripting sketch shows – Eric Sykes was probably the only other one to have done so – but Galton and Simpson had come up with something of an instant classic.

Another, arguably even more impressive (and now seriously under-rated) series, would follow one year later, exhibiting the same fine style and strengths, attracting the same high ratings and winning the same warm reviews.[45] The opening monologues carping about 'Thing' (which would inspire other performers from Larry Grayson and Ronnie Corbett to Paul O'Grady and beyond) were especially effective:

He said, 'Ah, yes, do come in. Do come in, won't you?' He said, 'Now tell me, which one are *you*?' I felt like one of The Beverly

Sisters! I said, 'Look – I'm not "one" of anybody! I'm on me own – "Howerd, F: comedian; BBC, for the use of". *[Sotto voce:]* And not very much lately, I might add!' So he said, 'Oh, yes! I remember *you*, yes.' He said, 'Very disappointing show.' He said, 'We must do better than *that*, mustn't we!' He said, 'Tell me, what have you got for us *this* time? Come on: fill me in!' I thought, 'Nothing would give me greater pleasure!' But I controlled meself. Then I took a liberty. I sat down. I said, 'Um, well, I've been thinking,' I said, 'I thought I might do more or less the same sort of thing I did before.' 'Oh!' he said. 'No! Oh, no, no, no, no, no! Oh, no, no, no, no, no, *no*!' He said, 'We can't have that.' He said, 'We must find the right *vehicle* for you,' And by the way he looked at me I think he meant a hearse! He said, 'You see, the trouble with *you* is that, um, you're so difficult to *categorise*.' He said, 'You see, you don't *fit in* anywhere. You're neither one thing nor the other.' I don't know *what* he meant by *that*! He said . . . he said . . . *[To the laughing audience: Please! There's too much tittering! Naughty tittermongers!]* No! He said, 'You're a sort of cross between Bertie Wooster and Harold Steptoe.' He said, 'You're terribly ill-defined.' I said, 'Well, I can't help me looks, can I?' He said, 'No, no, I don't mean *that*!' He said, 'You're not *with it* – you're not 1966.' He said, 'After all, you've got a sort of *musty* ambience of a bygone age. A sort of *mouldy* patina of incipient decay. A sort of fossilised—' I said, 'All right, don't go on!' I said, 'I got the drift!' Cor, blimey – I felt like something that Mortimer Wheeler had dug up! He said, 'Well, that's it in a nutshell.' He said, 'This is a technological age.' He said, 'You have to modernise, or get out. Modernise – or get out.' And with that he went up to his gramophone and he put a Henry Hall record on.[46]

'I think,' Ray Galton would reflect, 'that those two series were the best thing we'd ever written for Frank. To be honest, I think they were among the best things that he would ever do on television.'[47]

In addition to their own success on television with *Comedy Playhouse*, *Steptoe and Son* and *The Frankie Howerd Show*, the 1960s also saw Galton and Simpson branch out into movies: after writing *The Rebel* (a decent debut whose ill-advised title-change for the North American market, *Call Me Genius*, seemed to antagonise certain critics)[48] for Tony Hancock in 1960, they went on to supply the screenplays for *The Wrong Arm of the Law* (1963), *The Bargee* (1964) and *The Spy with a Cold Nose* (1966). They also wrote, yet again, for Frankie Howerd, but this time in the theatre – collaborating with Eric Sykes on the record-breaking West End revue *Way Out in Piccadilly* (in which Howerd co-starred with Cilla Black) in 1966, and then adapting the French 'wild west' satire *Du vent dans les branches de Sassafras* (re-titled *The Wind in the Sassafras Trees* and then *re-re-titled Rockefeller and the Red Indians*) for performances in Boston, Washington and Broadway.[49]

The momentum would be maintained deep into the next decade. *Steptoe and Son* would be brought back on both the small screen and the big; the *Comedy Playhouse* format would return, under the new banner of *The Galton & Simpson Playhouse*, for another exceptionally engrossing run (which included Leonard Rossiter in 'I Tell You It's Burt Reynolds' – one of the funniest half-hours of the 1970s); an adaptation of Joe Orton's black farce *Loot* would be made into a movie; a controversially *à la mode* new sitcom, *Casanova '73* (starring Leslie Phillips), would be introduced on BBC1; there would be several more shows and specials scripted for Frankie Howerd; and there would also be an admirably ambitious nine-part adaptation for BBC2 of Gabriel Chevallier's satirical novel *Clochemerle*. In addition to crafting these and other personal projects, they would also be obliged to monitor and advise on numerous foreign television versions of their own most famous productions.[50]

Throughout it all, the partnership, like the friendship, between Galton and Simpson remained remarkably stable and strong ('A pressure shared,' said Simpson, 'is a pressure halved').[51] Even during the many years that they spent inside the busy offices at ALS, where it was not uncommon for the various stellar talents to circulate and interact, this particular couple usually stayed, Ray Galton would recall, contentedly self-contained: 'Spike mainly wrote by himself. Eric wrote by himself. So both of them would come in to our office – not all the time, not every day, but quite often – and ask us to listen to what they'd just done and ask us what we thought about it. We, on the other hand, never went to them, because we'd got each other.'[52]

Galton and Simpson would always have each other. No two men could have been happier to be stuck inside the same room. It was, after all, the best possible place to be if you loved sitcoms.

Johnny Speight

Ninety per cent of my material comes from people in pubs.
I'm a recorder.

Every community needs someone to scrap and shout on its behalf. Every community needs someone who is willing to make a nuisance of him or herself. In the late 1950s and 1960s, British comedy, culture and society had someone just like that: Johnny Speight.

Johnny Speight was a working-class writer who refused to accept his supposed station in life. He was a writer who refused to encourage anyone else to accept his or her station in life. He was a writer who refused to respect anyone who expected, or demanded, that everyone else accepted their station in life. He spoke to people who had been told that they had never had it so good and showed them that, in reality, some of them deserved to have it much better, and some of them deserved to have it much worse.

He was also the sworn (and swearing) enemy of all forms of humbug and hypocrisy in modern society. Show him a snob or a sly dissembler, a bullying bigot or a blustering bore, and he would seek a way to reduce their words to what they really meant, and expose them for what they really were. He had a great ear for specious conceit: phrases such as 'It stands to reason'; 'It's human nature'; 'It's common sense'; and 'That is an actual fact' were mimicked and mocked by his satirical deconstructions, leaving nothing standing but naked shivering prejudice.

There were no hugs and kisses in his comedies, and no happy endings. He refused to sweeten the pill. He wrote about poverty, conflict, envy and ignorance. He noticed all of the dust and the dirt and the hurt. If there was corruption and injustice in his world, he always acknowledged it. 'I'm a grass,' he said, and he meant it.[1]

Speight was born on 2 June 1920 in the bottom half of a two-up, two-down rented terraced house at 111 Dale Road, Canning Town, east London – the first child of John Speight, a boiler scaler on the docks, and his wife, Johanna (née Sullivan). There was another family in residence upstairs, but as they, like the Speights, were similarly-natured Roman Catholics the arrangement caused relatively little friction between the floors. By the time that Johnny had been joined by a younger brother and sister, his parents were ready and able to move slightly up in the world – four streets away – and into a larger house all of their own (albeit still rented) that boasted no fewer than two downstairs rooms, three bedrooms, a scullery and a small but welcome back garden.

Johnny, as the eldest child, was given the dubious privilege of being the first one in the family to wear a brand-new pair of leather boots. The privilege was dubious because such items had to be tough enough at the start to be passed down the line not once but twice via his brother and sister. 'My mother would buy them two sizes too big and hope that you would grow into them,' Speight would recall. 'It took two years to grow into them and another two years to grow out of them. [. . .] I got the new pairs, but actually the other two were better off because I'd worn them in like.'[2]

Educated locally at St Helen's Roman Catholic Primary School in Falcon Street, he hated the experience from the start. It seemed to him like a small person's prison: '[T]he sentence was automatic. Nine years' hard labour. They decry dictators for putting people in prison without trial but we were shut up for most of the day without trial. There was no Court of Appeal either. We got no remission of sentence for good behaviour and there was no Parole Board to review our case either.'[3] One of the few things he would later admit to having learnt from his time 'inside' was 'the ability to look interested when one isn't'.[4] He was a bright and lively child, naturally inquisitive and instinctively argumentative, and he hated the emphasis on swallowing knowledge whole ('like some awful medicine') instead of discovering it piecemeal at a sensible pace: 'The captive child will endeavour to learn most things parrot fashion to escape the attentions of its gaoler, but this won't pass as education. For those who cannot escape over the barbed wire fences will surely escape into their own imaginations and dwell only on those thoughts that give them pleasure.'[5] This was precisely the strategy to which, year in, year out, the young Speight subscribed: 'I used to get completely immersed in my day-dreams. Well, my inner world was far better than my outer world, it was a gayer, more fascinating world and I was its star.'[6]

He was no school-room, or school-yard, joker: 'There was no time for comedy at my school.'[7] He would later admit, however, that, given his relatively short stature (unlike his future colleagues – Milligan, Sykes, Galton and Simpson – who shot up past the six-foot mark, Speight was destined to fall well short), stocky build and nervous stutter, a little humour would probably have helped: 'If you were born a handsome, good-looking feller who scored for the school team every Saturday you don't need comedy. But one day you look in the mirror and see your face and you say "Why? Why? Why me?" And if you're not going to cry you start laughing at it.'[8]

These early years were all about just going through the motions. School, he would say, remained nothing more than 'something to escape from': 'It seemed to me that the whole idea of school was to vaccinate the pupils with a little specially prepared culture in the fond hope that it would enable them to resist it for the rest of their lives.'[9] In his case, the vaccination failed to take and the craving for culture remained, even though it stayed largely starved of any formal stimulation. There were movies, there was music, there was radio and there was sport. Some stimuli existed, but precious little of it was to be found anywhere at school. He left, aged fourteen, feeling angry and frustrated, without any formal qualifications.

His initial ambition, he would claim, was to be a white-collar worker. 'If you were a white-collar worker you could knock off work and go out in the evening without having to wash.'[10] (There was no bath inside the Speight family home, so washing was always something of a problem.) His first paid position, however, was as a lowly lacquerer of spring clips: 'What they were used for I have no idea. All I know was that they had to be lacquered.'[11]

A succession of similarly meaningless menial jobs followed at several East End factories along the Silvertown Way, but the only enthusiasm that Speight exhibited during this period was reserved for his fledgeling amateur career as a jazz musician, playing drums in two minor, south London-based bands before forming his own outfit, Johnny Speight and His Hot Shots. When war intervened, he joined the Royal Corps of Signals and did his best to 'get out of anywhere where there was a chance of a gun being fired'.[12] He also did what he could to maintain his dubious reputation as 'the hottest drummer in Canning Town' by playing in Army unit bands, but his more formal soldierly duties still exposed him to the kinds of harrowing sights and scenes that would darken his outlook for the rest of his life. He was one of those detailed to cremate the enemy dead on the battlefields by pouring petrol over them and lighting fires – 'We couldn't bury them. There were too many and there was no bloody time'[13] – and, when he was demobbed, he returned to civilian life convinced that 'when old men start wars then those same old men should be made to go and fight them. It would save the lives of a lot of youngsters and get rid of decrepit senile old fools.'[14]

He was unsure as to what he could and should do with the rest of his life. School and war had shown him what he most definitely did not want to do, but, apart from jazz, the positive options were harder to find. He knew, however, that the pressure to get a 'proper' job was now on: 'I didn't have anything wrong with me like T.B. or any other disease I could fall back on.' He remained disinclined, none the less, to lose himself in a lifetime of manual labour: 'I was healthy and fit for work but I didn't consider the work fit for me.'[15]

He decided instead to resume his drumming, and so he contrived, by one means or another, to acquire 'the biggest set of drums in the area': 'I had the lot: swan neck cymbals, temple blocks, whistles, wood blocks, a tambourine for The Galloping Major and all that crap, castanets, maracas – I even had a football rattle for novelty effects.'[16]

Armed with this 'great Wurlitzer of drums', he joined a band called Howard Wynn-Jones and His Big Broadcast Band, and together they toured the local halls to no great or positive effect. 'When I think of the time and energy that could have been more profitably expended some other way,' Speight would reflect, 'it's heartbreaking really to see people desperately struggling to be something they can never hope to be. Their vain attempts to scale the heights of their dreams, giving glimpses of glorious high comedy to those who watch, but bringing them nothing but misery.'[17] Night after night, in darker and dingier dives, they would have to put up with booze-breathed old boys calling out for 'proper' dance tunes instead of more 'coon music': 'We're in a dance-hall,' they would shout, 'not in the fucking jungle.'[18] Speight would remember these types; he would respond to them one day.

When, eventually, the unit broke up, Speight auditioned for other bands, but he could not read music and it seemed as though he was competing with a veritable paradiddle of other drummers who were technically far more proficient. He did manage to impress a band composed entirely of dwarves, but, in spite of the fact that he would be sitting down at the back behind his drum kit, he was dismissed by their diminutive leader because he was still deemed to be too tall ('I was choked,' he would moan. 'I felt like saying to him, "*I* don't fit? It's *you* lot who don't fit"'[19]). Upping sticks and skins, he moved around the country in search of work, playing the odd gig here and there for up to a pound or two per night. Eventually, after some barren spells, he found a role for himself in a run-down jazz club just south of the centre of Manchester (surviving mainly on booze and bootlegged marijuana), and then, when that engagement ended, he travelled down to Clacton-on-Sea to drum in a pub by night and cook in a guest-house by day.

Speight stayed in Clacton-on-Sea for as long as he could stand it, which was not long, and then trudged reluctantly back to London. He had made no palpable progress; he had just worked as hard as he could to avoid sliding backwards. 'I was really struggling,' he later said, 'because guys playing great jazz even couldn't find an audience. I had as much chance of finding an audience for the music that I played as I had of growing two heads. What did I want two heads for anyway? I couldn't feed the mouth on the one I already had.'[20]

The idea of writing as a vocation came to Speight during his regular visits to Canning Town Public Library, where he was drawn to such authors as John Steinbeck (because Speight felt that he wrote of real people and believable worlds) and George Bernard Shaw (who, because of all of his well-known *bon mots*, Speight used to think was some kind of stand-up comic, like Tommy Trinder, until he saw a shelf-full of books and thought: 'Christ. He writes as well'[21]). Shaw's early semi-autobiographical novel *Immaturity* had an impact on Speight that he would liken to a 'divine revelation', acting as if 'a light had been turned on and every dark recess lit by sweet reason').[22] The more pages that he turned, he said, the more he thought: 'I'm not wrong after all. They're all wrong. What I think is right.'[23] Inspiration, at last, was at hand: 'The whole of life,' Speight would say, 'was made to look brighter and more hopeful than ever before.'[24] He proceeded to devour all things Shavian ('If God could write he couldn't write better than Shaw'),[25] as well as works by Strindberg, Chekhov, Wilde, O'Casey, H.G. Wells, William Morris, Godwin, Shelley, Keats and Ibsen (as well as the odd excerpt from Marx and Engels). Starved for so long of culture, he now gorged himself on a rich and wide literary range.

The only writing he was doing for himself at the time was limited to inscribing his name at the local Labour Exchange, but, with his musical efforts still falling on deaf ears, the chance to express himself through various literary endeavours seemed like an attractive and practicable alternative. 'I don't know why I thought I could be a writer,' he would say, 'but Shaw gave me the feeling that I could do it. He gave me the feeling that if you want to be something you have to have a go.'[26] He proceeded to experiment with short stories, newspaper articles, fierce polemics and playful flights of fancy, doing his best to keep his written sentences – like his spoken ones – as short, sharp and simple as possible ('I always try to slip out little words,' he would explain, 'before my stutter notices them').[27] Nothing was published, but strengths and weaknesses were identified and assessed and, slowly but surely, a style began to emerge.

Although he paid his way during this period by working from door to door – first to deliver milk and then to sell insurance – his writing was spurring him on. He tried to write about the things that mattered to him, the things that made sense to him, like those people – like himself – who were 'up against this business of trying to live without being exploited too much by the other bastards. Or having to work too hard at doing things you weren't the slightest bit interested in, just for a few bob to keep body and soul together so you could go on doing the same stupid things all over again, like bloody mice on a treadmill, going round and round and round again and not being able to get off the bleeding thing.'[28]

He joined a writers' group at the left-wing Unity Theatre in Mornington Crescent, where he chain-smoked, drank cognac and wrote several didactic plays that he later dismissed as 'a load of crap',[29] and also started scripting sketches and stand-up material in the hope of winning some commissions from professional comedians. No one seemed interested until the autumn of 1953, when an old Army friend – who was now working in the West End theatres as a masseur for, among others, Tony Hancock, Max Bygraves and Frankie Howerd – volunteered to arrange a meeting with one of his well-known clients. Speight was duly dispatched a few days later to the Prince of Wales Theatre in Coventry Street, where Frankie Howerd was currently appearing in a very popular revue called *Pardon My French*; the comedian, as keen as ever to find fresh sources of funny material, bought (for no great sum) the first joke that Speight ever sold – 'I'm livid – they're pulling down my house to build a slum!'[30] – and promised the budding writer that he would do what he could to help him kick-start his professional career.

Howerd proved as good as his word, and, after he introduced Speight to Eric Sykes, Spike Milligan and Galton and Simpson, Associated London Scripts signed up another promising new writer. Bearing in mind the calibre of its directors, Speight had imagined ALS to be a smart and rather *chic*-looking organisation – 'all chrome, lush secretaries and Jewish gold watches' – and so he was shocked to discover that it bore a much closer resemblance to 'a slum' in Shepherd's Bush but, none the less, he was thrilled by the enthusiastic reactions to his work (Eric Sykes had judged his first sample script to be 'absolutely scintillating')[31] and was grateful to be on the books.

The other, far more established, writers fascinated him as he considered how best he should try to fit in. He still felt like an ordinary working-class man from Canning Town, whereas Spike Milligan struck him as 'a bit mad', and Galton and Simpson puzzled and unnerved him by dressing up like futuristic dandies and reclining on the floor. Eric Sykes, with his 'camel-hair overcoat, a half-smoked cigar and an air of easy-come, easy-go', fitted much more closely with his image of what 'a successful writer should look like' – but that just made him seem even more of a hard act to follow.[32] Speight was also bemused, in the early days, by the fact that Beryl Vertue 'always used to be arguing with the greengrocer downstairs about his fruit display, asking him if he could make it less obvious as a lot of important people were coming from the BBC to talk to her clients'. There were times, he would later admit, when he 'wondered if I'd chosen right, and if there wasn't more chance of making money downstairs because, the way he sold it, it looked like fruit was here to stay.'[33] He started to feel much better, however, when Ray Galton revealed how much one of his suits cost – an astronomical amount as far as Speight was concerned – and looked forward to the day when he could afford something of a similar quality in a rather more conservative style.

His work was first heard on a 1955 BBC radio show entitled *Mr Ross – and Mr Ray*, starring bandleaders Edmundo Ross and Ray Ellington, and at the end of that year he began contributing scripts to the much higher profile *The Frankie Howerd Show*. 'You don't have to write all of those "Ooooh-aaahs" in,' the comedian told him. 'I'll put those in myself.' Speight just managed to stifle his instinctive sardonic response: 'Ah! This one can ad lib.'[34]

It was not long, of course, before Howerd changed his mind, as usual, and instructed Speight to ensure that all of the 'Oooh-aaahs' *were* included in anything that he submitted (it was a little game that he liked to play with most of his new writers), but their partnership soon blossomed into an outstanding creative relationship. Just as Eric Sykes and Galton and Simpson had done before him, Speight benefited early on from Howerd's exceptionally sharp eye (and ear) for detail when it came to shaping a comedy script:

> He was a *big* help to me as a writer. It was like a young journalist joining a newspaper and having a marvellous editor . . . Working

for a great stand-up like Frank was the same thing. I mean, Frank's attitude [towards a new piece of written material] was, 'Yeah, maybe a nice thought, but is it going to get a *laugh*?' You know, we all had such *trust* in him. We knew that if *he* said yes, it was OK, then it *was* OK.[35]

Howerd, in turn, appreciated Speight's gift for bitingly sarcastic one-liners, as well as his ability to write the kind of comic monologues (orchestrated with both men's shared stuttering rhythms) that contained so much of the performer's own refreshingly self-mocking spirit: 'It's not easy being a comedian,' went one of these routines. 'Some do it by wearing funny clothes. Some comedians have a funny face. Me? I have this curse of beauty!'[36]

Speight was the principal writer of the third series of *The Frankie Howerd Show* – which ran on BBC radio from 2 October 1955 to 22 January 1956 – as well as (in collaboration with his friend Dick Barry) the two television shows that followed towards the end of 1956. Howerd still could not resist soliciting the odd (unpaid) extra line from other writers within ALS, but Speight never objected: 'Frank was very generous in that respect,' he would reflect with real affection. 'He never left anyone out. He was willing to share our genius with the world. And I think he looked upon it as a comedy brook that flowed past his door, and he would put his bucket in and take out what he fancied for the day!'[37] Certain signatures, however, were hard to smudge, so the extra input was superficial.

It was an increasingly busy and exciting time for Speight. He married Constance ('Connie') Beatrice Barrett, a secretary from Dagenham, on 3 April 1956 (they would have two sons, Richard and Francis, and one daughter, Samantha). Later the same month, he began writing for Morecambe and Wise when they returned to television (after a period of licking their wounds following a disastrous debut series called *Running Wild*) as the resident comics on ATV's *The Winifred Atwell Show*. He then spent the summer writing for Peter Sellers and others in *The Dickie Valentine Show*. The more sensitive and perceptive that he became to each performer's strengths, weaknesses and personality, the more comfortable they felt with his material, and the more effective the performances became. He was learning quickly, and his reputation was rising rapidly.

Speight's writing career really started to advance in 1957 when he began a nine-year engagement as principal scriptwriter of ATV's *The Arthur Haynes Show*. Haynes – a 43-year-old comedian from Hammersmith whose career was finally sparking into life – came to television without an established comic persona, so Speight created one for him: an aggressive, argumentative, know-all tramp by the name of Hobo Haynes. This character, with his frowning hat, proud chestful of military medals and his index finger primed to prod, was capable of being unnerving as well as amusing ('Arthur had a marvellous, immobile face in which only the eyes moved – malicious eyes,' said Speight. 'You knew that tramp was going to con you the moment you saw him'),[38] and his comments could certainly cut.

Speight would go on to create various other types of anti-Establishment under-dog for Haynes to play (usually opposite his regular straight-man: the polished and posh-sounding Nicholas Parsons, whom Haynes always addressed as 'Mr Nichol-arse'), but Hobo, with his vaguely menacing bluff and bluster ('There I was, up to me neck in muck and bullets, fighting for me country, mate'), was the one who made Haynes into one of the biggest – and best-paid – stars on British television, and Speight into one of the best-paid writers. As one critic put it at the time, Haynes, when left to his own devices, was just 'an ordinary stand-up comedian [of] good ENSA standard', but, when playing Speight's 'obstreperous, slightly disreputable proletarian', he became exceptional. Hobo was a huge success.[39]

The inspiration for the character had come from a real-life tramp to whom Speight had once given a lift. This man had first surprised, then riled and then ultimately amused the writer with his mixture of snobbery, deference and chippy resentment: 'I prefer Bentleys,' he had said, settling back into the passenger seat of the shiny second-hand Silver Dawn Rolls-Royce that Speight had just saved enough to buy. 'A little Anglia offered me a ride, but I wouldn't take it. I mean you meet a better class of person in a car like this. Toffs like.'[40] The tramp never shut up: 'Shouldn't have to drive a Rolls if you own it,' he said. 'These cars are made for a servant to drive. All comforts in the back. Yer cocktail cabinet, yer telephone [. . .] all that's in the back for yer gentleman to use. I mean,' he went on, 'people who buy these cars don't have all that expensive education at Eton an' Harrow just to end up driving a car, specially a posh car like this. I mean, that's an underling's job. You'll never see the Queen drive herself, or any of yer nobs.'[41] Hobo spoke and acted just like that, and thus became both the target of and mouthpiece for Speight's attacks on those Britons – the snobs, the inverted snobs, the bosses and the brutes and the bigots – who in some way or other had gone bad.

It was also during this period that Speight wrote several powerful, class-conscious plays for television, including *The Compartment* (1961), for which he won the first of his four Screen Writers' Guild awards, and *Playmates* (1962). Peter Sellers had wanted to play the lead role in *The Compartment*, but, as happened so often with him and television projects, he kept on being distracted by more glamorous and lucrative offers from Hollywood and so the BBC, losing patience, ended up casting a lesser-known actor instead by the name of Michael Caine.

Broadcast by BBC TV on 22 August 1961, this tense psycho-drama featured a young working-class Cockney (Caine) and an older, somewhat aloof, middle-class man (Frank Finlay) occupying the same carriage on a train but failing to interact because of various social and cultural obstructions. When the older man remains haughtily distant and silent in spite of all the young man's efforts to engage his attention, the Cockney becomes increasingly angry and aggressive, and, eventually, is driven so mad with frustration that he threatens to kill his passively pompous tormentor. Caine relished the role because, as he later explained, 'it was basically a monologue with the other actor only speaking at the end when he pleads for his life,' and, on several other levels, it seemed so well-suited to his particular attitude, personality and talent: 'Here was something that would be the making of me as an actor on television, and I was so right for it. I was a Cockney, I had become an actor so I was more than likely insane myself and I hated the class system in this country – and here was my chance to have a swipe at it.'[42]

Caine – who was widely praised in the Press for his performance – also appeared in *Playmates*, which the television critic of *The Times* judged to be Speight's 'best work so far'. Focusing on a brief encounter inside a lonely country house by a strangely childlike man (Caine) and a ravening female predator (Sheila Burrell), the production was applauded for creating an overall effect that was 'less that of a study of two lunatics than of a parable on the impermanence of all human contact.'[43]

Speight would complement these two small-screen efforts with his first three-act play for the stage, *The Knacker's Yard* (a macabre comedy set in a sordid rooming house), which was performed in 1962 at the Arts Theatre in Great Newport Street despite incurring some severe censorship from within the Lord Chamberlain's office (the official censors of the London stage until 1968). 'The notices,' Speight would admit, 'were mixed. Those who liked it – and there were many – loved it, and those who hated it – and there were equally many – loathed it.' The writer, however, remained bullish, and regarded the differences of opinion as a sign that he was getting it more right than wrong: 'I'm one of those Englishmen who, as Shaw says, has only to open his mouth to be despised by other Englishmen.'[44] As a socialist writing truthfully about a class-ridden capitalist society, Speight said, it was inevitable that he would make plenty of enemies as well as win many friends.

Speight was actually by no means the only socialist at Associated London Scripts. Although Eric Sykes was a relatively apolitical conservative (in other words, a traditional English Tory), Spike Milligan (when he was not being some kind of quasi-Nietzschean-style misanthrope or an old-fashioned philanthropic liberal) had spells during which he raced back and forth between communism, anarchism, anarcho-syndicalism, utopian socialism, bourgeois socialism and revolutionary socialism, and both Galton and Simpson were committed modern socialists who, once *Steptoe and Son* was riding high in the ratings, were courted by Britain's Labour aristocracy. Speight, however, was the most self-conscious socialist amongst them, and was always ready to be seen and heard blowing the whistle on capitalist cant and corruption.

It was unfortunate, however, that Speight's own rather lumpy brand of socialism, for all of his disconnected references to Marx and Lenin – still bore such a strong family resemblance to Shaw's snobbish Victorian Fabianism – a strain of socialism that objected to capitalism more for functional than ethical reasons (it was wasteful more than it was unjust), and placed its faith in the well-bred wisdom of dynamic individuals drawn from the middle classes rather than invested in the long-term intellectual and cultural potential of 'the promiscuously bred masses' (not even a free and universal system of education, Shaw once declared disdainfully, could ever 'raise the mass above its own level').[45] Ordinary working people were still patronised by the Fabians – they were just patronised now in the name of the Left instead of the Right (there was nothing in Shaw's *Pygmalion*, for example, to suggest that the working-class Eliza Doolittle had it in herself to change who she was rather than just disguise who she was).

It was not too surprising, therefore, that Speight's own comments about the class from within which he had emerged sometimes sounded, though well meant, somewhat condescending. He would refer, for example, to the typical radio audience of the 1950s as being composed predominantly of 'simple people' who might not understand 'big words'[46] (contrast that with the relatively 'posh' Muir and Norden's insistence that this same radio audience was unlikely to be fazed by references to the likes of Picasso: 'They know *roughly* who he is,' Norden would reassure his sceptical bosses. 'They know he's not a clarinet player').[47] Speight would also relate with apparent affection such depressing instances of *nouveau-riche* loutishness as when the comedian Max Wall ('with wonderful disdain') spat out a mouthful of wine straight into the face of an innocent waiter just because it had not brought sufficient pleasure to his palate ('You ought to be locked up trying to sell filth like that').[48] It might have been the influence of Shaw's Olympian individualism, or the impact of his own recent and rapid progression to opulence ('Speight would talk up a good revolution,' his ALS colleague John Antrobus would recall with a smile, 'but he enjoyed a showbiz lifestyle'),[49] but, in spite of his genuine compassion for the working classes, he seemed to doubt that more than a few of them could follow in his footsteps –

which perhaps explains why his more class-based comedy, for all of its anger and urgency, often seemed so bleak.

When he tried to write less like Bernard Shaw and more like Johnny Speight, however, his humour often struck just the right balance between its bark and its bite. When, for example, he was called upon to help Frankie Howerd 'update' his material to suit the mood of the early 1960s, he knew exactly what he needed to do:

> Comedy, to have any point at all, has got to say something. I don't believe in a gag for the sake of a joke. I can't stand empty comedy. All great comedy has got some thought behind it. All the great comedians and comedy writers are having a go at society, trying to show what it is like. It was always in my writing. [. . .] I realised you can do more with comedy than with dreary plays but the thought is still there. You want to say something if you can. But first and foremost it's got to be funny.[50]

It was Speight who, quite brilliantly, provided the core political humour when Howerd performed at The Establishment club in 1962 and charmed a new generation of satirists. Without any of the heavy touches that sometimes undermined the impact of his plays, Speight's stand-up routines for Howerd were supremely effective, taking the news agenda and mocking it via a casual-sounding gossip over the garden wall:

> Why *should* I make jokes about Macmillan? Tell me. Why should I make jokes about Macmillan? I don't *know* the man. I don't know him. I mean, it's so unfair. And it's so easy. He's such an obvious target. Everyone has a go at Macmillan. After all, he's just one man against the Government. I mean, admittedly, well, I mean, I think he's silly to himself. I'm sorry, he's silly to himself. Well, I mean, his public image – I mean, let's face it, he's no Bruce Forsyth, is he? Pity, don't you think? Pity. I think it spoils him. He might be very nice, under that moustache. But it's a pity really, it spoils him. In any case, I mean, I've had no dealings with the man. I say 'no' dealings – there *was* this, little, er, *fracas*

we had about the Common Market. Wherever that may be. Well, no, we had a little argument . . . Well, no, ah, I thought, go to the top man, if you want to find something out – after all, we put him in. So I thought, right – he wasn't here, he was down in Chequers. Lovely place y'know. What? Oooh, a *beautiful* place! 'Cos, it goes with the job, that's why he's hanging on to it, naturally. You can't blame the man. No, I was, ah, no, *liss-en*, I was – no, honestly – I was out on a cycle rally, and we're passing – it can be fun, it can be fun – and we were passing by Chequers, and I thought I'll nip in. And I'm sorry, I told him. 'Cos I'm very forthright. I'm too stupid to be anything else but honest! I said, 'Harold, be careful, do! Don't rush, I beg of you. Don't *rush*!' But, you see, I don't think he got the message. No. I don't think he got the message. Of course, it's very difficult when you're shouting through a let-terbox.[51]

It was a style of political satire that, at the time, was refreshingly subtle, accessible and engaging, and it succeeded in personalising national party politics for an admirably broad and eager audience.

Speight contributed another delightfully deft piece of stand-up political deconstruction for Howerd's subsequent appearance on the BBC's late-night satirical show, *TW3*, in 1963. Whereas previous guest contributors had conformed to the conventional image of the 'angry young man' or the intellectual social critic, Speight helped Howerd to prick pomposity on both sides of the satirical divide – teasing the producer, Ned Sherrin ('Nice man. Underneath'); mocking the host, David Frost ('Yes. Hmm. He's the one who wears his hair backwards') and his on-screen team ('These days you can't be filthy unless you've got a degree'); ridiculing the more conventional political pundits, such as the notoriously austere Robin Day ('He's a strange man, isn't he? *Funny* man. Yes. Hasn't he got *cruel* glasses!'), before slipping into a routine that covered such topical themes as Harold Macmillan's controversial 'night of the long knives' (when he responded to the Government's unpopularity by sacking no fewer than six members of his cabinet) and the latest Budget of his Chancellor, Reginald Maudling.

Howerd did not speak like a superior satirist or a slumming political pundit. He sounded like one of the audience:

Everyone blames Macmillan for sacking half the Government last
year. You see. *Everyone* blames Macmillan. But, you see, I don't.
No. *I* don't blame *him*. I blame *her*. No, I do! It's Dot. Yes, *Dot*.
No. Dotty Macmillan. You can see what's happened: she's obviously got her knife into some of their wives and they've had to go,
y'see. And, you see, that's where Beryl – Beryl Maudling – was so
shrewd, because, I mean, she and Reg have this farm down in the
country, this *smallholding*, down in the country, y'see, and so obviously what Beryl does is she brings up a few eggs, and a bit of
pork, and a bit of, well, y'know, for Dot, you see, and keeps in with
her.[52]

The audience loved it, and loved him. Although it was a live show,
Howerd ran on, and on, and on: scheduled to do eight minutes, he
kept going – ten minutes, twelve minutes, and still more minutes –
clearly revelling in the spotlight. No one complained. No one wanted
him to stop.

It was a great achievement by Speight as well as Howerd. While the
more 'obvious', brightly signposted kinds of political satire were
being spotted and monitored closely and chronically by the guardians
of the country's Establishment, this cleverly intimate method of
addressing the same issues was arguably the most subversive contribution to the debate. What Speight did – via the charm and art of
Howerd – was to slip satire through under the radar, and take irreverence out of the hands of the élite and return it to the habits and
haunts of the broader audience.

Speight would do the same, in a less direct fashion, with his work
for Arthur Haynes, but he knew the potential was there for him to do
much more. By the early 1960s, he was growing tired of and frustrated
by the format of *The Arthur Haynes Show*, and was pushing hard for
greater freedom and flexibility. There was a 'silly convention', he said,
that anything he gave Haynes to say in character 'would be taken out
of character and attributed to Arthur Haynes the TV personality.'

This was particularly irritating, Speight added, because he was look-ing to 'delineate characters who would take the blame for their own abysmal ignorance and bigoted prejudice, i.e. the man in the street or in the Big House or the pretentious middle-class box who are respon-sible for some of the most stupid utterances of our time on race, religion, philosophy and politics.'[53] Another source of frustration was the fact that, as Nicholas Parsons would later acknowledge, Arthur Haynes was growing increasingly suspicious of the politics in Speight's scripts: 'Johnny's original material would sometimes disturb him to the extent that he would even try to resist performing it. He would argue that we should keep to more recognisable and pre-dictable material, and ask that less politics be brought in.'[54]

The result was that Speight was feeling straitjacketed. He wanted to write a show in which the focus was on the characters rather than the actors, as his colleagues Galton and Simpson were now doing so successfully with *Steptoe and Son*. 'I tried hard to get ATV to do a half-hour series on two tramps,' he later explained, 'but every time [it came close to being commissioned] Lew Grade would say, "Why change a successful format?"'[55]

The BBC offered Speight an escape. Towards the end of 1964, Dennis Main Wilson invited him to write an edition of *Comedy Playhouse*, the strand from which *Steptoe and Son* had emerged, and Speight did not hesitate to accept. This was his chance to create something real and raw that would work like a sort of 'kitchen-sink sitcom'. Eager to get started, he soon sketched-out the basic idea inside his office at ALS. 'It was exciting to be in on the beginning of things,' Beryl Vertue would recall. 'I remember him coming into my office one day and he said, "I've got an idea about doing something with a *family*. A father who's always arguing with his son-in-law." That turned out to be *Till Death Us Do Part*.'[56] The resulting pro-gramme (which reached the air in July the following year) was so unusual, intense and unapologetically unlovable that it was strangely hypnotic. It was a 'must-see' television moment, and, once the BBC's internal 'appreciation rating' for the show proved second only to that for the original pilot for *Steptoe and Son*, a series was promptly com-missioned.

Till Death Us Do Part (which will be discussed in greater depth in Chapter 9) was a spectacularly powerful antidote to all of the so-called 'gentle' comedies that were currently on television. As far as Speight was concerned, the term 'gentle comedy' just meant comedy that was 'not very funny, but almost always very boring'.[57] *Till Death*, in contrast, could hardly have seemed more alive, angry and aggressive, and it challenged the inhibitions not only of the viewers but also of the broadcasters. Speight believed in calling a spade a bloody bleedin' shovel, and he wanted his comedy to sound as real and as truthful as it looked. The consequence was that he fell foul, time and time again, of the censors.

This was certainly a 'golden age' for would-be censors. On 13 November 1965, during a late-night satire programme by the name of *BBC-3*, the theatre critic Kenneth Tynan startled his host, Robert Robinson, by suddenly uttering the long-dreaded 'F-word' live on air. Mary Whitehouse, Middle England's newly self-appointed moral guardian, reacted swiftly by alerting the nation's media to her displeasure and urging the Queen, the Postmaster-General and all of the BBC governors to spank the foul-mouthed critic's bottom (the prospect of which must have struck Tynan, given his private passion for sado-masochism, as more welcome than a round of applause). Newspapers were quick to echo her outrage, filling their pages with censorious articles and editorials on, as one of them put it, 'the naughtiest of all four-letter words'.[58]

The BBC stopped short of publishing an outright apology, but it did issue a fairly prompt 'expression of regret', while Tynan himself sought to assuage the public debate by pointing out, somewhat disingenuously, that he had used the expression not as a common expletive but merely as 'an old English word in a completely neutral way' during a discussion about censorship on the stage. The immediate meaning and motive, however, mattered far less than the lasting effect, which saw the most commonly perceived broadcasting sins switch from those to do with omission to those concerning commission.

When, therefore, the first series of *Till Death Us Do Part* reached the screen half a year after Tynan's undeleted expletive, it became the most obvious target for the anti-permissive polemicists. Mary

Whitehouse, who seemed to believe she only had to think her own thoughts to read the minds of everyone else who was wise and kind and decent, could not stand the new show, and could not stand Johnny Speight, either.

She had not been able to stand most of what was screened by the BBC (ITV, for some bizarre reason, left her far less distressed) since 1963, when she decided, as rapidly as Thomas Hobbes warmed to despotism while speed-reading Euclid, that British television needed to be 'cleaned up'. She pinpointed the appointment of Hugh Carleton Greene as Director-General at the beginning of the 1960s as the primary cause of broadcasting's supposed moral 'collapse'.

Greene's professed ambition had been to 'open the windows and dissipate the ivory tower stuffiness which still clung to some parts of the BBC' as well as 'encourage enterprise and the taking of risks. I wanted to make the BBC a place where talent of all sorts, however unconventional, was recognised and nurtured.'[59] Whitehouse, however, interpreted this as a clarion call to anarchy and debauchery, and proceeded to attack Greene for anything on the screen that she regarded as dubious in terms of taste. On 5 May 1964, she had announced, from the platform of Birmingham Town Hall, that she and her newly-formed 'Clean Up TV' acolytes were sending a telegram to the Queen and the Duke of Edinburgh, inviting them to give 'encouragement and support to our efforts to bring about a radical change in the policy of entertainers in general and the Governors of the British Broadcasting Corporation in particular', and added: 'In view of the terrifying increase in promiscuity and its attendant horrors we are desperately anxious to banish from our homes and theatres those who seek to demoralise and corrupt our young people.'[60] On 17 November 1965, after being snubbed by the Director-General on several occasions, she declared that 'nothing less than the removal of Sir Hugh Greene and those who support his policy will solve the present problem.'[61] Greene, to his credit, resisted the temptation to say 'likewise', and turned a dignified deaf ear. In the years that followed, however, she would remain a constant thorn in Greene's side, regularly contacting politicians to declare that, in her 'considered opinion', one programme or another – along with most editions of *Till Death Us Do Part* – urgently required to be re-viewed and then condemned for propagating and stimulating promiscuity and undermining 'the moral, mental and physical health of the country'.[62]

As a consequence, Whitehouse and Speight became each other's willing irritant. She would sit and count the number of swear words in every episode, while he had Alf Garnett read her book and agree with every comment. Her inability to understand irony, and his addiction to it, would mean that they were destined to continue clashing throughout (and beyond) the rest of the decade – and both of them, predictably, would always feel that the other received far too much time, trouble and respect from the BBC.

When, for example, the Corporation, in a well-meant attempt to balance the needs of one of its shows with the many threats and requests from all of the watchdogs, tried to 'ration' Speight to twenty-five 'bloodies' per episode (or four fewer 'bloodies' for every two 'tits'), he became apoplectic with indignation: 'It's ridiculous,' he complained. 'If bloody's a bad word, the more you say it, the more offensive it becomes.'[63] He had Alf sneer at the hypocrisy of it all – 'Look, if everybody in the country put two bob in a swear box every time they swore we'd pay off the national debt!'[64] – but still the scripts were snipped. So notorious did this 'bloody' count become that Peter Cook wrote an inspired parody of Speight's regular meetings with his producer, with Dudley Moore playing Speight and Cook his censorious superior:

> COOK: What I'm trying to say, Johnny, is that you've got twenty-seven bloodies in your script. We've led the way, *I* don't mind how many bloodies you have, that's fine by me . . .
> MOORE: It reflects life, dunnit? I mean, *I* use bloody the whole b-b-bloody time!
> COOK: That's true. You're welcome to use it in life and in the script. The only thing that worries me about this script is the number of bums you have.
> MOORE: So what's wrong with that? So I've got thirty bums in the script.

COOK: Thirty-one.

MOORE: Thirty-one, give or take a bum. The bums are all there for a dramatic cumulative effect. You're not going to tell me that bums don't exist?

COOK: No.

MOORE: I've got a bum, you've got a bum . . .

COOK: We've all got a bum, Johnny. I would not pretend that bums don't exist. But what I do ask you, Johnny, and I ask you this very seriously: does an ordinary English family sitting at home early in the evening want to have a barrage of thirty-one bums thrown in their faces in the privacy of their own living-room? I think not, I think not. I don't think we're ready yet to break through the bum-barrier.

MOORE: Don't give me that! Only two years ago, Kenneth Tynan said f-f-f—

COOK: I don't care what Kenneth Tynan said. That was a live, unscripted programme over which we had no control and I must tell you, Johnny, that it is very seldom indeed that we allow a bum to slip out before eleven o'clock in the evening.

MOORE: What miracle happens at eleven o'clock in the evening that takes the sting out of a bum?

COOK: Now then, *I* know it's illogical, *you* know it's illogical. It *is* illogical. But believe me, trust me: *I* believe in your bums. I'm going to fight tooth and nail to preserve your bums. I'll leave as many bums as I possibly can. Trust me, trust me. But there's one word that worries me even more than bum. And that is your colloquial use of a word for a lady's, er, chest.

COOK: You mean my comedic use of the word t-t-t- . . .[65]

In the end, in the Cook sketch, an amicable agreement was reached:

MOORE: I'll raise you one bum.

COOK: You're really driving me into a corner here, Johnny. Tricky. Look, I know you, you know me: why should we let one bum stand between us? It's a deal.

MOORE: I'm glad we could discuss this in an adult fashion.

COOK: Thank you for being so co-operative. And I'll whip this
script off to Sooty just as soon as I can.
MOORE: Well, bottoms up!
COOK: Cheers![66]

In real life, however, Speight kept on raging at all of the multiple
cuts and queries.

Till Death was, none the less, an immensely rewarding personal
success. Along with his various other writing chores, the show would
earn Speight at least £10,000 a year, along with all of the regalia of
fame that went with it, during the second half of the 1960s. It would
also extend his reputation and influence beyond Britain to Europe
and North America, and more or less guaranteed that, whatever else
he created, he would find a large audience and provoke a widely-
reported discussion.

Breezing into the Orme Court offices of ALS in the middle of each
morning, resplendent in the latest casual fashions by Blades or Mr
Fish, he would share a chat and a drink with Eric Sykes and Spike
Milligan, read the newspapers, reflect on the issues of the day, and
then, using his two index fingers, type out some more comic dialogue. 'Writing was a calling to Johnny,' said Sykes. 'He was a
compulsive writer; he had to write. And he had to write the truth.
Success didn't change that. Nothing would.'[67]

In spite (or perhaps because) of his extraordinary achievement
with *Till Death*, however, Speight would sometimes be guilty of putting out some ill-conceived and sloppily-executed projects during the
same eventful decade. John Antrobus, his occasional writing partner,
would later reflect: 'Johnny would never examine his work, he would
never rewrite.'[68] On some occasions, unfortunately, it showed.

One example of this was his play, *If There Weren't Any Blacks,
You'd Have to Invent Them*, an absurdist assault on middle-class
prejudice that was first performed at the Aldwych Theatre in
1965. A later, modified, 'made-for-television' version would win
an award at the 1969 Prague Festival, but the original script was
a well-intentioned but frustratingly undisciplined affair, full of
clumsy conceits and laboured assertions, that one critic summed up

as being 'depressingly glib and secondhand'.[69] In one scene, for example, a blind man accuses a young white man (who he has already decided is as 'black as a pot') of being Jewish:

BLIND MAN: So . . . you used to be a Jew, did you?

YOUNG MAN: It's none of your business what I used to be.

BLIND MAN: Don't get lippy now, Sambo . . . watch the old lip there. We're entitled to know what you are. We don't want your sort round here lowering our land values. *[He walks over and feels the young man's nose]* Yes, he's Jewish all right . . . I've tweaked enough of their noses to know that.

OFFICER: He hasn't got a Jewish nose. He doesn't look a bit Jewish.

BLIND MAN: You don't want to let his looks take you in. That's the trouble with you people who can see – you let 'em fool you with their looks.[70]

There were a few fine Speight 'riffs' – such as when a working-class character complains about the snobbishness of Heaven ('I mean, the only heaven we got is this Tory heaven . . . this Eton and Harrow one. This Lord God's place. I mean, there you aren't it . . . Lord God . . . Lord God . . . see . . . not Fred God or Harry God. A stuck-up, toffee-nosed God . . . a guvnors' God') – but too much of the rest resembled a callow drama school project in need of further revision.

His weakest effort of all was probably a contribution to *Comedy Playhouse* in 1967 entitled *To Lucifer – a Son*. Speight's basic idea was that the Devil (played by John Le Mesurier) was facing retirement and thus felt it was time that he sent his son (played by Jimmy Tarbuck) down to earth in order to acquire some practical experience in the business of Devilment. The problem was, however, that Speight – who was drinking fairly heavily at the time – found it hard to translate this idea into a complete and satisfactory script. According to a member of the production team, Haldane Duncan:

To Lucifer – a Son [. . .] was the biggest 'no-no' in the careers of everyone associated with it. To say the script was late is like saying a woman in the labour ward's period is late. I think we had a complete script by the end of recording, but we certainly missed every deadline on the way. The poor designer spent her days at the end of a phone in the workshops where the set was being built waiting for news; we couldn't cast anyone, we could only rehearse bits; everything was a shambles; and it was all down to Johnny not providing us with a decent script on time. I think the real Devil was watching and having a bit of fun and thinking, 'That'll teach 'em for trying to make fun out of my family.'[71]

Michael Billington, like most other reviewers of the time, savaged the show, describing it as 'like a bad dream' – 'witless, completely innocuous and astonishingly dull'.[72]

Speight's most notoriously problematic effort would be a series for the newly-formed London Weekend Television in 1969 called *Curry and Chips*. Part of the trouble was that Speight never seemed to be sure as to whether he wanted to communicate an important and coherent satirical point more than he wanted just to indulge and amuse his mates. Set in the staff canteen and on the factory floor at 'Lillicrap Ltd', a manufacturer of seaside novelties, the show starred a blacked-up Spike Milligan as 'Paki Paddy' Kevin O'Grady (who purported to be Irish on his father's side); Eric Sykes as Arthur, an obtuse but liberal-minded factory foreman; Sam Kydd as the malodorous Smellie; Norman Rossington and Geoffrey Hughes as a pair of racist white Liverpudlians; and the singer/actor/celebrity golfer and Pringle sweater-wearer Kenny Lynch as a coloured Pakistaniphobe. Apart from its predictably profuse use of racist terms and phrases (which earned the programme a complaint to the Race Relations Board from the union leader Clive Jenkins for being 'snide' and 'objectionable'), *Curry and Chips* was also accused of being too liberal with its use of profanities, with one viewer – a follower, needless to say, of Mary Whitehouse – complaining that a certain edition used the word 'bloody' on no fewer than fifty-nine separate occasions. Unlike with *Till Death*, where there was a real precision of purpose and a clarity of characterisation, *Curry and Chips* was a bewildering mish-mash of well-intended social commentary and offensively self-indulgent frivolity. The show was taken off after just six half-hour episodes, never to be seen again.

It did not help that, in those days, the booze loomed so large in Johnny Speight's life. 'I liked it,' he would later explain in the somewhat healthier 1970s. 'I enjoyed it. I was drinking more than quite a bit. I was drinking quite a lot! I believe in being a professional. In anything. Even in drinking I was a professional. I drank properly. And, gawd, I found that a professional drunk hasn't got much time for anything else except drinking. It was a phase I went through, you know? It's not a bad phase to go through – as long as you do go through it and don't stay in it.'[73] Speight would get through the worst of it eventually, but, for a while, it unbalanced his judgement and compromised some of his comedy.

There would always be some new variant of *Till Death* for him to attempt, but the same old problem always returned: some people felt that the comedy form countenanced the offensive nature of the content. It exasperated the writer, but he was never in the mood for revision or contrition. Responding to all of the 'liberal zealots' who attacked him and his work with such 'fundamentalist fervour', Speight complained:

> They miss the satire entirely, and blame me, as if I had endowed Alf Garnett, and other characters I may write, with all the unpleasantness they reveal. It seems they would prefer me not to draw attention to the nastier, more disagreeable side of people. They would prefer, if I must draw my characters from life, not to draw them with warts and all. How they expect me, or any other writer, to record truthfully all those bigoted, illiberal chauvinists and other xenophobic half-wits that plague us, without showing them in full cry, is beyond me.[74]

His duty, he insisted, was to write 'good, believable characters': 'To try and lift them right off the street with all their silly prejudices and other more major blemishes, and present them in a theatrical frame . . . here you are, this is what we're like . . . or some of us at least.'[75]

It was such a brave and hazardous ambition, but, even though some would judge the attempt to have fallen a fraction short, it would go far enough to inspire countless others to start aiming in the same direction. Speight showed that certain sitcoms could grow some teeth, acquire some bite and draw some blood. He grassed on the worst of us, and, as a consequence, he unnerved the rest of us. That was not his problem – it was ours.

Thanks to Johnny Speight, British television comedy would develop sharper eyes and ears, and a much, much, sharper tongue. For better and for worse, it would never be the same again.

A.N. Other's

We are your actual bona writers.

Spike Milligan, Eric Sykes, Galton and Simpson and Johnny Speight together formed the core of Associated London Scripts' activity, but there were many other writers around them in other rooms, creating shows, stories and routines that would help to entertain the nation. The name plates would change, but the fine writing kept on coming.

There was Dick Barry working sometimes on his own and on other occasions with Johnny Speight; Dave Freeman and John Junkin toiling away in tandem on one script; Brad Ashton and Dick Vosburgh tap-tap-tapping away on another; Lew Schwartz and Maurice Wiltshire rattling off gag after gag after gag; and, at certain hours on certain days, the likes of Peter Sellers, Tony Hancock, Harry Secombe and Frankie Howerd flitting from office to office reading scripts, sharing drinks, talking shop and playing darts.

One of the most eye-catching characters, in the earliest days of the company, was Larry Stephens. A former jazz pianist, cartoonist and Commando captain, he played a significant cameo role in the first phase of success for ALS. Born in Birmingham in 1923, he had returned from the war eager for a finer, funnier, more flexible kind of life, and decided to forge a new career as a writer of comedy. The recently demobbed Tony Hancock became an exceptionally close friend – he would even be best man at Stephens's wedding – and started relying on him as a reliable source of comic material. The pair became regulars at the Grafton Arms, where they came into contact with countless other comics and acted like an off-stage double-act.

'Larry and Tony were like brothers,' Spike Milligan would remark. 'I don't know how or where they met. They seemed to have come from nowhere. They shared the same digs and the same women and they both drank. They both liked to laugh at the human race and they'd have hysterical laughing bouts. Sometimes they didn't go to bed all night and I'd come in in the morning as I was writing a script for someone with Larry and there would be this hysterical laughter and the floor littered with newspapers and the two grotty tumblers and it was hurting their heads to laugh.'[1]

In 1952, the two of them developed an idea for a radio sitcom, in which Hancock would play the part of 'an estate-agent-cum-bachelor-town-councillor' who lived with his elderly aunt in a semi-detached villa in a small town on the south coast. Although the BBC commissioned Stephens to write a pilot script, and Hancock made it clear that he was keen to continue, the internal response was not sufficiently positive and the project was quietly dropped.[2]

Another radio project, however, had already borne fruit for Stephens. As Spike Milligan's regular collaborator during the early years of *The Goon Show*, he was usually to be found in his friend's office (first upstairs at Grafton's, then in a Shepherd's Hill flat and later at ALS), tapping away on the typewriter while Milligan roamed around the room, acting out a routine or improvising some dialogue. At ALS, at least, he struck the other inhabitants as a benign but quietly eccentric presence. 'Larry was a very nice man,' Beryl Vertue would remember, 'but very fastidious and very scared of dirt, always going round with white gloves on.'[3] Eric Sykes agreed: 'He was a lovely fella, Larry, but very, very quiet and rather shy. I don't think I ever heard him say more than two or three words at any one time in all the years I knew him, and he'd blush very easily when someone talked to him.'[4] An observer rather than a performer by disposition, he was invaluable as the kind of adviser who could stand back and consider a new idea or a fresh piece of comedy in a cooler, calmer, hour. As a writer, he could adapt and conform to a wide range of contexts and styles – sometimes so well, in truth, as to make his own contribution seem invisible – and seemed happy to serve bigger and bolder egos. '[H]e had a very bright mind,' said Alan Simpson. 'But he was a grasshopper – he couldn't finish anything.'[5] Although Milligan would later damn his old colleague with the faintest of praise, describing him as 'the highest-paid typist in the business',[6] Stephens did, in fact, add a great deal to the early scripts (Milligan would sometimes be fast asleep under his piano while Stephens continued to type out ideas), and also acted as an excellent foil to his far more excitable colleague.

Logical, perceptive and clever, he could capture Milligan's quick little ideas before they shot straight out of sight and then place them into a relatively coherent structure. His own keen visual sense – he even illustrated his scripts with vivid little drawings of certain goons – helped sharpen some of Milligan's characterisations and stimulated his already rich and lively imagination. Milligan would throw out all kinds of hit-or-miss suggestions; Stephens would retrieve the ones most likely to work. Milligan would sometimes get distracted or paralysed by all of the comic possibilities; Stephens would often find the most effective way to get him back on track and moving forwards.

His partnership with Milligan had foundered initially in the early 1950s – when he was drinking more than four bottles of rum and a couple of bottles of whisky each week, his colleague was descending into a desperate depression and (after clashing over scripts) neither man was on speaking terms with the other – but, after broken bridges were rebuilt, he returned to Milligan and *The Goon Show* in 1956, and the collaboration worked better than ever.

Stephens was probably at his busiest during 1956. Apart from co-writing *The Goon Show*, he also supplied the story and helped shape the screenplay for the short, goon-like movie, *The Case of the Mukkinese Battle Horn*. There were, in addition to this, countless last-minute rewrites of various comedians' scripts, innumerable short and sharp gags for a wide range of Variety shows and quite a few unofficial edits of troublesome television scripts. He also assisted Eric Sykes on a couple of episodes of ITV's *The Tony Hancock Show*. It looked, for a while, as though Larry Stephens was, somewhat belatedly, on the way up as a prominent writer. The drinking, however, got worse and the blood pressure got higher, and, in the next year or so, his health slipped into a sharp and inexorable decline.

Larry Stephens died of a brain haemorrhage on 25 January 1959, while he and his wife were on their way to dine out with Spike Milligan. He was aged just thirty-five. There was little coverage in the media, and no substantial obituaries, but, in both performing and writing circles, he was mourned sincerely, and he was missed.

Another, far more pivotal, figure from the earliest days of ALS – its first managing director, Stanley 'Scruffy' Dale – was destined to depart the company under highly acrimonious circumstances. He had never been every writer's cup of tea – especially not Spike Milligan's, who, upon hearing that Dale had lost a testicle while serving in the RAF during the war, merely muttered, 'I hope he dropped it on Dresden'[7]– and the tales of his incompetence (contracts were mislaid, offers of work forgotten and negotiations bungled) piled up throughout the 1950s. He had his good points – he could be loyal, supportive and sometimes even shrewd – but the combination of his chaotic lifestyle and amateurish approach to an increasingly professional kind of business meant that even his friends could sometimes find themselves bewildered by his bungling.

He also grew more and more secretive as the years at ALS went by. Leaving most of the writers in the more than capable – though greatly overworked – hands of Beryl Vertue and her assistants, he tried – *Broadway Danny Rose*-style – to interest various radio, television and theatre producers in his own motley troupe of 'talents' (among whom, on his circulated list, were 'Rusty – with his Pigeon Friends'; 'The Vipers Skiffle Group'; 'Jimmy Edmundson [the well-known comedian]'; 'Windy Blow – with his Balloons'; 'Mandy & Sandy – A Gal and Her Dog'; 'Bobby Collins – Personality Siffleur'; and a young comic and singer whom Scruffy had recently renamed 'Jim Dale').[8] He also began speculating as an independent entrepreneur, promoting a growing number of wrestling contests and, in response to the fashion in popular music for skiffle, launched a series of provincial talent contests that he modestly called 'Stanley Dale's National Skiffle Contest'.

On those occasions when he rose from his bed in his flat at

Holland Villas Road and ventured into the offices at ALS, Dale often amused and bemused those who saw him as he tried to attend to the most pressing needs of the likes of such old and loyal clients as Frankie Howerd. Brad Ashton, for example, would recall the extraordinary manner whereby Dale prepared to discuss a possible summer season for Howerd with the impresario Val Parnell:

> I remember seeing him one night – the door was ajar and he didn't know I could see, and hear, what he was getting up to inside his office – and he was in there on his own, playing out a meeting he had planned the following day with Val Parnell. He was sitting on the 'wrong' side of his desk, and he was going, 'Look, Val, okay, Frank isn't as big a draw as he used to be, I know that, but he's going to really wow your audiences, believe me, you're going to want him back again, and so I think you should start off with a lot more than what you're offering.' And then he got up and went round to the opposite side of his desk and he sat back, suddenly looked a bit bored, and he became Val Parnell: 'Yes, but as you yourself just said, he *isn't* such a big name now, and *I'm* giving him a big chance.' And Stanley just kept going back and forth around the table, haggling with himself! He'd go: 'Ah, you say that, but—' and then, 'Tch, come on, he's a—' and then, 'Look, Stanley,' and then, 'No, with respect, *you* look, Val . . .' And this was all a rehearsal![9]

It was at the end of the 1950s, when Howerd's career was in serious trouble, that Dale's dealings finally came under closer examination. Howerd suddenly discovered, to his horror, not only that a large portion of his savings had mysteriously disappeared, but now he also owed thousands of pounds in back taxes. 'Someone,' Howerd would moan, 'had clearly fouled things up in a big way.'[10] There was no doubt, however, that the 'someone' in question was none other than Scruffy Dale.

Several friends and colleagues had been warning Howerd about Dale for some time. Spike Milligan, in particular, had never trusted this peculiar character, and resented his continuing presence on the

board of ALS directors; after watching Dale branch out into other
fields of entertainment, he had grown more and more suspicious as to
where he was finding the capital to invest in such ambitious and risk-
laden ventures as nation-wide music contests and cultish-sounding
sporting events, and had started alerting others as to his concerns.
Howerd had also learnt, via a number of people at the BBC, that
Dale was getting increasingly remiss when it came to connecting the
Corporation with his client. As long ago as the spring of 1957, for
instance, Howerd had been alarmed to hear that an important letter
sent to him by a producer had taken two whole weeks to reach him –
all because Dale had forgotten that it was crumpled up in one of his
pockets. Howerd had been even more alarmed when he discovered
subsequently that one executive, reacting angrily to his supposed dis-
inclination to reply, had concluded that the comedian 'must either be
a very bad businessman, mentally unstable or just not interested' to
have allowed such a 'farcical' and 'insulting' situation to have
arisen.[11]

Howerd, blinded by a misplaced sense of loyalty along with a
residual feeling of indebtedness, had managed somehow either to
explain the various claims and rumours away or just block them out
of his mind. By the autumn of 1959, however, not even he was able to
remain any longer in denial, and the full extent of Dale's betrayal,
once confirmed, hit him – and ALS – hard.

First, there was the matter of from where Dale's money had
come. It soon transpired, after questions were asked and records
retrieved, that most of the money had come from Frankie Howerd,
Eric Sykes and, in varying amounts, several other members of ALS.
'He looked after Frank's money and he looked after my money, but
it wasn't a very good idea,' recalled Sykes ruefully. 'He was always
the one with the fist full of white fivers, and we were always the ones
who had to ask him for one of them.'[12] It was found out, following
some further frantic research, that Dale had taken Howerd's and
Sykes's money (and later some additional sums belonging to certain
others at ALS) and struck a 'secret' arrangement with their bank
manager to siphon off a percentage of their earnings and deposit
the funds in a separate account (set up in Dale's name) in order to

'protect them from themselves': 'You know,' he had told the bank manager in confidence, 'how irresponsible these show-business people are. It'll be gone in a week.'[13]

Second, there was the matter of where this money had ended up. The answer to this was rather more complicated.

Some of the money had gone into, of all things, a haulage firm that Dale had set up discreetly and then run surreptitiously from his base at ALS. 'It turned out,' revealed Brad Ashton, 'that he'd got these two Italian brothers in to help him run it, and they'd sometimes be coming into the office to see him and use the office phones, chat up their girlfriends and all of that sort of thing. Spike had hated their guts right from the start, but he could never quite find out why they were there.'[14]

Most of what money remained had been channelled into Dale's various projects as a budding promoter, and it was during his pursuit of this activity that he finally took one liberty too many. Dale had been managing a skiffle group fronted by his most promising young protégé, Jim Dale, and had secretly been benefiting from what he appears to have regarded as an ingeniously risk-free kind of arrangement: when the group made a profit, he pocketed it, but when it made a loss, his fellow directors at ALS were asked to make up the shortfall (according to Jim Dale's former producer, George Martin, Scruffy had his client 'tied up in more knots than I could count, and poor Jim never had the vaguest idea what his financial state was').[15] Eventually, Milligan and the others, exasperated by so many apparent anomalies in their accounting, decided that enough was enough, and, following an internal investigation, most of Scruffy Dale's countless shady deceptions were at last brought to the light.

Shortly after this, Dale disappeared abruptly from the metropolitan show-business scene. 'He disappeared,' explained Eric Sykes, 'because we got rid of him. We voted him out because of several "misdemeanours". But then he got a very prominent lawyer to represent him, and Associated London Scripts had to pay for that lawyer! And we ended up having to pay him £5,000 redundancy money! So he was really . . . well, he was somebody who wasn't very nice.'[16]

On 13 January 1960, the split was confirmed officially in a letter sent by Beryl Vertue to all the relevant broadcasters and impresarios: 'Stanley Dale has now left this Company and therefore his name must be struck off all your records.'[17] Although, in time, some of the tangible damage would be undone, the sense of betrayal, for some, would never go away, and Dale remained, darkly and definitively, *persona non grata*.

There were times later on its history when it looked as if ALS would lose another one of its members: John Antrobus. There was nothing corrupt about Antrobus. He was just someone with talent who started getting into trouble on a worryingly regular basis.

'I was flung [into ALS],' he would say, 'by a desire to be young, rich and successful. I was thrown in with men back from the war.'[18] Born in Woolwich on 2 July 1933, he had grown up in a military environment and lived through the war in which they had fought. Tall, thin and dark-haired with a vulnerable-sounding voice and rather haunted-looking eyes, he was from a different generation, but he understood where they had been and why they had gone elsewhere.

His father had been a Regimental Sergeant-Major in the Royal Horse Artillery, and the Antrobus family was stationed in Wiltshire, at the School of Artillery in Larkhill, on the edge of Salisbury Plain. John seemed set to follow in his father's footsteps – he was sent to the Military Academy at Sandhurst to finish his education – but he rebelled and dropped out of the Army life. He preferred to pursue a future writing comedy, so he went to be groomed at ALS instead.

He worked there with Spike Milligan on *The Goon Show*. He worked with Eric Sykes on *Sykes And A . . .* He worked with Johnny Speight on *The Frankie Howerd Show*. He worked with all of them and most of the others on *That Was The Week That Was*. He worked with the best in the business, and the experience was invaluable.

He began to write on his own for countless different kinds of performer and show, and wrote his first screenplay for a movie – a youth-oriented comedy, starring Anthony Newley, called *Idle on Parade* – in 1959. He also continued collaborating with others, supplying additional material to the first *Carry On* movie, *Carry On Sergeant* (1958), and assisting his colleagues at ALS on numerous other projects. He was working hard and doing well. As time went on, however, something appeared to be missing: 'I wanted to be an Angry Young Man, but I was far too good natured, still writing comedy for the likes of Morecambe and Wise.'[19] He was good at what he did – writing comedy, writing scripts – but it seemed to come too easily, so he mistrusted it. 'I was still determined to become a playwright,' he would reflect, 'and rather (sadly) looked down upon my easier talents.'[20]

For all of his efforts in radio, television and movies, he still craved the chance to create something for the stage. 'I was entranced by theatre,' he said, 'and particularly the Royal Court with its offerings from John Osborne, Arnold Wesker, Ionesco, N.F. Simpson and Anne Jellico.'[21] Towards the end of 1961, Bernard Miles, the actor turned manager of the Mermaid Theatre at Puddle Dock in the City of London, offered Antrobus his opportunity when, after being impressed by his skill and ambition, he decided to take a gamble and commissioned the would-be playwright to provide something – anything – for his theatre.

Meanwhile, however, Spike Milligan was approached by a dramatic group called Tomorrow's Audience (which included Richard Ingrams and William Rushton among its members), asking if he had a one-act play they could perform. Milligan did not, but he did remember a strange and funny idea that Antrobus had told him about bombs and survivors and strange and surreal transformations. He gave his colleague a call: 'What are you doing with that idea?' he asked. 'How about we write it up together for these lads?'[22] Antrobus agreed, the play was performed at the Marlowe Theatre in Canterbury on 12 February 1962, and the great drama critic Kenneth Tynan, who was in the audience, praised the production in his next newspaper column. Bernard Miles, upon reading the positive review, contacted Antrobus to inform him that this was the play that he had commissioned.

Antrobus and Milligan sat down and rewrote it – and kept on rewriting it – as the deadline approached. 'As the play got nearer and nearer production the scriptwriting got faster and faster,' Miles would recall. 'There were so many additions, alterations, take-outs, put-ins, extras – at the final analysis we had four secretaries, all with typewriters, all typing away at full speed and all of them well-trained, efficient girls begging to know, "Where do I put this in – what number is the page?"[23] It looked like complete and utter chaos from the outside, but both writers knew what they were doing, and, knowing that they were both in the grip of a creative high, were determined to realise their full vision on the stage. It was an intense and exhausting process, but, in the end, it seemed worth it.

Entitled *The Bedsitting Room*, the bleak and black satirical comedy opened at the Mermaid on 31 January 1963. Set in a post-apocalyptic Shepherd's Bush, nine months after World War III (which lasted for two minutes and twenty-eight seconds – 'including the peace treaty'), the play began as nuclear fallout is producing strange mutations in human beings. The title referred to the plight of a character called Lord Fortnum of Alamein (played by Valentine Dyall), who responds to radiation sickness by transforming himself into a bed-sitting room. Instead of seeking a cure, his doctor, Captain Martin (Graham Stark), responds to this unexpected occurrence by moving into the vacant premises created by his patient's mutation, and lives there rent-free with his fiancée (Marjie Lawrence) and her father, the Prime Minister, who has recently turned into a parrot (played by a parrot). The remaining plot, such as it was, concerned the fate of the first child due to be born after this terrible war. Spike Milligan appeared on stage – ad-libbing each night – as Mate, a roving traffic warden who carried a parking meter wherever he went and slammed it down in front of anyone he encountered, declaring, 'You can't park 'ere, sir.' A first-night review in *The Times*, hedging its bets in spectacular fashion, described the production as a 'gentle, riotous, blasphemous, reverent, tasteless, innocent, childish, adult, comical, desperate and once or twice oddly beautiful miracle play'.[24]

More confident and coherent critical encomia soon followed, the production transferred to the West End and the play became one of the 'must-sees' of London's theatrical season. '[O]ur mutual talents peaked to please the world,' Antrobus would say. 'SOLD OUT. HOUSE FULL. I had made it, with my friend Spike.'[25]

For Antrobus, however, the sense of elation would be short-lived:

'[F]rom the glittering heights, as I surveyed a glittering future, I was to fall like a stone into obscurity, alcoholism, debt and visits to mental hospital. It was me I would be visiting . . .'[26] Working in ALS alongside the likes of Johnny 'Effing' Speight and Spike 'Do Not Disturb – I'm Disturbed Enough Already!' Milligan had not had an entirely beneficial effect on the younger and more pliable man: 'Put bluntly I was impressionable, looking to build a whole new character for myself, one that even I could believe in. God is dead and satire is King and bollocks to the Establishment. Let's say I got carried away and had no idea of my true agenda which was to fix myself with all the trappings of success. I got on to Albert Camus, The Outsider. That's what I was, an existentialist!'[27]

The success of *The Bedsitting Room* – the plaudits, the tours, the revivals, the movie rights – would keep him flushed for a while but, as he later confessed, 'fame only fanned the flames of my Bonfire of Vanities. I was still trying to fix myself with money, applause, sex and rock and roll.'[28] An increasingly concerned Spike Milligan (who had come to regard Antrobus as 'a wayward son')[29] told him that he had developed 'a Jekyll and Hyde personality',[30] which must have struck Antrobus as more than a bit rich coming as it did from the infamously mercurial Milligan, but he still seemed set on confirming the diagnosis. 'I was intent on creating a myth of myself as the alcoholic artist. I still had some catching up to do on Brendan Behan . . .'[31]

There were plenty of 'incidents', and they began to occur increasingly frequently. On 29 October 1964, for example, the papers reported that the Literary Society of Queen's University, Belfast, had issued a statement dissociating itself from the behaviour of Antrobus, one of its guests at a debate over the motion that 'men should be angry', after he had stripped to the waist and, it was claimed, caused about a hundred people to get up and walk out in anger and/or disgust ('Later,' the reports added, 'he took down his trousers').[32] Not long after this, he broke into a live BBC broadcast of the arts show *Late Night Line-Up* – which, on that particular occasion, was hosting a symposium on writing comedy featuring the likes of Marty Feldman and Johnny Speight – and declared: 'I am the victim of political exclusion!' Although his visibly embarrassed ALS colleagues urged him to stagger off into the night, he seemed, for a few more seconds that seemed like hours, eager to stay and slur some more. Antrobus would remember: 'The floor manager crawled along the back of the podium, clutching at my trouser leg, asking me to leave, and as I had not prepared a speech – doing the whole thing impromptu – and had run out of steam, I allowed him to lead me off.'[33]

Milligan did what he could to put his friend's life and career back on track – 'He would always champion the underdog and do what he could to help the mentally sick,' said Antrobus. 'I qualified on both counts'[34] – but, as both of them knew, it was bound to be a long and hard battle that the younger writer was obliged to fight, on the whole, alone. The next two years saw him go in and out of various clinics and 'puzzle factories', drying out and soaking up advice. There were good spells and bad spells, relapses and fight-backs. It was when he finally stopped thinking that 'all else in the world was my problem and that's why I drank', and started to believe instead that it was actually the other way round ('an inside job'), that the spot of light at last appeared at the end of the tunnel.[35]

Antrobus would abandon the drink at the end of 1968, and remain clean and sober throughout the next few decades. He would team up with Ray Galton in 1997 to write the semi-autobiographical period sitcom *Get Well Soon*, and, in 2004, would even write a stage play about his days at ALS – *Of Good Report* – as well as (again with Ray Galton) a theatrical postscript to *Steptoe and Son* in 2005 entitled *Murder at Oil Drum Lane*. The memories had survived, and he did his very best to share them.

During the period in which Antrobus had been striving to bring his own brand of satire to the stage, three other ALS writers were finding crafty ways to mock the morals and mores of their society on the radio: Eric Merriman, Barry Took and Marty Feldman. While Antrobus often used the surreal to subvert, this trio deployed a kind of humour that many would categorise as 'camp'.

The somewhat misleadingly-named Merriman (who rather enjoyed a good moan and mutter) would be the first to arrive and start work. He was born into a show business-oriented family in Golders Green, north London, on 6 December 1924. His father, Percy Merriman, had led a First World War concert party, the Roosters, which recorded and broadcast in the early days of British radio. The young Eric, as someone eager to follow in his father's footsteps, started writing for Boy Scout magazines and then contributed sketches to Ralph Reader's Gang Shows. He was employed by the magazine *Picture Post* – a precursor of the likes of *Hello* – before joining the RAF in 1943 as an air gunner and navigator, where he also sang and drummed in the station dance band. Following his demob, he became involved in writing comic material, eventually via ALS, for such stage, radio and television performers as Vic Oliver, Dickie Henderson, Bernard Braden, Bill Maynard and Terry Scott, and would also provide some scripts for a young, gangling, bespectacled, middle-class stand-up comic called Barry Took.

Took – the son of a manager of the Danish Bacon Company – was born on 19 June 1928 in Muswell Hill, north London, in sight of the television masts at Alexandra Palace. He left grammar school at fifteen to brush the fringes of show business as an office boy at the Peter Maurice music publishing company in Denmark Street. In 1944, he left to become assistant projectionist at the Gaumont Palace, Wood Green, where he made his mark by showing Walt Disney's *Three Caballeros* upside down. Called up for National Service in the RAF in 1946, he made his daytime duties as a clerk more tolerable by blowing an out-of-tune trumpet each evening in the station dance band; realising that performing was much more fun than clerking, he also made himself producer of the station concert party, and wrote the odd routine. After demobilisation, he returned for a while to the sheet music trade while, by night, he tested himself as a budding stand-up comedian in various working men's clubs, and attended acting classes at the Toynbee Hall. In 1951, the Canadian talent scout Carroll Levis gave Took an audition, which the fledgeling performer not only passed but sailed through to the finals on Levis's radio series – ending up with a contract worth twelve pounds a week. Took turned full-time professional, making his debut at Hulme Hippodrome (billed as 'Lewisham's Lanky Lunatic'), and Levis made him compère of a touring revue called *Show Stoppers*. Realising that he was in dire need of fresh material, he started buying jokes and routines from Eric Merriman, and carried on with his stand-up career. In 1953, Took participated in a radio audition at the Nuffield Centre, where Dennis Main Wilson selected him to become a 'funny voice man' on *Pertwee's Progress* (which starred Jon Pertwee and also featured Dick Emery). More radio and stage work would follow, but, as time went on, Took grew more confident about his material (most of which he was now writing himself) and less confident about his performances. When he renewed his acquaintance with Eric Merriman, they started collaborating on scripts for other stand-ups and made plans to write a radio show all of their own.

The plans paid off: in 1958, a few months after Took had joined Merriman at Associated London Scripts, their first joint project, *Beyond Our Ken*, was broadcast by the BBC, and became a more or less immediate success. Featuring the avuncular, Cambridge-educated host Kenneth Horne and the versatile comic character actors Hugh Paddick, Betty Marsden, Ron Moody (later replaced by Bill Pertwee) and Kenneth Williams, with musical interludes from the singer Pat Lancaster and the close harmony group, the Fraser Hayes Four, this fast-moving, pun-laden show was full of funny characters, infectious catchphrases and smart little parodies of movies, plays and television shows (such as the *Panorama* spoof, 'Hornerama') as well as several recurring imitations of certain contemporary stars (including 'Fanny Haddock' – Betty Marsden's take-off of the TV cook, Fanny Craddock – and 'Hankie Flowered' – Bill Pertwee's impersonation of Frankie Howerd).

In 1959, after two series and forty episodes, the powers-that-be at the BBC were so impressed that they invited Took and Merriman to take over from Frank Muir and Denis Norden (who were departing for television) as the new scriptwriters of *Take It From Here*. This ought to have been a step-up for the pair, but in fact it led to a break-up: 'Merriman and I found ourselves constantly disagreeing as to what was good *Take It From Here* and what wasn't,' Took would recall. 'After much agonising and a lot of brooding silences it was decided that we should split the scripts and work alone.'[36] Merriman continued writing *Beyond Our Ken* on his own – crafting one hundred more consistently entertaining shows, over the course of five more series, before turning his attention to other projects on television (writing for Norman Vaughan – the new compère of *Sunday Night at the London Palladium* – as well as for Dave Allen, Terry-Thomas, Frankie Howerd, Tommy Cooper, Dick Emery, Max Bygraves and Beryl Reid, and, in 1965, he would also write and appear in his own short-lived BBC2 sketch show entitled *Call It What You Like*). Took, meanwhile, formed a new partnership with another performer-turned-author: a younger man – nearly six years his junior – from East Ham named Marty Feldman.

The pair had first met on a music-hall bill at the Empire Theatre in York during 1955. The diminutive Feldman (who, at the time, sported short blond hair and a neat little goatee beard) was appearing as one-third of an *ersatz* Marx Brothers-style act called 'Morris, Marty and Mitch'; Took (who was tall, thin and smartly-dressed) was there as a solo stand-up comic. They met and formed an instant rapport. 'We were both voracious readers and keen observers of the world around us,' Took would recall. 'We both had haunted the Soho coffee bars of the period and were both (awful) trumpet players. The only differences were that Marty was a Jew and a vegetarian and I was neither.'[37]

They not only complemented each other's style – Took was strong on outline and structure, Feldman was fast and fearless with detail and dialogue – they also boosted each other's confidence – the phlegmatic Took helped the excitable Feldman to relax (after developing a hyper-thyroid condition during 1961, which caused his eyes to bulge alarmingly, he became quite nervy and neurotic as a writer, but his partner adapted to his working habits and kept urging him on), and Feldman made Took feel that he could still be funny – or even funnier – when he was just being himself (an invaluable service to someone who, up until that time, had felt obliged to try to conform to a more 'music-hall' style of humour). It was a partnership, and a friendship, that promised much right from the start, and, right from the start, they found themselves very much in demand. They wrote for Frankie Howerd (a series on radio called *Frankie's Bandbox*) and for numerous other comedians and shows, and then began to acquire a higher profile when they contributed scripts first, in 1959, to the very popular television sitcom *The Army Game* and then, from 1965, to their own radio show – a sort of successor to *Beyond Our Ken* – called *Round the Horne* (which will be discussed in greater detail in Chapter 10).

Their creative schedule rarely changed: the working day began at 9.30am, when the two men met in Took's office to drink coffee and smoke some cigarettes (their joint consumption averaged about a hundred each day) while they chatted about what they had watched on television or in the theatre or cinema the previous evening and pondered those topics that were covered in the morning's newspapers. Then, at about 10.30am, they would get ready to start writing: sitting side by side at the desk, with the works of Shakespeare, the Bible and *The Oxford Dictionary of Quotations* close at hand, Feldman typed, Took scribbled in longhand, and, slowly but surely, a new script would begin to take shape.

The only minor 'spat' the two men ever had was over the ordering of their names. As producers, in the beginning, knew that Took was the senior partner in terms both of age and experience, they credited them as 'Took and Feldman'. Feldman, however, came to resent the fact that 'T' was being placed before 'F', so his colleague agreed to rename the partnership as 'Feldman and Took'. In 1965, however, as they prepared for the first series of *Round the Horne*, Feldman suddenly declared: 'Look, you know these people better than I do and you have written for them [before]. I think on this series your name should go first.'[38] 'Feldman and Took' thus went back to being 'Took and Feldman', and the two egos would stay unruffled.

For most of the 1960s, the union was near perfect. 'Writing with Marty was fun,' Took would say. 'He once said that when we worked it was as though we were merely the messengers and that the actual writing was done by a being called Barry Feldman or Marty Took who hovered over our heads and dictated what was written.'[39] In 1968, however, Feldman was given his own series as a performer on BBC2, and, although he and Took would write it (and also, in 1970, collaborate on the screenplay of Feldman's first major movie, *Every*

Home Should Have One), their respective ambitions began to diverge. Feldman wanted to concentrate on performing on television and in movies, while Took accepted an executive role at the BBC (overseeing, among other things, the formation of the *Monty Python* team). The partnership came, quite amicably, to a close. The back catalogue, however, would sustain a cult audience all the way into the subsequent century.

Comedy, however, was by no means the only thing that came out of Associated London Scripts. It was the main thing, without any doubt, but there was drama being produced, too.

One of the most notable figures who came to be associated with this particular area was Terry Nation. Although he started out as a stand-up comedian, he would re-invent himself, upon moving to ALS, first as a writer of comedy and then, with significant success, as a writer and editor of drama.

The Cardiff-born writer took a fairly long period of time to find a distinctive style and develop a viable specialist interest. Influenced heavily in the early days by *The Goon Show*, he found it easiest, during this formative period, to imitate the likes of Spike Milligan and Eric Sykes, writing bits and pieces for those shows and performers sent his way by his much busier role models. Like several other young writers at ALS, he also contributed material to *The Idiot Weekly, Price 2d* (1956), as well as, amongst other projects, collaborating with John Junkin on two series of *The Ted Ray Show* (1958–9). A bid to write a sitcom series called *Uncle Selwyn* (set in a Welsh village in the 1920s) foundered in 1960 when his pilot script was rejected for being too crude and derivative, but he did succeed in writing his first screenplay the following year: *What a Whopper!* – a cheap and cheerful vehicle for the pop star Adam Faith.

When Tony Hancock dropped Galton and Simpson in 1961, Nation was one of the other writers to whom he turned. Their collaboration was a friendly if sometimes frantic one – he acted as scriptwriter and chaperone when the comedian embarked on a provincial theatrical tour, and he also worked on several other projects once the performer turned his attention to his mid-term future – but it did little to reverse the depressing slide in Hancock's fortunes

('Tony wouldn't rehearse,' Nation would complain, 'and for the first time he was boozing while he was working').[40] After the 1963 series for ATV, *Hancock*, was eclipsed by Galton and Simpson's *Steptoe and Son*, the pair of them went their separate ways.

1963 proved a low point for Tony Hancock, but it would mark a breakthrough for Terry Nation. Having previously contributed adaptations of three classic science-fiction short stories to an ITV anthology entitled *Out of This World* (1962), he was invited to write some episodes for a new sci-fi television series called *Doctor Who*, the brainchild of Sydney Newman, the head of BBC television drama. Nation's initial inclination was to turn the offer down, as he was convinced that the programme was destined for the scrap heap. Friends and colleagues interceded to urge the writer to change his mind, and, to his credit, he listened. Changing his mind and taking the job, he would later say, was the shrewdest move he ever made.

His first script would see the debut of the Daleks (which will be covered in more detail in Chapter 10), and this and subsequent stories helped make his name as one of Britain's most promising new writers working within the genre. Now freed from the anxiety of being over-influenced by his comedy-writing heroes, he began to relax and his imagination flowed far more easily: 'The wonderful thing about science-fiction,' he said, 'is that if the author says a thing is so, then nobody can deny it.'[41] The confidence duly started to grow: he felt like his own man, his own writer, and he pushed on with his career.

Nation now all but abandoned comedy in favour of popular television drama. Throughout the rest of the decade, he wrote for one successful Lew Grade/ITV adventure series after another – including *The Saint* (starring Roger Moore), *The Baron* (starring Steve Forrest), *The Champions*, *The Avengers*, *Department S* and (at the start of the following decade) *The Persuaders!* – rising through the ranks, with the encouragement of his writer/producer friend Dennis Spooner, to become script editor and associate producer on some of the later programmes. In the 1970s, he would return to the genre of sci-fi, devising a thought-provoking post-apocalyptic series called *The Survivors* (BBC1, 1975) as well as the cult *Star Trek*-style saga *Blake's 7* (BBC1, 1978–81).

Other notable drama writers at ALS included the Australian-born Peter Yeldham, whom Beryl Vertue signed up in 1956. 'When I joined the agency,' he would recall, 'I was the only drama writer. It was a challenge for her, and a lucky break for me. I've never had a better agent':

> But for over a year nothing much happened, except near misses and rejections. I was on the point of giving up. We borrowed money for my wife and children's fares home: the idea was I would follow as soon as I could afford it. Then one morning in a basement flat we had in Earl's Court the phone rang. It was Beryl, who said Granada Television wanted me to write an episode of their crime series *Shadow Squad*. An hour later a delirious and disbelieving Beryl rang again. The BBC had bought a TV play. Two shows sold in the space of one morning, after a year of disappointments and frustration. We cancelled the idea of anyone going home. In the next few years I wrote plays for *Armchair Theatre*, *Play of the Week* and *BBC Theatre*, for series like *No Hiding Place*, *Probation Officer*, *Love Story*, *The Persuaders!*, the American series *Espionage*, and *Miss Adventure*, in collaboration with my wife Marjorie Yeldham, as a starring vehicle for the gifted comedienne Hattie Jacques.[42]

He kept on coming up with good, strong ideas, and Vertue kept on putting him in touch with the right sort of contacts:

> I think the best series I worked on in that early period was *Probation Officer*. Set in an East London district, it tackled adult subjects that had never been seen in television until then. There were four writers, and a bright and innovative producer, Antony Kearey, one of the best I have ever worked with. We had a story conference once a month, each chose a subject, then went away to write it. Unlike most producers at the time, Tony never insisted on 'treatments' or 'step-outlines', those rather plodding and destructive ways to ruin a good story. One day I said to him: 'An alcoholic wakes up in a crummy hotel room. He can't remember how he got

there, but he is still holding a bunch of flowers. Later, he remem-
bers they were for his wife, and it was their wedding anniversary.'
'Fair opening scene,' Tony said, 'what happens next?' 'Buggered if
I know,' I said. 'Go away and write it,' he told me. I did, and the
next year, 1963, I won the British Writers' Guild award for that
script.[43]

Such achievements may have been over-shadowed in the media coverage by all of the awards and plaudits being won by Milligan, Sykes,
Galton and Simpson and Speight, but they all made an impression on
a respectful and grateful industry. Drama, comedy, stage shows, television shows, plays and movies – they were all now coming out of
ALS.

While some of these projects were being developed by the likes of
Antrobus, Took, Feldman, Nation and Yeldham inside the various
offices, other ones were arriving from outside. Brad Ashton, for
example, had one land right in his lap:

I came back from lunch one day and there were these two guys in
my office. No idea who they were. So I said: 'Er, can I . . . help
you?' They said: 'Oh, we're waiting for Johnny Speight.' I said:
'But, um, this isn't his office.' They said: 'No, we know. We were
told to wait in here as the office was empty, you see, while Mr
Speight was out having lunch.' So I got talking to them, you know,
asking them what it was they actually wanted, and they said: 'Well,
we want to buy some Arthur Haynes scripts for a Dutch comedian
called Johnny Kraaykamp.' And after a while they got fed up waiting for Johnny and they asked me: 'Have *you* got anything
suitable?' I said: 'Well, no, everything I write tends to be written for
a particular person, so I've nothing that will fit anyone other than
I've written for.' So they said: 'Well, we just have to have this show
written for Johnny Kraaykamp, so why don't you come over and
meet him and see if you can write for him?' And that started me off
writing for twelve different countries for about thirty or so years.
All because of the fact that Johnny Speight was late back from
lunch![44]

Every office remained busy at ALS. Without the distracting presence of producers, executive producers, focus groups or press office representatives, the writers were free to get on with what they were there for: creating entertainment. The results were, more often than not, innovative, intelligent and enthralling. Quite a few, in fact, would turn out to be revolutionary.

4. The Output

Here you are, mate – add that lot up!

The Goons

ECCLES: My eyes aren't what they used to be.
SEAGOON: No?
ECCLES: No. They used to be my ears.

It was new. It was odd. It was special. It was unlike anything that had been heard on radio before. It was *The Goon Show*, and it would change our expectations as to what comedy could, and should, achieve.

The Goon Show stood the supposedly real world on its head – or set it back down on its feet; opinions, inevitably, would be divided, but, whichever one it was, the effect was splendidly subversive. Capturing the mixture of resentment, frustration, irreverence and relief felt by many whose lives had been stalled while their world was at war, the brave new spirit of goonery satirised the neurotic rigidities of rank and privilege, and mocked the solemn pomp and pose that went with wealth and power. The goon world would celebrate and cherish what was individual, unusual, vulnerable and eccentric; tolerate such wildly surreal nigglers, naysayers and ne'er-do-wells as teeth-rustlers, head-shavers and phantom batter-pudding hurlers; witness such strange sights as ships that turn into trains, shirt tails that explode without warning and fifty-ton Wurlitzer organs that hurtle through dusty deserts; cheer on adventurers who attempt to climb Mount Everest from the inside; and cultivate such comically exotic words and phrases as 'nadgers', 'needle nardle noo', 'the dreaded lurgi' and 'ying-tong-iddle-i-po'.

It all began in Jimmy Grafton's London pub during the first few years that followed the end of the Second World War. A warm and cosily ornate Victorian building, with etched glass partitions and gilt-embellished plasterwork, the Grafton Arms was the kind of pub where many up-and-coming entertainers who worked nearby would come in, claim a seat and a table and then treat the saloon or the snug as their cherished home-from-home (Terry-Thomas, Jimmy Edwards, Clive Dunn, Tony Hancock, Dick Emery, Graham Stark, Alfred Marks, Beryl Reid and Kenneth More were among the pub's current clientele). Michael Bentine began drinking, and joking, in there in the autumn of 1947, closely followed by Harry Secombe, then Spike Milligan and then, a short while later, Peter Sellers. Together, these four men, under the watchful eye of their worldly and witty barman, would spark a comic revolution.

By far the most privileged of the four, in terms of upbringing, was Michael Bentine. Born on 26 January 1922 in Watford, Hertfordshire, the second son of an English mother and Peruvian father, he was educated at Eton College, and intended to become an engineer and scientist, like his father, before war intervened and he joined the Royal Air Force as a volunteer aircrew cadet. In 1942, after being judged physically unfit for operational flying, he was offered an honourable discharge; he refused, so was given a commission in the RAF Operations Section of British Intelligence, where he stayed throughout the remainder of the hostilities. After demobilisation in 1946, he felt disinclined to submerge himself in anything particularly 'serious' (especially after witnessing during wartime the extent to which science had been made to serve politics), so he decided to try his luck as a professional comedian instead, and managed to pass an audition to perform for a six-week engagement at the Windmill Theatre (where he teamed up with an old pianist friend of his named Tony Sherwood to form an extremely odd, cod-Russian-speaking, comedy double-act called 'Sherwood and Forrest').

By the time that he first wandered in for a drink at the Grafton Arms, Bentine was about to make his debut on the West End stage (appearing at the Hippodrome alongside the twelve-year-old Julie Andrews in a comedy-musical called *Starlight Roof*),[1] and was already working fairly regularly in radio as a guest comedian on a range of Variety shows. A wild-looking, black-haired and black-bearded individual, whose predominantly visual act involved a strange range of antics with sink plungers, shooting sticks, an inflated car tyre inner tube and the broken back of a kitchen chair, Bentine seemed to have one foot in the drollery of pre-war music hall and the other one in post-war comic anarchy. He was indubitably bright and unusually well-read, which excited those who were eager for a more erudite kind of comedy, but was also playful and charming in a faintly quaint, Wodehousian sort of way, which endeared him to those who still preferred the unpretentious silliness of an earlier age.

He was also naturally, and tirelessly, inquisitive and inventive, which meant that his act would always evolve at an impressively rapid pace. 'It's pointless scrapping old material when it is new to the audience you are performing to,' he later explained, 'but the fascination is the creation of new stuff. It's one's reason for survival. The comedian who has decided ideas about comedy will eventually cease to create. You must be flexible or else you become a comedic dinosaur.'[2] It was an attitude that made audiences want to keep returning to see him, and then talk about him, and then bring other people to see him throughout those early years. Refreshingly unclassifiable, he seemed to be one of those up-and-coming performers who were sharpening the cutting edge of British comedy.

Off stage, Bentine, with his sparkling eyes, bright white smile, Old Etonian bonhomie and infectious, slightly wheezy, giggle, could be very good company indeed. His exotic-sounding pedigree, élite education, tall-sounding tales and disarmingly casual references to his stunningly protean skills could strike some, early on, as intimidating and somewhat implausible, but, as one of his friends from this period would recall, the initial sense of unease usually turned, sooner or later, to respect and admiration: 'He seemed to be capable of anything – he was an accomplished swordsman, a fine shot with a pistol, an expert with the longbow, a very good artist and an excellent cook. We could never fault his prowess in these areas, although we frequently tried, and if sometimes we became suspicious of this wealth of talent we had to accept the fact that he was indeed an extremely versatile young man.'[3] Jimmy Grafton, while acknowledging that Bentine had a slightly irritating habit of embellishing what should have been left unembellished, agreed: 'I was prone at first to quote Alexander Pope at him: "The bookful blockhead, ignorantly read,/With loads of learnt lumber in his head," but because of the extent of his real knowledge, I came to realise this was a calumny, and to regard him more in terms of Goldsmith's village schoolmaster: ". . . words of learned length, and thundering sound/Amazed the gazing rustics ranged around,/ And still they gazed and still the wonder grew/That one small head could carry all he knew"'.[4]

One of the people whom Bentine came to know and like while working at the Windmill was a young working-class Welshman by the name of Harry Secombe. Born on a council estate in a dock area of Swansea on 8 September 1921, Secombe was, in those early post-war days, a relatively thin but rather stockily-built, bushy-haired, very short-sighted young man with a strikingly big and bright Pickwickian personality. The son of a commercial traveller, he had served during the war in North Africa and Italy with the Royal Artillery (working his way up to the rank of Lance-Bombardier), and, in the latter stages, had also performed as a singer and comedian in a Combined Services concert party. Upon being demobbed in the spring of 1946, he had headed straight down from Wales to London in search of work in the world of theatre, and, after knocking on numerous doors and taking a brief detour through some run-down Northern clubs, he passed an audition in the capital to be one of the comics at the Windmill Theatre.

As Bentine and others had already discovered, being a comic at the Windmill was often a thoroughly miserable business, because most of the sad-faced men in raincoats who filled up the first few rows were there for the naked tableaux,[5] not the humorous routines that filled up the time between each new change of no clothes. The intimate little venue was, however, an excellent test of a performer's nerve, because if a comedian could overcome (or at least survive) the indifference there, he could probably overcome it anywhere, and Secombe was just grateful to have been handed such a challenge.

His act was, in truth, a wafer-thin affair, buttered thickly on both sides with a layer of creamy charm. He used to stride on to the stage to the sound of the band playing 'I'm Just Wild About Harry', and then, after producing a shaving jug, a brush and a blunt cut-throat razor, he would start demonstrating how a range of different social types (such as a soldier, a shy young gent and a stick-in-the-mud businessman) would carry out their morning ritual of removing the stubble from their cheeks and chins. He then closed the act by performing a parody of the movie stars Jeannette MacDonald and Nelson Eddy singing a romantic duet, his voice slipping back and forth from soprano to tenor as he made his merry way through the song. Before departing, he would do something that was destined to become a strange little signature of sorts: he blew his audience a quick but fruity raspberry: 'It was really a desperate attempt to give myself the bird before the audience did,' he later explained, 'and in most cases it worked.'[6]

Secombe began socialising with Michael Bentine towards the end of 1946, sharing a few drinks and an hour or two of gossip each night at Allen's Club in Great Windmill Street before moving on to chatter and laugh through the early hours of the following day in the nearby Lyon's Corner House. Bentine admired the energy and simplicity of Secombe's act, whereas Secombe was somewhat in awe of Bentine's breadth of reference and depth of invention.

It was not long before Bentine was helping Secombe out with fresh material. After several weeks of shaving himself on stage seven times a day, Secombe's cheeks were in danger of turning a permanent shade of scarlet, and the act was looking woefully stretched and strained. When, therefore, Secombe started getting offered the odd slot on such high-profile radio shows as *Variety Bandbox* (producers having seen the shaving routine once and assumed that there were probably several more cheerful skits where that one came from), Bentine came to the rescue, helping him to devise enough new gags and fresh routines to satisfy each engagement. A more lasting solution to his need for new material came one day when Bentine took him to the Grafton Arms for a lunchtime drink. Bentine introduced Secombe to the man behind the bar, who, upon learning that his new customer was another comedian, started chatting about Derek Roy. 'He's rubbish,' said Secombe. 'Who on earth writes his corny material?' 'I do,' replied Jimmy Grafton with a blush and a smirk. 'It might have been an embarrassing moment,' the publican-writer would later reflect, 'but instead we had a good laugh and some convivial drinking.'[7]

Bonding quickly over a glass and a giggle, Grafton agreed to come up with some 'corny' material for Secombe as well as Roy, and it would not be long before he also accepted an offer to become Secombe's agent and manager, too. Slowly but surely, a tight little comedy network was being developed.

Next to be netted was Spike Milligan. Bentine had known him socially for a year or so, bumping into him every now and again in Allen's Club, but Secombe had known and liked him for longer.

The two of them had first met – fleetingly – one dark night during the war, in April 1943 on the outskirts of Le Kef in Tunisia, when Secombe, based along with the rest of his detachment in a gully directly below a steep cliff, narrowly avoided being flattened by a heavy 7.2 howitzer that suddenly came hurtling down from above; evidently another unit, situated higher up the escarpment, had fired the gun without ensuring that it had been properly 'dug in', with the result that it had recoiled and rolled straight over the edge. As Secombe and the other shaken soldiers stood up and surveyed the damage, a dishevelled-looking figure in rumpled battledress emerged through the gloom brandishing a battered hurricane lamp: 'Anybody seen my gun?' he panted. It was Spike Milligan.[8]

They met up again in Italy late in the summer of 1945, when both men became part of a CSE unit based in a little village just outside Naples called Vomero. Secombe was contributing to sketches as well as supplying a solo comedy spot, while Milligan was performing with the Bill Hall Trio. 'I didn't know what to make of Spike at first,' Secombe later recalled, 'but when I discovered that it was he who had come looking for the 7.2 gun howitzer back in North Africa, we soon found that we had a lot in common.'[9] Both men were tired of war and desperate for fun; neither of them took much pleasure in telling the conventional kinds of jokes; but both of them delighted in producing a more 'offbeat' form of humour – pursuing the 'illogically sane thing that goes beyond the gag'.[10]

They were reunited again in London after both men were demobbed, and then began socialising whenever they could. It was only natural, therefore, that Secombe drew Milligan into the inner circle at Grafton's, and the fledgeling comedy trio grew into a quartet.

In the summer of 1948, however, a rather podgy-faced, dark-haired, bespectacled young man called Peter Sellers would arrive at the bar and the foursome became a quintet. Born in Southsea, Hampshire, on 8 September 1925, Sellers (unlike the others) came from a strong show-business background: his fiercely ambitious Jewish mother, Agnes 'Peg' Marks, belonged to the family responsible for bringing the first European-style revue to Britain (and was a descendant of the celebrated eighteenth-century prize-fighter Daniel Mendoza), while his far more easy-going Protestant father, Bill, was a piano-playing entertainer from Yorkshire. It was inevitable that Peter would follow in the footsteps of his parents: within weeks of being born he was being carried on to the stage at the King's Theatre in Portsmouth, where his mother and father were on tour, and, by the time he was a teenager, he could sing and dance, play the piano, ukulele, banjo and drums and mimic most people's voices, speech patterns and mannerisms with an accuracy that came close to being unnerving.

Serving during the war in India, Ceylon and Burma as an air-craftsman in the RAF, he established himself quickly as a popular concert party entertainer, playing the drums and performing impressions in the regular Gang Shows.[11] Soon after his discharge, he managed to find work at the Windmill (performing a routine about several shady street-market traders who sell each other a tin of sardines), but he was so eager to graduate into radio that he resolved, in a classic instance of showbiz *chutzpah*, to recommend himself – via the voices of the two stars (Kenneth Horne and Richard Murdoch) of the popular BBC sitcom *Much Binding in the Marsh* – to the producer Roy Speer:

I thought, being a senior producer, Speer would probably know Horne and Murdoch, you see, who were very big then. And I thought, if I click with the secretary, I'll get through, right? So I said, *[Adopts a deep, posh-sounding voice]* 'Oh, hello, I'm Ken Horne, is Roy there?' 'Oh,' she said. 'Yes, he is,' and I knew I was all right. So Roy got on and said, 'Hello, Ken, how are you?' I said, 'Listen, Roy, I'm phoning up because I know that new show you've got on – what is it? . . . *[Sellers then switched to an imitation of Richard Murdoch's voice hissing urgently in the background: 'Showtime, Showtime']* 'Showtime* or something. Dickie and I were at a cabaret the other night, saw an *amazing* young fellow called Peter . . . wotsisname? Sellers! And he was *very* good – probably have him on the show, y'know? Just thought I'd give you a little tip – little tip!' He said, 'Well, that's very nice of you.' And then it came to the crunch, and I said, 'It's me.' He said, 'What?' I said, 'It's me, Peter Sellers, talking, and it was the only way I could get to you, and would you give me a date on your show?' And he said, 'Oh, you cheeky young sod! What do you do?' I said, 'Well, obviously – impersonations!'[12]

The ruse worked, because Speer invited him for an interview, and, on 1 July 1948, Sellers made his debut on BBC Radio.

It was soon after this that he ventured, for the first time, into the pub that was the Grafton Arms. He already knew of Bentine from the RAF Gang Shows, and had formed a friendship with him and Secombe during their respective spells at The Windmill; he also, over a pint or two of good English ale, warmed more or less immediately to Grafton and Milligan, and so the gang of four became five.

There were some obvious common points of reference: fresh memories of military service (and military incompetence and pomposity) and even fresher ones of touring the halls, as well as a love of inventive comedy, imaginative movies and inspired jazz. The five men also found each other genuinely interesting as individuals, and so the sessions they spent together in the bar saw the bonds grow stronger and stronger and the badinage sharper and sharper. Jimmy Grafton would often arrange for a 'lock-in' after hours, when, as he later confirmed, the *craic* was cranked up to a headier level:

Apart from the consumption of liquor and the general conviviality, a variety of games were played, among them one devised to make use of an early tape recorder I had acquired, a rather massive affair in a wooden cabinet. On this we played a form of 'Consequences', now rechristened 'Tapesequences'. One of us would murmur into the microphone the beginning of a story, unheard by the others. This would be continued by the next person, having had played back to him only the last sentence recorded by the person before. Eventually the whole story would be played back for the amusement of all. Mostly they were absurd, sometimes scatological, but usually they produced enough hilarity to make them worthwhile.[13]

The machine was also used to capture some of Milligan's nonsense rhymes and Secombe's lewd limericks, Bentine's range of real and imaginary accents and Sellers's latest batch of vocal imitations. The group came up with bitter-sweet parodies of the old war reports that they used to endure when they were stationed abroad; savagely funny character studies of certain authority figures from their collective past and present; affectionate spoofs of current stage and radio shows; and plenty of wild and rambling conversations. There was no 'point' to these exercises other than to exploit, for their own private amusement, the extraordinary chemistry that circulated within the group.

There were plenty of reasons why, beyond the boundaries of the bar-room laboratory, these experiments seemed unlikely ever to result in something of substance, and the most obvious of these was the fact that all of the participants were starting to make some progress with their solo careers. Bentine, for example, had just started appearing regularly in Charlie Chester's peak-time radio show *Stand Easy*; Secombe could often be heard on *Variety Bandbox* and could also be seen, every now and again, on television Variety specials; Milligan was writing for, and acting in, the unhappy but relatively high-profile *Hip-Hip-Hoo-Roy*; and Sellers was popping up frequently in various editions of such popular radio shows as *Workers' Playtime*, *Ray's a Laugh*, *The Arthur Askey Show*, *Henry Hall's Guest Night*, *Petticoat Lane* and (via a sitcom-within-a-show called 'Blessem Hall') *Variety Bandbox*.

There were also some important distractions in their private lives: each man had now found a partner and was looking to put down some roots. Harry Secombe had met and wed Myra early in 1948, and they had their first child the following year; Michael Bentine had begun his second marriage, to the ballerina Clementina, in 1949; Peter Sellers would marry his first wife, the actor Anne Howe, in 1951, and Spike Milligan would do the same, with June Marlowe, the following year. Jimmy Grafton was not only already married but also had two small children to support by the time that the other four first came through his door. It was not the most appropriate time, therefore, for any of them to start devoting so much more time to 'the boys'.

A third factor that seemed destined to discourage the troupe from taking its playfulness more seriously was its current value as recreation: it was *fun*, it was *playtime* – it was what everyone looked forward to doing *after* finishing the week's work. 'It was always a relief to get away from the theatre and join in the revels at Grafton's on a Sunday night,' Harry Secombe would reflect. 'Spike, Peter, Mike and I were fast developing a team spirit and enjoyed bouncing ideas off each other. All the time Jimmy Grafton watched approvingly, sometimes curbing our excesses with a constructive suggestion.'[14]

It was this growing feeling of excitement, this mounting sense that what they were doing as a group was simply too good to waste, that made each man start considering pursuing a collective project. Three of them – Secombe, Bentine and Sellers – had already been given the chance to work alongside each other in Frank Muir and Denis Norden's cult comedy series *Third Division* (which ran on the BBC's Third Programme throughout December 1948),[15] and the experience had left them eager to collaborate again, with the welcome addition of Milligan, on a properly professional basis. Inside Grafton's pub, therefore, the play began to acquire a purpose.

Together, the four quick-witted misfits – the Watford-born Peruvian; the Indian-born Anglo-Celt; the Catholic school-educated Jewish-Protestant; and the raspberry-blowing, church-going, slowly expanding Welshman – combined with their friend and patron the publican-writer to conjure up some brand-new new comedy ideas. They took to calling themselves 'The Goons'. The initial inspiration for the name came, Spike Milligan would claim, from an old newspaper cartoon strip: 'Prisoners of war called their German guards goons, but I got it from *Popeye*. There was a creature called the Goon which had nothing in the face at all except hair. It had huge talk-bubbles with one little word in them like "Eeek!" It was very kind and gentle.'[16]

In addition to the continuing 'after hours' taped experiments, the group now started performing the odd impromptu routine for the regulars either in the saloon or an upstairs room at the Grafton Arms, and, by word of mouth, news of their antics began to spread. One or two curious producers arrived to see and hear for themselves what was so strange, funny and new about this comedy troupe, and, even though they judged the performances as being 'too way-out' to be considered for radio, they left, none the less, feeling very amused and rather impressed: there was something happening here, it seemed, that warranted being watched.[17] By the start of 1950, Jimmy Grafton (whom the others had dubbed 'Keeper of The Goons and Voice of Sanity', or 'KOGVOS' for short)[18] was using his internal contacts at the BBC to campaign for a pilot show for his 'Goons'. Seeing the popularity of Peter Sellers rise and rise, the cue was taken to pitch an idea that was packaged as a vehicle for him: *Sellers' Castle*. Scripted by Grafton and Spike Milligan, the proposed show was to feature Sellers as 'the twenty-third Lord Sellers' – the impecunious owner of a ramshackle country castle; included among the supporting cast was the impressionist Janet Brown, her husband the comic actor Peter Butterworth, Alfred Marks and Robert Moreton, as well as, of course, Bentine (as a mad inventor locked in the dungeons), Milligan (as an innocent idiot of a servant) and Secombe (as a wandering minstrel). Doubting his own production skills as the operator of an over-used home tape recorder, Grafton took the cast to a proper London recording studio called *Gui de Buire*, hired an old military friend turned BBC newscaster named Andrew Timothy to provide some linking announcements, and proceeded to tape a sample of part of the script.

When it was completed to everyone's satisfaction, Grafton set off to the BBC's Variety headquarters, just up the same road at Aeolian Hall in Bond Street, and played the tape to the producer Roy Speer. He liked what he heard, and asked if he could read the complete script. Grafton said that he could do better than that: he could bring the entire cast round to see him and give him a full-length private performance. Speer agreed to allow them all into his cramped little office, laughed all the way through the 'show' and then asked them at the end: 'Could you keep it up for a series?' They said that they could, so he said: 'Then I'll recommend it to the planners.'[19] Everyone went back to Grafton's, where the supplies of alcohol plummeted alarmingly.

News of a fairly sobering nature came a couple of days later, however, when the team was informed that the producer who had been assigned to the project was not Roy Speer but rather a man named Jacques Brown. Jacques Brown was, by the BBC's standards, an *enfant terrible* who was intent on recording shows without the presence of a studio audience. Grafton reasoned that the show was a brave experiment that would benefit from the sound of people laughing ('We were embarking on some way-out comedy and needed all the help we could get').[20] A compromise was, eventually, reached: Brown would record the show, *sans* audience, which would then be vetted by the team and, if necessary, re-recorded in front of a studio audience. Once the initial – cold and forced-sounding – recording had been completed, however, Jacques – unbeknownst to Grafton and his colleagues – played the tape straight back to the planners, who rejected it for sounding too 'crazy'. That, as far as most of the BBC's bosses were concerned, was that – the project had fallen stillborn from the press.

Fortunately, one of the people who heard it – Pat Dixon, a very experienced and respected radio producer (who had already worked with Secombe, Bentine and Sellers on *Third Division*) – disagreed with the decision and resolved to find something to do with this promising group of performers. Knowing that his colleagues were eager to persuade Peter Sellers to sign a long-term radio contract, he urged them to indulge the star by letting him and his friends record a brand-new pilot show. They saw his point and so, without much real enthusiasm, they commissioned a recording.

Settling down to write the script, Spike Milligan seized on the chance to create the world anew for himself and his friends. 'Spike looked at the world and decided it was peopled with idiots,' said Jimmy Grafton, 'and therefore he'd create his own parallel world of idiots.'[21] Assisted by Grafton and a former commando captain turned professional comedy scriptwriter called Larry Stephens (another friend from the saloon bar), Milligan proceeded to decon-struct and then reconstruct the conventional radio comedy show. There were false starts and absent endings; odd asides and sudden changes of pace; quick skits, spoofs and satirical swipes; and playful little moments when the content took note of the form ('The next part of the programme follows as soon as it has been written . . .'). Someone opened up a little tobacconist's shop, only to be caught by the little tobacconist; one minute the action took place at a Grand Prix in England, the next it moved to Italy and then moved back to England, where the well-known fictional hero Dick Barton found himself trapped in a gas-sealed sewer directly beneath a haddock-stretching factory in Park Lane; there was a trip to Egypt in search of the tomb of Tutankhamun, and then a quick visit to the Festival of Britain – where, to the strains of 'Land of Hope and Glory', messages of support were read out from loyal Commonwealth subjects in Australia ('We are divided from you by fifty thousand miles of land and sea. Let's keep it that way') and allies in America ('Yes, indeed, without doubt Britain *can* take it. Every dollar that we have sent to Britain, Britain has taken'), and then it was declared that the brave new post-war Britain could now raise its proud head to the skies and cry out: 'HEELLLPPPP!'. The script was just what Pat Dixon had expected it to be: unexpected.

Dixon chose Dennis Main Wilson, a very bright and passionate young protégé of his, to produce the show, and he proved himself to be the ideal person to defend such an unconventional and anti-estab-lishment project: 'During the war I saw the most horrendous things happen [and] I saw incredible bravery, and if you lived in that great mishmash of emotion and danger – incredible bravery and suffering –

you're not going to be put upon by some berk up on the sixth floor of the BBC who has got no balls do something worthwhile.'[22] The recording went ahead on 4 February 1951. 'After the show,' Harry Secombe would reflect, 'we weren't sure if we would get a series or not,'[23] but such anxieties were soon assuaged: the BBC agreed to give them a run of no fewer than seventeen half-hour shows.

The first argument, however, had preceded the first production. There had been a disagreement over what the title of the show should be: the team had wanted to call it *The Goon Show*, but the planners blocked that proposal on the grounds that, they claimed, it failed to shed light on the content. Their alternative – *The Junior Crazy Gang* – was dismissed by the performers because, they pointed out, their style of humour was brand-new and bold and different, and nothing like the old knockabout music-hall shenanigans associated with the veteran Crazy Gang itself.[24] Eventually, after many memos[25] and plenty of moans, an awkward compromise was reached: the show was called *Crazy People*, and billed in the following manner in the *Radio Times*:

CRAZY PEOPLE
Featuring
Radio's Own Crazy Gang
'The Goons'[26]

Broadcast at 6.45pm on Monday, 28 May, the opening show began with a predictably stuffy, bow-tie voiced announcer declaring: 'This is the BBC Home Service'. A fanfare of trumpets followed, and then a babble of incomprehensible voices. 'What is the zaniest comedy show on the air today?' asked the announcer. 'Er, *Today in Parliament?*' answered a Milligan idiot. 'No,' the announcer replied, trying to sound politely excited. 'It's those Crazy People, *The Goons!*' The next twenty-eight or so minutes were a mixture of planned and impromptu peculiarities that delighted some of the modest-sized audience and left the other part puzzled and bemused. What it made all of them do, however, was talk about what they had heard: the word started to spread that something very different was now on the air. '*The Goon Show* had a bigger effect than I ever dreamed,' Spike Milligan would come to reflect. 'There was an immediate reaction from young people who had come out of the war and found a new world after a restricted period of life.'[27]

The listening figures grew steadily throughout the series, from an average of 370,000 for the early episodes to a relatively respectable high of 1.8 million for the final few. Those who caught and stayed with the show from the start grew to know and love the recurring comedy characters, such as Michael Bentine's eccentric inventor Professor Osric Pureheart, the childlike Ernie Splutmuscle and the camp Flowerdew (both played by Peter Sellers) and the fictionalised 'Harry Secombe'. They also came to relish the extraordinary range of unusual sound effects, which included everything from a pair of supersonic feet to a single chewed leek. They even put up with the regular musical interludes (featuring the close-harmony singing group The Stargazers, the harmonica player Max Geldray or the Ray Ellington Quartet), which were about as unwelcome to comedy fans as Groucho Marx giving way either to Chico on the piano or Harpo on the harp.

A second, 25-episode series (billed on this occasion as '*The Goon Show*, featuring those crazy people . . .') followed in January 1952, and a broadcasting phenomenon began to evolve. There were two key changes in personnel – Michael Bentine left (citing a desire to pursue solo projects, although there had also been an increasing degree of creative tension between Milligan and himself),[28] and Dennis Main Wilson (who had come to identify himself so closely with his icono-clastic artists that his superiors suspected the gamekeeper had turned poacher) handed over production duties to Peter Eton – but both the team and the show re-emerged from this reorganisation seeming stronger than before.

The departure of Bentine (who had suggested a bit, accepted a bit and ad-libbed a bit) clarified the division of labour within the team: Milligan, from now on, was the main writer, Sellers was the main performer and Secombe was the main personality and link with the listening audience. The arrival of Peter Eton from the BBC's techni-cally more sophisticated Drama Department bestowed on the show a stricter sense of discipline: although he had no problem with comedy as such, he was hard to make laugh, hard to impress and hard to deceive, so he pushed all of the participants to improve. Eton was also an expert supervisor of sound effects and microphone technique, so he ensured that the show became a far more dynamic listening experience.

The third series (now billed officially as *The Goon Show*) was, as a consequence, a marked improvement, with less music, more comedy, better scripts, better performances and better production. That was promising, but it was just the start. The fourth series, which went out over thirty weeks from October 1953 to April 1954, would see the show begin the steady ascent right up to its peak in terms both of quality and popularity. The format was altered significantly – from two or three separate sketches to one continuous storyline – and so was the method of recording – from the old slow-speed acetate discs to the more up-to-date magnetic tape (which meant that, for the first time, the performances could be edited so as to remove any errors, dubious ad-libs or problems relating to timing). There was also, by this time, a familiar and well-liked coterie of comedy characters:[29]

Neddie Seagoon: Born in Broadcasting House and still trying to find his way out, Seagoon engages with the world by inquiring of it: '*What-what-what-what-what?*'. A short-legged, portly man of great honesty, integrity, stupidity and enormous appetite, he is a role model for every right-minded idiot, and an inspiration to every wrong-minded fool.

Eccles: Born in 1863, the only child of Ethel Cox, virgin. A part-time human being, whose adult height varies between 2" 6' and 18" 3' (depending on food, environment and bed size), he spent a dozen-and-a-half years at kindergarten before commencing his education at Mr Crollick's Establishment for the Chronically Fit. He has had 18,312 interviews for jobs so far, but has not yet had a job – he could find work as an idiot if only there wasn't so much competition. Spends his days walking around saying 'Hello dere' to anyone who will listen. Wears a 33-year-old Burton suit. Likes children. Children like him. Was the personal friend of a brewer's dray. Was also Home Secretary for three days – until someone discovered the printing error. Lives near 29 Scrot Lane, Balham. He was, is and will no doubt remain Bluebottle's best buddy. Clubs: none. Recreations: walking around saying 'Hello dere' to anyone who will listen.

Bluebottle: A keen reader-out-loud of signs, notes and stage directions, he is an impressionable young lad who can usually be persuaded to attempt the most dangerous of tasks for the meagre reward of a few dolly mixtures and a cheerful pat on the back. Plagued with bad luck, he is often on the receiving end of spectacular explosions, gunshots and physical attacks which leave him temporarily 'deaded'.

The Hon. Hercules Grytpype-Thynne: The son of Lord 'Sticky' Thynne and Miss Vera Colin (a waitress at Paddington Station), he is a suave, George Sanders-style cad who never tires of seeking new ways to swindle Seagoon. Educated at Eton Mixed Grammar School in Penge (where he was the subject of a police investigation into school homosexuality), he then spent two years at Oxford (where he was the subject of a police investigation into homosexuality in Oxford). Implicated subsequently in the sale of Regimental Silver Plate, he spent three years at Wormwood Scrubbs, where he was the subject of a prisoners' investigation into homosexuality in prisons. On release, he became a member of Harrow Labour Exchange, and then joined the Foreign Office, where he was the subject of homosexuality with a Masai goatherd. Awarded the OBE, he became a Private Secretary to a British Lord. Clubs: yes. Recreations: homosexuality.

Comte Toulouse 'Jim' Moriarty of the House of Roland: A deeply unscrupulous French idiot, international knotted-string consultant and Grytpype-Thynne's servile sidekick. He is often to be found scavenging in dustbins looking for food and muttering meaningless, foreign-sounding curses (*'Sapristi Bompetts!'*; *'Caramba le Ponk!'*). A nasty little man who is nothing but trouble.

Major Dennis Leonard Bloodnok, IND. ARM. RTD.: A corrupt military cad, pervert and idiot. Born in 1893 and educated at Repton, Eton and Oxford, he served during the First World War as a Colonel in the Rajputana Rifles, whom he hit with a big stick. Cashiered after military police traced him to Rangoon, where he was found wearing false testicles in a freak show, he rejoined the Army as a Major, seeing action and suffering wounds in the bedroom of Mrs Madge Feel. Cashiered during the Second World War for posing as an eccentric Hindu fakir who had gone white with fear, he rejoined the Army wearing a stocking mask, and, using his Masonic connections, rose once again to the rank of Major. As Seagoon's former commanding officer, he suffers from terrible bouts of flatulence, and is a total coward who will betray anyone or anything for money. Recreations: Piccadilly Circus.

Miss Minnie Bannister: The tipsy spinster of the parish, she has admitted that she once danced the Can-Can at the famous Windmill Theatre, and had a fling with a young Major called Bloodnok. When pressed, however, she merely screams and then refers all further inquiries to her current spokesman and companion of honour, Mr Henry Crun.

Mr Henry Crun: Henry Crun (full name: Henry Albert Sebastopol Queen Victoria Crun) is an elderly man of failing memory. He invents things, but can never remember what he has invented, or why. Persistent questioning will prove fruitless when it comes to refreshing his memory as to the identity of Mr Henry Crun; one will never elicit a response beyond the initial reply: 'Henry Crun?'

William 'Mate' Cobblers: An elderly cockney idiot who calls everybody 'Mate', he is the son of the road sweeper Fred 'Chopper' Cobblers. Left school at fourteen to join Thomas Crapper & Co. as tea boy. Joined Chislehurst Laundry as tea boy. Joined Woolwich

Arsenal as tea boy. Conscripted in World War I as Private in Sappers and Miners as tea boy. Rose to the rank of acting unpaid Lance Corporal – injured in action when a tea urn fell on his head. Discharged in 1918, since when he has wandered the streets of London telling people 'You can't park there, mate' or 'Oi, mate – put that cigarette out' or 'I dunno, mate – I'm a stranger round here' or 'Bloody foreigners' or 'Why don't you get yer 'air cut?' or 'I spent four years fighting for this country.' Now uniformed door-man at the BBC's Aeolian Hall. Informs all visitors: 'It's nothing to do with me, mate.' He has no mates.

All of the characters had come, in essence, from the mind of Spike Milligan (who used the likes of Grytpype-Thynne to exorcise the memory of those 'bloody scoundrels' with 'educated voices' and 'cowards charging around with guns' whom he and his father used to be obliged to address as 'Sir'),[30] but a few of their sounds, sayings and dispositions had crept out from the memories of his fellow performers – especially those belonging to Peter Sellers. Bluebottle, for example ('Pauses for audience applause; as usual, not a sausage'), owed much, Sellers would later confess, to an eccentric young gentleman – six foot four and rusty-headed – by the name of Ruxton Hayward:

Bentine was forever telling people that they were a genius. I don't know why he did this, but he'd say to anybody, after a few minutes of conversation, 'You're a genius!' And they'd usually believe it. Because Bentine, you know, is the only one who's had any real education out of the four of us. [. . .] So this fella came over one evening – I'll never forget it – he was tall and wide, he wasn't *fat* but he was *wide*, and he was dressed as a scout leader. In fact he *was* a scout leader. Bentine was appearing at Chiswick Empire [at this time] and I was at Shepherd's Bush Empire. [. . .] Anyway, the door opened and a fella said, 'There's some stranger, a geezer out there . . . well, I dunno what, but Michael Bentine sent 'im along . . .' So I thought, 'Well, I may as well see him.' Anyway, this tall fella, he'd got a little briefcase, and he'd got a scout hat on and he'd got a big red beard with all this, and red knees, and socks and all of the insignia, you know. And he said – and I'm not kidding, this is how he spoke – he said *[Adopts a strange, high-pitched, slightly quavering and tinny-sounding voice:]* 'Could I come *in* for a moment, please?' So I thought: 'What is *this*?' So I said, 'Er, yes, certainly, please, what can I do for you?' He said: 'I have just seen . . . Michael Ben*tine* a-*a*-t Chiswick . . . and he said that I am a genius.' Then he went on to ask me about doing a concert at the Sulgrave Road Boys' Club or something. So I said, 'No, you know, I don't think . . . it's, like, Saturday night . . .' You know, it was the last thing I wanted to do at that stage – especially if *he* was an example of what I was going to find down there! So he took this as a hint. He said: 'Er, there is a *fee* involved . . .' So I said: 'No, it's not a question of money, I assure you, really. I *would* come, but I just can't, you know, at the moment.' So he stood there for a second and he said: 'Oh, well. Just a thought!' He said: 'Do you know anyone else who I can see?' So I sent him along to see Secombe![31]

Similarly, Bloodnok was based in part on the kind of crusty old rum-soused officers whom Sellers encountered – and impersonated – while serving out in India, whereas William 'Mate' (apart from reminding BBC insiders of several rude and surly commissionaires) bore a fairly close family resemblance to an old man who worked in a furniture shop near the offices of Associated London Scripts in Uxbridge Road (whenever anyone asked him from what type of wood an item was made, he would always reply: 'That's *solid* wood, that is, mate'),[32] and an occasional visitor called 'Levis' (played by Harry Secombe) was modelled on the Canadian talent-spotter and impresario Carroll Levis, with whom Secombe had worked during the war.

One or two minor characters simply came into being by accident. Wallace Greenslade – the man who took over from Andrew Timothy as the show's announcer early on in the fourth series – found himself becoming a fictionalised version of himself once Milligan had spotted his potential as a comic foil. First, the others began to heckle him over the quality of his contribution; then he started to heckle them over the standard of the show in general; and then, eventually, he evolved into a thoroughly 'rewritten' character – and, in 1955, even starred in his own episode, entitled 'The Greenslade Story' (another real-life announcer, John Snagge, was dispatched to rescue Greenslade from a decadent life of celebrity: 'I've been given authority to offer you *four* pounds a week – and you can read the nine o'clock news at half past if you want to – *and* take your own time about it').

Little Jim – another peripheral yet memorable figure – was little more than a walking, talking catchphrase. Milligan had been eagerly deconstructing catchphrases ever since the days of the first series, when he took a random and, in the circumstances, quite meaningless line – 'More coal!' – and kept giving it to someone who would open a door, shout the phrase out loud and then shut the door again: the first time that it was uttered on air it was met with a deadly silence; the third or fourth time, it elicited the odd nervous chuckle; and by the tenth time, it started being greeted with plenty of laughter and applause. It was proof, as far as Milligan was concerned, that mechanical repetition, rather than organic and original comedy, had kept the older, more conventional, radio shows in business. By the time that Little Jim first popped up, however, Milligan had gone beyond satire and was revelling in the sheer absurdity of repeating lines whose only purpose was their purposelessness. The childlike Little Jim merely piped up to say: *'He's fallen in the wah-tah!'* Milligan would say that the phrase had come originally from an incident aboard the liner that was taking him and the rest of his family from India to England (his younger brother, who could not swim, crashed into the ship's pool as he tried to swing across it on a rope – thus prompting a little girl to observe almost absent-mindedly: 'He's fallen in the water!');[33] Peter Sellers would say that it had been inspired by his own son, Michael, who uttered the very same phrase when someone took an unexpected dip in the garden plunge bath.[34] Whatever the truth of his lineage, Little Jim grew into an unusually popular catchphrase on – and with – legs.

Eccles, on the other hand, was the character who most merited the title of 'the original Goon', because Milligan had been performing as him, in essence, ever since the days of *Hip-Hip-Hoo-Roy*. Inspired, at least in vocal terms, by the Disney cartoon character Goofy, Eccles became Spike's very own comedy tic. 'Eccles,' Jimmy Grafton would always maintain, 'is the real Milligan; his id or alter ego; a simple, happy soul, content for the world to regard him as an idiot, provided that it does not make too many demands upon him.'[35] The man himself agreed: 'I'm afraid he's right, yes, yes. That's it, man, you know. I don't want to think about earning money, I just want to be an idiot.'[36]

Conjuring up – and controlling – all of these characters proved to be, Milligan would recall, a repeatedly exhilarating and liberating experience: 'We had to create *The Goon Show* – a fantasy world. You could make characters do what you wanted because you were writing the script. You always win. You can't get arrested in a fantasy world unless you want to. For everyone who found reality a bug [. . .] *The Goon Show* was sheer therapy.'[37]

Each one of the trio behind this cast of characters contributed something special. Milligan provided the main tone, tempo and most inspired flights of fantasy; Sellers supplied the most broad and rich range of characterisations (on the odd occasion when he was unavailable for a show, it would take four or more other actors to cover all of his characters); and Secombe, as Neddie Seagoon ('the greatest straight man in comedy' according to Milligan),[38] was the rock-like character at the centre who held the show together, drew the listeners in and drove the action on. Together the three of them interacted to produce something that was even greater than the sum of its parts – a comedy show that came, in the words of Peter Eton, to represent 'a bold and melodramatic rearrangement of all life'.[39]

Every aspect of life, culture, politics and society would be grist to *The Goon Show*'s mill in the years that followed. The humour grew more dexterous and daring as each new series progressed. Jimmy Grafton dropped out as editor after the third series (acknowledging that his editorial input was now more or less redundant), and Larry Stephens stopped contributing on a regular basis mid-way through the fourth, and so, from the fifth series on, the scripts were shaped inside the offices of Associated London Scripts by Spike Milligan with the expert assistance of Eric Sykes. With stronger storylines and sharper routines, the show really started to revel in its own crafty freedom (prompting the *Observer* to hail it as 'the purest form of surrealist humour yet reached on steam radio').[40]

It parodied the clichéd, formulaic and pun-laden style of its popular predecessors, such as *ITMA* – even going so far in one episode as to recruit an old *ITMA* regular, Jack Train, to reprise his role as the Blimpish Colonel Chinstrap (catchphrase: 'I don't mind if I do!') to face one more flurry of ancient gags:

> SEAGOON: I wonder what they're up to.
> *[A shell drops down nearby]*
> BLOODNOK: Duck!
> *[Explosion followed by the sound of a hen clucking]*
> SEAGOON: That's no duck – that's a chicken.
> CHINSTRAP: By gad, sir, they're firing hens at us!
> BLOODNOK: A fowl trick!
> CHINSTRAP: Eggs-actly.
> MILLIGAN: We're being shelled!
> SEAGOON: *Stop cracking yokes!*[41]

It also demonstrated, seemingly effortlessly, how much funnier, more intelligent and, in a way, more *elegant* modern comedy now had the power to be:

> BLUEBOTTLE: What time is it, Eccles?
> ECCLES: Um, just a minute. I-I've got it written down here on a piece of paper. A nice man wrote the time down for me this morning.
> BLUEBOTTLE: Ooooh, then why do you carry it around with you, Eccles?
> ECCLES: Well, um, if, er, anybody asks me the time, I can show it to dem.
> BLUEBOTTLE: Wait a minute, Eccles, my good man—
> ECCLES: What is it, fellow?
> BLUEBOTTLE: It's writted on this bit of paper, what is eight o'clock, is writted!

ECCLES: I know that my good fellow. That's right, um, when I asked the fella to write it down, it was eight o'clock.

BLUEBOTTLE: Well, then. Supposing, when somebody asks you the time, it *isn't* eight o'clock?

ECCLES: Well, den, I don't show it to 'em.

BLUEBOTTLE: Oohhh.

ECCLES: [*Smacks lips*] Yah.

BLUEBOTTLE: Well, how do you know when it's eight o'clock?

ECCLES: I've got it written down on a piece of paper!

BLUEBOTTLE: Ohh, I wish I could afford a piece of paper with the time written on!

ECCLES: Oohhhh.

BLUEBOTTLE: 'Ere, Eccles?

ECCLES: Yah?

BLUEBOTTLE: Let me hold that piece of paper to my ear would you? [*Listens*] 'Ere – this piece of paper ain't goin'!

ECCLES: *What?* I've been sold a forgery!

BLUEBOTTLE: No wonder it stopped at eight o'clock!

ECCLES: Oh, dear.

BLUEBOTTLE: You should get one of them tings my Grandad's got.

ECCLES: Oooohhh?

BLUEBOTTLE: His firm give it to him when he retired.

ECCLES: Oooohhh.

BLUEBOTTLE: It's one of dem tings what it is that wakes you up at eight o'clock, boils the kettil, and pours a cuppa tea.

ECCLES: Ohhh, yeah. Um, w-what's it called?

BLUEBOTTLE: My Grandma.

ECCLES: Ahh. Ohh, here, wait a minute – how does *she* know when it's eight o'clock?

BLUEBOTTLE: She's got it written down on a piece of paper.[42]

In another episode, Sir Isaac Newton (played by Harry Secombe) was charged with the task of teaching Eccles about his law of gravity:

NEWTON: Now, just jump into the air.

ECCLES: Da, okay.

[FX: *jump effect*]

NEWTON: There – you see what happened? You jumped up in the
air but you came back down to earth again. Now: *why?*

ECCLES: Da – 'cos I live there.[43]

The sheer audacity of the show was, at times, truly astonishing. It
was not afraid, for example, to break one of radio's cardinal rules
and be silent – such as the episode in which several of the characters
stepped into the lift that took them all the way up to the top of a
mountain:

[*The sound of two doors clicking shut, followed by silence*]
[*More silence, other than a faint whirring noise*]
[*More silence, other than a faint whirring noise and the odd
nervous mumble and whistle*]

SEAGOON: This must be terribly boring for the listeners.

BLOODNOK: I know, I know, but what can one do in a lift?[44]

On another memorable occasion, Neddie Seagoon was offered a
range of silences to assist him with his rest cure:

CRUN: Now Neddie, this is where we give you complete silence.

SEAGOON: Oh. That's what my doctor prescribed.

CRUN: Oh. Is it National Health silence?

SEAGOON: Yes.

CRUN: Oh, dear. The National Health silence is a bit noisy, you
know. Why don't you have a private patient's silence?

SEAGOON: What does *that* sound like?

CRUN: It sounds like this:
[*A short stretch of silence*]

SEAGOON: Jolly good! I'll have some of that. Well, what size
silences have you got?

CRUN: Well, we've got the luxury one that goes from here –
[*Complete silence*]

CRUN: – to there.

SEAGOON: That's about the size I want.

CRUN: Oh, good. Minnie? Wrap up a full-length silence, please.
GREENSLADE: Ladies and Gentlemen, in case you, too, are interested in purchasing a quantity of silence, here are a few samples. First this:
[Complete silence]
GREENSLADE: And this for the ladies:
[Complete silence]
GREENSLADE: Or perhaps this is more in your line:
[Complete silence]
SPIKE: I don't like it! I don't like it at all![45]

Just as bravely, the show would sometimes pause the plot to allow a piece of dialogue (often featuring the chronically forgetful couple, Minnie Bannister and Henry Crun) to ramble on and repeat itself, pointlessly and perhaps almost boringly, to a fraction away from the point of no return:

OLD MAN: Gentlemen – people aren't coming to Brighton. They're frightened. I ask you to think of an idea that will revive the holiday trade and defeat the Phantom Head Shaver.
CRUN: I suggest that everyone entering Brighton be handed a bald wig and that he should sleep in that self-same wig.
MINNIE: Rubbish! If all the men wear bald wigs, the Phantom will attack the women!
CRUN: I fear that the ladies, too, will have to wear bald wigs.
MINNIE: Rubbish, buddy! Why should I wear a bald wig? I'm already bald!
CRUN: Well, wear a bald wig with hair on.
MINNIE: You-you can't have a bald wig with *hair* on, buddy!
CRUN: What-what-why-why not, eh? Why-why not?
MINNIE: Listen, if a bald wig had hair on, it wouldn't be bald!
CRUN: What? What? What? What? What? What?
MINNIE: Whoever heard of a bald-headed man with hair on, eh?
CRUN: Well, *I* have . . .
MINNIE: Who, eh? Go on, tell me – who? Who?
CRUN: No, no, no, I'm not going to tell you.

MINNIE: That's because you don't know anybody with a hairy bald head, do you!

CRUN: *Mnk . . .* I do, Minnie!

MINNIE: No, you *don't!*

CRUN: *Mnk . . . grnp . . . knp . . .* I *do*, Minnie!

MINNIE: Who? Go on, tell me!

CRUN: I don't see why I should tell you.

MINNIE: That's because you don't know anyone with a hairy bald head, do you!

CRUN: I do. I *do* know somebody with a hairy bald head.

MINNIE: Y'don't.

CRUN: I do.

MINNIE: Y'don't.

CRUN: *Mnk . . . DO!*

MINNIE: Y'don't!

CRUN: *[Starts suffering heart attack] Mnk . . . Grmp . . . Nuk . . . I . . . Mnk . . . I DOOOOO!*

MINNIE: Y-o-u . . . *DON'T!!!!!!!!*

[FX: Clash of sabres to mix with argument – two pistol shots – sabres continues – one pistol shot followed by silence]

CRUN: *Mnk . . .* I do!

MINNIE: You *don't!* Anyway, I'm going home – and I say you *don't* know a bald-headed man with hair on his head, so there! *Ha!*

[FX: Door slams]

CRUN: Pah . . . I do! I *do* know—

[FX: Telephone rings]

MINNIE: *[Distorted]* You don't.

CRUN: I do!

[FX: Receiver slammed down]

CRUN: I DO!

[FX: Door opens]

MINNIE: You don't!

[FX: Door slams shut again]

CRUN: I do, I—

[FX: Telephone rings – receiver grabbed off hook]

CRUN: *I-do-I-do-I-do-I-do-I-do-I-do-I-do-I-do! I-DO-know-a-man-with-*

a-hairy-bald-head! I-do-I-do- I-DO-know-a-bald-headed-hairy-man!
A-hairy-man-bald-headed! I-do-I-do! I-do-know-a-man-with-a-
hairy-bald-head! So there! I DO!

CALLER: Thank you. Can I speak to Mr Seagoon, please?
CRUN: *Ah-oh!* It's for you.[46]

Such audacity paid off, because (according to the producer, Peter
Eton)[47] a similar routine won the show the longest stretch of sustained audience laughter (over four minutes prior to editing) in its
history:

NEDDIE: I am just about to knock at the Minnie Bannister home
for Part Five of 'The Fearful Fu-Manchu Story'!
[FX: A knock on a door]
MINNIE: *[off]* Who's there?
NEDDIE: It's me.
MINNIE: *[off]* Henry, there's a man called 'Me' at the door.
CRUN: *[off]* 'Me'?
MINNIE: Me.
CRUN: He'll have to prove it. *[Raises voice]* You out there!
NEDDIE: Yes?
CRUN: *[off]* Prove you're me.
NEDDIE: All right: I'm Henry Crun.
CRUN: *[off]* Oh, that's me, Minnie, yes. Min – open
the door and let me in.
MINNIE: But you *are* in, Hen.
CRUN: *[off]* Well, you'll have to let me out again, won't you?
MINNIE: *[off]* Why?
CRUN: *[off]* Because I'm out there waiting to come in!
MINNIE: *[off]* Oh, very well.
[FX: Door opens]
NEDDIE: Ah, thank you.
[FX: Door closes. A brief pause]
NEDDIE: Now then, Mr Crun, I want to warn you that—
[FX: Knocking]
CRUN: Who's that out there?

MINNIE: *[off]* It's me. You've locked me out!

CRUN: Nonsense! Me just came in. He's here now.

MINNIE: *[off]* No, no, it's *me* – Minnie!

NEDDIE: Good heavens! Quick! That's the woman I'm here to protect. Open the door!

CRUN: Oh, very well, very well. But I must let Minnie in first.
  [FX: Door opens]

MINNIE: Thank you, Henry.

CRUN: That's all right, Min. Now, then, dear – what were you—
  [FX: Knocking]

CRUN: Who's there?

NEDDIE: *[off]* It's me. She isn't here.

CRUN: Rubbish, *rubbish!* She *is* here – aren't you, Min?

MINNIE: Yes, I'm here, Henry.

NEDDIE: *[off]* Well, you're not out here!

MINNIE: Oh. Are you sure?

NEDDIE: *[off]* Yes. Come out and have a look.

MINNIE: Right.
  [FX: Door opens]

MINNIE: You're right. I'm not here. *Help!* I'm lost! We'll all be
murdered in our beds! Oh!
  [Goes on having hysterics][48]

The achievement was all the more impressive because of the obsta-
cles *The Goon Show* had faced. Censorship was one problem, a
certain amount of internal scepticism and suspicion among the
powers-that-be at the BBC had been another, and a third had
involved technology.

Censorship had been an issue right from the start, and it would
never go away entirely, because of the continuing existence, and influence, of the BBC's notorious *Green Book*.[49] Introduced in 1949 by
the Corporation's then Director of Radio Variety, Michael Standing,
as a 'policy guide' for producers, writers and artistes, the text sought
to help clarify what moral risks were worth running in the post-war
era of broadcasting (one or two gags, themes and references of 'dubious' taste had recently caused something of a stir, and so the aim was

to deal with the matter internally before someone sought to deal with it externally). According to this well-meaning but somewhat snooty little manual, 'Music-hall, stage, and, to a lesser degree, screen standards, are not suitable to broadcasting,' because radio, unlike those other means of entertainment, could reach directly into the home. The BBC, as a servant of the whole nation, was obliged to avoid causing any members of the nation any unnecessary offence: 'Producers, artistes and writers must recognise this fact and the strictest watch must be kept. There can be no compromise with doubtful material. It must be cut.'[50]

In order to ensure that all of its employees understood what this 'doubtful material' might be, the manual proceeded to spell it out in sobering detail. There must, it said, be no vulgarity, no 'crudities, coarseness and innuendo', which meant 'an absolute ban on the following':

Jokes about –
    Lavatories
    Effeminacy in men
    Immorality of any kind

Suggestive references to –
    Honeymoon couples
    Chambermaids
    Fig leaves
    Prostitution
    Ladies' underwear, e.g. winter draws on
    Animal habits, e.g. rabbits
    Lodgers
    Commercial travellers

Extreme care should be taken in dealing with references to or jokes about –
    Pre-natal influences (e.g. 'His mother was frightened by a donkey')
    Marital infidelity[51]

As if that was not enough to completely obliterate the average red-nosed comedian's act, there was more: no advertising; no American material or 'Americanisms'; no derogatory remarks about any profession, class, race, region or religion; no jokes about such 'embarrassing disabilities' as bow-legs, cross-eyes or stammering; and, last but by no means least, no expletives (which not only meant no 'God', 'Hell', 'Bloody', 'Damn' or 'Ruddy', but also not even the odd 'Gorblimey'). Writers and performers were also urged to keep the jokes about alcohol and its effects to an absolute minimum.

Just in case these commandments left any dubious comic spirits still standing inside the Corporation, the manual went on to strike one final blow for decency. All performers were warned (without any further explanation) that on no account must there be any attempt to impersonate Winston Churchill, Vera Lynn or Gracie Fields.[52]

The Goon Show responded to these draconian restrictions by slipping through as much 'dubious' material as it could just under the censor's radar. One method involved the use of Cockney rhyming slang: the character of Hugh Jampton, for example, owed his name, supposedly, to a friend who was said to be a member of the studio audience – but, in reality, he owed it to an altogether different, and more substantial, sort of member (Hugh Jampton – Huge Hampton – Hampton Wick – Big Dick).[53] Another sly strategy was to quote only the punch-line of a well-known filthy joke, such as: 'It's your turn in the barrel.'[54] Then there were all of the many saucy euphemisms from Milligan, who – inspired by his reading of Rabelais – coined such suggestive but abstruse terms as 'a wizened gulper of mists' (as well as the names of such minor characters as the spy known as 'the Pink Oboe' and the carer called Frothpump who came to the aid of Mr Crun on his bath night).[55]

The Goon Show was even bolder, and more direct, in the way that it dealt with any doubters within the BBC. Ever since one ageing and befuddled grandee at Broadcasting House had been heard to inquire, 'What *is* this "Go On Show"?'[56] the team had made a point of mocking their own bosses on air. When, for example, one of their sober-sounding announcers declared smugly at the start,

'This is the BBC', Spike Milligan or Peter Sellers would respond with a sardonic comment such as: 'Hold it up to the light – not a brain in sight!' – and the refreshingly irreverent tone was set.[57] Similarly, when the show parodied George Orwell's *1984*, the authoritarian regime was renamed 'The Big Brother Corporation', and Neddie Seagoon was tortured inside Room 101 with clips from such anodyne mainstream programmes as *Mrs Dale's Diary, Life with the Lyons* and *Have A Go!*[58] When certain executives questioned the team's professionalism both before and during recordings, the performers made a point of announcing – on air – that they were going 'round the back for the old brandy' for the duration of the musical interlude (and they did: the bottle of brandy was 'hidden' inside an innocent-looking pint of milk). By no means everyone behind the scenes took exception to the routine teasing – and a fair few, discreetly, rather enjoyed it – but those who did object kept on trying, and failing, to bully the team into submission. 'I logged thirty attempts by them to stop the show,' Peter Eton would say of the BBC's so-called 'Bumbling Bureaucrats':

> For instance, one week Major Bloodnok was awarded the OBE for emptying dustbins during the heat of battle – just after two BBC executives had received the honour. I was called up and warned about committing further breaches of taste. On another occasion, Peter imitated the Queen's voice during the hilarious launching of an attempt to dislodge the pigeons from Trafalgar Square, and I was hauled up again. The officials threatened to take the show off altogether in the face of this further example of 'rank bad taste'. I believe it was only John Snagge's continued defence of the programme and insistence on Spike's right to freedom as a writer which saved us.[59]

Milligan and Co. used this hard-won freedom constructively – by testing the full potential of BBC radio's technology. The team had always been obsessive about their sound effects, never leaving any particular instruction – such as, 'They knock the door down' – open to the slightest kind of misinterpretation:

Long series of smashing door down noises – goes on and on . . .
give it variation in kind, i.e., first confident crashes on door with
axe. These all very long. Fail – then renewed. Then furious . . . then
frenzied . . . then heavy, full-blooded blows . . . furious sawing . . .
then hammering on door with fists . . . mad rattling of the door
knob . . . then four or five heavy blows . . . then a mad furious
hatchet attack on the door . . . Door opens. Sound of hinge.[60]

Even an ostensibly simple-sounding sequence, such as when one character was offered a cocktail, resulted in a complicated challenge in a
Goon Show script:

Make with the effects of eight jet planes, a police siren, the victim
of a maniacal strangler, the San Francisco earthquake and the
hydrogen bomb. It dies away in a strangled sob and hiss. The verdict on the cocktail is as follows – 'Quite nice.'[61]

The problem was that not even Milligan knew how to capture elec-
tronically the peculiar sounds that came alive inside his head – he just
knew when it had not yet happened. On one especially infamous
occasion, for example, he became so frustrated at his colleagues'
failure to come up with something that sounded exactly 'like a sock
full of custard splattering against a wall' that he marched off to the BBC
canteen, ordered a large earthenware bowl of egg custard (complete
with a sprinkling of nutmeg on top), removed a shoe and one of his
grey woollen socks, filled it full with the custard and then hit it
against a wall repeatedly; not even the real thing, alas, sounded to
him like the real thing, and so he emptied the custard back out, pulled
his sock back on, muttered a quick 'Shit!' and then returned to the
studio for another rethink.[62] Gradually, however, the BBC's sound
engineers (assisted, from the late 1950s onwards, by those specialists
attached to the Corporation's newly-formed Radiophonic Workshop)[63]
became more and more adept at translating the written words into
the desired sounds, and thus made *The Goon Show* into an increasingly rich and powerful listening experience.

All of this – the cleverness, the cheekiness, the subversiveness and the wonderfully imaginative and technologically inventive funniness – combined to make *The Goon Show*, for many people, an unmissable weekly event. The listening figures, as a consequence, continued to climb as the series and years went by, rising from an average of three million during 1954 to seven million by 1956.[64] The show that started out being described as an 'acquired taste', remarked the *Radio Times* with undisguised pride, 'has [since] been acquired by Royalty, statesmen, explorers, sportsmen, dons, film stars and listeners under eighteen and over eighty.'[65]

Avid fans of the show included a teenager in south Liverpool by the name of John Lennon ('he would drive me crazy with non-stop mimicry of the various accents,' his aunt would recall; 'he loved that play on words')[66] and a young boy in south-west London known officially as Prince Charles (to whom the Goons' style of humour appealed 'with an hysterical totality').[67] The Labour Party politician Michael Foot announced that Spike Milligan was now his 'favourite anarchist' (supplanting Proudhon and Kropotkin) and the critic Bernard Levin declared that The Goons were currently doing for their chosen medium what Gluck had done for opera – namely, 'they have added a new dimension'.[68] The Duke of Edinburgh, giving in for once to whimsy, chose The Goons to be his 'Royal Champions' for a charity tiddlywinks contest ('Goons versus Gown') at the University of Cambridge,[69] and hundreds of listeners – from abroad as well as within Britain – bombarded the BBC with comments, cartoons, suggestions and sample scripts about this most 'highly esteemed' of radio shows.

Its broad appeal owed something to its obliqueness. It managed, for example, to mock the political establishment without ever seeming 'political' – which was probably just as well, because there was no real message to defend beneath the mockery. Politically, Spike Milligan was someone who was far more sure of what he disliked than of what he admired, although there were times when he quite liked what he normally despised, and vice versa. 'Were his political opinions Right or Left?' John Antrobus would ask, before answering:

Left. Anarchic. And on Thursdays Fascist. He did not hold any particular party line. He could be passionately for a cause like

CND. I never knew him turn against any individual because of his or her colour, race or creed and he always showed respect for anyone's achievement and sympathy for their suffering. But he could make a general comment that I can only describe as bigoted. Once he had formed an opinion he found it hard or impossible to admit to being wrong and would rather lay another opinion on top of it and live the paradox.[70]

The show pitched its attack at a far more general level, knocking walls down not with a mind to building new ones, but just in order to see and breathe and roam free. Its irreverent energy was liberating to any individual, of any age and from any background, who had ever lived under another's thumb. 'Essentially,' Milligan would say of the show, 'it is critical comedy. It is against bureaucracy, and on the side of human beings. Its starting point is one man shouting gibberish in the face of authority, and proving by fabricated insanity that nothing could be as mad as what passes for ordinary living.'[71]

That, indeed, was the starting point, but there would never be an 'ending point'. There was no point in an ending. What *The Goon Show* started in the world of comedy would indeed go on and on: questioning things, experimenting with things and creating things. Nothing would ever again need to be taken for granted – not the scope and structure of any show, the potential of any medium nor the expectations of any audience. *The Goon Show* was one revolution that would never be betrayed or erased.

The programme itself (guided, after Peter Eton's departure towards the end of 1956, first by Pat Dixon and then the highly accomplished John Browell) continued until its tenth series in 1960, and spawned several spin-offs over the years: three short movies (*Down Among the Z Men* in 1952; *The Case of the Mukkinese Battle Horn* in 1956; and, in 1959, *The Running, Jumping and Standing Still Film*); five television shows (the one-off special *Goon Reel*, shown by the BBC in 1952; two editions on the commercial channel Associated-Rediffusion of *The Idiot Weekly, Price 2d* in 1956; one series, also on Associated-Rediffusion in 1956, of *A Show Called Fred*,[72] followed later the same year in the same place by a series called *Son of Fred*;

and two series on BBC TV, in 1963–4, of a puppet version called *Telegoons*); and numerous single and long-playing records (including the enduringly popular 'I'm Walking Backwards for Christmas' and 'The Ying Tong Song'). At the start of a new decade, after almost fourteen years together – and nine years (and over two hundred episodes) on air – the time had come for the trio to move on: Peter Sellers had a movie career to pursue; Harry Secombe was ready to accept more solo offers relating to music and theatre; and Spike Milligan was very, very, tired and keen to see The Goons go out at the top ('I didn't want to do what most shows have done and run the show until it had lost its energy and died – unfunny and unwanted').[73]

After The Goons came the most talented young fans of The Goons: a new generation of comedy writers and performers who wanted to preserve and promote the true spirit of great British goonery – not so much by imitating the achievement as by emulating the ambition. They, too, in their own distinctive way, would satirise their so-called superiors, look for the loopholes in the logic of grown-ups and sometimes begin things at the middle and then end them at the start. They, too, would surprise, delight and inspire their own loyal mass of young fans, who, in turn, would seek to do the same sort of things to their own. That, above all else, was the great legacy bequeathed by The Goons: they made each successive generation believe that it was time – that it was *always* time – for something completely different.

Sykes And A . . .

All we were after was laughter.

In the world of comedy, the centre needs to hold. The better and more stable the mainstream is, the more freedom there is on the periphery. *Sykes And A . . .* was one of those shows that maintained the good health of the mainstream. It was never 'dangerous', it never ran the range of risks that seemed rash, but it did, none the less, a very good job, and its job was to make the broad audience happy.

Sykes And A . . . was one of the best-natured, least pretentious and most successful British sitcoms of the 1960s. Featuring a succession of simple but delightfully engaging storylines, unobtrusive but cleverly effective direction and some technically brilliant comedy performances, it warmed the heart, made people laugh and did consistently well in the ratings. At a time when commercial television was churning out far too many comedy shows that pandered to the most basic kinds of tastes, *Sykes And A . . .* exemplified the BBC Light Entertainment Department's commitment 'to give the viewers what they want – but better than they expect it'.[1]

Set in and around 24 Sebastopol Terrace – a small, two-up, two-down, house in East Acton – it featured, as all fine sitcoms do, a 'trapped relationship': two characters who, for some unspoken reason, cannot ever seem to break away from one another. Eric Sykes played 'Eric', a playful, naïve, devious, eternal adolescent, and Hattie Jacques played 'Hattie' (often shortened to 'Hat'), a decent sort of soul who found most of the world around her far too brash and bewildering, and put up with Eric's antics because, however improbably, he was, after all, her twin brother. Both characters were unmarried (and rarely seemed to work), but each one laboured under the private delusion that the other was in greater need of grown-up guidance and help.

Johnny Speight (who was just starting to branch out into sitcoms after years of writing stand-up and sketches) had originally envisioned the relationship to have been that of a conventional husband and wife, but Eric Sykes, in a masterly intervention, changed it to that of brother and sister, and not just any old brother and sister, but twins – and not just any old twins, but identical twins. Aside from the obvious long-running visual gag of having the Rubenesque Jacques and the whippet-thin Sykes accept unquestioningly that they were as similar in looks as any two individuals of different genders could possibly be, the conceit also trebled the number of potential storylines available to the show, as, in addition to the basic two-handers, there could also now be episodes involving female friends of Eric and male friends of Hat.

Another masterstroke came with the casting of the show. The character of Hat, of course, had always been intended for Hattie Jacques, but it was still an inspired choice. Sykes had first encountered her during 1948, when, as a guest at the Players' Theatre (a small old-time music-hall situated underneath the arches in Villiers Street beneath Charing Cross Station), he saw her steal the show by striding on to the stage dressed in a surprisingly revealing Victorian costume and belting out a spirited version of 'My Old Man Said Follow the Van': 'Incredibly, at the end of the number, she leapt into the air and landed in the splits as softly as an autumn leaf.'[2] Like so many people before him, Eric Sykes left the little theatre that night pleasantly stunned by what he had seen.

Jacques was different – very different. She was big and broad, light and elegant, funny and flirtatious, and intriguingly self-aware and intelligent. She could sing, dance, act, star or support, do drama, do comedy, do a dazzling range of different voices, and she also had an abundance of effortless charm. She seemed to have it all, even though, by the conventional standards (and, more pointedly, the prejudices) of the time, she was not supposed to have much to applaud, as a star performer, at all.

Born in Sandgate in Kent on 7 February 1922, Josephine Edwina 'Hattie' Jacques had trained as a hairdresser and then spent two years during the war first as a Red Cross nurse and then as an arc-welder in a factory before turning in peacetime to entertainment for a profession. The Players' Theatre, with its unusually warm and cosy atmosphere, well-known repertoire, colourful costumes, good-natured audiences and cheerfully nostalgic attitude, proved an excellent place for her to acquire some confidence and experience on the stage, and, working alongside the likes of Clive Dunn, Ian Carmichael and Bill Owen, she soon established herself as an invaluable member of this post-war music-hall ensemble. John Le Mesurier, who met her there at the end of the 1940s and ended up marrying her in 1952, would describe her warmly as 'bright and witty and vivacious and an entertainer to her fingertips'.[3] Although unhappy and frustrated about her size, she refused to allow it to undermine the progression of her career, and always acted without any evident inhibitions (as Le Mesurier observed drily: 'It was as if, knowing she was bound to be noticed, she wanted to make a real job of it').[4] The strategy worked impressively well: good, versatile and reliable young character actors were always in demand, and Jacques was soon seen and heard far beyond the local club-like environs of The Players.

She was first heard regularly on radio at the end of the 1940s, playing the gluttonous schoolgirl Sophie Tuckshop in *ITMA*, before moving on to bigger and better roles written by Sykes for *Educating Archie* and by Galton and Simpson for *Hancock's Half-Hour*. She was first seen at the cinema in a couple of very minor and uncredited roles before making her 'official' debut in 1948 (alongside a couple of her colleagues from the Players' Theatre) in David Lean's adaptation of Charles Dickens' *Oliver Twist*, and then she went on to appear in her first three *Carry On* movies (*Sergeant*, *Nurse* and *Teacher*) during the final two years of the 1950s.[5] By the time that she was enlisted to act alongside Sykes on television, therefore, she was a well-known personality as well as a much-admired performer, and so brought her own lustre to the brand-new production.

She had also developed, by this stage, a very special kind of friendship with Eric Sykes that only seemed to need to be nourished by regular meetings inside the working environment of the radio and television studios: 'In all the time we worked together I only went to her house three times,' Sykes would say, 'and she came to mine maybe twice. We were very different people. Hattie loved being among people. There was always a crowd around her. She was as extrovert as you could get. I'm not like that. I'm basically shy. I like being alone. You couldn't say we had a lot in common, but she was a very great lady.'[6] What they did have in common came to the fore whenever the two of them shared a set: a finely-tuned comic sensibility that allowed each of them to anticipate, assist and complement the other, and thus enabled both of them to alternate, within the same episodes, between the roles of a comic and a feed. Once Hattie Jacques was on board, therefore, the high promise of the project seemed assured.

The choice of the actor to play the part of Eric and Hat's snide and snooty next-door neighbour, the owlish and alone-ish Charles Brown ('the last of my line'), was similarly swift and shrewd. Right from the start, Eric Sykes made it clear that he wanted no one else but Richard Wattis.

Richard Wattis was, as far as Sykes was concerned, the best available actor to bring the pompous, fastidious and quietly epicene character fully to life. Born on 25 February 1912 at Wednesbury in Staffordshire, and brought up in nearby Walsall, Wattis had idolised as a child the screen actor Robert Donat (with whom he corresponded, seeking sage advice), and, although aware of the fact that he would never have his hero's leading-man looks, he remained determined to pursue the same sort of glamorous-sounding profession. He dodged one potential humdrum career in electrical contracting and then dodged another one in chartered accountancy, and continued to act in whatever local amateur dramatic productions that he could find. After training at Croydon Repertory Theatre (alongside John Le Mesurier, Dennis Price, John Barron and the future theatrical agent Richard Stone), he spent the war serving in the Royal Medical Corps and then, upon being demobbed, began his professional acting career proper, finding supporting roles more or less immediately on the stage, in radio and also on television. It was in movies, however, that he seemed to become something of a fixture during the 1950s, popping up in production after production as a typical under-polished cog in post-war Britain's comically sluggish bureaucratic machine. Balding and bespectacled in his standard uniform of spindly pinstripe, he was the over-cautious civil servant, the pedantic colonial pen-pusher, the deeply conservative administrative assistant, who would ask politely how he could help you, then listen carefully to your request, and then inform you that he really was awfully sorry but he was afraid that he could not help you after all. He was junior counsel for the defence in *Kind Hearts and Coronets* (1949); a politician in *The Happy Family* (1952); a butler in *The Importance of Being Earnest* (1952); a lawyer in David Lean's *Hobson's Choice* (1954); a doctor in *The Green Man* (1956); an assistant hotel manager in Hitchcock's remake of *The Man Who Knew Too Much* (1956); and a Foreign Office official in *The Prince and the Showgirl* (1957). If anyone ever called out for 'Carruthers' in an office scene, most of the audience expected Richard Wattis to appear from the wings.

He was far more individualistic, interesting and discreetly sybaritic in real life. A cheerful, somewhat camp and relatively worldly *bon vivant*, he was a great thrower of parties and frequenter of high-class restaurants, a cultured quaffer of good vintage Haut-Brion and Aloxe-Corton and an avid student of history, the arts and literature (on *Desert Island Discs*, his choice of music included several songs from the musicals, a vintage recording by Marlene Dietrich and a snatch of Rachmaninov, while his one book was André Maurois's biography of Disraeli and his solitary luxury was a comfortable bed). He was also quite mischievous and a very good sport, so – rather as playful-natured John Le Mesurier (another familiar bureaucratic figure in 1950s cinema) would feel when the role of Sergeant Wilson in *Dad's Army* landed on his lap – he was delighted when Sykes asked him to play someone who was a little sillier, more vulnerable and, beneath the stuffy surface, far more amiable than the usual type of character he was offered.

The regular cast was completed by the signing of Deryck Guyler as Police Constable Wilfred 'Corky' Turnbull, the dim-witted local bobby on the beat with his own book of black-and-white rules (e.g.: 'Helmet on – "Constable"; helmet off – "Corky"'). Guyler, who was born in Wallasey (which was then in the county of Cheshire but is now classed as part of Merseyside) on 29 April 1914, was an old favourite of Eric Sykes's from their earliest radio days. After a brief spell working in his father's jewellery shop and then a year dabbling in theology at college, Guyler had drifted gradually into the world of entertainment, first by performing a modest Variety act – singing songs, telling jokes and (quite seriously) playing a customised washboard (it came with added bells, horns and cymbals) – around the local clubs and pubs, and then by appearing on a regular basis at the excellent Liverpool Rep. He joined the BBC's own repertory club[7] in the early 1940s after being invalided out of the RAF, and, in 1946, achieved a fair degree of personal fame via *ITMA* as the street-smart Liverpudlian Frisby Dyke (the first time, it is thought, that a recognisably Scouse-sounding accent had been heard on national radio).

Guyler went on to use his wonderfully deep, rich and lugubrious Northern voice to great effect in numerous other radio shows throughout the 1950s, including *Life with the Lyons* (1950–61), Eric Barker's *Just Fancy* (1951–57), Morecambe & Wise's BBC debut series *You're Only Young Once* (1953–4) and *Barker's Folly* (1959). It was Eric Sykes, however, who handed him the first real chance to establish himself on television (more of a chance, in fact, than was planned: the original intention had merely been to use Guyler's character on an occasional 'as and when' basis, but, as Sykes later explained, 'his popularity with the public grew more quickly than weeds on a bombsite and he became a regular member of the team').[8]

The preparation was now practically complete. Once Jacques, Wattis and Guyler were all safely in place, a brilliant young producer/director – Dennis Main Wilson – in control and the five scripts had been given a final polish (not just by their one acknowledged author, Johnny Speight, but also, unofficially, by two of his colleagues at ALS – Sykes and Spike Milligan – as well as by Frank Muir and Denis Norden at the BBC)[9] the show was deemed ready to reach the screen.

The series was called *Sykes And A . . .* so that the given topic of each episode could complete the title. The opening edition, 'Sykes And A Telephone', went out at 8.30pm on the night of Friday, 29 January 1960, and, judging from the uniformly positive critical response (no recording, alas, appears to have survived), set the tone for the briskly-paced and mildly farcical domestic comedy still to come (according to the review in *The Times*, the combination of Sykes's 'kindly gormlessness' with the 'unique and fantastic gifts' of Jacques and the 'graceful playing' of Wattis promised 'a great deal').[10] A second – six-episode – series was commissioned soon after this first one had begun, although Speight dropped out as scriptwriter and his duties were redistributed by Sykes among several of the others (including John Antrobus) at ALS. It was not until 1961 and the third series, however, when the BBC made it clear that it wanted Eric Sykes to be the sole writer responsible for all of the scripts,[11] that the show really settled down and found a single head and heart.

Sykes now took full control of what was already a very popular prime-time sitcom and proceeded to lift it up to a higher level. First, he clarified all of the characters, accentuating their distinguishing attitudes, and added a little more depth (and a few more lines) to the likes of Mr Brown and Constable Turnbull. Second, he modulated the pace more delicately, and allowed more moments when words were not needed, the camera could move in, and he and Jacques could use their eyes and facial expressions to convey thoughts and feelings and comedy (they became one of the first couples on television, for example, who just sat and watched television). Third, he started thinking about the various ways in which he could make more use of the situation of 24 Sebastopol Terrace, with Eric and Hat spending more time inside its four little walls (idling, arguing, chatting and playing). The consequence of such 'fine tuning' was that the show acquired a sharper focus as a sitcom, with more character and less action, and much more interplay between the actors. The show, in short, started to seem less afraid of doing 'nothing' except being funny.

The stand-out episode of this series (and, indeed, one of the best of the whole five-year run) was 'Sykes And A Bath,' (first broadcast on

25 January 1961) in which the presence of builders inside their home, and the disruption that duly ensues, forces Eric and Hat to seek alternative bathing arrangements:

> ERIC: *[On telephone]* Yes, hello, Mr Brown?
> BROWN: Yes, who's there?
> ERIC: Er, Mr Sykes.
> BROWN: Yes, what is it?
> ERIC: Is it all right for me to have a bath now?
> BROWN: Yes. As I'm constantly reminding you, Sykes: the sooner the better.
> ERIC: No, but, ah . . . in *your* bath?

Once the exasperated Mr Brown has consented, grudgingly, to Eric borrowing his bath, there follows a delightfully playful sequence in which Sykes, utilising all of the toy boats, bombers and battleships that he had brought with him from his own bathroom, improvises an increasingly anarchic conflict at sea ('Open the boom defences,' he begins, raising one side of the bath rack to allow his first two ships to venture out towards the taps, and then he turns his attention to one of his aircraft: 'Meanwhile, in a fjord – *brrrrrmmm* . . .'), which only ends when one of his big toes becomes lodged up the hot water tap. The bath, with Sykes trapped inside it, is then dismantled, removed from the house and carried shoulder-high down the street by six plumbers – a sight which causes some passers-by to remove their hats and lower their heads in a show of respect. A subsequent scene has Sykes sitting in the waiting room of the casualty department at his local hospital, with his big toe still connected to part of the bath, in between a sad-faced man (played by Bob Todd) with one hand stuck inside a vase ('I thought there was a pound note in there'; 'And was there?'; 'I dunno until I get me flippin' hand back out, do I?') and another unhappy character (John Bluthal) with the top part of his head trapped tight inside a tin pot ('What happened to you then, mate?'; 'It's obvious, isn't it?'). By the time that the episode had reached an end, the doctor had the tap stuck on the tip of his index finger, Eric had *his* index finger caught in the lid of the coal-hole and

Mr Brown had his right hand trapped in his next-door neighbour's letter-box.

It was all very Laurel and Hardy-like, and the viewers loved it for being so. Indeed, the episode not only drew in the millions at home (and won Sykes the 'Best Light Entertainment Artist' award from the Guild of Television Producers and Directors), but it also made a very favourable impact abroad. When, for example, it was shown in America a few months later as part of NBC's *International Showtime* series, the television critic for *The New York Times* declared the following morning that it had been half an hour of 'beautifully turned nonsense' that had 'demonstrated the universality of inspired silliness and showed the wondrous appeal of farce when the element of exaggeration is not overdone'. Predicting that the great success of this episode on US television 'should lead to a return engagement on these shores', the critic went on to say that both Sykes and the BBC deserved to be congratulated warmly for having 'come fairly close to an electronic variation on Hollywood's old two-reeler', and added that 'it would be pleasant to see more'.[12]

'Sykes And A Bath' also won third prize (and only missed out very narrowly on the gold prize) at the 1962 Alexandria Film Festival in Egypt (thus prompting it to be dubbed into Arabic and distributed throughout the Middle Eastern market).[13] According to Donald Baverstock (the BBC's current Assistant Controller of Programmes), who attended the event on the Corporation's behalf, the show had made its two Hollywood-produced rivals look 'stale and processed' by comparison, and the other television executives present were said to have been 'astonished' by the speed at which Sykes, Dennis Main Wilson and the rest of the team had made this and other episodes without compromising the high quality of performance and production.[14]

The burgeoning success of the show, however, brought with it certain problems. At one stage, for example, rumours began to circulate within the BBC that Hattie Jacques, after reflecting on the fact that the show was now set to run and run indefinitely, was wondering whether or not she should leave rather than remain and become typecast. Aside from her continuing contributions to the *Carry On* franchise, she was also accumulating a number of notable support- ing roles and cameos in other movies – including *School for Scoundrels* and *Make Mine Mink* (both of which were released in 1960) – so her career seemed interestingly poised. On 10 February 1961, two days after the end of the third series, Dennis Main Wilson jotted down the gist of a sobering conversation he had just had with Jacques's agent, Felix de Wolfe. It appears that de Wolfe (who felt – not for the first time nor the last – that people were taking advantage of his client's good nature) made the following six points:

1)   Jacques had to decide how much of her time (if any) she could and would devote to Eric's work now that she was in such a strong position to 'go all out for herself for big money and prestige'.

2)   She currently had two 'major' film offers on the table.

3)   She was paid more for her work in the recent ITV sitcom *Our House* than she had ever received for contributing to *Sykes*.

4)   She felt 'rather hurt' that the BBC had been making a fuss about Eric while she had been taken for granted.

5)   She was still, however, 'immensely pro' both the BBC and Eric Sykes.

Although de Wolfe would probably have preferred to see his client make a clean break from this and other potentially long-running tele- vision projects and concentrate instead on making more movies, Jacques herself was disinclined to go, and so, after receiving some reassuring letters and calls from several BBC executives, she instructed her agent to leave the matter alone.

While it therefore proved fairly easy, in the end, to persuade Jacques to stay on, there would still be one significant absentee when the fourth series commenced: a distinctly disappointed Richard Wattis. The reasons for this absence stretched all the way back to the autumn of 1960, when, shortly after the second series had been screened, Bush Bailey had written to the BBC's Booking Manager complaining about the agent who was representing Richard Wattis. After noting that the actor's fee for the most recent run of *Sykes and*

A . . . had risen by 75 guineas to 200 guineas per show (compared to the 150 guineas that Hattie Jacques currently received), Bailey reported that the troublesome agent was now pushing for more than 250 guineas per show for the next set of episodes. Bailey remarked that, while this would probably be tolerable, at a push, any subsequent increase most certainly would not. As everyone agreed, he noted, that Hattie Jacques was indispensable, he hoped that Eric Sykes could be persuaded to write Wattis out within the year, and either do without a next-door neighbour in future or else create a new one who could be played by a 'cheaper' actor. On 2 October 1960, Tom Sloan, the BBC's then acting Head of Light Entertainment,[15] wrote to Bailey saying that he had spoken to Sykes about the basic problem (without going into any great detail), and that Sykes had been 'disappointed' but 'understanding'.

'I understood all right,' Sykes would say; 'the accountants were gnawing at the woodwork.'[16] Angered by the intervention, but still committed to the show, he bowed, eventually, to the pressure and omitted Mr Brown from the fourth series – but he refused to replace Richard Wattis with another actor, and vowed to bring him back as soon as he could (and he did – although not until the show was revived in 1972).

The result was that, from the fourth series on, Deryck Guyler was given more to do, but there was also a tighter focus on the relationship between Eric and Hat that actually helped the overall quality of the comedy. Some of the most memorable moments, in fact, now came when nothing much seemed to be happening, and the two actors were left alone to mine all possible humour from out of the deep mundanity of domestic life:

HAT: [*Studying a newspaper crossword*] Four down: 'Animal, three letters'.
ERIC: Eh? Could be anything. 'Animal, three letters'? Er, cow.
HAT: It says 'feline'.
ERIC: Oh, well, you didn't *say* that, did you? Dog.
HAT: Cat.
ERIC: Pardon?

HAT: It can't be dog – it starts with a 'C'.

ERIC: It could be cow then.

HAT: With an 'A' in the middle.

ERIC: If you'd given me the facts! 'Three-letter word, starting with "CA"' – car!

HAT: A car isn't an animal, is it?

ERIC: That one of ours is – it's a pig.

HAT: That starts with a 'P'.

ERIC: That's not *The Times*, is it?

HAT: No, you remember – six across: 'Brother and sister born at the same time', five letters. Well, it's 'twins'.

ERIC: I put that in.

HAT: No, you put 'twits'.

ERIC: I was thinking of us.[17]

Although the rapport between Sykes and Jacques had always been, right from the very start, remarkable, it would now, as time went on, grow so close that Sykes would liken it to telepathy: 'We'd sit around the table on the Tuesday and read through the script, and sometimes, just as I was about to turn over the final page for the last bit of dialogue, Hattie would put her hand out and stop me, then she'd come out with her next line – and we'd turn over and there was that same line. She'd anticipated it just as I'd written it.'[18] Her keen intelligence and sound actor's judgement, Sykes would say, helped revive him whenever his writing seemed a little tired: 'Whatever I wrote she delivered as if it had been scripted by George Bernard Shaw, and if a line was really appalling she would suggest another one – strangely exactly the one I would have written had I thought about it first.'[19]

It was just as well that Sykes and Jacques had such a good understanding of each other, because, as the shows went out live, the need to get things right – or, failing that, at least make things *look* as though they were right – was, as Sykes later acknowledged, acute:

Our show was at 8.30 to 9 o'clock. It had to be written and performed to the exact second. If the show wasn't finished at the appointed time a dinner-jacketed announcer would appear on screen saying, 'Good evening, this is the nine o'clock news.' Indeed, some viewers must have thought he was part of our show. As a writer, I had a very difficult balancing job to do. For instance, if it was an exceptionally good audience, we'd be getting more laughs, in which case, with still two or three minutes of our show to run, up popped 'Good evening, this is the nine o'clock news.' So then we had to invent some way of letting the cast know whether we were running late or with time in hand, ergo the floor manager, in contact with the producer via his ear-phones, would stretch his arms out wide meaning we had time in hand, and if he whirled his hand round like cranking an old car, it meant, 'Get your skates on.' His antics were reminiscent of a batsman guiding down a jet fighter on to the deck of an aircraft carrier.[20]

Each actor had a private little sign, code word or phrase (Eric Sykes's was 'On top of which . . .') that alerted the others whenever he or she was struggling to remember the next line, and each had his or her own set of tiny tricks to suppress any build-up of laughter (Jacques – a great giggler – would usually lower her long eyelashes, glance down to one side, bite her bottom lip, brush away an invisible piece of cotton from the left-hand side of her dress and then continue with what she was saying; Sykes would normally just turn for a second to look quizzically at a corner of the set, turn back, clear his throat, touch an ear-lobe, prod a finger or pick up a prop and then slip straight back into the scene).

It helped that the production was in such a safe pair – two safe pairs, in fact – of hands. Dennis Main Wilson, with the able assistance of a young Sydney Lotterby (who would later not only take over as producer/director of this show, but also oversee such other popular sitcoms as *Yes, Minister*, *Butterflies* and *Ever Decreasing Circles*),[21] ensured that the show ran as smoothly as possible, maintaining an admirably healthy balance between planning and play. A passionate, thoughtful, unconventional but very responsible programme-maker, Main Wilson, like Sykes, was completely committed to the idea of making the mainstream better: 'Comedy is communication,' he said. 'If you dare step on the stage or in front of the cameras as a comedian it means that you have accepted the holy writ of entertaining the public. But not if you sit there entertaining yourself and believe that the less they laugh, the more stupid they are, the more clever you are.'[22] The director was also – again, just like Sykes – allergic to anything that detracted or distracted from the sitcom that was seen on the screen: 'The director's job on television in general, but in television comedy in particular, is solely to make sure that what is happening in front of the cameras is an entertainment. [. . .] If direction is noticeable it is bad direction. The camera is an ancillary thing. Is the show funny or not is the only thing that matters. And if it is funny, it is funny without cameras.'[23]

Everyone involved in the show was pulling in the same direction, and enjoying the process as it progressed. The *Sykes* set was a caring, as well as very professional, working environment: if, for example, one of the cast fell ill during the days leading up to the next show, Sykes would try to rewrite the episode so as to render their character bed-ridden or rooted to the settee. Similarly, if someone was unwell during rehearsal, the rest of the cast would leave them to rest while the others blocked out the relevant movements on their behalf. 'It was that kind of atmosphere,' Sykes would recall. 'We were all helping one another, and I think it shows. There are some shows – which I will not mention – that just didn't hit the mark, and that was because the people in them didn't particularly get on. And that comes through, because the camera is a great leveller, and it gets deep down.'[24]

Inevitably, given the routine exigencies and vicissitudes of live television as well as the sheer size of the complete output, not all of the episodes were entirely satisfying on every level, but the majority were admirably entertaining, and, at its very best, *Sykes And A . . .* was a genuinely exceptional sitcom. Indeed, several of its episodes would later be counted among the all-time greats in British television comedy.

'Sykes And A Stranger', for example, was a classic not once but twice: first, when broadcast on 21 April 1961, with Leo McKern playing a rough-and-ready ex-prisoner called Tom Grando who, in pursuance of a supposed childhood pact, returns to Sebastopol

Terrace to claim Hat as his fiancée, and then, when it was remade and broadcast again on 19 October 1972, featuring a truly treasurable small-screen *tour de force* from Peter Sellers. Cleverly structured and joyously performed, this was, on both occasions, a glorious mixture of fine writing and inspired acting.

McKern, predictably, played the role relatively straight as a quasi-Dickensian rogue, and injected a certain amount of tension into the scenes in which Eric, in a desperate bid to keep this thuggish-looking intruder away from Hat, puts on a wig and a hastily-purchased dress (ERIC: 'I'm buying the dress for my sister and she's an identical twin, so what fits her fits me.' FEMALE SHOP ASSISTANT: 'Oh! Well, couldn't she come in herself?' ERIC: 'Well, er, no – 'cause she's out buying me a suit') and tries to confuse him into believing that the real Harriet is actually the 'funny girl' who spends most of her time resting upstairs. Sellers, on the other hand, played the role purely for laughs: after coasting through the last rehearsal as planned, he took Sykes and Jacques by surprise on the night of the recording when he made his first entrance wearing a Brillo-pad wig, sporting several blacked-out teeth and speaking in a cod-Michael Caine accent (''Allo, darlin' . . .'). 'As soon as Hattie saw him, she'd gone,' Sykes would recall, 'so I turned round to look at Peter, wondering what had happened, and saw what he'd done to himself with all of the make-up and everything, and then I'd gone, too!'[25]

It was not the usual kind of show – it was more of a playful, semi-improvised routine by three very good old friends – but it was a joyful occasion to watch, and very, very funny:[26]

HAT: May I ask who you are?

GRANDO: Certainly, darlin' – this is who I am! Come 'ere!
  [Lunges at Hat, kissing her as he holds her tight]

ERIC: Geddoff! Jus-just come here! *[Grando takes one hand off Hat, grabs Eric by the wrist and spins him over the back of the sofa]*

GRANDO: Sorry to keep throwin' you abaht, mate, but don't you know who I am?

ERIC: Yeah, weren't you in *Peter Pan* with the crutch?

GRANDO: No, I'm Tommy Grando – little Tommy Grando! Don't you remember?

HAT: Wait a minute – didn't you run away to sea?

GRANDO: Yeah, that's right!

HAT: Tommy Grando!

ERIC: *Little Tommy Grando!*

GRANDO: An' we all used to play round the back of the old bakery there!

HAT: That's right, y-yes, we did!

GRANDO: Yeah.

ERIC: Little Tommy Grando!

GRANDO: Yeah, that's right. *[Suddenly sounding menacing]* Little Tommy Grando. You was always hittin' me, weren't you?

ERIC: Yeah, well, it's done you good, hasn't it? I mean, look at you now. *[To Hat]* Don't I say all the time? – 'I wish somebody had taken the trouble to hit *me* more often!'

GRANDO: Well, it's never too late, mate.[27]

This 'revived' episode would also show what a truly fine (but chronically under-appreciated) comedy performer Eric Sykes actually was. When, for example, after the slow-witted Grando has finally rumbled the deception and demands that Sykes removes and hands over his 'feminine' disguise (an awful early 1970s-style navy-blue dress with two bright red apples emblazoned across the breasts), he tries to resist, prompting a distressed Hat to cry out: 'Oh, Eric, let him *have* it – you can always buy another one!' Sykes hears this, looks at Hat incredulously and then, with a real sense of outrage in his voice, slaps his hands tightly over his chest and exclaims: 'With *two* apples?' It is a beautifully timed and delivered reaction – like a sublime little dance movement – and, in terms of technique, actually matches, on the night, the best that even Sellers has to offer.

Apart from the justly celebrated 'Sykes And A Bath', the other outstanding episodes would include 'Sykes And An Ankle' (first broadcast on 8 February 1961), in which, following a highly dubious stray biscuit-tin-related accident, a bed-ridden Mr Brown turns Eric and Hat into his full-time – unpaid – domestic servants; 'Sykes And

A Haunting' (13 March 1962) in which Eric and Hat, after being spooked by the supposed ghost of their escapologist Uncle Eduardo, spend much of the episode accidentally handcuffed together (thus leading to some splendidly choreographed routines in which the two of them attempt to eat their tea – Hat manages a few mouthfuls with her right hand while repeatedly pulling Eric's left hand away from his plate – and catch a bus – Hat just gets on in time while Eric is left to run after it at the back); 'Sykes And A Mouse' (21 March 1963), in which an eager Eric and an uneasy Hat try to trap a crafty mouse lodging in the skirting board of their lounge; 'Sykes And A Plank' (3 March 1964), in which Eric and Hat try to transport a long piece of timber through the town to the house of a friend of Hat's; and 'Sykes And A Golfer' (26 October 1965), in which, in a dream, Eric takes on and beats the then-prominent professional golfer Peter Alliss.

The BBC certainly appreciated the show. As the ratings soared and the plaudits piled up, there was much back-slapping in the board-room, and genuine respect and affection for Sykes and his team's achievement. On 26 February 1964, for example, Kenneth Adam, the BBC's current Director of Television, took the trouble to send a telegram to Sykes to congratulate him on his latest episode, 'Sykes And A Box', declaring that it had 'reduced the entire Adam family to a state of complete helplessness. Please do not be quite so funny again or permanent harm may be done.'[28] Similarly, Tom Sloan, who by this time was the BBC's Head of Light Entertainment, sent him a telegram on 9 November in the same year to applaud Sykes and the cast on the occasion of their fiftieth episode (a large party was thrown after filming).[29]

Eric Sykes, however, was far more sensitive than he seemed, and was never entirely convinced by the positive words. Indeed, in a com-pletely uncharacteristic outburst, he would later declare that, in his opinion, Ronnie Waldman was 'the first and last inspiring Head of Light Entertainment', and all of those who followed him 'were a dis-appointing bunch of trainee bureaucrats with a limited knowledge of what makes people laugh.'[30] This was, as he well knew, as inaccurate as it was unfair: Waldman was succeeded by none other than Eric

Maschwitz, an extremely urbane, talented and worldly man who was not only highly respected within the BBC for his previous achievements first as a pioneering editor of the *Radio Times* and then as a hugely influential Director of Variety for radio, but was also greatly admired in broader show-business circles as the creator and producer of numerous musical plays, sketches and revues, as well as the writer of several successful novels (starting with *A Taste of Honey* in 1924) and the lyrics to some exceptionally memorable popular songs (including 'These Foolish Things,' 'Good Night Vienna' and 'A Nightingale Sang in Berkeley Square') – hardly, therefore, a humourless trainee bureaucrat. Maschwitz's own successor, Tom Sloan, was, it is true, an administrator rather than a programme-maker, and was far too much of a worrier ever to be mistaken for an unbroken ray of sunshine (he was the dutiful Dulwich School-educated son of a Scottish Free Church Minister, and usually needed at least a whisky or two before the smiles rose above his spreadsheets), but, none the less, he did enough things right to preside over a period in the BBC's history that would later be regarded as a 'golden age' of television comedy.[31] He, in turn, was followed by Bill Cotton Jnr – the man who brought Morecambe and Wise to the BBC and had the inspired idea of teaming them up with the producer/director John Ammonds and the writer Eddie Braben; the man who put together *The Two Ronnies*; the man who encouraged and defended the groundbreaking *Dave Allen At Large*; and, somewhat ironically, the man who commissioned several new series of *Sykes* (to revise a line from Churchill: some trainee, some disappointment).

No doubt the normally eminently good-natured Sykes himself, in a cooler hour, would have acknowledged the full extent of his exaggeration. It was really Tom Sloan, and Sloan alone, whom he had some real (though far from extreme) cause to resent. He had distrusted the decent but sometimes rather dour and businesslike executive ever since he heard, shortly after filming the pilot edition of *Sykes And A . . .*, that Sloan had praised – in private – all of the actors except Sykes himself (who was said to have been 'acted off the screen' by Richard Wattis).[32] If this undeniably strange observation had not been bad enough, Sloan proceeded to compound it, in

Sykes's eyes, by appearing to take the show's subsequent success –
and its sole writer's remarkable industry, consistency and rare professionalism – for granted ('I believe,' Sykes would later complain,
'that when our series was on television Tom decided it was a good
time to go out to dinner').[33] It was more bad man-management than
bad judgement by Sloan, because (if the many positive comments
preserved in the BBC's archive are anything to go by) he genuinely
did, in his own very quiet and understated way, admire and respect
both the show and its writer and star, but, none the less, some
damage was certainly done: Sykes would never feel properly appreciated – by some executives – for all of his exceptional efforts.

More pointedly, he also came to feel that the show – not so much
in spite of as because of its increasingly broad and strong appeal –
was being routinely mistreated. On 1 December 1964, for example,
Sykes wrote a long letter to the BBC's Director of Television, Kenneth
Adam, detailing the frustrations he had experienced during the run of
the most recent series. He was particularly angry, he said, about the
way in which the show had come to be used as a ratings weapon, and
scheduled on Friday evenings when, traditionally, so many people
were out: 'The *Sykes* shows are just a half hour in a long viewing
week to the BBC, but to me it has been my career, and it is horrifying
to feel it is being jeopardised in the battle of the ratings.'[34] On 10
December, the Controller of BBC1, Donald Baverstock, having heard
about the letter, wrote to Adam, asking him to make Sykes aware of
how much the BBC still appreciated his talents.[35] Adam (a genuine
fan of Sykes) did just that later the same day.[36] On 14 December,
Sykes wrote to thank the executive and assure him that it was all
'water under the bridge',[37] but it would not be long before the nig-
gling sense of unease returned.

In August 1965, Sykes began discussing his hopes for his next series
(the ninth in five years) with Donald Baverstock's successor as
Controller of BBC1, Michael Peacock. Noting, somewhat sardonically, his preference to see the episodes go out when most of their
potential audience was likely to be in, he suggested either Tuesdays or
Thursdays at 8pm or, failing that, 7.25 on Sundays as the best new
slot for the show. Peacock, perhaps anxious to underline his own

authority, disagreed, and said that he would schedule it at 7.30 on Tuesdays. It was a fair enough compromise, but it meant that *Sykes And A . . .* would now be competing for viewers with ITV's increasingly popular hospital soap *Emergency – Ward 10*, and the *Sykes* team was not best pleased.

The scheduling was actually a kind of a compliment – the BBC had just launched a new policy[38] that involved pitting its most popular sitcoms head-to-head with ITV's soap operas, and Peacock wanted a guaranteed audience pleaser to compete against one of the commercial channel's strongest prime-time performers – but, for a writer who was finally beginning to tire of the need to keep on conjuring up, week after week, fresh comedy and new situations, it was just one more reason to question his, and his show's, future. The last thing that anyone wanted to see was a slow and depressing decline.

The ninth series, which ran from 5 October to 16 November 1965, still performed very creditably indeed – well enough, in fact, for the BBC to offer Sykes another lucrative long-term contract – but its tired and disenchanted writer and star had already decided, after discussing the matter with the rest of the team, that enough was enough: it was time to go out while the show was still at the top. No one, after all, was going to be left stranded: Hattie Jacques had other projects to pursue (and was also busy reorganising her private life following her recent divorce from John Le Mesurier); Deryck Guyler was being lined up to provide regular support for Michael Bentine in his forthcoming series for ATV, *All Square*;[39] both Dennis Main Wilson and Sydney Lotterby had been lured away to produce other BBC programmes; and Sykes himself wanted to make more use of his creative freedom at ALS and start planning a move into movies. It felt as though it was time.

On the day of the final broadcast, therefore, Sykes held a press conference to announce that he would not write another series for the BBC or any other channel until, as he put it, the television ratings war had ended. There followed a fortnight of conversations and correspondence between Sykes and the BBC, and it seems that every effort was made to persuade him to pause and reconsider, but, calmly and politely, he stood his ground. On 3 December, Sykes wrote to

Kenneth Adam, reaffirming his decision and adding: 'I feel it is important to get my hat and coat.'[40]

After five intensive years, it was over, but its job had been done – and done well. *Sykes And A . . .* had been one of the sitcoms that had shown the mainstream the best way forward.

Hancock & Steptoe

British. Undiluted for twelve generations. One hundred per cent Anglo-Saxon, with perhaps just a dash of Viking . . .

First came Hancock: a great character. Then came the Steptoes: a great relationship. The former brought the British sitcom into being. The latter brought it to maturity.

Galton and Simpson were responsible for them both. They put together the big picture: the foreground and the background, the broad strokes and the fine detail, the fiction and the fact. With *Hancock's Half-Hour*, they created a novel context for comedy; with *Steptoe and Son*, they created a novel context for comedy and tragedy as well as a fair amount of real life.

Hancock's Half-Hour was, in a sense, a Janus-faced kind of enterprise, because, on the one hand, it was looking back on the old star-centred vehicles of the past while, on the other, it looked forward to the new, character-driven format of the future. It featured a star, Tony Hancock, but it had him play a character, 'Tony Hancock'. Part evolution and part revolution, as any good and true revolution must be, the show changed as it preserved, building on Hancock's success in Variety to create a new home for him, and countless others like him, in the genre of situation comedy.

It all started when Hancock met Galton and Simpson. The date was 9 December 1951, the location was inside a BBC studio – the Paris Cinema – in London's Lower Regent Street, and the occasion was during a rehearsal for the radio show *Happy-Go-Lucky*: 'Did you write that sketch?' asked Hancock as he relaxed in a seat in the shadowy auditorium. 'Yes,' Galton and Simpson replied as they walked down the aisle. 'Very good,' said Hancock. The writers thanked him and moved on, and the comedian remained in his seat, but the connection had been made: it would not be the last time that they would hear from Tony Hancock.

His was quite a promising acquaintance for them to have commenced, because Tony Hancock was one of British radio's fastest-rising stars. Born in Small Heath, Birmingham, on 12 May 1924, he had spent much of his childhood in Bournemouth, where his father (himself a semi-professional entertainer) kept a small hotel often frequented by well-known performers from the local seasonal shows. Inheriting the familial ambition to seek out some kind of a career in show business, he put up with periods spent away at boarding schools in Swanage and Reading, and then began looking for ways to entertain as a budding comedian. There were plenty of formative appearances in RAF Gang Shows during the war, and then a six-week spell at The Windmill soon after the return of the peace, but his first major breakthrough occurred in 1949 when (after impressing the producer Dennis Main Wilson at a BBC audition) he began appearing regularly in such popular radio shows as *Variety Bandbox* and *Workers' Playtime*. His career progressed further in the summer of 1951, when he joined *Educating Archie* (scripted by Eric Sykes with assistance from Sid Colin) as tutor to Peter Brough's ventriloquial doll, Archie Andrews, and his muttered catchphrase, 'Flippin' kids', soon began to draw widespread attention and repetition. His additional duties during that same year on Derek Roy's *Happy-Go-Lucky* would prove to be little more than a brief and frustrating distraction, but they did at least cause him to encounter the up-and-coming writing partnership of Ray Galton and Alan Simpson.

He got back in touch with them at the start of 1952, a short while after the unlamented demise of *Happy-Go-Lucky*. With a booking arranged for a forthcoming edition of *Workers' Playtime*, he needed some new material, so he asked them if they could oblige. It was, Alan Simpson recalled, a welcome surprise:

He said, 'I don't know what you charge, but I'll give you half of what I get – how's that?' Well, Derek Roy was giving us eight guineas for a single spot but Tony said, 'I get fifty quid.' So we thought to ourselves, '*Twenty-five quid?* Bloody hell! That's three times what we've been getting!' So we went to Derek Roy and said, 'Tony Hancock's given us twenty-five pounds for a single, can we have a raise?' But Derek just said, 'Oh yeah, but come on boys, who gave you your first break?' And he wouldn't raise it – well, he put it up to ten, grudgingly, but that was it. Talk about comics being mean – they really were in those days![1]

The fledgeling collaboration was resumed later that same year, when the writers were called on to complete the last six scripts of a concert party-style series, featuring Hancock as support for Charlie Chester, entitled *Calling All Forces*.

Hancock's success in this, in addition to the increasingly popular *Educating Archie*, eventually persuaded the BBC, at the beginning of 1953, to give him a more prominent role alongside each week's guest compère in a revamped Variety show (produced by Dennis Main Wilson and written by Galton and Simpson) called *Forces All Star Bill*. The opening edition, broadcast on 6 January with Ted Ray as its first guest, set the tone swiftly in terms of Hancock's somewhat naïve and slow-witted on-air *alter ego*:

HANCOCK: Well, Edward, it's happened. After twenty-eight years of bachelorhood, brisk walks, PT and cold showers, Hancock the impervious has had his armour pierced by a member of the opposite mob.

TED RAY: Tony, you don't mean a woman?

HANCOCK: Can you think of anything more opposite?

TED RAY: Why, Tony, that's wonderful. Does she reciprocate?

HANCOCK: *[Shocked]* Ted, please, I've only just met her!

TED RAY: Tony, don't look now but your brain just stuck a white flag out the top of your head. Who is this girl, anyway?

HANCOCK: My fiancée, Joan Heal.

TED RAY: Joan Heal? She's a lovely piece of crackling! Your *first* girlfriend? Shouldn't you have got something for a *beginner*? Where did you meet her?

HANCOCK: Last week, at Broadcasting House. She was waiting
for one lift and I was waiting for the other. Then she opened her
gates, stepped in and went up, and I opened my gates, stepped in
and . . .

TED RAY: You went up.

HANCOCK: No, I went down – the lift wasn't there. And as I was
lying there, Ted, my mind began to wander.

TED RAY: You can't blame it, there's a lot of space in there.

HANCOCK: *[Ignores him]* I started thinking to myself, 'Hancock,
my boy, this girl is just your type.'

TED RAY: How do you mean?

HANCOCK: She was breathing.[2]

It was while they were working on this show, however, that Galton
and Simpson began seeking to shape a more distinctive comic character for Tony Hancock – and the sense of satisfaction that came
through the attempt to do so would lead them to consider creating a
special space for him all of his own.

Still inspired by the best of the American radio situation comedies
to which they had listened during their years together in the sanatorium, Galton and Simpson now felt ready to craft something similar
for Britain. Their ambition was to devise a comedy show that was
coherent rather than fragmentary: a half-hour show that, instead of
accommodating the usual hit-or-miss mixture of monologues,
sketches, special guest spots and musical interludes, would concentrate on one continuous storyline, and rely on character and
situation, rather than on jokes and catchphrases and funny voices, to
elicit all of the laughs. One difference from the typical American
model would be the shift away from the husband-wife-and-kids
domestic environment in favour of a focus on one, ordinary, flawed
individual.

They wanted to build the show around Tony Hancock because,
through working and socialising with him, they had come to admire
him as a performer as well as like him as a person, and could see how
much more talent there was to be tapped. 'We just thought he was
one of the greatest comic *actors* of the time,' Ray Galton would

recall. 'For instance, he could pick up a script and read it, word perfect, first sight – give it the full monty as a performance the first time he'd seen it.'[3] They also felt that, given the time and freedom to write for a personality rather than just a performer, they could produce a role that was tailor-made for the particular talents of their friend. 'We created a character in his own image,' reflected Alan Simpson, 'so that, by the time we got it right, the character sounded like Tony.'[4]

Dennis Main Wilson – who had listened to and liked the idea – asked them to design a format that he could propose to his bosses as a practicable new programme option. What they came up with was a one-page outline centred around Hancock, with a smarter and more confident male friend, a girlfriend and a shady-sounding acquaintance. Armed with this brief but clear description, the mercurial Main Wilson wrote a typically strong-minded memo to the assistant head of his department on 1 May 1953, stressing his commitment to Galton and Simpson's desire to write a show for Tony Hancock that would be founded on 'reality and truth rather than jokes, merry quips, wheezes [and] breaks for crooners who have no reason to be on the show anyway.'[5]

Several anxious months would follow, with no one knowing quite what the future held, until good news arrived at the start of the following year. A draft contract was finally dispatched to Hancock on 6 January 1954, but, after further discussions with him and the writers, Dennis Main Wilson still felt the need to send another explanatory memo to his superiors, pointing out that they should appreciate and embrace the radical nature of the enterprise: 'The comedy style will be purely situation in which we shall try to build Tony as a real life character in real life surroundings. There will be no "goon" or contrived comedy approaches at all. We shall be experimenting with a "semi-domestic Hancock" in the new series of *Star Bill* which will give you some idea of the eventual approach we shall make.'[6] The executives agreed, and the official contract (which stipulated that the star would be paid fifty guineas per show for a series that was scheduled to commence at the end of October 1954) was duly signed by Hancock. The next task was to refine the central character and select the supporting cast.

'Anthony Aloysius St John Hancock' was certainly not the whole real-life Hancock, nor was he nothing but the real-life Hancock, but he was definitely made up from the bits of the real-life Hancock that most made his writers laugh. '[W]e just took what we wanted from him and invented the rest,' Galton would later explain, 'such as being very gullible and only half read, the sort of guy who reads all his information from the colour supplements.' They also, acknowledged Simpson, added a little of themselves to his outlook and attitude: 'Both of us were really self-educated, always trying to better our-selves, perhaps by reading philosophy. So we had Hancock doing things like that, but of course he was always unsuccessful at it.'[7]

As the process of characterisation continued, Galton noted, the comedian was quite willing to trust the judgement of his two writers: 'Most of the things that we gave him to say were really dragged up from our past, our childhood. Tony was the consummate artist – his timing was impeccable and everything else – but he never contributed anything [to the scripts]. Sometimes he would say, "Oh, I don't like it," or something like that, but he didn't make any suggestions. Because I remember him saying, "Look, you're the writers, I'm the artist."'[8]

The other aspect to be inserted into the Hancock persona related to the class-based frustration, aggression and bewilderment of some-one who, deep down, knew his place, but still hoped to leap up to a better place. As Simpson later reflected: 'The Hancock character was aspiring to get up the ladder a bit. He was never a working-class character, but he wasn't much above it.'[9] This was certainly a theme, and an outlook, that would strike the right social chord: 'At a time when the citizens of Britain were being assured that they had never had it so good,' one critic would write, '[Hancock] was the inade-quate one who was missing out and wanted to know why. He was the puritan who always suspected that someone somewhere was having a good time. He was the man doomed to be forever out who desper-ately wanted to be in.'[10]

The next step, said Galton, was to decide on a suitable situation:

When we thought about a place to put him – roots – Cheam came up, because I used to deliver milk up there on a horse and cart on Saturdays. Cheam: I used to think, 'God, this is posh! It really *is* posh!' So we agreed that was a good place to put him – Cheam. But he couldn't be in Cheam proper, so we put him in *East* Cheam – the bad part of Cheam, if there is such a part. And then, of course, we added to that 'Railway Cuttings', which was the wrong side of the tracks.[11]

When it came to deciding who should join him on the other side of these tracks, the writers were prepared to wait. They knew that the defining details of each one of Hancock's coterie of friends would be determined to some extent by the character and calibre of the actors the show could attract. Neither Galton nor Simpson was interested in forcing someone to conform to a stereotype. Both of them wanted to get to know the people before cultivating the full nature of each persona. The key thing, therefore, was to secure the right kind of personnel.

The role of Hancock's more worldly and upbeat male friend (partly inspired by a character in US radio's *The Phil Harris & Alice Faye Show* called Frank Remley)[12] was given to another former cast member of *Happy-Go-Lucky*, the comedian and actor Bill Kerr. Born in South Africa on 1 January 1922, but brought up from an early age in Australia (in Wagga Wagga, New South Wales), he had arrived in England shortly after the war. Performing a slow-talking, sad-voiced stand-up act that always began with him announcing, 'I'm only here for four minutes . . .,' his various engagements on both the Variety circuit and the odd radio show brought him into contact with, among others, Spike Milligan, Harry Secombe, Peter Sellers and Eric Sykes (with all of whom he became good friends), and, off stage, he was known to be quite an ebullient and amusing raconteur. Galton and Simpson had first met him socially at the Buxton Club – a popular place in London's West End for actors to mix and relax – and had warmed to his self-deprecating wit.

There was far more of a problem finding a suitable female friend for Hancock. At this early stage in their careers, Galton and Simpson, by their own admission, had found it relatively difficult to write for 'straight' (as opposed to out-and-out funny) women – there were always doubts as to how broad or subtle to make the humour for female characters, when the majority of audiences, in accordance with the sexist standards of the time, preferred their comedy fairly coarse but their women fairly demure – and, apart from the odd female comic who could 'act a bit', there were few likely candidates around. The very talented Geraldine McEwan had been a regular in *Forces All Star Bill*, but she had left to pursue more substantial roles in the theatre. Her successor in the subsequent series, however, had been another good young character actor, Moira Lister, and she was still available. South African-born but now London-based, the 31-year-old performer had most often been cast as the coldly attractive and quietly calculating type – such as the self-centred, two-timing wife in the recent movie *The Cruel Sea* and the scheming personnel manager in the Norman Wisdom vehicle *Trouble in Store* (both of them released in 1953) – so Dennis Main Wilson felt that she would be more or less ideal as the strong-minded woman looming large in the soft-headed Hancock's life.

Casting the last of the main characters was relatively straightforward. As one of the facets of Hancock's radio personality that Galton and Simpson were keen to accentuate was his childlike gullibility, there was a need for someone to play the lovable rogue who would fleece him week after week, and the writers thought more or less immediately of an actor named Sidney James. 'We knew what he looked like,' said Galton, 'and we knew his work, but we didn't know his name. So we had to go and see *The Lavender Hill Mob* again, just to wait for the cast-list. "That's the one we want, Sidney James."'[13] Yet another South African, James – born Sidney Joel Cohen in, of all places, Hancock Street in Johannesburg on 8 May 1913 – came from a show-business extended family, but, after changing his surname to the less 'ethnic' sounding 'James', he had tried a wide range of alternative vocations (including, he would later claim, those of coal heaver, diamond digger, hairdresser, dance tutor and boxer) before conforming to his parents' expectations and serving in an entertainment unit during the war. Following demobilisation, he had gravitated to Britain and begun a new career as a character actor, specialising in working-class hard men with either Cockney or American accents. When, therefore, Dennis Main Wilson got in contact and explained the kind of role that Galton and Simpson had in mind, he knew it made sense: it was an offer too good to refuse.

With Kerr, Lister and James now safely in place, there was just one more member of the team to find: the 'odd job man' who could be relied on to supply a wide range of cameo roles, including the odd policeman, doctor, judge, clerk, elderly man and eccentric. Although Alan Simpson was on hand to play the occasional 'A.N. Other' ('He'd done a concert party,' his writing partner would recall. 'He liked the idea of performing'),[14] there was still a real need for a 'proper' character actor who could vary his voice, alter his dialect and slip up and down the social ladder. Unsure of whom to consider, Dennis Main Wilson sent out requests to all of the various theatrical agencies, and a representative from one of them, Peter Eade, called back with an interesting suggestion: there was a very versatile 28-year-old actor named Kenneth Williams, he said, who was currently playing the Dauphin in a new production of George Bernard Shaw's *Saint Joan* at the Arts Theatre in Great Newport Street; it would be well worth paying a visit.

His curiosity suitably aroused, Main Wilson agreed, so he set off one evening to take in the play. The intention was that, if he liked what he saw, he would try to grab a quick chat with the actor backstage. He later recalled:

> I go backstage – and I'm going to do this young man the biggest favour he's ever had in his life – and I'm told, 'Oh, he's very busy – you'll have to wait.' So I go round the corner to the bar . . . and this tall, elegant, Irving-Garrick-type actor laddie comes in, and *booms* at me – 'Well, what do you want?'
>
> So I said, 'I'm a BBC Producer–' Williams said, 'Mmm – I don't like the wireless . . .'
>
> So I bought him a large light ale . . . and he said, 'Well, what's it all about?'

So I said, 'We've got this great idea for a great show' – and *I* am trying to *placate* him!

We were half-way through this and Ken Williams collapsed into a fit of giggles, and said, 'I don't care, I'll do it – what is it?'

He took me in for about half-an-hour . . . a very powerful personality, of enormous warmth.[15]

The producer went back to Galton and Simpson and announced excitedly: 'I have a great person for the show.' 'We liked him,' said Simpson, 'and gave him the part of "The Snide" in the first show. Ken did his now-famous "Good evening" and the place erupted. So much for no catchphrases or silly voices!'[16]

Right from the start, Simpson remembered, there was an excellent working atmosphere among the cast: 'Sid James, Bill Kerr, Kenneth Williams and Tony Hancock – [they were] four of the biggest laughers. They used to really guffaw – raucous laughter. If we had a read-through on a radio show, they didn't see it until the day. And if they found something that tickled them, all four of them would be rolling about. You'd think, "It's lovely – we did that."'[17] The only performer who encountered any problem early on was, Simpson would recall, none other than Sidney James:

You wouldn't think it now, but when Sid was first asked to do the show on the radio, he was quite anxious about it. He came down to one of the recordings [of *Star Bill*] we were doing at the Garrick Theatre to meet us all. And he said, 'I'm very worried – you see, I've never done radio before, and I don't think I can do it.' So Tony said, 'Why?' And Sid said, 'I dunno, I just don't feel comfortable with it.' So Tony said, 'It's easy – it's a piece of cake. You haven't got to *learn* anything. These two go away for a week and write it, and all we do is come in on the day and read it.' So he said he'd give it a go. Then, when he turned up on the first day, he'd be playing in front of the microphone, with his script held up in front of his face, and he had his hat down over his eyes and he was shaking like a leaf! After a couple of weeks, when he realised that he was getting laughs, the hat came off, and he was perfectly OK. But, originally, he was absolutely petrified about doing radio. Films: no problem. But radio: a real worry at the start.[18]

The very first episode of the very first series (introduced by its star's breathless stutter as '*H-H-Hancock's Half-Hour*') was broadcast on the BBC's Light Programme at 8pm on 2 November 1954. Entitled 'First Night Party', it began with Hancock and Bill Kerr discussing the invitations to his pre-show celebratory soirée ('Get 'em all on my side – the national newspapers, the BBC. I'm inviting all the radio critics and the high BBC officials'). Moira arrives and points out that Hancock's flat is not fit to hold such a party, and Bill suggests that they get his estate agent friend, 'smooth-talking Sidney' ('as honest as the day is long'), to sort out a more suitable venue. Sid duly obliges, providing them with the crowbar that can get them into a palatial apartment in Park Lane, and preparations continue with the arrival of Hancock's French chef (''Iggins! Half past seven, lad – give the ox another turn on the spit'). Sid and his Runyonesque associate Coatsleeve Charlie volunteer to act as butlers and proceed to pick the pockets of most of the guests, and, as the glasses chink-chink and the chatter continues, the effects of Hancock's bath-tub gin begin to kick in. Just as the drunken antics threaten to cause serious damage to the property, the owner, Lord Bayswater (played by Kenneth Williams), arrives. 'Do you realise who I am?' he barks. 'I'm afraid your mime wasn't very helpful,' Hancock replies as the other guests attempt to beat a hasty retreat. The following morning, there are no favourable mentions in the papers, but there is a 'stop press' announcement about the arrest of sixty-five hooligans for housebreaking: police are still looking, the report added, for a fat little man by the name of 'Ted Ray'.

It was an uneven opening effort, but the audience reaction was cautiously optimistic. The BBC's official (internal and unpublished) report, based on some bald facts and the brief responses of a sample group of listeners, declared:

Twelve per cent of the adult population of the UK heard the show. The previous week *The Al Read Show* at the same time was heard by 25 per cent. Tony Hancock was given a great welcome by the vast majority of this sample audience who were delighted that he should have his own programme. Although the low appreciation index (52 as opposed to the average variety 'Gang' show of 62) suggests an unenthusiastic response to the show as a whole, there appears no doubt that its star enjoys widespread popularity.[19]

What listeners particularly liked, it seemed, was the fact that there were no 'moaning crooners', 'shrieking choirs' or 'blaring dance bands', and, although some felt that the script could do with considerable improvement, the majority looked forward to the rest of an enjoyable debut run.[20]

The reaction within the BBC was more enthusiastic because, a mere month into the opening run, plans were already being hatched to arrange a bizarre-sounding long-term link-up between Hancock and The Goons. In a memo written on 7 December 1954, Peter Eton, the current producer of *The Goon Show*, responded to internal suggestions that his show should start sharing a running gag (reminiscent of the fake 'feuds' between Jack Benny and Fred Allen and W.C. Fields and Charlie McCarthy that had proven so popular on American radio) with *Hancock's Half-Hour*. 'This would be an excellent touch of showmanship,' he said, 'but would involve me in the additional expenditure each week of five guineas for Tony's fee for a short appearance – possibly only half-a-minute – in *The Goon Show*.' It appears, therefore, that the plan was taken no further mainly because of the limited budget: 'I have had to turn down this idea,' Eton wrote, 'as I have no money to spare.'[21] The odd little option had gone: Eccles would never fall foul of Sid, and Hancock would always steer clear of Grytpype-Thynne.

The show continued to evolve throughout its sixteen-week opening run, with its audience rising steadily from 4.51 million in its first week to 6.39 million for the last and, a mere two months later (in April 1955), a second series was set to commence. Then, however, the problems started.

First, Moira Lister was unable to participate because she had fallen pregnant, so she was replaced by a 22-year-old actor from Liverpool named Andrée Melly (the sister of the jazz singer and journalist George) in a hastily-written role as Hancock's new girlfriend from France. Then, just days before the date of the first recording, a far bigger problem occurred: *Hancock's Half-Hour* 'lost' Tony Hancock.

He had been locked into a long and gruelling run in *The Talk of the Town* at the Adelphi Theatre, and, slowly but surely, had worked and worried himself close to an emotional and physical breakdown. His spirits then slipped a little lower still, it seems, when his old RAF friend Scruffy Dale – not only the managing director of Associated London Scripts but now also a predictably disorganised part-time promoter – persuaded him to make an (unpaid) appearance at a ball that was being hosted by Dale's bank manager in Hendon; when another special guest, the comic actor Jimmy Edwards, received rather more attention than he did, an extremely tired and somewhat emotional Hancock beat a discreet retreat and trudged off home to his fifth-floor flat in Queens Gate Terrace.[22] The following evening at the Adelphi, instead of completing his performance and then going off for a meal before bed, he walked out early into the night and just disappeared. When Dennis Main Wilson arrived armed with the first script of the new series, the old stage-door keeper told him: 'If you're looking for the boy, sir, 'e's gone.'[23]

The puzzled producer searched all of the usual West End pubs and clubs in vain, but was woken up in the early hours of the following morning by a telephone call from an old friend of his who was now a Chief Superintendent of Special Branch at Scotland Yard: Hancock, he was informed, had been spotted at the airport boarding the last plane bound for Rome. Another report came a few hours later: upon arriving in the city, the comedian had booked into a local hotel and then driven south in a hired car to rest and recuperate at the pretty little village of Positano on the Neapolitan Riviera. Back in Britain, Main Wilson was left to come to terms with the fact that, when the first episode of the new series of *Hancock's Half-Hour* was recorded, H-H-H-Hancock was going to be A-A-A-Absent.

Unable to postpone the series until its star felt able and willing to return, the producer discussed the matter with Galton and Simpson and then, with the clock ticking loudly, secured the services of a last-minute replacement: his old *Goon Show* colleague Harry Secombe. The series thus started on time, with the incongruous-sounding introduction: 'We present *Hancock's Half-Hour*, starring Harry Secombe, Bill Kerr, Sidney James . . .'

In this and the next two hastily rewritten episodes, the uncomplaining Secombe (who, ironically, did actually live in Cheam) helped hold the action, and series, together, as he and the other characters went by accident on an excursion to Paris (where they met Andrée and brought her back home with them to Britain), became embroiled in a plot by Sid to steal the Crown Jewels and then allowed Bill to buy a three-legged horse which Sid proceeded to run in the Britannia Steeplechase. By this stage, Secombe had settled into the show so well that he was sounded out, discreetly, about the possibility of continuing for the remainder of the series, but he declined: 'I admit I was tempted,' he would later reveal, 'but Tony was an old friend and I had enough on my plate with *The Goon Show*, so that was that.'[24]

Hancock finally returned to the country midway through the first week in May ('like a little dog,' Main Wilson would say, 'with his tail between his legs')[25] – just in time to appear in the fourth half-hour of his own series. After telling reporters that he would have to be 'very leisurely' about his next few broadcasts,[26] he met Secombe privately and thanked him for what he had done during his open-ended absence, but offered no explanation as to why he had disappeared (nor, indeed, would he ever offer any explanation to anyone else on his team – not his producer, his writers or his fellow performers). It was left to Galton and Simpson to explain the absence of his character in the next rewritten script – he had, they said, been sidelined by a severe cold, but they sent him off to visit Harry Secombe in Wales (down whose coal mines he was now supposed to have returned) to acknowledge his debt and vow never to miss another show.

The remainder of the series went by without further disruption, but, understandably, there was an awkward feel about the season. A greater degree of stability and coherence was regained for the third set of episodes (which ran from October 1955 to February 1956), but it would not be until the fourth series (starting in October 1956) that *Hancock's Half-Hour* really found its feet.

Recent changes had helped guide the show in the right direction. Andrée Melly, for example, had 'lost' her improbable French accent for the start of her second season in the show, and, more tellingly, the dynamics between all of the characters had developed in certain significant ways. The key revision, in this respect, concerned Bill Kerr's character, who had gradually lost most of his wit and some of his influence as Sid James began to assume a much more relevant role. 'Once he'd settled into his character there was no stopping him,' Kerr would reflect without any hint of resentment. 'He became the main feed for Tony, while my character hung around the periphery.'[27]

The great breakthrough, however, occurred a few episodes into the fourth series with the arrival of Hattie Jacques. Andrée Melly had left because, as Galton and Simpson had never been convinced about Hancock having a regular girlfriend, her role had grown increasingly peripheral and underwritten. Hattie Jacques was brought in to play a much more clearly-defined female character: an aggressive but incompetent secretary by the name of Grizelda 'Grizzly' Pugh.

Miss Pugh did not exactly match all of the requirements that had been outlined in the ad that Hancock placed in the local tobacconist's window:

SECRETARY WANTED: Blonde, nineteen years old, 37-22-36 or nearest offer. Live-in. £5 a week (more if can type).

Indeed, Miss Pugh did not even match her own application details:

Twenty years old. 36-23-35. Has several times been mistaken for Anita Ekberg. Typing speed: eight words a minute.

She did, none the less, succeed in getting herself noticed. 'She sounds perfect!' Hancock exclaimed. Even when Bill pointed out the bit about eight words a minute, he was undeterred: 'That's all right,' he said brightly. 'I'll just have to dictate a bit faster to keep up with her.' When she actually arrived, however, Hancock (though willing to agree that her being mistaken for Anita Ekberg was indeed a major mistake) was distinctly underwhelmed: 'Hop it – before I set the dogs on you!' Her own far more convincing threat of violence soon changed his mind, and Miss Pugh was engaged without further delay. 'Let's get down to business, shall we?' asked Hancock glumly. 'Your hours are half-past nine to five-thirty'. Miss Pugh corrected him: 'They're eleven to half-past four'. Hancock allowed himself a couple of seconds' hesitation before responding meekly: 'Of course they are – I don't know what came over me.'

Jacques – an old friend and colleague of Hancock's from their days together on *Educating Archie* – was just what the show had needed. 'Whatever we wanted she would do it – and be funny at it,' Galton recalled. 'She was a good actress, a great comedienne with a wonderful presence and perfect timing.'[28] Before she arrived on the scene, it had been a little mechanical – Hancock chats to Bill, one of them has an idea and then both of them seek out Sid for some dubious assistance – but now there was a healthy sense of fluidity and unpredictability: sometimes Miss Pugh would boss the others, and sometimes she would stand and comment sardonically on them from a safe distance; Hancock might start mocking her appearance, or she (with a more brutally wounding wit) might start mocking his; there were, in general, a richer mix of interrelationships, more options for each plot and rather more 'bite' to the badinage.

The fourth series featured several episodes that would end up being counted among the best and most cherished in the whole of the Hancock canon. 'The Wild Man of the Woods', for example, was a wonderfully funny little story about Hancock's bid to try something akin to Thoreau's existential sojourn at Walden Pond: 'I, Anthony Hancock, philosopher, guide, adviser and wicker-bottom chair repairer, have decided that civilisation has failed us, and I have therefore come to the conclusion that I, to be honest with my principles, must from henceforth renounce the world!' This decision to surrender all of his worldly goods, live deep and suck out all the marrow of life in the local woods leads him to set up camp in 'the depths' of the wilderness inside a bus shelter on Clapham Common, and then (following a brief but humiliating period of hospitalisation) try again in a tiny 'lump of forest' rented from none other than a suddenly sympathetic Sidney James ('Hurry, hurry, hurry – get your tickets! Get your tickets for the coach trips to see the wild man of the woods! He's naked! He's hairy! And what's more, he's British!').

Other memorable editions included 'Michelangelo 'Ancock' (about Hancock's attempt to win a 'best new statue design' competition held by the town council – using Miss Pugh as the model for his masterpiece 'Descending Angel'); 'The Diary' (which was partly inspired by James Thurber's short story and movie *The Secret Life of Walter Mitty*, and featured the much-loved sequence about Hancock's old life as a 'skylarking' test pilot); and 'The Last of the McHancocks' (which saw Hancock battle against Seamus McNasty and Bonnie Prince Sidney in the Highland Games for the right to reside at an ancestral Scottish castle). The storylines, the dialogue, the characterisations and the acting were all coming together and the show was really starting to flourish.

Instead of settling for further progress in radio, however, the team turned its attention to television. It was a period when everyone seemed to be turning his or her attention to television. The live coverage of the Coronation of Queen Elizabeth II in 1953 had been the catalyst: the television audience for that event rose, for the first time in UK history, to almost double the size of the radio audience. The establishment of commercial television in Britain in 1955 further accelerated the switch-over. Television, by the mid-1950s, was the exciting new broadcasting medium. The burgeoning popularity of *Hancock's Half-Hour*, Ray Galton recalled, made it an obvious candidate to make the transition from the speaker to the screen:

All of a sudden, everybody wanted to work in television and Tony, ourselves and the BBC were very keen, so we did our first series live in 1956. It was very successful, but it meant learning our trade all over again. Around this time Hancock was under contract to Jack Hylton to do another stage revue, which he didn't want to do, so Jack said, 'If you do a television series for me at ITV, I will let you out of your contract.' Eric Sykes started writing it, but he was also writing his own show [*Pantomania*] so he was a bit pushed, so Ray and I were asked if we would contribute to it. We said, 'Yes, of course,' but we were under contract with the BBC, who said 'No way.' But then it was pointed out that it was in the BBC's best interest that Tony had a successful series, because a flop on ITV would only harm his reputation. So the BBC let us write the last three episodes as long as we didn't take a credit for them. So that's what happened. Hancock was free of his contract and able to return to the second series for the BBC. The only problem was, ITV had doubled our money, so the BBC had to match it. From then on we never looked back.[29]

The *Hancock's Half-Hour* of the small screen was not quite the same as the *Hancock's Half-Hour* of the radio. It had been decided that the cast of the latter would look too crowded on the former, so Bill Kerr was omitted right from the start and both Hattie Jacques and Kenneth Williams were limited to just a handful of appearances each. 'To us,' Ray Galton later explained, 'it seemed impossible to write a show to include them all, every week, on the screen. So we decided to simplify it.'[30]

Other changes to suit the particular needs of the visual medium were kept to the absolute minimum. As far as the embellishments to the central character were concerned, they did not amount to much more than a Homburg hat and an astrakhan-collared coat. As far as their writing technique was concerned, they merely stopped writing such lines as 'Pick that bucket up,' and started writing such lines as 'Pick that up.' 'That,' Ray Galton would recall, 'was about the only concession to television that we made.'[31]

The first (six-episode) series went out live on BBC TV every fortnight from 6 July to 14 September in 1956, attracting an average of more than six million viewers. Produced and directed by one of the BBC's best young programme-makers, a 31-year-old Bristolian by the name of Duncan Wood, the show was stressful to shoot – Hancock would sometimes have to perform a scene (under hot studio lights) with his next change of clothing hidden beneath his current outfit, and, if he or anyone else fluffed a line or misplaced a prop, there was no way of cutting the error or altering the camera angles –

but it seems to have satisfied the viewers, who were left wanting more of Hancock on the screen.

Far from undermining the radio show, however, the success of the television show seemed to spur the original programme on. The fifth radio series was the best yet. Writing at the top of their form, Galton and Simpson created a remarkably audacious set of scripts that, apart from supplying the characters with several richly comical situations, also dared to deal with the sense of nothing rather than something: indolence instead of action, silences instead of sounds, purposelessness instead of plots. There were still a number of strong and busy storylines during the run – such as 'The Unexploded Bomb', 'The Foreign Legion' and 'The Americans Hit Town' – but there were certain other episodes in which the conventional rules of the sitcom were turned upside-down and the characters were allowed just to 'be'. The best example of this was the gloriously story-free 'Sunday Afternoon at Home', which began (so improbably for the sitcoms of the time) precisely as it meant to go on:

HANCOCK: *[Yawns]* Ah, dear . . . Ah dear, oh dear . . . Ah, dear me. *[Yawns again]* Stone me, what a life! What's the time?

BILL: Two o'clock.

HANCOCK: Is that all? *[Sighs]* Oh dear, oh dear . . . Ah, dear me. I dunno. *[Yawns again]* Oh, I'm fed up!

SID: Oi.

HANCOCK: What?

SID: Why don't you shut up moaning and let me get on with the paper?

HANCOCK: Well, I'm fed up!

SID: So you just said.

HANCOCK: Well, so I am!

SID: Look – so am I fed up and so is Bill fed up. We're all fed up. So shut up moaning and make the best of it!

HANCOCK: *[Sighs again]* Are you *sure* it's only two o'clock?

BILL: No, it's, er, one minute past two now.

HANCOCK: One minute past two. Doesn't the time *drag?* Oh, I do hate Sundays. I'll be glad when it's over.

Nothing really happened in the rest of that half-hour – which was what made the episode so refreshingly and memorably real. Never before had the sheer boredom of ordinary life seemed so thoroughly entertaining: Hancock attempted unsuccessfully to persuade the others that part of the patterned wallpaper resembled, in a certain light and at a certain angle, an old man smoking a pipe ('Screw your eyes up. Stare hard. Squint a bit. That's it. Now concentrate on that bit by the serving hatch!'); Sid tried to scribble all over his newspaper ('I thought I'd fill-in all the "o"s and the "d"s and the "p"s and the "g"s on the front page'); Bill failed to raise any interest in a game of 'Beat Your Neighbours Out of Doors' (mainly because of his admission that he had absolutely no idea as to how it was played); and Miss Pugh endured a brutal critique of how she had cooked the latest Sunday lunch ('I thought my mother was a bad cook but at least her gravy used to move about!'). The arrival of Hancock's next-door neighbour, Clark, did seem to hint at a particle of a plot – only for him to prove himself to be the biggest bore of all ('I do impressions, y'know . . .').

The show was very special. The acting – by all – was technically superb, the dialogue beautifully judged and the use of 'dead air' – which was such a broadcasting taboo at the time – brilliantly bold and inspired. It all added up to a subtle revolution for radio comedy, and the whole team knew it. 'Hancock and the others were knocked out by the idea of doing half an hour of nothing happening,' Alan Simpson recalled. 'It's the only time I can think of when we were conscious of the fact that we were exploring new ground.'[32]

There would be one more series on radio. Running from September to December in 1959, it kept the standard high with such first-rate episodes as 'The Poetry Society' – which saw Hancock's attempt to impress his fellow members of the East Cheam Cultural Progressive Society eclipsed by the most unlikely pair of instinctive existentialists. He began with his usual expression of a pretension of surplus disorder: HANCOCK: 'We're the *avant-garde* of the New Culture. We're dedicated to setting up a new order of things; determined to establish a new set of values; to break away from the bonds that threaten to stifle the cultural and creative activities of Man's mind.' This then prompted the usual down-to-dirt response from Sid: 'Blimey: another load of layabouts!' The debate began:

> HANCOCK: We are not layabouts. We are artists, mush. Writers, poets, thinkers. All men who are seriously perturbed about the state of the world at the moment.
> SID: And what are you lot going to do about it?
> HANCOCK: We are going to show the world the real truth, by setting them an example, developing our superior intellects. Culture, mate – that's where the hope of the world lies! And a more cultural mob than us you wouldn't find outside the Chelsea Embankment. Twenty-seven throbbing intellects, raring to go!

After dismissing Bill's request to join them – 'This isn't a ping-pong and darts club!' – and denouncing Sid's 'dead reactionary' lack of interest – 'The struggle of the human race is nothing compared to your struggle up to the two-bob window at Cheltenham, is it?' – Hancock welcomes his new leader, Gwegowy ('Just "Gwegowy" – we never use surnames in our group, they're very bourgeois'), into his home, along with all of the other self-proclaimed intellectuals.

Gwegowy gets the poetry session going:

> 'TIN CAN' *by Gwegowy*
> *Splish, Splash, Splonk . . .*
> *Wooden shoes, red socks,*
> *Coffins, tombstones and tranquillisers.*
> *Aspirins and driving tests, jet planes and skeletons,*
> *Frog singing to egg-timer;*
> *Calendars and candles upside-down*
> *Plastic apples on coconut trees . . .*
> *Splish, Splash, Splonk.*

Once Bill has been adopted by the other bohemians as their very own 'little savage', he is moved to come up with something abstract himself:

'INCANDESCENCE' *by William*

Hic, Hack, Hoc!
Rinky-tinky on purple grass.
Shafts of light – hobnailed boots
Tramping down the bamboo that grows
Upwards, downwards, sideways into the concrete cosmos.
Life is mauve
I am orange
Hic, Hack, Hoc!

An outraged Hancock exclaims: 'What a load of rubbish! You *buffoon!* "Rinky-tinky on purple grass"? What does *that* mean? I have never heard such unadulterated codswallop in all my life!' Appalled to find that Bill's effort has actually impressed the group – to such an extent that they appear ready to appoint him their new leader – Hancock cries out: 'Don't make any hasty decisions, listen to mine – listen':

'THE ASHTRAY' *by Anthony*

Steel rods of reason through my head!
Salmon jumping – where jump I?
Camels on fire – and spotted clouds.
Striped horses prance the meadow wild
And rush on to drink at life's fountains deep.
Life is cream, I am puce . . .
Ching, Chang, Cholla!

Gwegowy stuns Hancock with his response: 'How *dare* you revile the group with such shallow, trivial nonsense!' When pressed for an explanation of his poem, Hancock splutters: 'What does it *mean?* W-Well, I should have thought that was obvious. It's a plea for the, er . . . well, no, it's more of an outcry against the . . . er, . . . it's an outcry against the licensing laws. Well, now, now, now, let's er . . . let's split it up a bit. Now then, you take, for a start, the camels on fire under the spotted clouds: now there's a provocative line if ever I've heard one. In that I've summed up the whole situation in the Gobi

251

desert. And "life's fountains deep": well, it's a plea for more water-holes. That's why the camels are on fire, they're gasping – they haven't had a drop to drink since they left Kabul! It's a very long trip, Kabul.' When pressed about the concluding 'Ching, Chang, Cholla', he says: 'Well, they're the drivers – you won't get any change out of them! No, they couldn't care less. As long as they've got their striped horses they're quite happy.' Turning to Sid for support against the new supporters of Bill ('Tell them what a *poltroon* he is!'), he is horrified to find that his shifty friend, having studied the Society's rule book and discovered that leadership will be remunerated, has written a poem all of his own:

> 'LIMBO' *by Sidney*
> *Mauve world, green me*
> *Black him, purple her*
> *Yellow us, pink you.*
> *Lead pipes – fortune made.*
> *Six to four, coming second*
> *Green country, Blue Harringay and White City;*
> *Hic, Haec, Hock!*

Hancock panics:

> *It's a funny old world we live in*
> *But the world's not entirely to blame*
> *It's the rich what gets the pleasure*
> *And the poor what gets the blame.*

It fails to turn the tide, and he is expelled from his own soirée: 'Put me down, I'll have the law on you! Layabouts! Get back to work! Useless members of society! *Parasites!*'

Galton and Simpson would return to this pretension-puncturing look at pseudo-intellectualism the following year, when they wrote the screenplay for Hancock's first movie-star vehicle, *The Rebel*. Cast as a bowler-hatted London clerk who abandons his mind-numbing job in order to live out the life of a painter in Paris, he creates his pictures by sloshing paint over his canvas and then riding over it on his bike, and, in true Hancock fashion, seeks to assimilate himself into the Left Bank's intellectual élite with the usual boastful bluster: 'So, anyway, I said to Dali, "Salvador," I said . . .' It was still Hancock, in character, but it was Hancock alone, without Sid or Bill or Miss Pugh, and the first obvious sign that, if he had not quite out-grown the sitcom, he was close to outgrowing his cast.

The television show, meanwhile, was going from strength to strength, establishing itself as one of the most popular and critically admired programmes on British television. John Cleese, who was an avid fan, would recall how keenly each new episode was anticipated: 'Say it went out on Friday: you began to think about it on Sunday night – you'd think, "Ooh, there'll be another *Hancock* on Friday!" I think, probably to a greater extent than almost any other comedy show I can remember, people arranged their week round *Hancock*.'[33] By the time of the sixth series, in 1960, it was being watched by more than ten million viewers each week. 'Tony Hancock was the first actor to empty the pubs,' his friend and occasional colleague Clive Dunn would remember. 'Ten minutes or a quarter of an hour before he came on, the publicans will tell you – *whoosh* – he would empty the pubs. What an achievement *that* was.'[34] In such episodes as 'The Missing Page' (in which Tony and Sid become obsessed with tracking down the absent ending to Darcy Sarto's hardboiled detective thriller *Lady Don't Fall Backwards*), 'The Ladies Man' (featuring a classic analysis of Hancock's problems with women: RECEPTIONIST: 'Do they laugh at you?' HANCOCK: 'Yes!' RECEPTIONIST: 'In which way?' HANCOCK: 'In the worst possible way!') and 'The Reunion Party' (focusing on Hancock's ill-advised attempt to rekindle some of his old wartime friendships), the combination of exceptionally good writing with two masterful central performances produced some of the best comedy that had so far been screened on British television, and the rapport between Hancock and Sid James was shown to be better than ever.

It came as quite a surprise, therefore, when Hancock announced that he would return for the next series without the services of Sid James. He needed a change, he said – a clean break not only from the character of Sid but also from the environment of East Cheam. It was, he insisted, purely an artistic decision, but it still left Sid James feeling extremely confused and hurt. Galton and Simpson did try to soften the blow by devising a new sitcom for him early on in 1960 entitled *Two's Companies* (in which he was set to co-star with Miriam Karlin), but, although most of the scripts were written, the project was dropped after James announced, somewhat late in the day, that he had lost enthusiasm for the series.[35] The subsequent project that did win his commitment later the same year, *Citizen James*, would be handed over to the up-and-coming scriptwriting duo of Dick Hills and Sid Green after Galton and Simpson had written the initial series – thus enabling them to return to work on their project with Hancock.

The new show – which began on 26 May in 1961 – was re-titled *Hancock* and, in the opening episode ('The Bedsitter'), Hancock was all that there was. '[W]e thought: right, if you want to be on your own, you will be on your own,' Ray Galton recalled. 'There was no one else in it. We had to use our ingenuity to do it without it becoming boring; we decided you could have people ringing up on the phone and could hear people outside his bed-sit and gradually the story evolved.'[36] Now based in Earl's Court ('In those days,' Alan Simpson would explain, 'Earl's Court was very cosmopolitan and having a bed-sit in that part of London was almost a cliché'),[37] Hancock was trapped with no one but himself.

It worked. It worked supremely well. Hancock *became* his own sitcom. The camera just watched as he sat around the bed-sit being a human being. As brilliant as the performance was, however, it was all carefully choreographed by Galton and Simpson's script, which contained the following kind of detailed directions:

[Hancock looks at his feet and wiggles them] He then puts one foot vertically with the heel resting on the bed. Then he puts the other foot on top of it with the heel resting on the toes. He takes the bottom foot out and places it on top of the other one with the heel again resting on the toes. Now his two feet are a couple of feet off the bed. One on top of the other, thus causing a strain on

his stomach muscles. These give way and his feet collapse on the bed. He rubs his stomach and winces. TONY: 'Getting old.'[38]

It was a performer's dream – two writers who knew exactly what would and would not suit the voice, expressions, gestures and personality of their subject – and, in turn, it was a writer's dream – a performer who could take every single line, sign and direction that he was given and make the most of every little nod and nuance. '[Galton and Simpson] worked so well with Hancock,' Beryl Vertue would recall. 'You'd hear them talking together, and it was like hearing snatches of the next script. They were him and he was them. They observed him so closely, they knew exactly what suited him and what didn't. It was quite magical.'[39]

The series never flagged. 'The Bowmans' poked fun at *The Archers* ('Oh dear, what a shame – they've all fallen down that disused mine shaft!'); 'The Radio Ham' was a glorious solo *tour de force* ('Friends from all over the world! Not in this country, but all over the world!'); and 'The Lift' reminded people, as if they needed it, that the team could still create top-class ensemble comedy (WOMAN: 'I think I'm going to faint!' HANCOCK: 'You can't, dear, there's no room.' MAN: 'I'm a doctor.' HANCOCK: 'Yes, we all know you're a doctor – you've been talking about nothing else ever since you got in here! I don't understand you. *I* don't go round telling people what *I* am all the time.' MAN: 'I think we've all reached an opinion as to what *you* are!'). Then came something that was, if anything, even more special – 'The Blood Donor':

> HANCOCK: Well, I'll bid you good day, then, thank you very much.
>   If you want any more, don't hesitate to get in touch with me.
> DOCTOR: Where are you going?
> HANCOCK: To have me tea and biscuits.
> DOCTOR: I thought you came here to give us some of your blood.
> HANCOCK: Well, you've just had it!
> DOCTOR: That's just a smear.
> HANCOCK: It may be just a smear to you, mate, but it's life and
>   death to some poor wretch!

DOCTOR: No, no, no – I've just taken a small sample to test.

HANCOCK: A sample? How much do you want, then?

DOCTOR: Well, a pint, of course.

HANCOCK: A *pint*? Have you gone raving mad? You must be joking!

DOCTOR: A pint is a perfectly normal quantity to take.

HANCOCK: You don't seriously expect me to believe that? I mean, I came in here in all good faith to help my country. I don't mind giving a reasonable amount. But a *pint*? Why, that's very nearly an armful! I don't mind that much *[points to the tip of his finger]*, but I'm not having it up to here! I'm sorry, I'm not walking round with an empty arm for anybody. I mean, a joke's a joke . . .

DOCTOR: Mr Hancock, obviously you don't know very much about the workings of the human body. You won't have an empty arm . . . or an empty anything. The blood is circulating all the time. A perfectly normal healthy individual can give a pint of blood without any ill effects whatsoever. After all, you do have *eight* pints, you know.

HANCOCK: Now, look, chum. Everybody to his own trade, I'll grant you, but if I've got eight pints, obviously, I *need* eight pints – and not seven, as I will have by the time you've finished with me. No, no, I'm sorry, I've been misinformed. I've made a mistake. I'll do something else. I think I'll be a traffic warden . . .

As always with *Hancock*, people were quoting lines from this episode for days – and in some cases weeks and months – after the broadcast, but few at the time knew just how much care had been invested in each little comic line. As Alan Simpson would later reveal about the most repeated phrase of all:

The line that went out was: 'A pint? Why, that's very nearly an armful!' Which gets a nice laugh. But Ray and I used to take care over rhythms. We used to spend a lot of time working out just how we wanted the sound of the line, the rhythm of the line, to be. One 'and' too many, one 'but' too many, one syllable too many, can kill a line. It's like poetry. So that line probably started out as: 'That's an armful!' Which in itself is quite an amusing concept – to talk about blood as being an armful or a legful. And then one of us probably said: 'That's *nearly* an armful!' Which is better because it's a little bit more precise. And then the other one would have topped it up by saying: 'That's *very* nearly an armful!' Now, 'very nearly an armful' is much funnier than 'that's an armful'. It's the same gag, but [the key thing is] being specific on a stupid way of assessing things.[40]

A great deal of care also went into the direction. Although videotapes cost £100 each at the time and were not reusable once cut – a fact that caused the BBC to discourage all but the most straightforward kinds of recording – Duncan Wood still proved himself an innovative producer/director, experimenting with new editing techniques as soon as they became available[41] to provide breaks between scenes, hide the presence of extra cameras and omit the more obtrusive kinds of mistake.[42] Always very much in charge of all aspects of his studio (Spike Milligan once said that the big, broad-shouldered director 'would have made the perfect Tank Corps sergeant'),[43] he timed each rehearsal meticulously so that it lasted precisely 29.5 minutes (so as to allow enough room on the night for likely audience laughter without upsetting the pace and the flow) and trained his actors to collaborate with his cameramen so that every key expression was captured in quick little close-ups ('Television,' he said, 'lives and breathes in faces').[44] The ultimate ideal, he always stressed, was to preserve a sense of artistic immediacy while achieving technical perfection. With *Hancock*, he came admirably close to realising the ambition.

The novelist and critic J. B. Priestley would celebrate these most recent small-screen shows as Hancock's crowning glory:

He was beautifully equipped for the job: a superbly controlled mobile face; expressive eyes, lightening up or darkening; a voice, always wonderfully timed, answering to every demand; he had it all. And though he deliberately avoided pathos, despising the 'little

man' appeal, there was still this suggestion of depth. His pretensions as this TV character were absurd, making us laugh every
week (and would make us laugh again next week, month, year),
and yet this was somebody close to mass man of today, coming out
of the faceless crowd, hopeful, near to glory, for some minutes,
before the lid comes on again, before he shrugs his way back into
the dark.[45]

Shifting the emphasis a little, Denis Norden applauded the writers for
perfecting the character they had crafted: 'Galton and Simpson didn't
write a series, they wrote a novel. They created a most marvellous
person and Tony filled it out like no other person in the world could,
capturing every tiny nuance. But he didn't exist before Galton and
Simpson and he didn't exist after they left.'[46]

The challenge was as clear as it was intimidating to both the actor
and the writers: follow that. Galton and Simpson were bright enough
and brave enough to do so, and they would go on to not just match,
but arguably even surpass, this extraordinary achievement – but they
would do so without the contribution of the talented Tony Hancock.
One Sunday during the autumn of 1961, he brought the collaboration
to a sudden close.

He had taken to spending a great amount of time at the offices of
Associated London Scripts in Cumberland House, where Beryl
Vertue was now acting as his (as well as his writers') agent.[47] Galton
and Simpson were writing a new movie for him, as he had requested,
but he seemed increasingly unsure about the project. When they were
about a third of the way into their first draft, he told them that he
wanted a more 'international' sort of story, so they wrote him a
second screenplay – only for him to change his mind yet again and
ask them to come up with something else. 'It was almost as though
he was willing Ray and Alan not to write a script he would like,'
Beryl Vertue remembered. 'He kept saying things to me like, "I'm sure
I'm not going to like it." He seemed to have conditioned himself not
to like it.'[48] Eventually, after Galton and Simpson had spent six
months working on the project without pay, Hancock summoned
them, along with Vertue, to the flat he was renting at the time in a

building called the White House near Regent's Park. There was something that he needed to say.

'It was a very dramatic meeting,' Ray Galton would recall. 'A terrible slap in the face.' The three of them sat down opposite Hancock and, without any delay for small talk, he told Beryl Vertue that he no longer wanted her to represent him; from now on, he said, his brother, Roger, would be looking after his professional affairs. What, if anything, he then said, or failed to say, to his writers, while a stunned Vertue tried in vain to fight back the tears, remains a matter of some debate. According to Galton, he informed the two of them that they were free to go off and write for someone else on television, and he would call them if and when he needed them. According to Simpson's recollection, on the other hand, Hancock was not so forthcoming: 'He had nothing to say to Ray and I. The point of the meeting was mainly to announce that he was leaving the agency.'[49] As, however, it was their agency as well as Beryl's, it certainly sounded as though he was effectively leaving them, too. One way or another, it was over.

'He could be ruthless,' Galton reflected, 'and he was.'[50] Hancock would never offer them any proper explanation for the split. 'I don't know exactly why he did it,' said Beryl Vertue, 'except that I felt it went in the pattern of Bill Kerr and Kenneth Williams and Sid James. He didn't want to *rely* on them.'[51] *Private Eye* would mock the conceit (in one comic strip, it pictured 'Tony Halfcock' dropping Kenneth Williams, then Sid James, then Galton and Simpson, and then, finally, God),[52] and Spike Milligan, after Hancock had committed suicide in 1968, would claim with glacial glibness, 'One by one he shut the door on all the people he knew; then he shut the door on himself.'[53] It was by no means as neatly simplistic as that – but, then, nor was it any more logical, either. He was confused and insecure, but he was also very, very stubborn. The BBC tried hard to make Hancock change his mind, as did many of his friends and colleagues, but he remained adamant that it was time to move on, so he did – and so did Galton and Simpson.

Invited soon after the split by Tom Sloan, BBC TV's then *de facto* Head of Light Entertainment, to write ten unrelated half-hour pieces under his new *Comedy Playhouse* banner, Galton and Simpson saw the proposed series as a golden opportunity to graduate from serving comic performers to guiding serious actors, and start creating the kind of scripts that could move as well as amuse. They accepted Sloan's offer, and duly proceeded to prove themselves absolutely right.

Comedy Playhouse, remembered Simpson, would provide him and his partner with the ideal antidote to *Hancock*: 'After nine years of comedians, we thought, "That's the lot – we're going to have only straight actors now." Because actors are good, you see – they don't ask where the next gag is coming from. They don't count the jokes.'[54] Previewing the project in the *Radio Times*, Galton said excitedly: 'This series can be a real turning-point in our writing career. In these half-hour shows – they're really one-act plays – we dream up our own characters, and the actors playing them have to fit the writing instead of the other way round. If the series succeeds, this is the kind of thing we want to do from now on.'[55]

Their producer/director, once again, was Duncan Wood, and he agreed and identified completely with their current ambition. 'Working with a name comic,' he said, recalling his experience of making *Hancock*, 'you start with a set of limitations – no, that's not fair – a set of assets, which are limited. Everything has to be geared to presenting the comedian.' Looking forward to *Comedy Playhouse*, he said: 'In a comedy playlet [. . .] you present the script as interpreted by actors and you have to put comedy actors in far more of a directorial strait-jacket than comedians.'[56] Armed with more cameras and more clout, he could not wait to make a more polished kind of programme.

The series began on 15 December 1961 with *Clicquot et Fils* (which co-starred Eric Sykes and Warren Mitchell as a couple of crafty undertakers), followed by *Lunch in the Park* (a vehicle for Stanley Baxter) and then *The Private Lives of Edward Whiteley* (featuring Tony Britton as a dedicated bigamist). When it came to writing the fourth programme, however, Galton and Simpson experienced the same problem they had encountered back in the days when they were scripting shows in the sanatorium: they ran out of ideas. It was understandable: whereas with Hancock, they had been obliged to come up with a fresh storyline for each new show, they were now having to dream up a whole new cast of characters and a brand-new situation – as well as a completely new storyline – for every one of the self-contained half-hour shows, and the strain was taking its toll.

'We'd get the most terrible blocks,' Galton would recall. 'On Fridays, when we were meant to have everything in, we were sometimes still lying on the floor, not even started.' On this particular occasion, the two men sat in silence inside their office at ALS and just thought and thought and thought. Four days came and went without a sound except the ticking of a clock. Then, at long last, Ray Galton felt moved to make a suggestion: 'I said to Alan: "What about doing a thing about two rag-and-bone men?" After eight hours' silence, he said: "What did you say about rag-and-bone men? Shall we start that?" And so we did.'[57] Simpson continued: 'We just started writing, "FIRST RAG-AND-BONE MAN . . . SECOND RAG-AND-BONE MAN . . ." We didn't even know who they were, didn't know their names or anything. We just wrote for about ten pages, half a script, and then we stopped and said, "Right, now we'd better work out who they are and what is it all about." So we read back and it turned out that one of them was older than the other one, and then one of us said, "Father and son?" and that was immediately it – we knew that was it.'[58]

There was an obvious 'family resemblance', Simpson would later acknowledge, to another pair of characters they had created: 'A lot of people think that [the relationship in] *Steptoe and Son* was an extension of [the one that had existed between] Hancock and Sidney James, and it was in many respects. You had the same dichotomy, the same attitudes were there in both sets of characters. Both Hancock and the young man Steptoe thought there was a life above what they knew, and the other two didn't. You know, Sid James's attitude was: "If it doesn't run and you can't eat it, it doesn't exist."'[59] Where the new relationship clearly differed from its predecessor, however, was in the grittiness of its situation and the dark and raw emotions that it provoked. Galton and Simpson's script – which they entitled 'The

Offer' – was as tragic as it was comic: an ageing, widowed, arthritic and irascible working-class man waiting at home while the rest of his time passed him by, and his 37-year-old bachelor son, still living and working at home, desperate to escape and better himself but not quite able to break the bonds borne of flesh, blood and bone.

Writing for someone much older than themselves, as well as for someone more or less the same age, proved no real problem for Galton and Simpson: 'We'd grown up in the company of quite a few older people, you see,' Simpson would explain. 'When we were in the sanatorium, we lived alongside much older people who'd served in the war. So older people met younger people in there on a level basis. Your experiences were shared throughout the generations.'[60] It was obvious, however, that Galton and Simpson – because of the truth they had placed in their scripts – would need serious actors, rather than comic personalities, to accommodate such shadows and light.

Both writers shot straight to the same conclusion when it came to casting the role of Albert, the father: it had to be Wilfrid Brambell. Brambell (who was born on 22 March 1912 at Rathgar in Dublin) was a graduate of Dublin's legendary Abbey Theatre, learning his craft in pioneering productions of works by, among others, George Bernard Shaw. After touring with ENSA during the Second World War, he had resumed his theatrical career in England, working in numerous repertory companies while accepting a wide range of supporting roles in radio plays, television serials (including *The Quatermass Experiment* in 1953 and *Our Mutual Friend* in 1958) and movies (such as Carol Reed's 1947 IRA drama *Odd Man Out* and, the following year, Charles Crichton's Ealing comedy *Another Shore*).

Galton and Simpson had seen him on numerous occasions in recent years, including, in 1959, as an elderly tramp (he was actually aged only forty-seven at the time) in a television play by Clive Exton called *No Fixed Abode*. 'This was,' Ray Galton remembered, 'exceptionally well acted by Brambell and fitted our ideas for Albert perfectly. We had also seen him in *Widowers' Houses* [by] George Bernard Shaw, all the other Clive Exton stuff, so we knew Brambell was good. There was no fear of his letting us down.'[61]

The writers were similarly in agreement about their first choice actor to play Harold, the son: Harry H. Corbett. Born on 28 February 1925 in Rangoon, Burma, Harry Corbett (the middle 'H' – which stood for nothing, or 'hanything' – would only be added much later to distinguish him from his well-known 'Sooty' puppeteer namesake) was the son of a British Army officer. Following the death of his mother when he was aged just three, he was sent to England to be raised by his aunt in Manchester. When, while still a young child, he was taken to the Manchester Opera House to see the popular comedian Leslie Henson, he became fascinated by all facets of the theatre, and soon started nursing an ambition to work in some capacity or other on the stage. After serving during the war as a radiographer in the Royal Marines, he duly embarked on a career as an actor, joining the Chorlton Repertory Company in Manchester before moving on to the Bristol Old Vic, the Langham Experimental Group and Joan Littlewood's self-consciously politicised Theatre Workshop at London's Stratford East.

One of the country's earliest exponents of the so-called 'Method' school of acting (which involved drawing on one's own memories, feelings and experiences in order to replicate the emotional conditions under which a character might operate in real life), there was something undeniably edgy, unpredictable and exciting about Corbett that rapidly won him the deep-felt respect of most of his peers. 'Whenever he was on television,' Alan Simpson would recall, 'the whole of the acting profession who weren't working, which is about eighty per cent of the acting population of London, dropped whatever they were doing and went to a television set.'[62] He was heading a two-week season as *Macbeth* at the Bristol Old Vic when the *Comedy Playhouse* script came through his door. Fortunately for Galton and Simpson, who were not too sure that he would be interested, Corbett could not have seemed keener: 'I'd looked at television, and all I saw that was making any kind of good – what's the word? – "social comment" were the Hancocks, the Eric Sykes, this kind of half-hour comedy programme. Oh, I did envy them!'[63] He did not hesitate, therefore, to accept a role in 'The Offer'.

Galton and Simpson had their two first-choices on board (which was bad luck for J.G. Devlin and Ronald Fraser, because they were the next two on the list), and the ensuing rehearsals (which ran from 28 December 1961 to 3 January 1962) could not have gone more smoothly. The only problem arose on, of all days, the day when the show was due to be shot. Whereas Wilfrid Brambell, as a jobbing actor, was no stranger by this stage to a television studio set up for the purposes of light entertainment, it was still an unnervingly unfamiliar environment for a drama specialist like Harry H. Corbett. As Ray Galton recalled: 'When you're rehearsing, you're in Boy Scout huts or tents or anywhere you can find, and you get into the studio only on the day of recording. And on the day we got there, Harry turned round from looking at the sets, and asked, "What are all those seats?" "Well, they're for the audience". "An *audience?* I shall have to rethink my entire performance . . ."[64] He soon settled down, however, and, like Brambell, proceeded to give a masterly example of acting.

Recorded 'as live' on 4 January 1962, 'The Offer' reached the screen at 8.45pm the following evening. Featuring no characters other than Steptoe and his son, and a cluttered and claustrophobic set that seemed more suited to a play by Samuel Beckett than a conventional British sitcom, the next half-hour would prove to be a real 'water-cooler' moment for popular television. It began with a shot of a rag-and-bone man on his cart, being pulled by a tired-looking horse down a scruffy little London lane and into a junk-ridden yard, where he was met by a shorter, older man. Shutting the wooden gates to reveal the clumsily painted sign, 'STEPTOE AND SON: SCRAP MERCHANTS', the old man turns back and starts fussing over the horse while grumbling at his own flesh and blood: 'Have you been out all day just for this?' he snaps. 'What sort of totter are you?' The younger man is clearly used to such a cold and ungrateful reception ('Don't start, Dad . . .'), but something about his manner suggests that, on this particular day, his skin is finally wearing thin:

HAROLD: Here, look – you moan about the way I treat the horse, you moan about the way I go out totting . . . *you* go out – go on – I don't mind staying here in the yard, sitting round the fire drinking cups of tea all day long . . . go on, *you* get up on the plank, you're so good at it . . . I'm sick and tired of sitting up there *[Points to the horse and cart]* watching that great backside all day long. *You* go out tomorrow!

ALBERT: You know I can't get out in the cart no more, not with my legs.

HAROLD: Yeah, well, that's it then, ain't it . . . you don't want to say nothing, do you, otherwise I'll jack this lot in and be off. I'm sick and tired of you, and the yard, and the horse and the cart!

ALBERT: Yeah? What do *you* know – what could *you* do?

HAROLD: Don't worry about me, mate – I'll be all right. I-I've had an offer!

ALBERT: Get out of it!

HAROLD: Oh yes I have. And it don't include you or that rotten horse, see? OK? All right? Well – watch it!

ALBERT: What offer? Who from?

HAROLD: Never you mind. I'll go an' feed the horse.

ALBERT: You don't want to go taking no offers. We've got a good business here!

HAROLD: You're *worried* now, ain't you!

The old man reacts by faking his fear about his weak heart, but this time the son is having none of it: 'You've been moanin' about your heart for forty years – every time you can't get your own way! You've had fifteen heart attacks to my knowledge!' Then, changing tack, the old man tries to reassure him about the security that comes from his fixed position in the family tradition – 'I built this business up for you – it'll be yours when I'm gone. And then, when your son comes along, you won't have to change the sign, either: "Steptoe and Son"' – but this serves only to remind the son of how much that tradition has held back his life – 'Well, I ain't got a son, have I? I ain't even got a wife!'

Pale in the shade of the prison-house that is his home, the fully-grown boy sees every little attempt to improve his condition crumble down alongside all of the rest of the rubbish. When, for example, he sits down to drink the 'non-vintage Beaujolais' that he found on his rounds, he discovers that it has been filled full of paraffin:

ALBERT: Maybe it won't matter. Maybe you won't taste it. I knew a man who drank methylated spirits. He swore by it!

HAROLD: Look – I'm not an alcoholic, mate, I'm a *connoisseur!*

ALBERT: Well, if you don't want it, I'll have it. I don't mind a drop of paraffin!

HAROLD: Oh, you *dirty* old man!

Driven to the end of his tether ('I'll never make a name for meself 'ere; 'ere I'm just "and Son"') he declares that he is going to put all of his possessions on the cart and take up the mysterious offer. Picking out those extra items that might suit his upwardly-mobile ambitions – such as a tatty old armchair ('Oh yes, that will look very nice in my study, that will. I think I'll have it re-covered in red leather, with brass nails all round it') and a battered golf bag with one solitary club inside ('That's essential, that is – all company directors play golf. That's where all the big deals are done, on the golf course') – and loads them on to the cart. When, however, he tells his father to fetch the horse, the old man, sensing his chance, stands firm:

HAROLD: I got to have the horse, otherwise how am I going to move my stuff out?

ALBERT: That's *your* problem, isn't it? You're not having the horse!

HAROLD: Well, keep your rotten, stinkin' horse! It don't bother me, mate. I'll move it on me own. I never got nothing in the past from you, so don't do me no favours. I don't want none now. That don't bother me – I'll soon have that on the move. *[He gets in between the shafts and takes one in each hand]* I'm sorry it had to end this way, but I'll come and see you, when the pressure's off. Cheerio, then.

ALBERT: Cheerio.

[Harold strains at the shafts. Nothing happens.]

HAROLD: Is that brake off?

ALBERT: Yeah.

HAROLD: Well, I'll be off, then. Right? Cheerio.

ALBERT: Cheerio.

HAROLD: No 'ard feelings?

ALBERT: No.

HAROLD: It's the only way. If you don't look out for yourself, you don't deserve to get on. I was in a rut, you see. If I don't go now, I'll never go.

ALBERT: Cheerio, then.

HAROLD: Cheerio, then.

[Harold strains harder and harder. The cart does not budge.]

ALBERT: I'll, um, go and open the gates, shall I?

[Harold strains and strains, gradually getting weaker. He relaxes, then has another go, panting with the effort. Eventually he starts whimpering.]

HAROLD: Move! Move, you rotten, stinking cart! *Move!* I got to *go!* I got to get away . . . move . . . *move . . .*

[The cart stays where it is. Harold breaks down and slumps over one of the shafts, sobbing.]

HAROLD: I can't go . . . I can't get away . . .

[Albert goes over to him, stands looking at him for a moment, then puts an arm round him and helps him up.]

ALBERT: I'll go and put the kettle on and make a cup of tea, shall I? Get the old sausages going. You like sausages *[choking up]* don't you? *[He starts leading his son back into the house]* It's a bit late to start going anywhere now, anyway, isn't it? I mean, it's getting dark – you'd have to put the lights on.

HAROLD: I'm still goin' . . . I'm not stayin' . . .

ALBERT: 'Course you aren't. You can go some other day. On a Sunday, when the traffic's not so heavy. We'll unload the cart in the mornin', don't you worry about that.

HAROLD: I'm not stayin' 'ere . . . I'm going to take that offer . . .

ALBERT: 'Course you are. They'll keep that offer open for you. You can go another day. Or you can stay with your old dad and wait till a better offer comes along. I mean, look at the way you're saving up stock here. You'll be a force to be contended with. I mean, the more you have to put down, the better offer you'll get, see? You stay with your old dad.

It was an astonishingly good script, brought to life by two extraordinarily realistic, honest and vulnerable performances that had one laughing one moment and close to tears the next. There had been no fixed 'good' character and 'bad' character – the viewers' sympathies had switched back and forth across the two generations as the struggle, and the emotions, kept twisting and turning – and no neat and simple solution. As a sitcom, it had been unexpectedly dramatic, intense and unusually engaging. As television, it had quite simply been unforgettable. Even the writers were impressed with what they had witnessed. Alan Simpson recalled: 'We saw [at the end that Harry H. Corbett] was actually crying. The tears were rolling down his cheeks. And we looked at each other and thought, "Oh my God, this is *acting!*"'[65]

The powers-that-be at the BBC were, if anything, even more positive about the show. 'Tom Sloan had been watching the rehearsals,' Galton recalled. 'And he came up to us and said: "You do realise what you've done here, don't you? You've got yourselves a series!" So we said: "No, no thank you very much, we've just done ten years of Hancock and the last thing we want to do next is commit ourselves to another long-running series." But he kept on about it, and finally we said: "OK, if Harry and Wilfrid agree, we will do it" – thinking that they never would.'[66]

They did. Although both men expressed some reservations, initially, about the risk of becoming typecast, neither of them could resist the chance to return so soon to such rich and vivid characters.[67] There was also, already, a real chemistry between them as actors: although as different from each other as chalk and cheese in real life – Bramble was a closet homosexual who liked to collect antique silver trinkets, take long and languorous annual holidays in Hong Kong, attend the odd show-business cocktail party and dawdle over long liquid lunches (he would choose whisky and lager as his luxuries on *Desert Island Discs*);[68] Corbett was a promiscuous heterosexual, a committed socialist and somewhat earnest searcher for theatrical truths – and although they also differed from each other in terms of their styles of acting – Brambell was an old-school 'learn it and do it' performer, whereas Corbett liked to 'feel' his way into a scene by experimenting with alternative interpretations – somehow, when they worked together on the set, they met in the middle, the fit was perfect and the effect immense. The proposal of a series, therefore, was far too good for either actor to resist.

After Galton and Simpson had added the odd little detail – such as placing the Steptoe residence not far in spirit from the original home of ALS in the fictional Oil Drum Lane in Shepherd's Bush ('That,' Galton would say, 'was our little homage to the fact that in Victorian times anything to do with modernity was captured and put on street signs. You had names like Electricity Lane, and there was a place in Hammersmith called Pumping Station Lane, which I loved. Oil Drum Lane sounded worse!')[69] – the first series of *Steptoe and Son* was ready to be filmed.

Broadcast during January and February in 1963, it was an immediate popular and critical success – so much so, in fact, that the BBC took the unprecedented decision to repeat it soon after the run had finished. 'The series was an even bigger hit the second time round,' Ray Galton would recall. 'It was the biggest thing in the country. It was amazing, and we weren't even aware of it. Alan and I were on holiday, and Harry H. Corbett joined us down in southern Spain, exclaiming: "It's unbelievable. I can't go anywhere." So we had no reason not to do any more!'[70]

The second series, by some quirk of television scheduling, went out on 3 January 1963 on the same night as a new series from Tony Hancock (his first not to be scripted by Galton and Simpson – not because he had failed to ask them, but because they were now too busy to oblige)[71] was screened on ATV. The Press made the most of the apparent coincidence, and *The Times* even went so far as to bill its review as 'Mr Hancock v. His Writers',[72] but, as both series progressed, *Steptoe* put the other show in the shade ('[T]he papers had a field day,' Alan Simpson recalled. '*Hancock* got hammered by *Steptoe*').[73] Watched each week by an estimated twenty-two million people,[74] it contained some instantly iconic scenes and images – such as the sight of Albert, sitting naked (save for his black hat) in his tin bath in the middle of the living room, singing 'These Foolish Things' while searching through the murky water for the pickled onions that have dropped from his jar – and plenty of memorably spiky exchanges between father and son – such as when (in the episode entitled 'The Stepmother') Harold, after discovering that Albert is planning to remarry, takes his turn to keep their relationship trapped:

ALBERT: I loved your mother!

HAROLD: You *said* you loved this one!

ALBERT: Well, so I do – I love both of them.

HAROLD: You can't have it both ways! Oh, it may be very conven-ient for you while you're down 'ere alive, choppin' and changin' your affections, but what happens when you and this new one go? What happens when you get up there? Which one are you going to go with? You can't go with *both* of them. They don't allow that sort of thing up there, mate! They're very particular up there!

ALBERT: W-well, the vicar said it would be all right. *[Thinks to himself for a few seconds]* Aaah, thousands of people get mar-ried twice! *Three* times!

HAROLD: Not to my Mum they don't!

The plaudits kept on coming. Gale Pedrick, the man who had given Galton and Simpson their first break, declared: 'In half a lifetime of writing for television and about it, I cannot remember a series which has made a firmer and more rapid impact';[75] Duncan Wood wrote in an internal BBC memo: 'Alan Simpson, Ray Galton, Harry Corbett and Wilfrid Brambell are four of the most creative artists I have enjoyed working with. They should be contracted for ever';[76] and a critic in *The Times* said that the show 'virtually obliterates the divi-sion between comedy and drama'.[77] At the same time that the music industry was hailing the arrival of 'Beatlemania', television was cel-ebrating 'Steptoemania': apart from the millions of people who were watching the show itself, there were also records being released (including a single of Ron Grainer's theme tune, 'Old Ned' – which won him an Ivor Novello Award – and several albums of excerpts from the show) and 'novelisations' published; the Duke and Duchess of Bedford invited anyone in Britain bearing the name of Steptoe to take tea with them and Wilfrid Brambell in the grounds of Woburn Abbey (four hundred parched and peckish Steptoes turned up); and, on 4 November in 1963, Corbett and Brambell appeared in character as Steptoe and Son on the same Royal Variety Performance, fittingly, as The Beatles (and, shortly after, a recording of their contribution – 'Steptoe and Son at Buckingham Palace' – spent twelve weeks in the UK singles chart).

The two stars coped with the success of the show in different ways. Brambell enjoyed his fame greatly – but then, as Alan Simpson would remember, he could choose, when it suited him, to leave his *alter ego* behind in the studio:

> The first thing he did when he came off the set was have a wash and shave, put his proper teeth in – because he used to have a rendered-down pair of teeth for the part that were all blackened up with holes and gaps in them – have a shampoo, comb his hair, put his suit on and get himself ready to go. He was absolutely immaculately dressed – always – off set. I mean, beautifully creased trousers, smart shirt and tie, shiny shoes: really dapper. And he used to wander out with the audience all around and nobody would recognise him.[78]

Corbett, on the other hand, found it a struggle to escape from his on-screen persona – 'Harry was better dressed on the set than he was off,' said Simpson, 'so they all recognised him immediately!'[79] – and, as someone who preferred to avoid the spotlight, he was sometimes driven to don disguises in the futile hope of fooling his legion of fans ('Harold is not me,' he would protest. 'Harold only exists on paper').[80] Both men, however, genuinely appreciated the fact that so many people cared so much about what they were doing, and neither was inclined to give up being part of something so good.

The show would go on to run, in all, for eight series, from 1962 to 1974, regularly attracting audiences of twenty million or more, and would also spawn two movie spin-offs, six radio series, one touring show and a hugely successful American television adaptation.[81] Indeed, so great would its popularity become that an episode scheduled for the evening of the 1964 General Election came close to being delayed (at the request of an Opposition Leader – Harold Wilson – fearful of its damaging effect on voter turnout) until after polling had ended ('the BBC told him to get stuffed,' Alan Simpson recalled, 'in the nicest possible way, of course').[82]

What, then, was so special about *Steptoe and Son*? It is tempting to say: 'everything'. It re-defined all of the key ingredients that people associated with the British sitcom. First of all, there was the realism (at least in the conservative terms of the television comedy of the time) of the setting: it took viewers away from the old lace-curtained cosiness of previous sitcoms and right into the gritty, grubby, gloomy working-class milieu of a rag-and-bone man's ramshackle home in Shepherd's Bush; second, it featured a daringly dark, tragi-comic 'trapped relationship' between a dour, habit-hardened proletarian and a socially sanguine, would-be *petit bourgeois*; third, it was based on the kind of writing that was capable of pathos and poignancy as well as sauce and slapstick; and finally, instead of resting on pre-existing theatrical comic personae, it based itself on newly created characters that needed to be played by professional actors. In short, *Steptoe and Son* changed the sitcom genre for good – and definitely for the better.

It also struck a chord with the British people. Appearing at a time when new tensions were emerging between the young and the old, especially in terms of the growing differences between their respective cultural tastes, lifestyles and social aspirations, the world of *Steptoe and Son* was one with which all ages and classes could identify.

It was a very British world: a world populated by stubbornly proud traditionalists and increasingly exasperated innovators. As a furious Harold would exclaim, after seeing yet another plan for progress sabotaged by his craftily conservative father: 'You frustrate me in everything I try to do. You are a dyed-in-the-wool, fascist, reactionary, squalid, little know-your-place, don't-rise-above-yourself, don't-get-out-of-your-hole, complacent little turd!' (An outburst that failed to provoke his father into uttering a response any sharper than: 'What d'yer want for yer tea?'). Both characters had their own familiar social faults: Albert – the supposed conformist – could not bear to share a space with his so-called 'superiors', while Harold – the supposed rebel – could not wait for the chance to join and – more likely than not – serve them. One way or another, the contradictions made sense to class-conscious Britons.

It was a world in which there was always a ready put-down to puncture any pretension. If, for example, Harold's language grew too highfalutin (e.g., 'Your mere presence tends to impinge upon my aesthetic pleasures and moments of relaxation'), Albert could be relied on to offer a plainer translation ('In other words: I get on your tits!'). Similarly, whenever Harold's dreams of a better life drifted too far from his working-class reality – such as when he imagined transforming his shared junkyard hovel into a fashionable salon, a 'powerhouse of intellectual thought' so full of 'choice wines, superb food and elegant conversation' that the likes of 'C.P. Snow and Bertrand Russell will be busting a gut to get in' – vulgar Albert would always step in to bring him crashing back down to earth: 'Oh *yeah!* There'll be plenty for them to do here: table tennis, rat hunting. I can see you all now, going for long tramps across the yard deep in intellectual conversation and horse manure.'

It was also a world in which, when it most mattered, no one, being typically British, could bring themselves to say what they really felt. Albert would do his best to hurt Harold – 'You can't wait to hear the first shovel-full of dirt hit the coffin, can you? I wouldn't be mourned, I know that. You'd be dancing on my grave!' – and Harold would do his best to hurt Albert – 'Oh, you poor old man! You ain't got nothing to live for, have you? Here, cut your throat, put yourself out of your misery!' – because both men hoped that the show of hate would help hide the love.

All of British life was there, at its most essential and intimate, and that was why *Steptoe and Son* made us blush almost as easily and as often as it made us laugh. It was not the show that brought the British sitcom to life; but it was the show that brought real life to the sitcom.

Everyone involved with it knew that they were part of one of British television's stellar events. Harry H. Corbett, for example, when he was looking back on the first few series, was understandably proud of what the show had achieved. He enthused about the Everyman quality in the character of Harold:

He has his dreams all day, and so do we; it's in all of us, and we never lose it. And he's a man in the grip of that terrible dilemma – how long do you stand by your duties and let life slip away from you? There are so many people in the same situation. A lot is written about the problems of teenagers and old folk, but the thirties have their troubles too, and to me *Steptoe* is basically an exploration of this theme.[83]

He also praised the show as a whole for the depth and breadth of its scripts:

The rag-and-bone men [theme] didn't mean a thing. I wasn't interested in a documentary about rag-and-bone men. Never have been. I don't give a damn whether their prices are right, wrong or otherwise. That's dismissed. That's thrown out the window. It just gave us a perfect format and set-up to range and slash all over the place. I mean, Harold, his domestic work is over and done with in five or ten minutes. [Then] it's all about politics, about sex, about general economics, about a thousand and one things, about the Church, about anything you wish to mention. But it's certainly not about the rag-and-bone business. Now, none of that, surprisingly enough, relies on double takes, pratfalls, Joey-Joeys, grimaces or whatever you wish to call them. They rely on words and timing. Do you notice the *pace* of it? It's very, very delightfully slow and truthful to the subject matter.[84]

The writers, while quite happy to agree, were also keen to stress that, for all of their various innovations, this was still a sitcom that tried equally hard to be funny as well as profound. 'We didn't sit down and decide to write a show that said something that needed to be said,' Alan Simpson would explain. 'But if you are writing about real people in real situations, this inevitably comes into it and people say, "Ah, social significance!" But it's not deliberately socially significant. The first thing is that it's got to be funny. That's not a cop-out, it's a starting-point.'[85]

The consistently high standard of writing – by the standards of television during any decade then or since in any country – was remarkable. It was not just the comedy and the context, but also the sensitivity and compassion, that impressed. One episode in the second series, entitled 'Sixty-Five Today', was especially subtle and insightful about the tensions – relating to age and love and culture and class – between the two generations.

The occasion is Albert's birthday, and most of the episode focuses on his and Harold's respective attempts to hide the real affection that each one feels for the other. The sequence begins when Harold gives his father a pair of leather gloves: Albert's face lights up as he looks at them, and Harold – feeling a smile coming on – turns his back and wanders away: 'Do you like 'em?' he asks his father from a safe distance. 'They're all right,' the delighted Albert tries to reply without giving away a trace of emotion. Then comes the birthday card: although Harold, with his cultural pretensions, pretends to regard the item as more of an empty gesture than a genuine expression of warmth, Albert reads the words inside with uncharacteristic care:

> *Happy birthday, father dear,*
> *Here is my wish most sincere:*
> *You've stuck to me throughout my life*
> *In times of trouble and of strife*
> *And so I wish for you, dear Dad*
> *Long life and happiness from your lad.*

Albert is genuinely choked by the sentiments, while Harold appears taken aback – and somewhat embarrassed – at the emotional effect they have had. Harold then reveals that a birthday treat is planned up the West End: 'We're going to start with cocktails at a very fashionable bar, then tickets for a show and then dinner at an exclusive restaurant I have chosen.' Unfortunately, however, the attempt to share his upwardly-mobile pleasures ('We are not mixing with the *hoi polloi* tonight') with his set-in-his-ways father ('I won't enjoy it if it's too posh'), falls horribly flat: Albert hates the cocktail lounge ('I'm thirsty – I don't want one of them little drinks. I want something with *guts* in it!'); he hates the visit to see *Richard III* at the Old Vic ('A right load of rubbish *that* was!'); and he hates the food in the high-class Chinese restaurant, too ('"Bird's nest soup"? *Bird's nest? Eeuuww* – the dirty devils!').

Once the two men are back outside on the street, they go their separate ways off into the night. Each one looks more angry with himself than with the other: Harold because he realises he has been trying to impress his father rather than please him, and Albert because he realises that he could have made more of an effort to pretend that he was impressed – and both of them know that another rare chance of warm togetherness has been wasted. The episode ends with Albert walking home alone, unaware that his precious new gloves have dropped down on to the pavement behind him.

Editions such as this would help underline the importance of the show. Writing in 1966, Frank Muir (in his capacity as the BBC's then Head of Comedy) would single out *Steptoe and Son* as the exemplar of Britain's distinctive 'organic' style of sitcom. Contrasting it to America's tradition of what he called 'formula' comedies ('A formula for the show is established and most of the creative effort goes into getting the pilot programme right. Teams of less inspired writers are then engaged to produce scripts to the given formula. Further development of the characters is normally discouraged by the producer and a kind of endless rewriting of the pilot programme is aimed at'), Muir observed that an 'organic' and 'hand-made' comedy like *Steptoe* embodied 'an original view of life, a comic attitude which is the product of [one or a pair of writers'] mind and talent and cannot be written satisfactorily by anybody else'. He then stressed the value of such shows to the health of the medium in general:

[Organic comedy has an] enormous potential as a winner of viewers. And with successful comedy you not only win their – as it were – eyeballs, you can also engage their minds and their affections. This is done with other forms of telly, to be sure – *Coronation Street, Double Your Money, Crackerjack, The Black and White Minstrels, Dr Finlay's Casebook*; all these have pleased many millions for many seasons. But none of them have touched the heights of delight achieved by *Steptoe and Son*. And none so quickly. Comedy can be a national talking point overnight.[86]

Muir's immediate superior, Tom Sloan, would later pay tribute to *Hancock's Half-Hour* as well as to *Steptoe and Son*. Looking back on the 'golden age' of BBC entertainment over which he had presided, he said that *Hancock* had been 'the breakthrough that situation comedy needed in this country', while *Steptoe*, he added, was already a 'classic' in its own time: 'Was it a psychological study of old age and frustration? Was it a real and tender interplay between a father and son? Maybe it was, but it certainly wasn't written as such. It was a series of well-constructed scripts involving two actors who breathed life into the words and made them real, and it was funny. Above all, it was hilariously funny.'[87]

The achievement of Galton and Simpson, everyone agreed, was immense. To change the nature of the sitcom, and capture the imagination of the public, not once but twice was – and remains – an unprecedented feat. They gave the world *Hancock* and *Steptoe*. No lover of comedy could have failed to be grateful.

Looking back on these two great shows, the writers themselves would declare a personal preference. Alan Simpson remarked: 'We got a tremendous kick out of writing *Hancock*, particularly when we had a good one. We used to look forward to going down to the read-through because they laughed and fell about so much. It was great. But *Steptoe* is ours. We've got two good actors but it is our thing, whereas on *Hancock* we were just Tony's scriptwriters. Sometimes we got mentioned, sometimes we didn't. And the *Steptoe* situations are much more realistic, deeper, less fantastic.'[88]

Both of these sitcoms, however, were, in their own ways, crucial to the development of British comedy. They were also invaluable models as to how a programme could be made to be as popular as it was progressive. 'Let us not lose sight of the fact,' Galton and Simpson would say, 'that the primary purpose of a television comedy series is to entertain.'[89] Neither *Hancock* nor *Steptoe* ever failed to fulfil this basic duty – but they would also take the trouble to make us think, and feel and reflect. Every decent sitcom that followed would owe an immense debt to them for that.

Till Death Us Do Part

It stands to reason . . .

At the end of 1964, Johnny Speight submitted a script for an episode of *Comedy Playhouse* that had an immediate impact on everyone who read it. It featured a family, as most other sitcoms did, but this family, unlike all the others, was full of tension, anger, bitterness and hate. No one said: 'Hi, honey, I'm home!' They were more likely to say: 'Go to bloody hell!'

Entitled 'Till Death Us Do Part,' the script seemed like the nightmare that the BBC's internal censors had been dreading ever since the bad old days of the head-shaking, finger-wagging, tut-tutting *Green Book*. The script made fun of sex, race, religion, royalty, class conflict, political parties and most of the great and the good. The language was bad, some of the sentiments were worse and the overall tone was strikingly dark, harsh and bleak. Every page seemed like a slap in the face as far as the comforting image of a consensual and deferential post-war Britain was concerned: the generational divisions were vast, the cultural divisions stark and the ideological divisions intense. It was uncomfortable to read, and quite offensive and upsetting in places, but there was something else about this script that made it stand out: it seemed so real.

In the middle of the 1960s, the British people *did* argue with each other. There *was* class conflict, racial prejudice and passionate political debate. It was just that there was relatively little of such people and things currently being shown on British television, and, outside of the extraordinary *Steptoe and Son*, next to nothing in peak-time comedy shows. *Till Death Us Do Part* promised to change that – and change it for good.

Tom Sloan, the BBC's Head of Light Entertainment, read the script, and so did Frank Muir, the Head of Comedy, and Dennis Main Wilson, the current producer/director of *Comedy Playhouse*. Of the three of them, the relatively cautious and conservative Sloan (with his strict Presbyterian background) seemed the most likely to take offence, and to some extent he did, but he was fair-minded enough to acknowledge the pertinence of the approach and the high quality of the comedy. 'It was raw, it was honest, it was brilliant in its characterisations and it was funny,' he would reflect. 'What was different was that it had something to say – and it was worth hearing.'[1] At the time, however, he was by no means sure that he wanted to see it survive beyond the initial half-hour slot, but he felt that, as an experimental episode, it was a worthwhile risk for the BBC to run.

Frank Muir was not quite so ambivalent. As a fellow writer, he was quick to congratulate Speight on pursuing such a bold and powerful vision, and expressed his admiration for the muscularly structured dialogue, although he advised Speight to cut down on both the range and quantity of swear words and concentrate instead on a few well-placed 'bloodys' to supply the scenes with the requisite grit.[2] Dennis Main Wilson, meanwhile, was by far the most positive of the trio, declaring that he was delighted with the material and felt that it had more than enough potential to develop into a full-length series.

The script featured four main characters: a white, working-class, ill-educated, Tory-voting, middle-aged East End bigot named Alf Ramsey; his stoical wife, Else; their slightly saucy young daughter, Rita; and their left-wing layabout future son-in-law, Mike. There was very little action, and precious little plot, but, inside the claustrophobic little set, the dialogue fizzed, buzzed and sparked with an immense amount of vim and venom.

Dominating the centre of the screen was the character of Alf: a man whose whole outlook was determined by his desperate fixation on three basic absolutes: God, Queen and Country. His God was an omniscient and omnipotent Englishman who looked after his own and supported West Ham; his Queen was a bit like his God, only female and visible at Christmas-time, when she could see straight through the television screen at who was standing up and who remained seated; and his Country was good old England, the jewel in the crown of the Great British Empire and the saviour of the civilised world. He thought in black and white about blacks and whites, labour and capital, law and order and tradition and modernity: everything – morally, politically and culturally – was cased in a debate that demanded an either/or, 'us' or 'them' conclusion. Clearly unnerved and alarmed by the way that his secure and reassuring pre-war world of order, deference and respect was crumbling at such a rapid rate, he raged at all that was new, permissive and foreign, and reasserted what he believed to be just and right.

The result was that he served as a lightning conductor for all that was contentious in contemporary British society: immigration, racial assimilation and multi-culturalism; the prospect of European integration; class mobility; youth counter-cultures; republicanism; secularism; feminism; sexual permissiveness; censorship – they all helped to fuel Alf's thundering polemics. A beacon of bigotry, he seemed set to show us all up.

The nearest there had been to him, in terms of personality, was probably Pa Glum – the boozy, bullying, strangely verbose male chauvinist pig (played by Jimmy Edwards) who lived with his wife, Ma (who was nothing more than an occasional 'noise off'), their spectacularly stupid son, Ron (Dick Bentley), and his very plain and needy fiancée, Eth (June Whitfield), in the 1950s mini-sitcom *The Glums*. A segment of Frank Muir and Denis Norden's very popular *Take It From Here*, the Glum family was – unusually for that era – a comically dysfunctional domestic unit:

MR GLUM: If you think for one minute I'd allow my only son to engage himself to a female of *your* ilk . . .

ETH: What's wrong with my ilk?

MR GLUM: The ilk that brings a lad home this hour of the night. Engaged? I should cocoa!

ETH: But I *love* him, Mr Glum.

MR GLUM: That is quite irrelevant! How can Ron *consider* getting engaged to be married? He can't even support *himself*! *Look* at him. Can you ever envisage him being in a position to keep a wife and home? Gaw – if it wasn't so laughable, it'd be comic.

ETH: Well, I happen to believe he will be able. I've known Ron long enough now to have every confidence in him. After all, we've been walking out for six months, Mr Glum.

MR GLUM: Then you can just walk out *again*. Through that door!

RON: No, Dad.

MR GLUM: Go on – off out of it! And if I ever catch you hanging round this boy again – I warn you. I have intimate connections with the Vice Squad.

ETH: Vice? Mr Glum, I am not used to being spoken to like *that* and I don't intend to. You might as well know now – bullying won't help you.

MR GLUM: Oh, I'm a bully now, am I? That's nice, isn't it? Being name-called by a chit of a girl within the privates of your own home. Well, I'm not bandying words with you any further. Ron, kindly inform this person her presence is no longer desirable here.

RON: Right ho, Dad. Eth, Dad says your presents are no longer desirable here.

ETH: Then you just inform your father, Ron, you inform him that this is the 1950s, we're not living in Victorian times and if I want to see you I shall continue to see you, and no amount of threatening is going to make any difference!

RON: Right. *[Trying to remember it all]* Dad, Eth says this is the 1950s, er, we're not living in . . .

MR GLUM: Victorian times.

RON: Victorian times. And . . . er . . .

MR GLUM: And if she wants to see you, she will continue to see you.

RON: And if she wants to see me she will continue to see me. And . . .

MR GLUM: And no amount of threatening is going to make any *difference*.

RON: And no amount of threatening is going to make any *difference*.

MR GLUM: She . . . said . . . *what*? Never known such defiance! In
that case, Ron, I forbid *you* to see *her*. Understand? Hereafter,
you are never to see her again!

ETH: *[Appalled]* Ron . . .?

RON: It's all right, Eth. Leave it to me. *[Bravely]* Dad, if you think
you can keep Eth and me apart, you're wrong. There is no possible way you could stop me from seeing my Eth.

MR GLUM: No? Suppose I take your *trousers* away from you and
hide them?

RON: Oh yes, that's a good way.[3]

'The Glums in *Take It From Here* were a great influence,' Speight
would confirm. Although Pa Glum was by no means as outspoken
and prejudiced as Alf, Speight acknowledged that the character of Alf
'came down from him.'[4] The big difference was that, whereas Glum
was clearly a comical persona for Jimmy Edwards and was never
meant to cause any real offence, Alf was shaped to resemble a genuine contemporary sociopath, and primed to cause as much offence
as he possibly could.

Dennis Main Wilson realised, therefore, that the casting had to be
absolutely right if Alf was going to be brought fully, believably and
unashamedly to life:

My original casting was Peter Sellers to play Alf, except Peter was in
a down period – this is when he disappeared and lived in Ireland with
his lady [Britt Ekland]. And my second choice was Leo McKern,
with whom I'd done a couple of wild shows with Eric Sykes. Leo had
just come back from Hollywood, made a fortune, and bought himself a triple-screw luxury diesel yacht and was cruising up and down
the Channel trying it out. We tried 'Come in number 19!' but it
wouldn't work. And my third choice was Warren Mitchell.[5]

Johnny Speight would remember the list slightly differently, claiming
that another experienced character actor, Lionel Jeffries, was also
seriously discussed ('He would have been different but could have
done it just as well'),[6] but, in the end, they agreed to go for Mitchell.

Born Warren Misell in Stoke Newington on 14 January 1926, he represented a knowingly ironic choice – as a left-leaning Spurs supporter from North London with a Russian-Jewish heritage – to portray a reactionary West Ham fan from the East End who was so proud and fiercely protective of his Little English lineage. The actor, however, relished the chance to get under the rhino-like hide of such a profoundly unlikeable and contradictory character.

Mitchell (as he would later rename himself)[7] had been attracted to acting from an early age, attending Gladys Gordon's Academy of Dramatic Arts in Walthamstow when he was just seven. While reading Physical Chemistry at the University of Oxford, he had met and subsequently served in the same Royal Air Force unit as Richard Burton, who encouraged him to develop his acting skills. Upon being demobbed, Mitchell enrolled at London's Royal Academy of Dramatic Art (where he studied alongside Paul Eddington and Dorothy Tutin), and performed in the evenings at the left-wing Unity Theatre (the same place to which Johnny Speight would soon start contributing plays).

Prompted by the onset of his premature baldness to concentrate on character – rather than leading role – acting, he soon earned a reputation for his versatility, playing an array of exotic outsiders, chippy labourers and stuffy bureaucrats on radio, television and in movies as well as in numerous plays and revues on the stage. He was a regular on the wireless for a season of *Educating Archie* (and also contributed several memorable cameo performances to *Hancock's Half-Hour*), and began appearing on television during the second half of the 1950s (alternating between drama – he was the young Sean Connery's trainer in the boxing drama *Requiem for a Heavyweight* in 1957 – and comedy, such as his leading role the same year in the ATV sitcom *Three 'Tough' Guys*). He was more of a peripheral figure in the cinema, however, and was usually limited to playing corrupt or sinister foreigners (including an Italian priest in Eric Sykes's 1962 comedy *Village of Daughters*, a Russian spy in Morecambe and Wise's 1965 big-screen debut *The Intelligence Men* and an Asian cultist in The Beatles' recently-completed movie *Help!*). When the call came from Speight and Main Wilson, he was appearing on stage, at the

Vaudeville Theatre in the Strand, as a Jewish-American con man named Solomon Bozo in a darkly comic romp called *Everybody Loves Opal*.

Mitchell was just what Speight had been waiting for, and searching for: an actor – not a comedian like Arthur Haynes – who knew how to be funny and how to be straight, and was not afraid to be mocked, disliked or even hated by the audience if it was likely to help the show. He was Speight's Wilfrid Bramble or Harry H. Corbett – someone who was willing and able to turn his character into flesh and bone, and make every word, every nuance and every expression seem unnervingly alive and real. Warren Mitchell was up to playing this extraordinary bald-headed, baggy-trousered, big-mouthed anti-hero.

When it came to casting the part of Alf's long-suffering wife, Else, Dennis Main Wilson chose a 34-year-old London-born character actor named Gretchen Franklin. Coming from a large and well-established theatrical family (both her father and grandfather, for example, had toured the halls with well-honed musical-comedy acts), Franklin (who would later find greater fame as 'Ethel Skinner' in *EastEnders*) was a very experienced and versatile performer who had appeared on the same bill as Gracie Fields, founded a tap-dancing troupe, worked in several West End revues and acted in numerous movies (including the 1957 mystery *Bullet from the Past* and the race relations drama *Flame in the Streets* in 1961) and television shows (ranging from period dramas such as the BBC's 1959 production of *Bleak House* to a co-starring role alongside the fine northern comedian Dave Morris in a sitcom – also broadcast in 1959 – entitled *The Artful Dodger*). Unselfish and lacking any obvious vanity, Franklin was one of those crafty supporting actors who knew how to make the most out of each fleeting scene. She seemed well suited, therefore, to a part that, although relatively short on lines, required plenty of telling little comic reactions.

Selecting the daughter, Rita, was, for a time, more of a problem. The character said little, and did even less, but she had to look right, and, crucially, she had to seem more than just a mere cipher. Eventually, after all kinds of performers had been considered and then discarded, Main Wilson tried, tested and liked a young, budding actor named Una Stubbs. Born on 1 May 1937 in Leicester, she had featured as a dancer both on the stage and in various television shows since the middle of the 1950s, but had branched out into acting in 1962 when she was chosen for a prominent role in the Cliff Richard movie musical, *Summer Holiday*. She was a quick learner and, like most dancers, a very disciplined performer, and she certainly fitted the bill: a fashionable-looking young woman who could still tweak at her father's taut heart-strings while cuddling up to her boyfriend. Main Wilson felt that Stubbs deserved her chance.

The final piece of the jigsaw was found when Anthony Booth was cast as Mike, the mercurial son-in-law. The son of a merchant seaman, Booth was born on 9 October 1931 in the Wavertree district of Liverpool, and, even as a boy, had harboured an ambition to act in both the theatrical and political spheres. 'I thought actors were rogues and vagabonds,' he would say. 'People with no respect for society. That's the company I wanted to keep. I wanted to change society.'[8] After leaving school and enduring an unhappy period working for Cunard in an office at the city's Pier Head, and then an equally unrewarding spell of national service in the Royal Corps of Signals, he returned home and joined the Crosby Amateur Dramatic Society. This decision, he would later say, marked a major turning-point in his life: 'For the first time I knew beyond doubt what I wanted to do.'[9] He started touring in a number of northern repertory companies before finding work at theatres in Manchester, Liverpool and London. Meanwhile, as a passionate political activist, he also began campaigning on behalf of the Labour Party. Regular work in television soon followed, both as a writer (for such shows as *TW3*) and actor (more often than not as an edgy young villain or rebel in such shows as *Dixon of Dock Green, Z Cars* and *The Saint*).

He first met Johnny Speight in London during 1964 at the end of a mass rally for the Labour Party. The two men would soon discover, over a pint or two of beer, that they had much in common: both came from working-class Catholic backgrounds; both had a voracious appetite for culture and current affairs; both were committed socialists; and both of them definitely liked a drink. Explaining that his friend Michael Caine was no longer available to play an argumentative young character in his forthcoming television pilot, Speight handed Booth a copy of the script and asked him to consider taking over the role. Nursing a hangover, the actor read through the text the following morning and, as soon as he had finished, called the author to say that he accepted: 'The challenge excited me and I knew if it was ever shown the programme would generate enormous controversy.'[10] Speight promptly rewrote the role for a Scouser instead of a Cockney, and Tony Booth was duly cast.

The resulting programme was broadcast at 8.50pm on Thursday, 22 July 1965, and, as Dennis Main Wilson would recall, was hailed as a huge success:

Johnny and I went drinking in the White Elephant in Curzon Street that night. All our friends had seen it and hooray: champagne! And in the Elephant you get next morning's papers round about half past eleven in the evening. The crits were super, so we decided not to leave the Elephant, and we stayed there and drank champagne all night and then had breakfast. Turned up at the BBC Club bar at lunchtime, still on champagne, and all our friends came up and said: 'Wow, follow that!' [They said] it was aggressive – within the first three pages we'd destroyed Harold Wilson, we'd destroyed Ted Heath, anybody in charge in Britain. [. . .] It was a total breath of total fresh air. It had never been done before and it was flat out. [. . .] And the audience didn't know what had hit them. So we are back [the following week] – it's now lunchtime-ish – in the BBC Club bar, on a Wednesday. And Wednesday is [the day of the weekly] programme board meeting, to review last week's output by all the bosses of BBC Television. And our mates were buying us drinks, and in came Tom Sloan, who was the head of my department – entertainment. Johnny Speight, who had this stutter, bless him, [. . .] went up to Tom and he said: 'A-a-a-a what about that for a bloody series, mate, eh?' Tom froze and actually said: 'Over our corporate dead body do we make series out of subversive murk like that!' And my heart sank. [. . .] Luckily, down from the same board meeting came the Controller of BBC 1, Michael Peacock, and the Controller of BBC2, David

Attenborough. And David giggled and nudged Peacock and said: 'If you don't want it on One, I'll have it on BBC2!'[11]

Peacock promptly commissioned a series for BBC1, Sloan cooled down and wished it luck, and *Till Death Us Do Part* was guaranteed a future.

An ecstatic Dennis Main Wilson was convinced that he and his team were now set to make something truly extraordinary: 'I'd started with *The Goon Show*, I'd done *Hancock's Half-Hour*, I'd done the first all-girls' show, *The Rag Trade*, which was about trade unions. I'd done some wild shows, all experimental so far, and this was going to be the big one.'[12] When, therefore, he bumped into Frank Muir a few weeks later in the bar at Television Centre, he could hardly contain himself as he revealed his plans for a ground-breaking, Orson Welles-style opening sequence that, he announced with bright and widened eyes, was going to be shot from high above London in a helicopter. Muir put down his glass of white wine, raised his eyebrows and reminded Main Wilson that he had already exceeded his budget for the entire run and the actual series had not even started. *'Bugger the budget!'* barked the maverick producer, who protested that it would only cost the Corporation an extra four hundred pounds to realise this brilliant little dream. Muir smiled weakly but sympathetically: he rather liked the idea, and he admired Main Wilson, so he said that they could go ahead with the shot. The conversation, however, did not end there. 'I'm afraid there's a problem,' said Main Wilson, who was now blushing slightly and glancing down nervously at his feet. 'The four hundred pounds only stretches to a single-rotor chopper,' he mumbled, 'and in that we are only allowed to fly over the Thames, that is, over water. To fly over land we have to have a twin-rotor job.' Muir tried hard not to gasp. 'And how much would that cost?' he asked. Main Wilson shuffled awkwardly and said, 'The twin-rotor chopper comes in at eight hundred and fifty pounds per hour.' Muir thought to himself for a moment, wondering where any spare funds might be found, sighed deeply and then said: 'Go ahead with your shot.' Main Wilson shook his hand vigorously, patted his arm and started smiling: 'Thanks so much. I knew I could count on your support.' Then he paused, threw Muir a shy look, took a quick breath and added: 'The fact is I did the shot last Thursday. It didn't work.'[13]

The following week, therefore, Main Wilson and Speight went back up in the helicopter:

> We did a flight over Wapping in a chopper. [We were] looking for an area which would encompass all the location sequences – the area we were going to describe. And it had to have a bit of a play-ing field, a pub round the corner, a church not too far away. It had got to be near the docks, got to be near the river. It had to be in Wapping High Street if possible. So we did that. And we then per-suaded them to let us go back to opposite Big Ben, and I said to the pilot: 'When I say "go", split us from opposite Big Ben to the end of Wapping High Street, where it becomes a dog leg and becomes Garnett Street, where the cement silo is.' He got that and we did it in one minute twenty-three seconds – which is brilliant because it's one minute forty-three for Big Ben to strike the hour and chime eleven, and that was the opening titles.[14]

Speight, meanwhile, was still busy working on the scripts. Tom Sloan had let it be known that he wanted fewer swear words and less of a scatter-shot approach to the social and political satire, and, while nei-ther Speight nor Main Wilson was inclined to follow such restrictive instructions, they knew that it would be sensible for them to be seen to make the odd little symbolic concession. One such revision was to have Alf call his wife a 'silly moo' instead of the more obviously offensive 'silly cow', and Main Wilson also promised to keep an eye on the number of 'bloodys' that were uttered in each episode. Sloan was far from satisfied, but he did his best to bite his tongue and leave them to it.

Other changes centred on the casting. Gretchen Franklin revealed that she would be unable to continue in the role of Else because she was still appearing in *Spring and Port Wine* and the theatre management would not agree to release her. Apologetically, she recommended her friend Dandy Nichols to Dennis Main Wilson as an ideal replacement, and, as it happened, the producer/director was quick to agree.

Born in Hammersmith on 21 May 1907, Daisy Nichols (as she was known originally) was one of the cleverest and craftiest character actors in Britain. After learning a range of skills in Cambridge Rep and ENSA, she had gone on to establish herself as one of the most trustworthy supporting players in Britain's post-war movies and television, bringing a subtlety and attention to detail that would lend an air of authenticity to a succession of maids, chars, down-trodden wives and nosy neighbours. Dennis Main Wilson had seen and admired her in countless productions, including such movies as the Ealing comedy *Hue and Cry* (1947) and Richard Lester's 'swinging London' snapshot *The Knack . . . and How to Get It* (1965), as well as the odd episode of such television shows as *Emergency – Ward 10, Ask Mr Pastry, Maigret, Armchair Theatre* and the Harry Worth sitcom *Here's Harry*.

He knew that she would slip effortlessly and unobtrusively into the role of Else, and go on to make it her own. He also knew that she would be a stabilising presence both in the rehearsal rooms and the studio. In contrast to her often cold and aloof on-screen personae, Nichols was actually a very caring, rather maternal figure who always came on to the set carrying a 'remedies' bag full of countless types of potential cure-alls ready for any ailing members of the cast. She was also a consummate professional. 'I learnt so much from working with her,' Main Wilson would say. 'We were talking about audience laughter, and she said, "Darling, the whole art is: you make the buggers laugh when you want them to laugh but, even more important, you make them stop when you want them to stop, so you can carry on". This is what actors are for; they're not just there to play a script. Once they are on, they are directing themselves – and the audience.'[15]

There was one other small but significant change for Johnny Speight to make. Since the pilot episode had been broadcast, the long build-up had begun for the 1966 World Cup Finals that were being held in England, and, as the manager of the host nation happened to be none other than Alf Ramsey, and as the final itself was due to take place during the opening run of *Till Death Us Do Part*, it was deemed inappropriate to have another 'Alf Ramsey' ranting on the BBC about, amongst other controversial things, the many flaws and failings of foreigners. Speight's 'Alf Ramsey' was therefore renamed 'Alf Garnett' for the forthcoming series.

The tireless Main Wilson, however, was not quite finished yet. While Speight thought long and hard about each one of his characters, Main Wilson fussed over every aspect of the set:

> I called in my set designer to discuss what kind of house they lived in. And it was to be a twelve foot square front room with a scullery out the back, with an earthenware sink, a bath in the scullery with a lid on where you keep all the crockery, a copper where you heat up all the hot water to hand-bail the water into the bath and run the cold tap, and a bog out the back, and a tiny garden, and a front door that opened into a hall and the stairs go straight up and you turn left into the front room. In the front room there's got to be a two-seater settee, two armchairs, a piano, a dining table, four chairs and a sideboard, in a twelve foot square room. That [would become] our trademark; that was it. That in fact was the exact floor plan and the furniture arrangement of my Mum and Dad's house, and they never spotted it. And they thought the Garnett family lived in the most dreadful circumstances![16]

Proving that there were no hard feelings since the incident with the helicopter (as well as demonstrating how supportive BBC executives could be during this era), Frank Muir would make a point of praising all of Dennis Main Wilson's prodigious efforts during this period, declaring that it 'was almost impossible to overstate [his] contribution': 'Dennis did nothing by halves. In the early days he almost lived with Johnny Speight to help get the *Till Death* scripts out on time, and even wrestled Johnny out of Annabel's nightclub in Berkeley Square in the early hours of one morning to make sure that there would be a script for rehearsal later that day.'[17]

It was worth it. All of it was worth it.

The first episode of the first series – the aptly-titled 'Arguments, Arguments' – was screened on Monday, 6 June 1966, at 7.30pm.

While BBC2 showed a sober documentary on Britain's Polish community, and ITV concentrated on the cobble-stoned cosiness of *Coronation Street*, BBC1 filled its screen with half an hour of raw and noisy working-class desperation. The characters shouted and screamed at each other, sulked, smoked too much, drank too much, swore too much and never seemed to listen to what anyone else was saying. Picking up from where the pilot show had left off, it showed a family at war with itself:

> RITA: He blames *everything* on Labour. He'd blame the weather on 'em if he could!
> ALF: No one's talkin' about the *weather*, Miss Clever Dick.
> ELSE: No. But we haven't had no decent weather. Not since they've been in. I noticed that.
> ALF: Look, as a cabinet minister of the realm –
> ELSE: Rain, rain, rain it is . . .
> ALF: You're perfectly entitled –
> ELSE: And gales. Terrible gales . . .
> ALF: On a ministerial level –
> ELSE: And *snow* in April!
> ALF: *Why don't you shut up, yer silly mare?* I've lost the thread of me argument! I've lost the thread, 'ere, ain't I!

It treated public authority figures with blatant disrespect:

> ALF: They sit up there, them MPs, in that Houses of Parliament, copping their twenty thousand a year . . .
> MIKE: 'Twenty thousand a year'? *Twenty thousand a year?* Listen, you don't half talk a load of cobblers, don't you? Twenty thousand a year? Listen, old Wilson don't even get twenty thousand a year, and he's the Prime Minister!
> ALF: Listen: what they *tell* you they get, and what they bung in their pockets – they're two entirely different things, innit?
> MIKE: What are you talkin' about?
> ALF: Perks! Perks! That's what I'm talkin' about!
> MIKE: Perks?

ALF: You blue-eyed virgin! *Perks!* Listen: you don't think that they can afford to live up there the way they do on what they're supposed to be earning, do you? What? Off to the Scilly Isles every five minutes?

It also had its wryly self-knowing moments:

ELSE: I just don't want no more arguments, that's all.

ALF: 'Arguments'? Who has arguments?

ELSE: You do!

ALF: What are you talkin' about? We don't have *arguments*. Discussions, yeah. We have *discussions*. We don't have *arguments*.

ELSE: Look, I don't care what you call it, it's argument.

ALF: It ain't argument, I tell yer!

ELSE: What is it then?

ALF: Look: in a discussion, see, when you have a discussion, right, you put your salient points of view to each other, right? See? Look: you put your pros, don't you? Then you put your cons, don't you? Then – then – you like debate with any points of contention arising out of yer polemics. See? Now do you understand what discussion is?

ELSE: Yeah. It's arguing!

ALF: *It ain't bloody arguing, yer silly moo!* All arguing is shouting an' hollering, innit?

ELSE: Well you're shoutin' and hollerin' now!

ALF: *I AIN'T BLIMMIN' SHOUTING AN' HOLLERING!*[18]

The critical response was, in general, extremely positive – *The Times*, for example, greeted it warmly, declaring that the series promised to be 'noisy, honestly vulgar and at times hilarious'[19] – but the BBC also received an unusually high number of public and private complaints. The episode had, for example, described the Leader of the Opposition, Edward Heath, as a 'grammar school twit' – an act of supposed insolence which, at the time, was deemed serious enough for officials at Conservative Central Office to request a transcript from the BBC in order to consider whether the insult merited some form of retributive action; the Corporation agreed to send them a copy of the script, but pointed out that Mr Heath had only been called a 'twit' and not, as some papers had reported, a 'nit' – a fact that seemed, oddly enough, to appease the angry officials.[20] The Press, however, was fascinated by the show's power to provoke, and looked forward to more 'political dynamite' during the rest of its opening run.[21]

The show did not disappoint. It took on everything. While most sitcoms of the time had a timeless quality to them, *Till Death* seemed like a slightly warped supplement to the latest national newspaper.

Garnett raged with rabid paranoia about each topic to invade the front page. One early episode, for example, explored – or at least interfered with – the topic of immigration and the gradual collapse of Alf's precious British Empire. In one particularly uncomfortable but deftly executed scene, Garnett gave the British public a glimpse of a blood donor that was as shocking as Tony Hancock's had been funny a few years before:

ALF: *[Whispers]* What's the *coon* doin' 'ere?

MIKE: *[Looks down the row at a black man]* Giving blood, the same as us.

ALF: *[Puzzled]* What, you mean, for other coons, like?

MIKE: No, for anyone.

ALF: What? You mean they bung his blood into anybody?

MIKE: Yeah. Why not?

ALF: *[Raises his voice]* 'Why not'? *[Suddenly noticing that the black man is now looking his way, he nods and smiles nervously]* How d'you do![22]

In another episode, Garnett gave a jaundiced guide to modern domestic politics:

ALF: Yer million unemployed, that's what I'm talkin' about . . .

MIKE: Lies! Lies!

ALF: . . . Caused as a consequence of his Selective Employment Tax.

MIKE: Whose?

ALF: Your darlin' Harold – that's whose! He's clobbered the firms
for that twenty-five bob per person per week – put a million out
of work over it – an' now he's got to pay that million unemployed ten pound a week each dole money! I mean, there ain't
even no sense in it, is there? I mean, he's grabbed it in with one
hand and now he's got to pay out ten times as much with the
other! An' you call him a bloody economist! I wouldn't trust 'im
with a jam jar of threepenny bits! And another little thing, too:
what's that million unemployed going to be *doing* at home all
day, eh? What are *they* going to be up to, eh?

MIKE: Come on, tell us.

ALF: I'll tell yer! Talk about the population explosion, cor blimey –
they'll be breeding like rabbits, they will! And that's going to
cost 'im more money, ennit? What with your family
allowances . . . an' . . . an' . . . free orange juice an' all that . . .

MIKE: Look, just a minute, just a minute . . .

ALF: Never mind 'just a minute'! And your doctors – they're gonna
want overtime for deliverin' all them babies!

ELSE: *[Idly cutting patterns as she listens]* And your midwives.

ALF: *Shuddup!* And then I suppose we shall have to have another
bloody war to get rid of a few of 'em![23]

He also discussed religion:

MIKE: You and your God! Who *is* this God, eh? Well, come on:
what's He *like*? Come on – tell me!

ALF: *[Sounding uncomfortable]* Er . . .

MIKE: Tell me: what's He *look* like? *Describe* Him.

ALF: *[Defensively]* I-I know who He is. I-If you want me to
describe 'im . . .

RITA: Yeah, come on, what's He like?

ALF: Well . . . He's like your Queen. That's who He's like. He's
like your Queen . . . only higher. Much 'igher.

MIKE: Yeah – and about as useful!

ALF: *[Leaps up]* You bloody blasphemous Scouse *git*![24]

He also pondered on the relation of race to modern science. Responding to the news that Christian Barnard, the heart surgeon, was following his first transplant operation (on a patient named Louis Washkansky) with another operation that would involve taking a heart donated by a man of mixed race and placing it in the body of a white man, Alf was outraged:

ALF: Look, you take the case of this Washkansky fella. Now, why did he die, eh? The *operation* was successful, wasn't it? But the reason why he died was that his own *body* rejected the fine heart that them doctors had put into 'im. Because: why? Because Washkansky was a *Jew*, wasn't he? Now, if yer doctors had a *Jewish* heart to put into 'im, he'd have been all right, wouldn't he? His body would have accepted *that*, see?

MIKE: Look, that's rubbish!

ALF: It's *not* rubbish, is it? Look: Washkansky's body was Jewish, wasn't it?

MIKE: Yeah.

ALF: Every single part of it, right? Every single organ. Jewish. He's been brought up Jewish from birth, wasn't he? Well, I mean, if he's Orthodox, y'see, if them organs of his are Orthodox Jewish organs, well, I mean, they're bound to reject a *Christian* heart, ain't they! I mean . . . it wouldn't be like what they would call 'kosher', is it? Well, it's the same way a Christian would reject a Jewish heart. The same as when you put a black heart in a white body now! I mean, I don't wish the fella any ill luck . . .

MIKE: Oh, that's very nice of you.

ALF: I hope he gets away with it. But . . . every single white organ in 'is body, I mean, ain't gonna want to mix with a black heart, are they? And even if they do . . . I mean, what sort of life is he goin' to lead in South Africa? With your Apartheid? Eh? I mean, he won't even know what *toilet* to use![25]

He also reflected on love, sex and the institution of marriage:

ALF: The whole country seems to have gone sex mad! I mean, they had two bishops on the telly, bold as brass, *talkin'* about it! I mean, when I was young, you-you never heard people going around talkin' about sex like that! Not in public, anyway.

ELSE: It used to go on, though . . .

ALF: I know *that*. It went on, I know.

ELSE: Yer, well, the other night on the telly . . . I didn't know where to put my face. Well, I didn't even know the clergy *knew* about them sort of things!

ALF: Well, things they were saying . . . I looked at you, didn't I?

ELSE: I turned away.

MIKE: What were they talking about then?

ALF: Eh? What? Blimey, what *wasn't* they talkin' about!

MIKE: Look, it's 1967 – you've got to talk about them sort of things!

ALF: Not in full view of everyone, though! I mean, you go talkin' about things like that on the telly an' you're goin' to *encourage* it, ain't yer?

ELSE: Some of 'em don't need much encouraging, if you ask me.

ALF: I mean, that sort of thing . . . I mean, it can act like an aphro-*daisy*ac, that sort of thing.

MIKE: *What* sort of thing?

ALF: That book yer church has brought out – *Sex Before Marriage*.

RITA: Oh, you're old-fashioned, Dad!

ALF: 'Old-fashioned'? Listen, we was decent-brought up, we was! Me and your Mum. I mean . . . I never, well, we never . . . she and I . . . I mean, I never attempted to *touch* your mother until after we was married.

ELSE: *Well* after![26]

He also responded to the campaign for sexual equality:

ALF: Look, no argument is going to turn a cabbage into a steak, is it? God – *He* – He put woman here just for man, didn't he?

RITA: *What?*

ALF: Yeah. It's in yer Bible! Yer Garden of Eden! All God done there was made Man: Adam. But God, see, in His infinite wisdom, realised that He couldn't expect Man to run the Garden of Eden on his own. So He, God, He took a rib an' made Eve. So she could clean . . . an' wash up . . . and look after Adam's house for him. So, y'see, if it hadn't been for Man, an' Man's need for a home help, Woman wouldn't have got born at all, in the first place. *[Points at Else]* An' if *she* was a bit faster around the house perhaps my pants wouldn't be as dirty as she bloody makes 'em out to be! Because, then, she might have a bit more time to wash 'em a bit more often!

ELSE: Yes, perhaps I could – if you took 'em off a bit more often instead of livin' in the bloody things for a fortnight![27]

Garnett talked – and talked – about all of the hot topics of the time. Nothing seemed beyond the show's reach – no matter how complex, contentious or delicate the subject-matter was conventionally deemed to be.

There was even an episode that revolved around television's coyest taboo: the lavatory. Lavatories were rarely seen or discussed on television in those days (apart from the odd brief comical shot in *Steptoe and Son*) – indeed, the basic human need to use them was never even acknowledged – but when Alf Garnett contracted a stomach bug the smallest room finally assumed centre stage on the small screen:

ALF: I've been on and off all day at work, I have . . . *[Gets up]* Blimey, I gotta go!

ELSE: 'Ere – you're not going out the back, are you?

ALF: Where d'yer think I'm going?

ELSE: You can't use that – it's blocked up!

ALF: Eh?

ELSE: It's blocked up. It's been blocked up all day, it has.

ALF: Ah, blimey! That's you and your bloody tea leaves, innit! I've *told* you about bungin' 'em down there, 'aven't I!

ELSE: It's nothing to do with tea leaves!

ALF: *Course* it's yer tea leaves!

ELSE: I've been putting 'em down there for years!

ALF: Yeah? Well, now look what's happened! *[Doubling up with discomfort]* Blimey, what am I supposed to . . . I mean, haven't you got the plumber in?

ELSE: He can't come round till tomorrow.

ALF: Well, what am I supposed to do till then?

MIKE: Hang on.

ALF: *Shuddup!*

ELSE: If it's urgent, Mrs Carey says that we can use hers next door.

ALF: Well, why didn't you say so in the first place, then?

[*Alf rushes across the room towards his copy of Mary Whitehouse's* Clean Up TV *book]*

ELSE: What do you want now?

ALF: I want something to *read* out there, don't I?[28]

The critics queued up to analyse and appreciate the nature and impact of this extraordinary creation, and none of them was more thorough, nor more enthralled and effulgent, than T.C. Worsley in the *Financial Times*:

If, instead of appearing in this transient medium, [Alf Garnett] had been the central figure of a stage comedy, he would instantly have been recognised as a major comic creation to be discussed and re-visited and revived over and over again. [. . .]

Who, then, is this Alf Garnett and what is he? Why, he is the rampaging, howling embodiment of all the most vulgar and odious prejudices that slop about in the bilges of the national mind. Whatever hidden hates, irrational fears and superseded loyalties stand in the way of our slow stumble towards a more civilised society, Alf Garnett is the living, blaspheming expression of them. He is everything most hateful about our national character – xenophobic, illiberal, racist, anti-Semitic, toadying, authoritarian. He's a flogger, a hanger, a censor, a know-all and a Mister-Always-Right. He is a positive anthology of unconsidered bigotry. [. . .]

In Alf Garnett, Mr Speight brings out fully into the light of day all the absurdity and irrationality of prejudices that even the most enlightened of us probably harbour somewhere in the sink-pipe of our minds. [. . .]

This is the public service that Mr Speight is performing – cleansing the Augean stable of our national vices of mind. And it wouldn't be as effective as it is if Alf Garnett were not the wholly outrageous figure of Mr Speight's invention. It's no use complaining that he is offensive. He is, indeed, just as completely offensive as everything he embodies is offensive. The one exposes the other. And it takes some audacity of mind to make him so extreme as he is. That is Mr Speight's special quality – that audacity of mind which is prepared to go further than any of us would dare to go.

It is in his tirades, his superb flow of uninhibited invective, that Alf Garnett really reveals himself. They are the special point of the series, they are what we wait for and treasure.[29]

As a social satire *Till Death* was stunning. As a sitcom, however, it was perhaps, in the conventional sense of the format, a little forced. The 'trapped relationship' at its centre seemed more of a puzzle than in, say, *Sykes And A* . . . or *Steptoe and Son*. While one could see what, in spite of the tensions, held Eric and Hat together (sibling affection and mutual incompetence), and Albert and Harold together (repressed love, hidden fear and material deprivation), it was not quite so obvious what necessitated the continuation of the chronically fractious Garnett family unit.

There was not the slightest intimation of love between husband and wife, and no obvious reason, other than indolence, for the continuing presence under the same roof of their daughter and her lover. The bonds between them, as a consequence, appeared to owe more to habit than logic (as Speight would later acknowledge, the character of Alf 'doesn't really need people around him').[30]

The dynamics, however, worked from week to week like a well-oiled comic machine. Alf's dazed-looking wife, Else, for example, was an ice-cool exemplar of the repressive-aggressive response. She would sit there, in the background, saying nothing, paying seemingly little attention, and then, like a Venus Fly Trap snapping itself shut on an idle insect, she would throw away a remark that stopped her husband sharply in his tracks. His daughter, Rita, was similarly subtle, shuffling her pleas for tolerance with her snarls of contempt so that he never quite knew where, in her affections, he stood. The son-in-law, the edgy and mad-eyed Mike, was very close to being a mirror-image Alf – as instinctively left-wing and permissive as Alf was instinctively right-wing and prudish, and, in his own way, just as unsure and uneasy beneath the carapace of prejudice.

Arguably, the one problematic relationship, in terms of the emotional weight of the show, was that between Alf on the one side and Rita and Mike on the other. This young couple were so relentlessly shrill, smug and self-righteous that, on some occasions, they made Alf seem – of all things – vulnerable, and thus encouraged, by default, a measure of audience sympathy for the old boorish brute. Without them, or with a more well-rounded and emotionally complicated couple, Alf might have been better exposed as the monster that he actually was, and not misrepresented merely as a bear that was regularly baited. As it was, however, one still had to be unusually obtuse or impetuous to mistake the treatment of Alf's views for something the show condoned instead of condemned.

Someone who did appreciate this distinction was none other than the Queen, who, like the rest of her immediate family, had become one of the show's most fervent fans ('This is the gentleman,' said Prince Philip when introducing Johnny Speight to Princess Anne, 'who writes your mother's favourite show').[31] Someone who most definitely did not, to an infamous extent, appreciate the distinction was Mary Whitehouse – a person who would do her utmost to get the show binned and banned.

Right from the start of *Till Death Us Do Part*, Whitehouse had regarded the programme as a major threat to her idea of a clean and decently broadcast Britain. Speight, in turn, had come very quickly to consider Whitehouse as his very special *bête noire* against whose rugged abuse he could keep on sharpening his biting wit. Every time, therefore, that she issued another moralistic edict, he responded with another satirical retort. In one early episode, for example, one of Alf's drinking friends remarked that, after seeing Whitehouse complaining yet again about 'hardcore' pornography on TV, he had sat up all night in the hope of seeing some for himself, and was most disappointed when it failed to appear. Betraying a bewildering blindness to irony, however, Whitehouse proved incapable of critical self-reflection, and kept on cranking up the criticisms.

On 17 January 1967, during an interview with BBC Radio 4's *The World at One*, Speight finally snapped, accusing Whitehouse of outrageous arrogance, hypocrisy and intolerance. Whitehouse responded the following day by issuing a writ against Speight and the BBC for libel: she claimed that Speight had 'implied' that she and her followers were actually 'fascists' who were concealing their true political beliefs under the cloak of a moral campaign. On 27 July, following some inconclusive legal discussions, the BBC and Speight agreed, reluctantly, to pay a 'suitable sum' to Whitehouse for the remarks that Speight had made.[32] The war, however, would rage on, with Speight infuriating her further by making Garnett one of her most avid fans:

ALF: Listen, that woman, that Mary Whitehouse, is concerned for the moral fibres and the well-being of this beloved country!

MIKE: *[Blows raspberry]*

ALF: Never mind about that *[Blows raspberry]*. It's being rotted away by your corrupt films and your telly! And your bloody BBC's the worst of the lot with that *Top of the Pops* and the *evil* painted youths dressed up like *girls*, and-and that middle-aged peroxide albino clunk-click *ponce* they've got in charge of it!

ELSE: I like it.

ALF: Yeah, *you* bloody would, wouldn't you! And-and-and their seductive music, with-with their singing about . . . *[Gets embarrassed]* men's fings an' that . . .

RITA: *[Sarcastically]* Oooh!

ALF: Driving the youth of the country to crime . . . and-and mugging – *[Looks around]* where's my bloody pipe gorn? – and-and

bestialities and-and rape and-and b-bloody gypsies . . . an'
refusing to go in to work . . . and-and-and-and bloody livin' off
the dole and-and havin' no respect and mocking their elders –
and calling me bloody skin-'ead!

Whitehouse would sit there, listening to this monster heaping praise
upon her, and then complain all over again. 'She was our biggest
publicist,' Warren Mitchell would say. 'Every time she protested to
the BBC, we got another million viewers.'[33]

The scripts – which were often being written or rewritten right up
to the last possible minute – continued to be remarkably sharp and
socially pertinent. Keynote political speeches by the likes of Harold
Wilson, Edward Heath and Enoch Powell were soon dissected and
discussed on the screen; opinion polls on such issues as the future role
of the Royal Family drew rapid and spiky responses; and the references to economic disputes, moral squabbles and cultural trends were
invariably kept up to date. Room was also found, as Warren Mitchell
would remember, for some playful yet pointed in-jokes:

> Johnny wrote one of the greatest lines. The son-in-law says, 'Dad.
> Hitler killed over six million Jews.' And Alf starts off saying, 'Oh
> yes, granted, he had his faults . . .' I'd have given anything to have
> written a line like that . . . but I did say to Johnny, 'You are racist in
> every episode, but you never say anything about the Jews.' And
> Johnny said, 'I don't like to, on account of you being Jewish.' So
> they wrote one wonderful episode where my son-in-law accuses me
> of being Jewish and says my real name is Solly Diamond the fish-
> monger. He says, 'Look, you use your hands, Dad, 'cos you're
> Jewish.' So I had to play the whole episode with my hands stuck in
> my pockets.[34]

The scripts alone made the show watchable, but the high quality of
the acting made it enjoyable. Dandy Nichols, for example, was a law
unto herself, and one of the best and most subtle scene-stealers in the
business. She could fascinate just by making the most fleeting adjust-
ment to her spectacles or the most furtive sideways glance. She could

make you feel that you were watching her *think*, and she could make you wonder, while Alf was ranting, what those lonely thoughts might be. She could also, when the mood took her, unsettle any other actor who was foolish enough to displease her. On one fractious occasion, for instance, she and the rest of the cast were rehearsing a scene in which, as usual, Alf was raging against everything from Arsenal Football Club to the Asian-run corner shop when, all of a sudden, Nichols (who had been leaning against the wall by the fireplace) straightened herself up, wandered past Warren Mitchell and sank into an armchair on the other side of the set. 'Dandy!' barked a furious Mitchell. 'What did you move for? Right in the middle of my speech you wandered vaguely right across me. You had no motivation for moving, Dandy. None. If you'd looked chilly and had seen a woolly on the chair, then right, we'd have known what was in your noddle. But to just wander across me . . . You were at position A and you moved, all of your own accord, to position B. Why?' Nichols looked at him impassively and said: 'I was at position A and I farted, so I moved to position B.'[35]

Mitchell's own performance, right from the start, had been mesmerisingly stark and brave, but, as the first series gave way to a second and then a third, the strain of playing such a tightly-bound bundle of bigotry and bile began to take its toll. 'I've come to hate the character,' he would say, 'to the point where I have to swallow hard before I can make him speak':

> I know it is brilliant writing, truthful and perceptive. I know that the whole point is to mirror the ugly prejudices in people. But I'm the one who has to do it. It is no joke. People tend to identify you with the character. One chap came over to me saying, 'I'm glad you had a go at the Queen and the coloureds.' – I told him, 'You stupid so-and-so, I was having a go at you!' He looked quite stupefied. This sort of thing worried me. [. . .] The more popular he became, the more he offended me . . . the awful chauvinism of the man was beginning to wear me down. And his drunkenness and 'all-women-are-rubbish' stuff is a joke that needs a pretty strong stomach to play indefinitely.[36]

There had always been tensions between Mitchell and the other members of the cast, and they seemed to worsen with each new run. 'You can be in failures and everybody loves each other,' Warren Mitchell would reflect after the final series was over, 'but when we were in a success like *Till Death*, it generated so much heat. We all hated each other at times, and loved each other – not often, but occasionally. I suppose it was true that Dandy Nichols and I did not get on well. She is a brilliant actress but Johnny was obsessed with the character of Alf and he wrote reams for me and Dandy had very little to say. She got very bored, as did the other members of the cast because they had very little to do compared to me. I think that listening to Alf week after week in rehearsal, Dandy did think of me as Alf and I understand that.'[37]

According to Tony Booth, when Mitchell was particularly edgy and irascible during a certain rehearsal, the ever-thoughtful Nichols reached into her 'remedies' bag and gave the actor a 'downer' to help him relax and sleep at the end of the day: when, however, he spent the rest of the afternoon in a disturbingly manic state, and then, quite uncharacteristically, came in late the following morning, it transpired that Nichols had 'confused' her downers with her uppers and given Mitchell a 'black bomber': 'I caught Dandy's eye and she winked. This was no accident. This was Dandy's brilliant and inventive retaliation against the aggravation Mitchell continually inflicted on all of us.'[38] It was clear that things were falling apart.

In February 1968, after three series, twenty-four episodes and two specials, the BBC – or, to be more specific, Tom Sloan – decided that the time had come for *Till Death* to depart. Sloan would later explain his decision by saying that, in his opinion, the comedy had become forced and the polemics had grown too crude: 'Where a rapier would have scored its point,' he remarked as he looked back on the celebrated show, 'it used a cutlass and only when the edge became dull, and a bludgeon substituted, did I cry "Halt".'[39] Johnny Speight was appalled, complaining to the Press that his show had been undermined by increasingly 'savage censorship' before suffering from the cruellest cut of all. Sloan responded by calling the writer's claims 'utter rubbish', and retorted that Speight had eventually, and knowingly, gone 'beyond the broad tolerance given to him' by the BBC.[40] Whatever the rights and wrongs of the decision – and opinion at the time appears to have been divided (some feeling that the show had indeed grown a little jaded and somewhat repetitive, while others believed that much still remained that deserved to be mocked) – there was an unprecedented amount of praise for what Speight and his show had achieved over the past three years.

On the morning after the final episode had gone out, a leader in *The Times* declared:

> The objection to *Till Death Us Do Part* is not that it is a malicious, lying attack on the English race, but that, alas, it is terribly true. Lives like that are led; marriages as sour as that of Alf and Elsie exist. There are those who toady to any authority, while announcing that, like other Britons, they never will be slaves, whose patriotism ineffectively disguises dread of the unknown, and terrified resentment of the new.[41]

A remarkable number and range of other newspapers and magazines followed this with their own reflections on the achievement and significance of the show. The London *Evening Standard*'s Milton Shulman observed:

> The fascination of Alf Garnett [. . .] lay in his ability to act as a distorting mirror in which we could watch our meanest attributes reflected large and ugly. Like some boil on the back of the neck that one cannot resist stroking or touching, this social aberration demanded the nation's attention. Some 18 million viewers – half of Britain's adult population – watched him weekly wallowing in the hates and fears and prejudices most of us have tucked away in some genteel niche of our psyche. [. . .] The difference between Alf and most of us is that he brandishes his decadent and violent ideas in the foul-mouthed linguistic setting that suited them best. He was too uncultivated and ignorant to realise that if he disguised them under a veneer of propriety, they would have been acceptable in some of our best drawing-rooms.[42]

A critic in *The Stage* remarked:

> From its beginning, *Till Death* introduced a vigorous new element
> into television comedy. It did not rely on jokes or funny situations
> but on the extreme attitudes and prejudices of its central character.
> [. . .] Although he was superficially a working-class character, Alf's
> brand of bigotry and dogmatism can be found anywhere. It was
> with these recognisable, far from humorous, and exaggerated fail-
> ings that Johnny Speight attacked unthinking acceptance of many
> of our society's standards and establishments. Somewhere, some-
> time, we have all heard one of Alf Garnett's tirades and have come
> away feeling smug about our own liberalism. Such a programme,
> with its vigorous realism of language, was certain to arouse the
> anger of those who, perhaps unconsciously, want to impose their
> own morality on viewers.[43]

George Melly added his own views in the *Observer*:

> [T]his Falstaff among programmes [. . .] managed [. . .] to contain
> general and universal truths within a particularised and temporal
> shell. By creating Alf Garnett and his wife, Johnny Speight has
> added two figures to the small pantheon of immortal comic mon-
> sters, the Père and Mère Ubu of the Welfare State, and in time this
> will appear to have been his great achievement. But it has had a
> more didactic function. He probed, with an admirable contempt
> for our sensibilities, into the social sores and abscesses which we
> have tried to ignore in the vain hope that they might cure them-
> selves. He is, in fact, a moralist and, like all true moralists, became
> the object of hatred and denigration to those who confuse moral-
> ity with 'good taste'.[44]

The *Daily Mirror* tried to sum these tributes up:

> No television character has sparked off such adjectival excesses as
> has this hairless malingerer with the distorted, hypocritical view
> of life, people, religion and Her Britannic Majesty. 'Brilliant',

'Despicable', 'Crude', 'Perceptive', 'Harmful' [and] 'Timely' are sample comments taken from the large dossier on *Till Death Us Do Part*. Alf Garnett was compulsive viewing for millions, even for those unfortunate ones who relished this confirmation of their own intolerance, unable to see the parody behind prejudice. Conceived by Johnny Speight, it was 'think' entertainment on a devastating level. Behind every belly laugh was that nagging thought: 'Is there a hint of Alf in me?'[45]

The memory of *Till Death Us Do Part*, understandably, would not go away. It had become part of television's conscience; a voice that had kept it critical. If anything, it took the absence of the show for it to be appreciated as fully as it deserved. Thanks to what it had said and done, the small screen now seemed bereft without something so outspoken and so extreme. It needed another big mouth. It needed another pest.

Johnny Speight – who described *Till Death* as 'the longest play I have written'[46] – would revive the show for four more series during the 1970s (and then, in 1985, brought Garnett back for six more series in a revamped production entitled *In Sickness and In Health*), and also wrote two feature film spin-offs – *Till Death Us Do Part* (1969) and *The Alf Garnett Saga* (1972). Many other writers, who had been inspired by what Speight had achieved, would attempt to follow in his footsteps and fashion their own forms of sharp-witted social satires. *Till Death* had made it possible. *Till Death* had made it seem like a public service.

'I didn't create Garnett,' Speight always insisted, 'society created him. All I did was report him.'[47] He did so brilliantly. He turned out to be the best and most responsible grass in the business.

Soldiers, Satire and Sci-Fi

Resolutely on the side of the angels . . .

The Goon Show, Sykes And A . . ., Hancock's Half-Hour, Steptoe and Son, Till Death Us Do Part: together, they certainly added up to an extraordinarily impressive list. They were by no means the sum, however, of the significant output of ALS. Ever since the mid-1950s, the company had been responsible for countless other productions and performances in multiple kinds of media, and, by the start of the 1960s, it was well established as one of Britain's major suppliers of high-class popular culture.

Whenever the country's radio, theatre, movie or television producers were searching for new ideas, formats or scripts, they thought, without any hesitation, of calling ALS. It came as no surprise, therefore, when, amongst other projects, ALS was asked to helped shape and sustain British television's first military-themed sitcom, *The Army Game*. It was not just, in this instance, that ALS was such a reliable source of good material; it was also because so many of its writers had themselves been marked by military life.

The Army Game was a calculated attempt by commercial television to attract the kind of massive prime-time audience that the BBC seemed able to summon at will with its own distinctive sitcoms. Sensing that the national mood was ready, after a few years of peace, for a light-hearted look at contemporary military life, and knowing that such a set of 'trapped relationships' would accommodate a broad enough range of characters to appeal to the rich and the poor, the north and the south and the young and the old, the planners went to work. The portents were unusually good: when the BBC imported the brilliant American post-war military sitcom, *The Phil Silvers Show* (featuring the scheming US Army Sergeant Ernest G. Bilko and his motor-pool platoon of work-shy gambling addicts), in April 1957, the response, in terms both of reviews and ratings, was extremely positive. ITV duly responded two months later with its own home-grown version, *The Army Game*.

Sid Colin, a writer who had begun his entertainment career as a guitarist, singer and songwriter with the popular RAF dance band, Ambrose and the Squadronnaires (one of his most famous songs, 'If I Only Had Wings,' became one of the forces' favourite tunes), was the man responsible for devising the new show. Having written previously for television series featuring the likes of Terry-Thomas, Alfred Marks, Arthur Askey and Ted Ray, and assisted Eric Sykes on the long-running radio series *Educating Archie,* he had seized on the chance to develop something stamped with his own signature for a potentially huge prime-time viewing audience.

Unlike the so-called 'organic' form of sitcom that the BBC was known to favour, Colin wanted a much more gag-driven format that would guarantee the commercial channel a steady flow of hearty laughs. Realising, therefore, that each thirty-minute episode would devour page after page of new material, he arranged to share the writing duties with a growing number of colleagues from (among other places) ALS, including, for the first two series, Larry Stephens, Maurice Wiltshire and Lew Schwarz; and then, for subsequent runs, John Antrobus, Barry Took, Marty Feldman, Brad Ashton and John Junkin.

Based loosely on the Boulting Brothers' 1956 movie satire *Private's Progress* (which featured Terry-Thomas struggling to control his 'absolute *shower*' of a platoon), the series followed the fortunes of a mixed bag of army conscripts based at Hut 29 of the Surplus Ordinance Depot at Nether Hopping in a remote part of Staffordshire. At the forefront of this troupe of misfits were the fragile-footed Pte 'Excused Boots' or 'Bootsie' Bisley (played by the diminutive comedian Alfie Bass), the always-hungry Pte 'Cupcake' Cook (Norman Rossington), the camp Pte 'Professor' Hatchett (Charles Hawtrey), the tall and thick Pte 'Popeye' Popplewell

Steptoe and Son: 'Pinter with shorter pauses and more laughs.'

Till Death Us Do Part: 'cleansing the Augean stable of our national vices of mind'.

Beyond Our Ken: a big radio show for 1950's *Little Britain*.

The cast of *Round the Horne*: Hugh Paddick, Kenneth Williams, Kenneth Horne, Betty Marsden and the announcer Douglas Smith.

TW3: 1960s satire reaches the small screen.

Eric Sykes takes centre stage with the cast of *Educating Archie*.

The sci-fi that kept on selling: Terry Nation and his Daleks.

The Goons reach BBC TV in 1963 as the puppet Telegoons.

'Hello dere!' A Goon meets a Telegoon.

A Telegoons *TV Comic* tie-in from 1964:
one of the many ways in which Beryl Vertue helped promote the
productions of ALS.

Red Foxx and
Demond Wilson
in the US TV
version of *Steptoe
and Son*.

All in the Family: America's celebrated adaptation of
Till Death Us Do Part.

The extraordinary
Beryl Vertue – agent,
manager, producer
and pioneer: 'How
extraordinary my life
has become just
because I said, "Oh,
all right then," all
those years ago'.

'Grovelling bastard!' Milligan accepts an honorary Knighthood from one of his biggest fans, Prince Charles, in 2000.

A genuine national treasure: Sykes receives his CBE in 2005.

(Bernard Bresslaw), the Bilko-style East End schemer Corporal Springer (Michael Medwin) and the bellowing Sgt-Major Bullimore (William Hartnell).

The fact that, when the show began, National Service was still compulsory in Britain (and the Second World War had only ended twelve years before) meant that most viewers – regardless of age or background – could identify easily with the basic situation, and sympathise with the plight of the men who were being ordered and organised and bullied about. Right from the opening episode (which went out on 19 June 1957), the sitcom seemed to find just the right mood: it featured tensions between working-class, middle-class and even one or two upper-middle-class figures; it pitted the new desire for greater freedom, prosperity and social mobility against the old culture of discipline, deference and rigid social distinctions; and it treated most serious and official things with a certain degree of cynicism. As an ensemble comedy, there were plenty of opportunities for each character to catch the eye and the ear of the public, and, as each series progressed via unusually long, American-style, thirty-nine-week seasons (featuring, behind the scenes, Nicholas Parsons as the regular warm-up man), the familiarity bred contentment. *The Army Game* soon grew into one of television's most popular and reliable shows – never surprising nor particularly inspiring but, while each edition was on, consistently engaging and inoffensively entertaining.

Thanks to the weekly repetition, a large part of the population was able to use the programme as one of their common points of pop cultural reference: Pte Popplewell's plaintive protestation, 'I only *arsked*,' for example, became a national catchphrase and also provided the title for a 1958 feature film based on the television series. The theme tune also proved so popular that, when released commercially in the same year, it reached number five in the UK singles chart. The broad appeal and simple structure of the show would even help encourage the establishment of the *Carry On* franchise, because the first movie in that sequence, *Carry On Sergeant* (1958), would feature several of the sitcom's actors, a number of very similar characters and one or two elements drawn directly from its old storylines.

A number of cast changes from 1958 onwards would, however, undermine the show's early popularity and, following the departure of a few more favourites, hasten the programme's demise. The first actors to leave, because of the lure of other work, were the pivotal trio of Hawtrey, Bresslaw and Hartnell. Hartnell's place was taken by Bill Fraser as the brusque bruiser Sgt Claude Snudge (a character that would prove popular enough – along with Alfie Bass's 'Excused Boots' Bisley – for a spin-off series called *Bootsie and Snudge* in 1960 written by Barry Took and Marty Feldman). Harry Fowler was drafted in as another Cockney shyster; Frank Williams (who would later appear in *Dad's Army* as the fey and flustered vicar) arrived as an epicene and ineffectual officer; and Dick Emery joined for one series as a character called Pte 'Chubby' Catchpole. Some of the old coherence, however, seemed to have gone, and, in the summer of 1961, the show was brought to a close. The fashion had simply faded.

Television comedy had grown significantly sharper, edgier and more ambitious during *The Army Game's* four-year run. By 1961, the keenest appetite was for satire. The very witty, bright and biting revue *Beyond the Fringe* (co-starring Peter Cook, Alan Bennett, Jonathan Miller and Dudley Moore) had just opened at London's Fortune Theatre following its celebrated debut at the Edinburgh Festival; in October of the same year, Peter Cook and his old friend Nicholas Luard opened up their nightclub, The Establishment, in Soho; and, at the end of the same month, the first issue of *Private Eye* went on sale. It was only a matter of time, therefore, before this new brand of humour – intelligent, irreverent and politically informed – reached the small screen.

It had arguably already done so, in a furtive fashion, via the early comedy of Johnny Speight. His work on *The Arthur Haynes Show* might have seemed, at first glance, quite conventional, but, as time went on, the range of social and political references had become striking, as had the increasingly critical tone. Speight then went on to show television producers how the new satire boom could be brought to a broad viewing audience when, in 1962, he (with a little help from his friends at ALS) conjured up a sublime piece of political mockery for Frankie Howerd to perform at The Establishment.

The BBC's liberal-minded Director-General, Hugh Carleton Greene, saw the new satire as something that suited his avowed ambition to open the windows, let in the fresh air and make the Corporation embrace and engage with contemporary life. He let it be known, therefore, that he wanted to see the BBC develop and broadcast a show that would prick pomposity in public life and question received opinion. His words were made swiftly into deeds. Although the project was, in practice, a cross-departmental effort, the resulting programme would formally be the responsibility of Grace Wyndham Goldie's Talks and Current Affairs department – which freed the show from any Light Entertainment anxieties about the dangers of seeming too 'serious', but burdened it with the worries of those hardened news reporters who were wary of the intrusion of any apparent 'frivolity'.

Overseen by Ned Sherrin, the 31-year-old former producer/director of the current affairs magazine programme *Tonight*, the new show's regular cast was to include the presenter David Frost; the actors Roy Kinnear, Lance Percival, William Rushton and Kenneth Cope; the journalist Bernard Levin; and, providing the musical interludes, the singer and actor Millicent Martin. A huge list of potential scriptwriters was compiled (the names included the future Labour politician Gerald Kaufman, Christopher Booker and Richard Ingrams from *Private Eye*, Frank Muir and Denis Norden, Michael Bentine, Dennis Potter and Peter Cook), and Associated London Scripts was identified as a major supplier of a broad and steady stream of monologues, sketches and up-to-the-minute topical material.

The first edition of *That Was The Week That Was* went out live at 10.50pm on the night of Saturday, 24 November 1962. Nothing quite like it had ever been seen before on British television. Flouting the convention that television should not acknowledge that it is television, the show made no attempt to hide its cameras, allowed the microphone boom to intrude and often revealed other nuts and bolts of studio technology. The show also adopted a relaxed attitude to its running time: loosely-structured and open-ended, it seemed to last just as long as it wanted and needed to last, even if that meant going beyond the advertised time for the ending.

The real controversy, of course, was caused by the content. Coinciding, by a stroke of satirical good fortune, with the coverage of the politically-charged Profumo affair,[1] *TW3* (as the show came to be called) did its research, thought its arguments through and seemed unafraid of anything and anyone. A politician would not just be mocked: his or her voting patterns, poor attendance record and extra-parliamentary interests would be brought to the public's attention. Every hypocrisy was highlighted and each contradiction was held up for sardonic inspection. No target was deemed out of bounds: royalty was reviewed by republicans; rival religions were subjected to no-nonsense 'consumer reports'; pompous priests were symbolically defrocked; corrupt businessmen, closet bigots and chronic plagiarists were exposed; and topical ideologies were treated to swingeing critiques. No one was spared.

Most of the media admired and revered it. *The Times*, for example, praised the show for its tone of 'sulphurous wit', its lack of 'snide self-satisfaction', its eschewal of 'random sniping [and] assaults on already demolished enemies' and its reflection of 'sharp, imaginative minds, who know the world they are ridiculing', and then went on to declare:

> *Private Eye* may lash out in all directions and provoke nothing more than a chorus of bland cooings: but let the BBC do something similar – as they did last Saturday – and they arouse the public to close on a thousand telephone calls and a threat of legal action. It is not irresponsible to state that this is exactly the kind of effect that a satiric programme should have.[2]

Hugh Carleton Greene was thrilled with *TW3*. He would say:

> Its audience became national in every sense, both in size and in distribution. Women liked it as much as men; the old as much as the young; the provinces as much as London. Nothing could be more misleading than the suggestion that it was a wicked metropolitan programme corrupting the innocence of Scotland, Wales, Northern Ireland and the more distant parts of England. It has

been suggested that it matched the national mood of wry dissatis-
faction. However that may be, it proved that an intelligent
programme of sharp humorous comment on current affairs could
hold an audience of many millions and could, as the headmaster of
a comprehensive school in Yorkshire told me, encourage an interest in current affairs among people both young and old who had
previously been too apathetic to read the newspapers with any
attention.[3]

It was not just another programme for this exceptional Director-
General. It was a beacon that illuminated the BBC's best new
intentions:

> It was frank, close to life, analytical, impatient of taboos and cant
> and often very funny. It was capable of being mature and compas-
> sionate – the full text of the programme which followed the
> assassination of President Kennedy was read on the motion of
> Senator Humphrey into the record of the United States Senate –
> and it was resolutely on the side of the angels. It dropped some bad
> bricks from time to time, but items which I for one should regard
> as not only defensible but positively good aroused as much offence
> as its undoubted mistakes.[4]

After one and a half exceptionally popular but also intensely controversial series, however, the show was cancelled at the end of 1963.
It was an unusually delicate time politically for the BBC: its Charter
was coming up for renewal, and all kinds of public figures, bruised
and bloodied by *TW3*, were lining up to inflict their revenge on the
Corporation; then, inevitably, there was Mary Whitehouse and her
'Clean-Up TV' cult, along with various other censorious cliques and
cranks, who were busy calling for the Director-General's head (and
some had even resorted to sending threatening letters to his family at
his private address); and, as 1964 was set to be a General Election
year, it was feared by some insiders that the show's political content
would prove too much of a problem.

According to Grace Wyndham Goldie, neither the Chairman of

the Board of Governors nor the Director-General had wanted to lose *TW3*: 'They enjoyed the sharp cutting edge of its mockery; were proud of having given it so much freedom; and defended it when it was attacked.'[5] Regular editorial interference seemed too cowardly – and contradictory – to be an option for saving the show. The problem hinged, as far as Greene was concerned, on a straightforward either/or: either keep giving the programme its head, or cut that head off – to attempt to interfere with an independent show, he reasoned, would be to betray it. A reluctant Greene decided, therefore, on the guillotine:

> The BBC had always been a target for those who could not bear to hear the expression of their opponents' views in a controversy. Now it was also a target for the defenders of taboos, especially those which surrounded public discussion of sexual matters. But we were also under fire from people who thought the BBC too timid. As I said at the end of 1963, 'It was in my capacity as a sub-versive anarchist that I yielded to the enormous pressure from my fellow subversives and put *TW3* on the air; and it was as a pillar of the Establishment that I yielded to the fascist hyena-like howls to take it off again.'[6]

There was far more outrage than delight at its premature demise. There were rumours of party political dirty tricks, religious inter-ference and unacceptable pressure from certain interest groups, and, although no such claims were proven, the sense of loss was palpable, and the show was mourned at length by other broadcasters, who presented the production team with a special BAFTA award at the end of its final run. The programme's influence, however, would con-tinue – inspiring a new tradition of satirical shows about news and current affairs that began with Johnny Speight's BBC1 special for Frankie Howerd, *A Last Word on the Election*, in October 1964 ('It's partly his own fault, I think,' he said of the newly-defeated Prime Minister, Alec Douglas-Home. 'Oh, yes. I think he's silly to himself. I'll tell you why: it was going round, all this talking, and he *would* bring *politics* into it . . .'),[7] then continued on the same channel with

Not So Much a Programme, More a Way of Life (1964–5) and *BBC-3* (1965–6), and then ran all the way through to, and beyond, *Have I Got News For You* (1990–).

The climate, during the mid-1960s, was changing on radio as well as television, and, once again, ALS writers were involved. Barry Took and Marty Feldman's *Round the Horne*, for example, was at the forefront of a new generation of comedy shows that, following on from The Goons, struck most of their blows with the left hand, eschewed the old clichés, tried to invent instead of imitate and embraced a more youthful form of irreverence.

Round the Horne came into being during 1964, after Took and Feldman were invited to devise a new series for Kenneth Horne (using the same cast as its popular predecessor, *Beyond Our Ken*) after Took's former partner Eric Merriman had abruptly severed connections with BBC Radio in an atmosphere of considerable acrimony (according to Kenneth Williams's diaries from the period, 'Merriman had incurred the wrath of the BBC').[8] When Took and Feldman carried on with the new show, a furious Eric Merriman – feeling, not entirely unfairly, that too many of the new characters bore too close a resemblance to those from *Beyond Our Ken* – seriously considered taking legal action for plagiarism, but he was persuaded to walk away.

Took and Feldman went on to produce their best and most masterful piece of work. Broadcast for the first time in 1965, *Round the Horne* featured playful parodies, satirical sketches and a repertory of comic characters, including the world's oldest dirty old man, J. Peasmold Gruntfuttock (Kenneth Williams); the libidinous English folk singer Rambling Syd Rumpo (also played by Williams); the hopeless chat show host, Seamus Android (Bill Pertwee); and the two old-fashioned 'luvvies' – ageing juvenile Binkie Huckaback (Hugh Paddick) and Dame Celia Molestrangler (Betty Marsden) – in their regular roles as the terribly British, *Brief Encounter*/Noël Coward-style lovers Charles and Fiona:

CHARLES: I know.
FIONA: I *know* you know.

CHARLES: I *know* you know I know.
FIONA: I *know* you know I know you know.
CHARLES: Yes, I know.

or:

CHARLES: Everything is the same . . .
FIONA: . . . and yet . . . somehow different.

Smart, pacy and endlessly inventive, the humour was charmingly impertinent, mocking all aspects of the Establishment while also poking fun at the latest *nouvelle vague* ('That's your actual French, that is').

The show soon became a national institution – as Barry Took would discover, to his great surprise and delight, while stuck in a traffic jam one Sunday lunchtime. 'I suddenly realised that everyone was listening to *Round the Horne*,' he would recall. 'It was incredible. Everybody had their windows open, the same sounds were coming out and everybody was laughing. A snarl-up had turned into a festival. It was unforgettable.'[9]

Much of the show's great appeal came from the fact that it managed to maintain such a fine and knowing balance between sauciness and subversion. Sometimes it sounded as though it was definitely 'up to something', and at other times it sounded as though it was just 'messing about'; the censors had drawn a line in the sand, but, like a Donald McGill seaside postcard, *Round the Horne* proved brilliantly adept at washing the trace away. Rambling Syd Rumpole, for example, kept on coming up with things from his 'ganderbag' (always set to the tune of 'My Darling Clementine') that seemed so cryptically crude as to short-circuit any watchdog's radar:

> *Joe, he was a young cordwangler,*
> *Monging greebles he did go,*
> *And he loved a bogler's daughter*
> *By the name of Chiswick Flo.*

> *Vain she was and like a grusset,*
> *Though her ganderparts were fine,*
> *But she sneered at his cordwangle*
> *As it hung upon the line.*
>
> *So he stole a woggler's moulie,*
> *For to make a wedding ring –*
> *But the Bow Street Runners caught him*
> *And the judge said he will swing.*
>
> *Oh they hung him by the postern,*
> *Nailed his moulie to the fence –*
> *For to warn all young cordwanglers*
> *That it was a grave offence.*
>
> *There's a moral to this story:*
> *Though your cordwangle be poor –*
> *Keep your hands off others' moulies*
> *For it is against the law. Oh!*[10]

Even more artfully devious were the camp couple Julian and Sandy, whose liberal use of gay code words and phrases – known collectively as 'polari' – amused and delighted a homosexual community that, until the law was finally changed in 1967, was still considered illegal. Polari (sometimes spelled 'palare') was a kind of private slang – evolved from a rich mixture of Latin, Romanes, Yiddish and Cockney elements – that had passed gradually over the course of a century or so from common theatrical usage into a more specialised kind of gay subculture. 'Bona' meant 'good' and 'fantabulosa' – 'wonderful'; 'lattie' meant 'house'; 'ogles' meant 'eyes', 'onk' – 'nose', 'willets' – 'breasts', 'luppers' – 'fingers' and 'lallies' – 'legs'; 'omni' meant 'man', 'polone' – 'woman' and 'omni-polone' – 'effeminate man'; and 'charpering omni', whispered urgently through the shadows, meant 'a policeman on the prowl'. A good deal of the effect of polari came from the manner in which it was spoken, so when a phrase was slipped into an otherwise 'ordinary' conversation it often acted as a verbal nudge, wink or goose. Took and Feldman relished every opportunity to do just that via the hugely popular Julian and Sandy sketches, and, as a consequence, not only preserved a great deal of material that would otherwise have been spotted and censored, but also persuaded many heterosexual listeners to laugh with, instead of at, this eminently likeable couple of characters.

In the following sketch, for example, Kenneth Horne served as the 'straight man' (in every sense) for the pair as they launched their 'Keep Britain Bona' political campaign:

HORNE: Hello – is there anybody there?

JULIAN: Oh, hello – I'm Julian and this is my friend, Sandy.

SANDY: Oh, hello, Mr Horne, how bona to vada your dolly old eek! Yes, we are the Universal Party – so-called because we're at it right, left and centre! Shake hands with your prospective member!

JULIAN: That's me, Mr Horne.

HORNE: You, Julian?

JULIAN: Yes, I stand behind the working man.

SANDY: Yes, and I stand behind Jule – I'm his campaign manager.

JULIAN: He's an old campaigner, Mr Horne.

SANDY: Mmm, he don't tell no lies.

HORNE: Er, no. Now why have you formed your own party?

SANDY: That's a good question.

JULIAN: Well, we couldn't see eye to eye with the other parties. The Labour Party because we disagreed about the prescription charges.

SANDY: And we fell out with the Conservatives because blue isn't our colour.

JULIAN: No – makes me right washed out.

SANDY: Right washed out, it does. No, we didn't like the curry of their favours. We was Liberal with our favours for a while. Then we felt personally betrayed by the actions of our Liberal member.

JULIAN: Yes.

HORNE: Oh, what did he do?

JULIAN: I can't bring myself to say it, Mr Horne. He . . . He . . . He went and got married!

SANDY: Don't carry on, Jules!

JULIAN: I can't help it!

SANDY: Jules, pull yourself together! It's to no avail! What's done is done! Now blow your nose on your rosette.

JULIAN: So then we thought: they've all let us down so it's time for a change. We formed our own party.

HORNE: And what are your policies?

JULIAN: Well, we have a three-pronged manifesto.

SANDY: Yes, we have. Three distinct prongs it's got. Show him, Jule – get out your manifesto.

JULIAN: Yes. Our points are these. One: Double the building pro-gramme so that there are latties for all.

SANDY: Latties for all!

JULIAN: Yes.

SANDY: Two: Remove American missiles from our shores.

JULIAN: Yes, particularly that one, er, what's it called? 'Polari', that's it.

SANDY: And our third prong: free crow's feet cream for all!

JULIAN: Yes – irrespective of race, creed or sex!

SANDY: Yes. That's your incentive bona.

HORNE: And what about old-age pensions?

SANDY: Don't you worry, Mr Horne, duck, we'll see you all right.

JULIAN: We'll make special provision for the over sixties.

SANDY: Yes, and the smaller sizes won't be left out, neither.

JULIAN: I think I can confidently say that I expect a huge poll.

SANDY: Mmmm, his name's Vladimir.[11]

The show, in spite of its craftiness, still attracted more than its fair share of complaints, but most of them were patently unsure as to what they were claiming had caused the offence: the words were all so weird, and the laughter so loud, that the self-appointed moral guardians came to suspect practically everything of being secretly salacious and therefore kept on sending in their criticisms – just in case. Took and Feldman responded by turning the tables on those who complained, admonishing them through their sketches for possessing such filthy minds:

> PADDICK: Come in.
> [FX: Door opens]
> PADDICK: Ah, Horne.
> HORNE: You sent for me, sir?
> PADDICK: Yes, as Controller of Thought, Word and Deed at the BBC, I'm afraid I have to reprimand you over the use of certain words and phrases in your show, which are capable of misinterpretation.
> HORNE: I'm surprised to hear that, sir. Was it something the Fraser Hayes Four sang, sir?
> PADDICK: No, I'm referring to *double entendres* contained in last week's show.
> HORNE: What specific phrase did you have in mind?
> PADDICK: Well, last week in your show, you distinctly said 'Hello'.
> HORNE: Well, what's wrong with that?
> PADDICK: Come off it, Horne! We all know what 'Hello' means! We all know what it *suggests*! It suggests, '*Hello*, what's *this* I can see through the keyhole? It's a scantily clad female doing an exotic dance with a ball of wool!'
> HORNE: Good heavens, is that what it suggests?
> PADDICK: That's what it suggested to me. Immediately. And later in the programme, you said you were going to introduce someone 'without further ado' – which suggests immediately that there had been *some* ado going on previously – and what *sort* of ado, might I ask? I know what sort of ado *I* had in mind! Which brings me to your name –
> HORNE: My name? What's wrong with Kenneth Horne?
> PADDICK: Everybody knows that ground-up moose's horn is an aphrodisiac. The very title of your show is an incitement to loose living and carrying on – I've found. You'll have to change your name.
> [ORCHESTRA: signature tune]
> P.A.: Ladies and Gentlemen, for the next thirty minutes it's: *Round the Larksleigh-Fortinbrass!*[12]

*

Marty Feldman (who moved on to make his own television show on BBC2) was replaced for the final series in 1968 by not one but two new writers – Johnnie Mortimer and Brian Cooke – while Barry Took stayed on to see it all through to the end (which came with the premature death of Kenneth Horne in 1969). As with *TW3*, however, the memory of *Round the Horne* would endure and inspire countless new shows on television as well as radio, and would even be revived itself on stage, in a 2004 tribute by Brian Cooke, called *Round the Horne . . . Revisited*.

The other significant strand in 1960s popular culture to which ALS contributed was the genre of science fiction. The decade in which human beings first ventured out into space saw the cultural responses grow more imaginative, pertinent and passionate – including, on British television, the BBC's new serial, *Doctor Who*.

Launched towards the end of 1963, the programme brought the niche to the masses. It featured a mysterious and somewhat irascible time-traveller (played by one of the former stars of *The Army Game*, William Hartnell), and his three young assistants – granddaughter Susan (Carole Ann Ford) and her science teacher, Ian (William Russell), and history teacher, Barbara (Jacqueline Hill) – and promised to follow them as they moved from place to place in time and space in their unlikely-looking spaceship – a midnight blue, 1950s-style police box that was actually an unusually commodious time machine known as a TARDIS (an acronym of 'Time And Relative Dimension In Space').

Starting on Saturday, 23 November, at 5.15pm on BBC1 (just after *Grandstand* and just before *The Telegoons*), the series sought to appeal to the broadest possible family audience, aiming to strike a tone that would excite the younger viewers while making the older ones sit back and think. A mixture of action and adventure with ideas and speculation, it was different enough to attract a relatively large (approximately 4.4 million)[13] and unusually curious audience. Unfortunately, however, this debut – decent enough though it was in terms of ratings at that time of night – was vastly overshadowed by the continuing reaction to the previous day's assassination of the American President John F. Kennedy; this, combined with a widespread power cut during the broadcast, prompted the BBC to repeat the programme the following Saturday, immediately before the next episode (which was seen by an estimated 5.9 million),[14] and *Doctor Who* was at last on its way.

Following the initial scene-setting sequence, the second (seven-episode) serial in the show's opening run was written at ALS by Terry Nation. Known at various stages in its development as 'The Survivors' and 'Beyond the Sun', his script reached the screen bearing the title 'The Mutants', and made an instant and extraordinary impact.

The story began with the TARDIS landing in a petrified forest on the planet Skaro, a seemingly moribund world with high levels of radiation. All is still and silent: a strong breeze is blowing, but the leaves on the trees never rustle; the ground is covered in dust and ashes, yet flowers of a sort are still growing. The curious Doctor, drawn deeper and deeper into this peculiar world, cannot resist exploring what appears to be a deserted city in the distance, but, upon arriving, discovers that he and his trio of fellow travellers are not actually alone after all: they are captured by sinister metal creatures who glide silently through the corridors and walkways like metallic ghosts – the Daleks. The survivors of a deadly nuclear war with their enemies the Thals, the Daleks have mutated into creatures dependent upon their surrounding protective cases to move and keep them alive. Beyond the boundaries of the city, meanwhile, the scattered Thal survivors – who are peaceful, physically perfect, human-like creatures – are fast running out of food and supplies. With the TARDIS temporarily out of action, the Doctor and his companions have to persuade the Thals to compromise their pacifist principles and fight the ruthless Daleks (who are planning to detonate another nuclear bomb) before it is too late.

As soon as each episode was over, everyone seemed to want to talk about the Daleks, but, ironically, this was the one aspect of Terry Nation's script that was not entirely his own. Although the concept (like the name) was definitely his, the look was, to a great extent, the work of someone else: a BBC designer named Raymond P. Cusick. Cusick had learnt his trade through working on such shows as *Sykes*

And A . . ., *Hugh and I* and several mini-series before assuming a more pivotal role on *Doctor Who*. The notion of Nation's 'hideous and machine-like' Daleks fired his imagination.

Cusick knew what he did not want: the stereotypical masked man dressed up in a silver suit with some kind of aerial on his head. What he had to do was dream up what he *did* want – and then work out how, on a limited budget (of about £62 per Dalek),[15] he could afford to bring it into being. Noting Nation's description during a telephone conversation of the monsters as gliding about like the Georgian State Dancers – who seemed to glide across the stage by taking tiny steps with feet that were concealed under long, wide dresses – Cusick's first attempt (using a pepper pot from the BBC canteen as an initial point of reference) was to construct a conical, one-armed creature that, by some means or other, would slide or hover across the screen; he followed this by fashioning a shorter, two-armed design featuring a diamond-patterned 'skirt' section and a large camera lens poking out of the dome. Nation had described each monster as having hands shaped like clamps, but, in his next attempt, Cusick decided to give them one sucker-arm and one gun-arm, and then, as he studied the overall look, he judged the design to be more or less ready for the screen.

His next task, however, was to find a way to enable the construction to *reach* the screen. His first thought was that an operator might be able to move about inside on a child's tricycle, but it was soon found that no tricycle was small enough to fit within the fibreglass casing. Under growing pressure to meet his deadline, Cusick had to compromise in the short term and settle for either rolling the creatures around on nylon castors or using wheels connected by bicycle chains to hand cranks, while room was still found for a hot and sweaty human operator (attired in a T-shirt, 'lightweight slacks' and plimsolls)[16] to hide inside and manipulate the various rods and plungers. The basic effect, however, still struck Cusick as encouragingly sharp and powerful, and he felt confident when it came to testing it in front of an audience. 'Before rehearsals started,' he would recall, 'the cast and other members brought their children along and they were shown the Daleks and talked to the Dalek operators, but then when rehearsals started the operators got into the Daleks and started moving, and at that point all the children screamed and ran out of the studio!'[17] He had made his monsters.

Cusick's creative role, therefore, was crucial, but Terry Nation was the one who gave the Daleks their distinctive collective personality. In an interview with the *Radio Times* in 1964, Nation summed up the 'essence' of the Daleks as being most reminiscent of the Nazis whom he had dreamed of and dreaded during his youth: 'They are utterly brutal, totally without moral responsibility. They cannot distinguish between good and evil.'[18] Nation knew exactly what he was doing: with each mechanical move of their metallic carapace, each upward thrust of their taut little eye stick and each synthesised shriek of *'Exterminate!'*, he had plenty of viewers twitching, squirming or sinking into – or behind – the living-room sofa. The *frisson* of fear was there.

Nation seized on it. More Dalek fictions would follow, and, within less than a year of their debut, the newspapers began talking about 'Dalekmania'. There would be Dalek dolls, Dalek cartoon strips, Dalek 'novelisations', Dalek wallpaper, Dalek crockery, Dalek jigsaws, Dalek quizzes, Dalek board games, Dalek records ('I'm Gonna Spend Christmas With a Dalek' by The Go-Go's), Dalek playsuits and even Dalek baby plates.[19] Thanks in large part to Terry Nation, science fiction in Britain became part of pop commerce as well as pop culture.

The art, however, remained the primary ambition, and Nation (once he had realised that the public would not allow him to kill off his creatures for good) was keen to see his monsters come back to life in bigger and, ideally, better-funded media. In 1965, for example, Nation would transfer the Daleks to the stage, collaborating with his *Doctor Who* colleague David Whitaker on a play entitled *The Curse of the Daleks*, which opened at Wyndham's Theatre in London on 21 December. The reviews were generally very favourable. *The Times*, for example, judged the Daleks to be 'no less compelling on the stage than the television screen', and found the drama to be very effective: 'Simultaneously exploiting the properties of the whodunit and science fiction, the authors have concocted an ultimately exciting adventure.'[20] A movie version was released during the same year – *Doctor Who and the Daleks*, starring Peter Cushing as the idiosyncratic Time Lord – and it found a similarly appreciative audience.

Buoyed by all of the success, Nation (who, after taking on the *Doctor Who* job to help pay the rent, was now the proud owner of a fifteen-room Elizabethan mansion near Teynham in Kent) would move on to write other kinds of science fictions, and cause the formation of several more sci-fi cults. The popularity of the Daleks in *Doctor Who*, however, would prove more than enough to ensure the acceptance of his legend, and provide the inspiration for a succession of new stories that would stretch on into another century.

It all added up to a remarkable achievement for ALS. Whatever the public had craved throughout the past decade – sitcoms, satire, sci-fi, sketches or stand-up – the company had created. No other group of writers had made so many people so happy so often. Although the team would not last for ever, what ALS did next ensured that its legacy most certainly would.

5. The Exit

BRIAN: Look. You've got it all wrong. You don't need to follow me. You don't need to follow anybody! You've got to think for yourselves. You're all individuals!
FOLLOWERS: Yes, we're all individuals!
BRIAN: You're all different!
FOLLOWERS: Yes, we are all different!
DENNIS: . . . I'm not.

The Legacy of ALS

*At the time, you don't think you're a pioneer. You just think
you're doing your job.*

In 1962, *The Times* published an important article about the state
of British humour entitled 'New Race of Humanisers of Popular
Comedy'. Surveying the current scope and styles on show, the report
declared that popular comedy had grown up: 'The permissible range
of comedy has been substantially enlarged: television satire is no
longer confined to the sterile exercise of satirising television; comedians are no longer restricted to exploiting one fixed personality –
they can even change character; the old pressure to pack in the max-
imum number of laughs has been relaxed.'[1]

A new era, it was said, had begun: '[T]he age of the catch-phrase
and the quick-fire gagman has departed and has been succeeded by a
race of performers and writers who have humanised comedy and
who rarely use gags at all.'[2] Comedy was now so much richer and
deeper, and had moved in the direction of drama.

'The change might not have been so successful,' the report added,
'had it not been for the foundation some eight years ago of
Associated [London] Scripts, a company that has numbered on its
books [most of] the young men of British comedy who managed,
while working within the framework of the commercial system, to
bring about an internal revolution.'[3] Such praise was, by this time, a
fairly common event for ALS – even though *Steptoe and Son* had only
just started and *Till Death Us Do Part* was still to come.

Something else, however, was happening inside the offices of
Associated London Scripts that was starting, with little or no coverage

in the Press, to revolutionise the ways in which Britain's most popular programmes were produced, promoted and protected. The brilliant Beryl Vertue was, in her own very pleasant manner, busy questioning all of the things that everyone else had accepted as givens.

'They wcrc all such exciting times,' she would say, 'because there were so many "firsts".'[4] One such 'first' concerned how shows – or certain elements within particular shows – were marketed. In those days, television seemed disinclined to treat even its best programmes as anything particularly 'special'. They went on air, went off air and then, if they were not repeated, they were often simply wiped to make way for what was due next. Television treated itself as a chronically evanescent form of entertainment: it did not seem to realise how *treasurable*, at its best, it could be. Avid fans of certain shows had nothing to keep, nothing to cherish, nothing to return to – except their own memories.

Vertue responded to this absence. She could see how well loved the likes of *Hancock's Half-Hour* and *Sykes* had become, and she began to investigate how that affection might better be engaged and sustained by the programme-makers. One idea, she would recall, that sparked a major revolution in this area concerned the merchandising of memorabilia:

Merchandising at the BBC began because of us. There wasn't a department for it in those days, there was just one man called 'Roy' something, who just sort of 'looked into' merchandising issues as part of his job. It was all very new, so we all had to get it together as we went along. I had the idea to do something about the Daleks and *Doctor Who* in America, because Terry Nation was writing the programmes then, and so I went to New York – such a big thing for me in those days – and I told a toy manufacturer there about it and he got hugely excited, saying if the series was on the network over there he'd be able to make all of these toys and licence them. The networks didn't know what I was talking about, however, so that attempt came to nothing, but this toy manufacturer still kept sending me all of these presents, these *huge* toys – like great big cars and a massive one-man band and God knows what else – for my two small children. They were all free gifts, but of course when they hit customs I got charged for all of this, and I couldn't really afford to keep paying for them, so each time another one arrived I'd be thinking, 'Oh God! How much will it be this time?'[5]

It was not long, however, before Vertue and the BBC had developed some practicable strategies and fans could buy their own mementoes of their favourite shows. Apart from the astonishingly wide range of Dalek and *Doctor Who*-related memorabilia, consumers could also buy, among other things, a *Hancock's Half-Hour* board game (made by Chad Valley); *Telegoons* glove puppets, dolls, comics and colouring books (published by a company called Tonwen); two *Steptoe and Son* jigsaw puzzles (produced by Tower Press); and a growing number of single, extended and long-playing vinyl records featuring original or re-recorded shows, scenes and sketches.

The massive and lucrative industry that television and radio-related merchandise would later become – all of the tie-in books, cassettes, videos, CDs and DVDs, and all of the various figurines, watches, plates, posters, pens, pads, bags, badges, key fobs, calendars, T-shirts and mobile phone downloads – grew out of this ALS initiative. Every future fan – and, indeed, every future commercial operator in this area – would thus owe Beryl Vertue a very real and significant debt.

Vertue, however, was by no means finished there. Even more importantly for the long-term interests of the industry, she clarified the nature of the ownership, and pioneered the marketing, of programme format rights. She recalled: 'When we used to do the contracts, they always had this clause about selling the programmes overseas – so the copyright all moved. And in the very early days I thought, "Well, they'll never sell those programmes overseas; they won't understand them." So I just started crossing the clauses out. But it turned out that, because of me going "scribble, scribble, scribble" over those clauses, the writers and us kept the format.'[6] It all started, said Vertue, with the first dramatist at ALS, Peter Yeldham:

I was just looking for ways to help Peter. I had the idea that, if you couldn't sell certain plays and programmes and things in Britain, the writers could, if the idea and the script and everything were good, do their own productions. So I did sell a play of Peter Yeldham's to Germany. That got me thinking: 'What else can we do?' I'd got this bee in my bonnet that this would work, so I decided that I would go round to all the television stations in the different countries in Europe – which was a huge adventure for me because I'd only been abroad once before, and certainly never been there before on my own – and see what I could do. Alan and Ray, in particular, got quite excited about me doing this, and they bought me some new clothes so I would look smart. I bought a hat, too, because I'd seen an advert on a bus that had said: 'To get ahead, get a hat!' And I got all the names of where these television stations were from different embassies – because I didn't have a clue – and I wrote to them all, saying, 'Could I have a meeting, please?' Then off I went to Europe in this new red coat, with a bit of black fur on it, and a hat![7]

It definitely was a very big, and exhausting, adventure: 'It turned out to be quite an effort, because, unlike in Britain with just the BBC in London, these other countries had networks all over the place. In Germany, for example, I went to one in Cologne and one in Stuttgart and one in Hamburg and one in Mainz and one in Munich, and then I went to one in Austria, and then I went to France – *that* was a waste of time! – and so on and on.'[8]

Eventually, her hard work began to pay off, and some ground-breaking deals were struck: 'Germany was the first place where we were successful. They had much more money than we were used to getting at home, and so they paid the writers very well for these scripts. It was quite hard selling them comedy, because they couldn't always understand why it was funny, so I used to act it out and try to make them see.'[9] Whatever Vertue did, it must have worked and they got the joke, because they bought the rights to *Hancock* and then, later on, the ones to *Till Death Us Do Part* as well. She would also sell the format of *Hancock's Half-Hour* to Finland (where it was remade as *Kaverukset* in 1961) and, some years later, to Norway (where, as well as in Denmark and Sweden, it would run for many years as a hugely successful sitcom called *Fleksnes Fataliteter*).

The breakthrough had been made, and, as Vertue would explain, the list of interested countries began to grow:

> Where we were very successful with the programmes was in Holland. They did very well indeed with their own productions. When they did *Steptoe and Son* [as *Stiefbeen en Zoon* in 1963], they invited Alan and Ray and me over to Hilversum to see their version of the programme and meet the artists, and when we got off the plane we were taken across the runway in a horse and cart, and then straight into a press conference with this barrage of cameras and a huge crowd of journalists! We hadn't encountered something like that before – it was really splendid.[10]

Suddenly, it seemed, the shows were the stars, and the writers were in charge. Vertue came back to London from Hilversum more convinced than ever that her new policy held huge potential:

> That experience in Holland gave me the idea that you could do this – sell formats abroad – not just every once in a while, with special cases, but actually as part of your usual service for a show. Any good show. So after that I thought, 'I'll try it in America.' And I did. I sold the formats of *Till Death Us Do Part* and *Steptoe and Son*, which both became huge in America, because I managed to find a wonderful writer/producer called Norman Lear. He was very smart and very shrewd. He understood very well what had made these programmes work so well in the UK, and then took the essence of what made each one work and then made it into something 'American'.[11]

Steptoe and Son became *Sanford and Son*, starring the veteran comedian Redd Fox as an ageing, Los Angeles-based, African-American junkman with Demond Wilson as his frustrated son, and would run from 1971 to 1977, attracting very appreciative reviews and peaking at number two in the network ratings. 'Our contribution to *Sanford and Son* was very limited,' Ray Galton would say. 'We just gave our permission for them to use our scripts and characters in the adaptation. The first series was something like fourteen programmes, eleven of which were based on our shows. After that it was turned into a gang show and we had nothing to do with it. They brought in aunties, friends, next-door neighbours . . . but it was still our idea, just!'[12]

Till Death Us Do Part was remade as *All in the Family*, starring Carroll O'Connor as Archie Bunker, and would run for longer in the US – from 1971 to 1983 – fare even better, sensationally so in fact – topping the ratings for six consecutive years and winning innumerable awards – and spawn no fewer than three high-profile spin-offs (*Maude*, which featured the future *Golden Girls* star Bea Arthur as Mrs Bunker's outspoken, hyper-liberal cousin; *The Jeffersons*, starring Sherman Hemsley and Isabel Sanford as a pre-Cosby *nouveau riche* African-American couple; and *Gloria*, which followed Sally Struthers as the Bunkers' young, independent-minded daughter). Suddenly, other US television producers started looking to Britain for fresh ideas, and, even if one or two of the next few promising-sounding imports (such as *Dad's Army*)[13] petered out at the pilot stage, the all-important breakthrough had been made by ALS.

Vertue would continue to champion the policy of selling basic format rights – right the way through to the 1990s, when, on behalf of her own company, Hartswood Films, she would make headlines on both sides of the Atlantic for striking a lucrative deal to sell *Men Behaving Badly* in the US to the production team of Carsey-Werner-Mandabach, and, in 2003, *Coupling* to the giant network channel NBC – and the rest of the television industry would follow gratefully in her footsteps. It all came, she later reflected modestly, from that 'little idea' she had at ALS:

> It *was* pioneering, but, at the time, you don't think you're a pioneer. You just think you're doing your job. Because I was just trying to be a good agent and doing what I could to maximise the work. All I thought was, 'Hmm, that's a good idea – if I can't sell something *this* way, I'll try to sell it *that* way.' It just seemed at the time

like a common-sense approach. It turned out in the end, I suppose, to be quite a bright thought.[14]

Beryl Vertue never seemed to stop having these bright thoughts.
She looked to strengthen the independence and influence of ALS (as
well as bolster its bank balance) by advising her fellow directors to
become shareholders in one of the best of the new regional ITV
companies, Yorkshire Television.[15] She also, in the mid-1960s, started
looking to help her colleagues assume greater control in movies, too:

> In those days, all the major Hollywood film studios had offices in
> London – Paramount, Columbia, Twentieth Century-Fox and so
> on – that were really all going concerns; they weren't just post
> offices. So they'd always alight on us and ask who our best writers
> were – there was a growing interest there. And on one day in par-
> ticular, this producer came and said he'd got this book and he
> wanted some really good writers to adapt it, so I put him in touch
> with Galton and Simpson. Then I watched this man go to
> Columbia and get the money to pay for the book and the writers.
> And I thought to myself, 'Just a minute: if I knew what that man
> knew, *I* could do that! So that's why I started to say that I thought
> we ought to start getting into films. It was really so that we could
> be more involved in our own work, by getting money from the
> source, so to speak, rather than going through these intermedi-
> aries.[16]

Having convinced her colleagues of her prudence, she pushed ahead
with typical shrewdness, commitment and enthusiasm:

> So we formed Associated London Films, and then Alan and Ray
> wrote a film script called *The Spy with a Cold Nose*. I kept read-
> ing in *Variety* about a man called Joe Levine, who was a very
> successful American producer who had this film called *Hercules
> Unchained*, and it kept saying 'boffo' or 'huge box-office' in
> *Variety* whenever it was mentioned, so I got his address and sent
> the script to him. Then I phoned him to tell him I'd sent it – it

didn't dawn on me that he might not accept my call, because I'd never called America before, but he did take it – and then he called back to say he'd read it, and liked it, and 'would I like to go to America and talk about it?' That was literally the first time I went to America. So they paid for me to go to New York to meet him and his partner, who was called Leonard Lightstone, to discuss the film. He said that they wanted to do it, and I said that the script was owned by Associated London Films so we would like to produce it. Then he went on talking about various other things and eventually I thought to myself, 'I'm going to have to come clean here.' So I said to him, 'Actually, I don't know *how* to produce it. We haven't done that yet. So, what I thought was, if *you* did it, I could be "Associate Producer" or something, and watch how you do it.' Well, he and his partner thought that was ever so funny. He said, 'Well, I don't know. Let's let her do it – you never know, she might be good at it!' Then they laughed away again, and that's exactly what happened. I had a contract for £100 a week and a chair with my name on it, and we went into films![17]

It did not take long, however, for Vertue – who was such an exceptionally quick learner – to crave more of a 'hands-on' opportunity to acquire some practical experience: 'They seemed to be doing everything. That was understandable but, after a while, it upset me. I kept going home to my husband and saying, "Everything's going on and I'm not *doing* anything!" I was used to being at the centre and making everything happen, and so all of this sitting about every day in my chair that had the name on it was making me a bit embarrassed. But then one day I suddenly thought, "Actually, if *I* hadn't done what *I* had done, none of you would have a job." So I bucked up after that!'[18] She continued to watch, listen and reflect, and, as the long and elaborate process went on, she began to feel more confident about the prospect of pursuing future projects on her own: 'It was a good experience. It was an exciting way to learn and move us on a bit.'[19]

Vertue went on to do just that. She moved ALS on a bit:

Then Eric Sykes – who'd been wanting to direct for a quite a while – came up with his idea for *The Plank*, which was wonderful. Making that was one of the really happy times in my life, because it was so funny. I mean, Eric and Tommy Cooper: gosh, the lunchtimes were a riot! I got the money for that from Bernard Delfont, who had all of these theatres and wasn't in films at all, but I needed the money – the budget was £23,000 – and he knew everybody who was going to be in it. He said, 'Oh, I don't know about that, Beryl. What are you going to *do* with it?' I said, 'Well, I thought that Rank have always got this second film – you go to see the big film and they always have a little film as well. So I thought that *they* would buy it.' And in the end he said, 'Yes, I'll give it to you,' and he gave us the £23,000, all of which he most certainly got back, and Rank did buy it. It did very well. Rank said how '*useful*' it was because whatever their big film was, *The Plank* always went with it.[20]

There was yet more from Vertue still to come. Having broadened the business and extended its interests, she thought that the logic was for ALS to now keep on moving and expanding, and so, bearing in mind the ambitions of many of her writers, she turned her attention to the theatre. ALS had actually been producing stage plays by some of its members, such as Johnny Speight, since the start of the 1960s via 'ALS Presentations Limited', but, by the middle of the decade, Vertue began contemplating establishing a 'proper' ancillary company, this time called Associated London Theatre, to complement the activities of the newly-formed Associated London Films.[21] The problem was, she realised, that ALS would require some external financial help if they were going to make a serious attempt at further progress:

I just found by this time that we were all getting on and being busy with one thing or another, but we still didn't have the money to be producers. Because ten per cent of an agency doesn't enable you to produce anything. The other thing was that, although there were other really good people around, I was just so busy doing all these millions of things, and still having to check on how much toilet paper we had and goodness knows what else, I thought, 'If only we could be with somebody else, we could grow in an organic way. I didn't want us to be with another agency – that would just mean we'd be a bigger agency. I wanted us to be with someone who'd help us to develop. So I mentioned this to our lawyer, Oscar Beuselinck.

The lawyer, Vertue recalled, had some interesting news to share:

As it happened, a man called Robert Stigwood, whom I'd never heard of and never met, had said to Oscar Beuselinck that he wanted to expand his own interests laterally into film and television. Stigwood, at that time [the start of 1967], had gone to Brian Epstein to run NEMS Enterprises – NEMS was ever so important then because of The Beatles – and he took The Bee Gees and The Cream with him there. So Oscar introduced us. We met a number of times, and I was really fascinated by this man; we talked about philosophies and all kinds of things, and he seemed to me to be really very clever and interesting. He was also quite curious about Associated London Scripts, so we talked about that and what we'd done and now hoped to do. It was all very casual and relaxed – there wasn't any plan – but we both got to know where the other was hoping to go, and we started to think of how we could help each other get there.[22]

The 33-year-old Stigwood was certainly ambitious: since merging his own management company with NEMS and assuming joint control alongside Brian Epstein, he had been trying to buy Epstein out and establish himself as the company's sole managing director. Epstein, by this time, was tempted: after five incredibly challenging, eventful and intense years of looking after The Beatles (who had recently stopped touring and, he feared, might not need him any more) as well as numerous other musical acts, he was worn out, barely sleeping, self-medicating to a dangerous degree and still pursuing an extremely hazardous private life as, like Stigwood, a promiscuous but closet homosexual. He often resorted to undergoing deep-sleep therapies at The Priory (the rehab clinic at Roehampton that catered to many a stricken celebrity), and it was during one of his brief stays there that he decided to sell his controlling interest in NEMS to Stigwood and his partner (and fellow NEMS director) David Shaw for the cut-down price of just £500,000. He gave the two men until September 1967 to come up with the money.[23]

Epstein could not have been thinking properly, because The Beatles alone had been 'bid' for the previous year by a consortium of American businessmen for $20m, and there were also question marks hanging over Stigwood and Shaw: the former was still an undischarged bankrupt in his native Australia, while the latter had been named publicly at the start of the previous year in connection with a major bond-washing scandal.[24] It did not take Epstein long, once he was back out of the clinic, to change his mind and declare that the deal could not include either The Beatles (who had told Epstein: 'If you somehow manage to pull this [deal] off, we can promise you one thing. We will record *God Save the Queen* for every single record we make from now on and we'll sing it out of tune. That's a promise. So if this guy buys us, that's what he's buying')[25] or Cilla Black (whom Epstein regarded as a special personal protégé), but Stigwood was undeterred; he felt that he was heading in the right direction, and continued talking informally to possible future partners – including Beryl Vertue at ALS.

Vertue listened and liked what she heard:

> Eventually, it came to the point where I told Alan and Ray and Eric and Spike and Frankie Howerd about this idea, and they were vaguely interested to varying degrees but were just waiting to see what happened. Then an offer – to buy part of the company, and, if that went well, perhaps buy all of it at some later stage – was made by Robert and NEMS, and we got involved in proper business negotiations, with bits of paper floating about, but then, very suddenly, Brian Epstein died [on 27 August 1967]. His brother, Clive, was so flummoxed by all of this that the last thing he wanted to do was expand NEMS any further.[26]

Stigwood and Shaw made their move and staked their claim on

NEMS – as did a number of other directors – but, as the pair had failed to find (or at least produce) the £500,000 before Epstein died, the offer was deemed withdrawn by NEMS' lawyers. Stigwood and Shaw were paid off with £25,000 and given back full control of the clients they had brought in (including The Bee Gees, Cream and Oscar Beuselinck's son, Paul – a young singer who would later be better known as Paul Nicholas), and, in November 1967, they left to pursue their interests elsewhere.[27] 'Robert Stigwood leaving was disappointing for us,' said Beryl Vertue, 'because, when he went, our deal fell apart. I thought, "Oh, that's a shame. That had sounded really good." But that seemed to be that.'[28]

It was not long, however, before the situation changed again and, as Vertue would recall, the deal – or at least a new one very much like it – was suddenly back on the table:

A few months went by, and then one day I got a call from someone called David Shaw, who was the financial partner of Robert Stigwood, and he said that Robert had formed a new company and would be interested in talking to us again. So I said, 'What is this company called?' He said, 'The Robert Stigwood Organisation.' So I said, 'Well, it's not the same as NEMS, is it?' You know, even after Brian Epstein had died, NEMS was still very, very, important and prestigious in those days. So I responded to this by saying, 'No, thank you, I don't think so.' But he then said, 'Look, why don't you just come for a meeting?' I said, 'Oh, I don't know . . .' This would be the second big thing in my life that I very nearly blew: the first was almost not bothering to go on the trolley-bus to Shepherd's Bush back in 1955, and now the second one was almost saying that I wouldn't be bothering to go to this meeting. So he said, 'Well, will you just come and meet Robert? Just come and have a bit of a chat. Will you do that?' I said, 'All right.' So off I went, and in about ten minutes we were talking just like we were before. I thought to myself, 'You're being really stupid, Beryl, here. You're fussing about what's the name of the company, when what is really important and fascinating is the man himself.' So I was back where I was before: hugely enthusiastic.[29]

The problem Vertue had now was to win the support of her fellow directors:

> That did prove quite a problem, and I knew it would be, because not everyone had the same aims, and, besides, this offer wasn't from NEMS, you know. So I had to do a bit of persuading there. Eventually, some of them got a bit more enthusiastic, and some of them didn't: Galton and Simpson and Frankie Howerd and I went. Eric Sykes didn't want to go, though, and neither did Spike Milligan, who said, 'I don't think I want to be a director of *things*. I think I'll just stay put in Orme Court.' And so he and Eric stayed in Orme Court, and we all went off to the Robert Stigwood Organisation at 67 Brook Street.[30]

The split – which would be made official on 26 February 1968 when a £2m merger with RSO was reported[31] – was not an amicable one. Inside the offices at Number Nine Orme Court, the final meeting, towards the end of 1967, was heated, angry and desperately unhappy. Spike Milligan and Eric Sykes felt betrayed. Milligan, his agent and manager Norma Farnes would later recall, exploded with rage: 'Stigwood, he said, wanted to buy the talent to gain respectability. Getting into his stride, Spike reminded everyone that ALS had been started to nurture all concerned. Now the rats were deserting a very happy and successful ship. Let them go; they could sell their souls for gold if they wanted, the traitors. He was staying put. "On my own, if need be."'[32]

Eric Sykes felt very much the same. Although, many years later, he would admit that he and Milligan had been so immersed in their own respective writing projects at the time that, had a bomb blown up in the next but one Bayswater street, neither of them would probably have responded with anything more than an absent-minded mutter of 'Come in.' This particular bombshell had exploded in their own street, under their own feet, without any prior warning, and the shock had been immense. So much of the negotiations, Sykes felt, must have gone on before in secret, that the actual suggestion of a move struck him as 'a fait accompli', and that cut him to the quick.[33]

'I found it hard to take in the audacity of such shenanigans being carried on without my knowledge; after all, Associated London Scripts was the brainchild of Spike and me. In no uncertain manner I told [Vertue, Galton and Simpson] I was not about to leave ALS and I was sure that Spike [was] of the same mind.'[34]

An outsider might well conclude that both parties were in the right (or at least not in the wrong): Vertue was only following the business logic of someone who was responsible for managing a growing agency in an increasingly competitive market, and, by doing what she had done, she had made it much more likely that Galton and Simpson and others could pursue their future ambitions in a number of different media; Milligan and Sykes, on the other hand, had reached a stage in their lives where they felt that they had earned the right to do as they wished, stay true to their principles and refuse to play the game the world's way. The split, in a way, made sense to both groups, even though the fact of it, at the time, caused so much hurt and sadness.

Beryl Vertue, Frankie Howerd, Ray Galton, Alan Simpson and their young assistant Tessa Le Bars duly moved off to join RSO ('leaving the better half of ALS behind them,' a still-bitter Eric Sykes would say),[35] where they would continue to flourish. Spike Milligan, Eric Sykes and Norma Farnes stayed at Orme Court, where they would stay happy. Vertue did try to persuade Farnes – her most able colleague as a budding agent and manager – to join her at RSO, but Farnes politely declined: 'I knew she was right in everything she said, but I could not leave Spike on his own.'[36] Years later, as the still-loyal supporter of both of these two proudly independent writers, she would have no regrets: 'Eric Sykes once said that at Number Nine we had grown into a family and it was true.'[37]

Associated London Scripts would live on for several more years, in name, as part of the Robert Stigwood Organisation, but, after the split, the original, 'real' ALS had gone. Its influence, however, would never stop. The anarchic spirit of *The Goon Show*, for example, would inspire, directly or indirectly and to varying extents, *Monty Python's Flying Circus*, *The Hitchhiker's Guide to the Galaxy*, *The Young Ones*, *Vic Reeves' Big Night Out*, *The League of Gentlemen*,

Brass Eye and countless other strange and bold new comedies. The high-quality mainstream writing of *Sykes And A . . .* would set a standard to which the likes of *Dad's Army, Ever Decreasing Circles* and *One Foot in the Grave* could aspire. The beautiful, truthful, characterful scripts for *Hancock's Half-Hour* and *Steptoe and Son* would encourage the creation of *Fawlty Towers, Porridge, Frasier, I'm Alan Partridge, The Royle Family, The Office* and many, many other well-observed and sharply written sitcoms. The clever and playful irreverence of *Beyond Our Ken* and *Round the Horne* would be echoed by such subsequent productions as *The Fast Show* and *Little Britain*. Johnny Speight's grown-up and grittily articulate social, cultural and political satires would enable *Yes, Minister, Absolutely Fabulous, Spitting Image, Drop the Dead Donkey, Have I Got News For You, The Day Today* and *The Thick Of It* to sharpen their blades and stick in their knives. The overall impact has been immense: to adapt a line from Auden, each great ALS writer 'is no more a person now but a whole climate of opinion'.[38]

Some might claim, looking back, that the writers at ALS benefited from being around during the age of the mass mainstream audience, but that would be a lazily specious and profoundly disrespectful form of argument. There never was any great and static mainstream audience, and neither – in spite of the self-serving assertions of some niche broadcasters today – was there ever a nation full of white, Anglo-Saxon, Protestant, middle-class, middle-aged, middle-brow, cardigan-clad conservatives waiting patiently for the next big cosy mainstream thing. The 1950s and 1960s were decades of immense and intense social, cultural and political dissent, divisions and unrest. To please most of that nation most of the time really was an extraordinary *achievement*. It was an achievement that came about because of great talent, great industry, great intelligence and great heart.

Some comedy lovers' memories would prove short and their sense of history depressingly slight – every now and again, for example, documentaries bearing such titles as *When Comedy Changed Forever* would appear to hail another recent Goon-type show as 'revolutionary'[39] – but the majority would never forget, and the respect and gratitude would always remain. Successive generations of fans would cherish the scripts and the recordings; the Establishment – somewhat ironically – brandished the baubles (Milligan would get an honorary KBE, Sykes a CBE and Galton and Simpson and Beryl Vertue each got an OBE), and younger writers, performers and producers paid proper homage.

Eddie Izzard would style Spike Milligan 'the godfather of alternative comedy' as well as 'a giant of comedy and creation',[40] while John Cleese would call him 'the great god of us all'.[41] Sir Peter Hall hailed Eric Sykes as 'our greatest living vaudevillian', while he was lauded inside the House of Commons for being 'one of the comedy geniuses of our time'.[42] Galton and Simpson were praised by the BBC for being 'a true national treasure'.[43] As for Johnny Speight, the entertainment executive Paul Jackson would remark: 'There are very few writers who can claim to have created a character who embodied a spirit of a generation. Johnny Speight did this with Alf Garnett. He will always be remembered as the man who created a comic icon for the age.'[44]

It was all so richly deserved. Without, in sum, the likes of Spike Milligan, Eric Sykes, Galton and Simpson and Johnny Speight, there would have been far too little in comedy of anything that really stretched the mind as well as the mouth.

This is the very special legacy of ALS. None of its old buildings requires a plaque: we commemorate it each time that we laugh. As Beryl Vertue would reflect, no house would ever hold more fun:

> When I look back now, I just think how extraordinary my life has become just because I said, 'Oh, all right then' all those years ago. It was hugely, hugely hard work, but very, very exciting as well. Being with all of those very clever people, and good *fun* people, too – what times we had together. And I think we were a pretty unique company. In the beginning, everyone called us 'The Fun Factory' – which the boys used to hate! – but I guess that's sort of what it was, and from it came such huge talent. It really was very special.[45]

ALS Output

A Chronology

For a key to the writers' initials, see page 353

1954

RADIO:
The Goon Show *(SM, LS, ES)*
Educating Archie *(ES)*
Hancock's Half-Hour *(RG, AS)*
The Frankie Howerd Show *(ES, RG, AS)*

TV:
The Big Man *(ES)*
Happy Go Crazy *(DV)*

THEATRE:
Mother Goose *(ES)*

1955

RADIO:
The Goon Show *(SM, ES, LS)*
Hancock's Half-Hour *(RG, AS)*
The Frankie Howerd Show *(ES, SM, JS, JA, DB, TN)*
Mr Ross – and Mr Ray *(JS)*
Man About Town *(SM)*
Christmas Crackers *(JS, JA, DB, TN)*

TV:
The Howerd Crowd *(ES)*
Max Bygraves *(ES)*
Secombe Here! *(ES, SM)*
The Harry Secombe Show *(ES)*
The Benny Hill Show *(DF)*

Great Scott – It's Maynard! *(LSZ, EM, JS, DF)*

1956

RADIO:
The Goon Show *(SM, ES, LS)*
Hancock's Half-Hour *(RG, AS)*
The Frankie Howerd Show *(JS, JA, DB, TN)*
Back With Braden *(RG, AS)*
Floggit's *(DF, JJ, TN)*
Curiosa and Curioser *(SM)*
Puss in Gumboots *(JS, DB)*

TV:
Hancock's Half-Hour *(RG, AS)*
Frankie Howerd *(JS, DB)*
Dress Rehearsal *(ES)*
Jimmy Logan *(ES)*
Opening Night *(ES)*
A Show Called Fred *(SM)*
Son of Fred *(SM)*
The Idiot Weekly, Price 2d *(SM, ES, DF, JJ, TN)*
Max Bygraves *(ES)*
The Max Bygraves Show *(ES)*
The Tony Hancock Show *(ES, LS, RG, AS)*
Alfred Marks Time *(DV, BA)*
Evans Abode *(JS, DB)*
The Winifred Atwell Show *(JS, DB)*

The Dickie Valentine Show *(JS, DB)*
Pantomania *(ES)*

MOVIES:
The Case of the Mukkinese Battle
Horn *(SM, LS)*

RECORDS:
The Bluebottle Blues/I'm Walking
Backwards for Christmas *(SM)*
Bloodnok's Rock'n'Roll Call/The Ying
Tong Song *(SM)*
My September Love/You Gotta Go
OWW! *(SM, ES)*

1957

RADIO:
The Goon Show *(SM, LS)*
Hancock's Half-Hour *(RG, AS)*
Floggit's *(DF, JJ, TN)*
Variety Playhouse *(TN, JJ)*
Askey Galore *(DV, BA, JS, DB)*
Son of Mother Goose *(JJ, TN)*

TV:
Hancock's Half-Hour *(RG, AS)*
Hancock's Forty-Three Minutes *(RG,
AS)*
Eric Sykes Presents Peter Sellers *(ES)*
The Army Game *(LS, MW, LSZ)*
The Howerd Crowd *(ES)*
Frankie Howerd *(JS, DB)*
The Arthur Haynes Show *(JS)*
Alfred Marks Time *(DV, BA)*
The Max Bygraves Show *(ES)*
Cooper – Or Life With Tommy *(DF)*
Early To Braden *(RG, AS, JA, DF, JS,
EM, MW)*
Jimmy Logan *(ES)*
Summer's Here *(DV, BA)*
These Are The Shows *(RG, AS)*
Evans Above *(JS, DB)*
Drake's Progress *(MW)*
Friday the 13th *(JJ, TN)*
Mostly Maynard *(EM)*
Scott Free *(LSZ)*

The Jimmy Wheeler Show *(JA)*
A-Z *(RG, AS)*
Pantomania *(DV, BA)*
Man and Music *(SM)*
Closing Night *(ES, AS, JS, DF, DV)*

RECORDS:
Eeh! Ah! Oh! Ooh!/I Love You *(SM)*
Whistle Your Cares Away/A Russian
Love Song *(SM)*

1958

RADIO:
The Goon Show *(SM, LS, JA, MW)*
Hancock's Half-Hour *(RG, AS)*
Beyond Our Ken *(EM, BT)*
Fine Goings On *(JJ, TN)*
The Deadly Game of Chess *(JS)*
Pantomania *(JS)*

TV:
Hancock's Half-Hour *(RG, AS)*
The Peter Sellers Show *(ES)*
The Army Game *(LS, MW, LSZ, JA)*
The Arthur Haynes Show *(JS)*
Alfred Marks Time *(DV, BA)*
The Ted Ray Show *(DF, JJ, TN)*
The Jimmy Logan Show *(ES)*
The April 8th Show (Seven Days
Early) *(RG, AS, JS, JA)*
Tony Hancock *(RG, AS)*
Frankie Howerd In . . . *(JS)*
The Frankie Howerd Show *(ES)*
Educating Archie *(MF)*
Charlie Drake In . . . *(DF)*
Drake's Progress *(MW)*

THEATRE:
Mr Venus *(RG, JS)*
Large As Life *(ES)*

1959

RADIO:
The Goon Show *(SM, LS, MW)*

Hancock's Half-Hour *(RG, AS)*
Beyond Our Ken *(EM, BT)*

TV:
Hancock's Half-Hour *(RG, AS)*
The Army Game *(LS, MW, LSZ)*
The Arthur Haynes Show *(JS)*
Alfred Marks Time *(DV, BA)*
The Ted Ray Show *(DF, JJ, TN)*
The Arthur Askey Show *(DF)*
The Cyril Fletcher Show *(JS)*
Educating Archie *(MF)*
Gert and Daisy *(LSZ)*
Charlie Drake In . . . *(DF)*
Tell It To The Marines *(DV, BA)*
Shadow Squad *(PY)*
Crime Sheet *(PY)*
Gala Opening *(ES)*

MOVIES:
The Running, Jumping & Standing
    Still Film *(SM)*
Idle on Parade *(JA)*

RECORDS:

Goon With The Wind *(SM)*

1960

RADIO:
The Goon Show *(SM)*
Beyond Our Ken *(EM)*
Frankie's Bandbox *(BT, MF)*

TV:
Hancock's Half-Hour *(RG, AS)*
Sykes And A . . . *(JS, ES, SM, JA)*
The Army Game *(MW, LSZ, BT, MF)*
Ladies and Gentle-Men *(JS, RG, AS,*
    BT)
The Arthur Haynes Show *(JS)*
Alfred Marks Time *(DV, BA)*
Arthur's Treasured Volumes *(DF)*
Armchair Theatre *(PY)*
Citizen James *(RG, AS)*

MOVIES:
The Rebel *(RG, AS)*
Jazz Boat *(JA)*

1961

RADIO:
Beyond Our Ken *(EM)*
It's a Fair Cop *(JJ, TN)*

TV:
Sykes And A . . . *(ES)*
Comedy Playhouse *(RG, AS)*
The Army Game *(MW, BA, JA, BT,*
    MF)
Bootsie and Snudge *(BT, MF)*
The Arthur Haynes Show *(JS)*
Spike Milligan *(SM)*
Alfred Marks Time *(DV, BA)*
The Sid James Show *(DF)*
The Anthony Newley Show *(RG, AS)*
Colonel Trumper's Private War *(BT,*
    DV)
Bresslaw and Friends *(DV, BA)*
Roamin' Holiday *(ES)*
Top Secret *(PY)*
Echo Four Two *(PY)*
Ghost Squad *(BA, MW, PY)*
The Missing Links *(JA)*
The Compartment *(JS)*

THEATRE:
The Compartment *(JS)*

MOVIES:
What a Whopper! *(TN)*

1962

RADIO:
Beyond Our Ken *(EM)*
The Arthur Haynes Show *(JS)*

TV:
Sykes And A . . . *(ES)*
Steptoe and Son *(RG, AS)*
Comedy Playhouse *(RG, AS)*

Bootsie and Snudge *(BT, MF)*
The Arthur Haynes Show *(JS)*
Mess Mates *(LSZ)*
Playmates *(JS)*
Out of This World *(TN)*
That Was The Week That Was *(ES, JS, BA, JA, DN)*

THEATRE:
Frankie Howerd at The Establishment *(ES, RG, AS, JS)*

RECORDS:
Eric, Hattie & Things!!!! *(ES)*
The Bridge on the River Wye *(SM)*

1963

RADIO:
Beyond Our Ken *(EM)*

TV:
Sykes And A . . . *(ES)*
Steptoe and Son *(RG, AS)*
Comedy Playhouse *(RG, AS)*
Bootsie and Snudge *(BT, MF)*
The Telegoons *(SM, MW)*
The Arthur Haynes Show *(JS)*
Hancock *(TN)*
Shamrot *(JS)*
Scoop *(BT)*
Espionage *(PY)*
Doctor Who *(TN)*
That Was The Week That Was *(ES, JS, BA, JA, DN)*

THEATRE:
The Bed-Sitting Room *(SM, JA)*
Swing Along (JS)

MOVIES:
The Wrong Arm of the Law *(JA, RG, AS)*

RECORDS:
Frankie Howerd at The Establishment & At the BBC *(JS, RG, AS, BT, MF)*

1964

RADIO:
Beyond Our Ken *(EM)*

TV:
Sykes And A . . . *(ES)*
Steptoe and Son *(RG, AS)*
Frankie Howerd *(RG, AS)*
The Arthur Haynes Show *(JS)*
The Graham Stark Show *(JS)*
The Telegoons *(SM, MW)*
Room at the Bottom *(JA)*
Milligan's Wake *(SM)*
Muses with Milligan *(SM)*
A Last Word on the Election *(RG, AS, DN)*
A Touch of the Norman Vaughans *(LSZ, EM)*
A World of his Own *(DF)*
The Five Foot Nine Show *(DF)*
Deep & Crisp & Stolen *(DF)*
Scott On . . . *(BT, MF)*
Room At The Bottom *(JA)*
Story Parade *(TN)*
Miss Adventure *(PY)*
The Saint *(TN)*
Doctor Who *(TN)*

THEATRE:
In Praise of British Revue *(JA)*

MOVIES:
The Bargee *(RG, AS)*

RECORDS:

How to Win an Election (or not lose by much) *(SM)*

1965

RADIO:

Round the Horne *(BT, MF)*
The Naughty Navy Show *(SM)*

TV:
Sykes And A . . . *(ES)*
Steptoe and Son *(RG, AS)*
Till Death Us Do Part *(JS)*
Muses With Milligan *(SM)*
The Arthur Haynes Show *(JS)*
The Val Doonican Show *(EM)*
Max Bygraves Entertains *(EM)*
BBC 3 *(DV)*
A World of His Own *(DF)*
The Saint *(TN)*
Doctor Who *(TN)*

THEATRE:
You'll Come to Love Your Sperm Test
  (JA)
The Curse of the Daleks *(TN)*
If There Weren't Any Blacks You'd
  Have to Invent Them *(JS)*

MOVIES:
The Cuckoo Patrol *(LS)*
The Big Job *(JA)*

1966

RADIO:
Round the Horne *(BT, MF)*
Steptoe and Son *(RG, AS)*

TV:
Till Death Us Do Part (JS)
Frankie Howerd (RG, AS)
East of Howerd (ES, RG, AS, JS)
The Arthur Haynes Show (JS)

Hancock at the Royal Festival Hall
  (RG, AS)
Watch the Birdies *(PY)*
The Baron *(TN)*
Doctor Who *(TN)*

THEATRE:
Way Out in Piccadilly *(ES, RG, AS)*

MOVIES:
The Spy with a Cold Nose *(RG, AS)*

1967

RADIO:
Round the Horne *(BT, MF)*
Steptoe and Son *(RG, AS)*

TV:
Till Death Us Do Part *(JS)*
Sykes Versus ITV *(ES)*
To Lucifer – a Son *(JS)*
Before the Fringe *(RG, AS)*
Mr Aitch *(RG, AS, DF, JJ)*
The Baron *(TN)*
Spike Milligan's Sad/Happy Ending
  Story of The Bald Twit Lion *(SM)*

THEATRE:
Way Out in Piccadilly *(ES, RG, AS)*

MOVIES:
The Plank *(ES)*

Guide to ALS Writers involved:

ES – Eric Sykes; SM – Spike Milligan; RG – Ray Galton; AS – Alan Simpson;
BA – Brad Ashton; BT – Barry Took; DB – Dick Barry;
DF – Dave Freeman; DV – Dick Vosburgh; EM – Eric Merriman;
JA – John Antrobus; JJ – John Junkin; LSZ – Lew Schwarz; JS – Johnny
Speight; LS – Larry Stephens; MF – Marty Feldman; MW – Maurice Wiltshire;
PY – Peter Yeldham; TN – Terry Nation

List of Programmes

[Episodes marked * are thought, at the time of writing, missing believed wiped. It should be noted, however, that, as rare copies are still being recovered either by the BBC's admirable 'Treasure Hunt' project (http://www.bbc.co.uk/cult/treasurehunt/) or by various international 'old time radio' (OTR) services, this list is subject to change.

THE GOON SHOW (BBC Home Service)

Series 1 (Billed as '*Crazy People*')

(Regular cast: Peter Sellers, Harry Secombe, Spike Milligan, Michael Bentine, The Ray Ellington Quartet, The Stargazers and Max Geldray)

01: No Title *
First broadcast: 28/05/1951
Script: Spike Milligan and Larry Stephens, edited by Jimmy Grafton
Producer: Dennis Main Wilson

02: No Title *
First broadcast: 04/06/1951
Script: Spike Milligan and Larry Stephens, edited by Jimmy Grafton
Producer: Dennis Main Wilson

03: No Title *
First broadcast: 11/06/1951
Script: Spike Milligan and Larry Stephens, edited by Jimmy Grafton
Producer: Dennis Main Wilson

04: No Title *
First broadcast: 18/06/1951
Script: Spike Milligan and Larry Stephens, edited by Jimmy Grafton
Producer: Dennis Main Wilson

05: No Title *
First broadcast: 25/06/1951
Script: Spike Milligan and Larry Stephens, edited by Jimmy Grafton
Producer: Dennis Main Wilson

06: No Title *
First broadcast: 02/07/1951
Script: Spike Milligan and Larry Stephens, edited by Jimmy Grafton
Producer: Dennis Main Wilson

07: No Title *
First broadcast: 09/07/1951
Script: Spike Milligan and Larry Stephens, edited by Jimmy Grafton
Producer: Dennis Main Wilson

08: No Title *
First broadcast: 16/07/1951
Script: Spike Milligan and Larry Stephens, edited by Jimmy Grafton
Producer: Dennis Main Wilson

09: No Title *
First broadcast: 23/07/1951
Script: Spike Milligan and Larry Stephens, edited by Jimmy Grafton
Producer: Dennis Main Wilson

10: No Title *
First broadcast: 02/08/1951
Script: Spike Milligan and Larry Stephens, edited by Jimmy Grafton
Producer: Dennis Main Wilson

11: No Title *
First broadcast: 09/08/1951
Script: Spike Milligan and Larry Stephens, edited by Jimmy Grafton
Producer: Leslie Bridgmont

12: No Title *
First broadcast: 16/08/1951
Script: Spike Milligan and Larry Stephens, edited by Jimmy Grafton
Producer: Leslie Bridgmont

13: No Title *
First broadcast: 23/08/1951
Script: Spike Milligan and Larry Stephens, edited by Jimmy Grafton
Producer: Leslie Bridgmont

14: No Title *
First broadcast: 30/08/1951
Script: Spike Milligan and Larry Stephens, edited by Jimmy Grafton
Producer: Leslie Bridgmont

15: No Title *
First broadcast: 06/09/1951
Script: Spike Milligan and Larry Stephens, edited by Jimmy Grafton
Producer: Dennis Main Wilson

16: No Title *
First broadcast: 13/09/1951
Script: Spike Milligan and Larry Stephens, edited by Jimmy Grafton
Producer: Dennis Main Wilson

17: No Title *
First broadcast: 20/09/1951
Script: Spike Milligan and Larry Stephens, edited by Jimmy Grafton
Producer: Dennis Main Wilson

Special: Cinderella *
First broadcast: 26/12/1951
Script: Spike Milligan and Larry Stephens, edited by Jimmy Grafton
Producer: Dennis Main Wilson
(with Lizbeth Webb as Cinderella, Graham Stark as Prince Charming, The Goons, The Stargazers, The Ray Ellington Quartet, Max Geldray and the Augmented Dance Orchestra conducted by Stanley Black)

Series 2

(Regular cast: Peter Sellers, Harry Secombe, Spike Milligan, Michael Bentine, The Ray Ellington Quartet, Max Geldray, The Stargazers – episodes 1-6 – and Andrew Timothy as announcer)

01: No Title
First broadcast: 22/01/1952
Script: Spike Milligan and Larry Stephens, edited by Jimmy Grafton
Producer: Dennis Main Wilson

02: No Title
First broadcast: 29/01/1952
Script: Spike Milligan and Larry Stephens, edited by Jimmy Grafton
Producer: Dennis Main Wilson

03: No Title
First broadcast: 05/02/1952
Script: Spike Milligan and Larry Stephens, edited by Jimmy Grafton
Producer: Dennis Main Wilson

04: No Title *
First broadcast: 19/02/1952
Script: Spike Milligan and Larry Stephens, edited by Jimmy Grafton
Producer: Dennis Main Wilson

05: No Title *
First broadcast: 26/02/1952

Script: Spike Milligan and Larry
Stephens, edited by Jimmy Grafton
Producer: Dennis Main Wilson

06: No Title *
First broadcast: 04/03/1952
Script: Spike Milligan and Larry
Stephens, edited by Jimmy Grafton
Producer: Dennis Main Wilson

07: No Title *
First broadcast: 11/03/1952
Script: Spike Milligan and Larry
Stephens, edited by Jimmy Grafton
Producer: Dennis Main Wilson

08: Her *
First broadcast: 18/03/1952
Script: Spike Milligan and Larry
Stephens, edited by Jimmy Grafton
Producer: Dennis Main Wilson

09: No Title *
First broadcast: 25/03/1952
Script: Spike Milligan and Larry
Stephens, edited by Jimmy Grafton
Producer: Dennis Main Wilson

10: No Title *
First broadcast: 01/04/1952
Script: Spike Milligan and Larry
Stephens, edited by Jimmy Grafton
Producer: Dennis Main Wilson

11: No Title *
First broadcast: 08/04/1952
Script: Spike Milligan and Larry
Stephens, edited by Jimmy Grafton
Producer: Dennis Main Wilson
(Without Spike Milligan)

12: No Title *
First broadcast: 15/04/1952
Script: Spike Milligan and Larry
Stephens, edited by Jimmy Grafton
Producer: Dennis Main Wilson

13: No Title *
First broadcast: 22/04/1952
Script: Spike Milligan and Larry
Stephens, edited by Jimmy Grafton
Producer: Dennis Main Wilson

14: No Title *
First broadcast: 29/04/1952
Script: Spike Milligan and Larry
Stephens, edited by Jimmy Grafton
Producer: Dennis Main Wilson

15: No Title *
First broadcast: 06/05/1952
Script: Spike Milligan and Larry
Stephens, edited by Jimmy Grafton
Producer: Dennis Main Wilson

16: No Title *
First broadcast: 13/05/1952
Script: Spike Milligan and Larry
Stephens, edited by Jimmy Grafton
Producer: Dennis Main Wilson

17: No Title *
First broadcast: 20/05/1952
Script: Spike Milligan and Larry
Stephens, edited by Jimmy Grafton
Producer: Dennis Main Wilson

18: No Title *
First broadcast: 27/05/1952
Script: Spike Milligan and Larry
Stephens, edited by Jimmy Grafton
Producer: Dennis Main Wilson

19: No Title *
First broadcast: 03/06/1952
Script: Spike Milligan and Larry
Stephens, edited by Jimmy Grafton
Producer: Dennis Main Wilson

20: No Title *
First broadcast: 10/06/1952
Script: Spike Milligan and Larry
Stephens, edited by Jimmy Grafton
Producer: Dennis Main Wilson

21: No Title *
First broadcast: 17/06/1952
Script: Spike Milligan and Larry
Stephens, edited by Jimmy Grafton
Producer: Dennis Main Wilson

22: No Title *
First broadcast: 24/06/1952
Script: Spike Milligan and Larry

Stephens, edited by Jimmy Grafton
Producer: Dennis Main Wilson

23: *No Title* *
First broadcast: 01/07/1952
Script: Spike Milligan and Larry
Stephens, edited by Jimmy Grafton
Producer: Dennis Main Wilson

24: *No Title* *
First broadcast: 08/07/1952

Script: Spike Milligan and Larry
Stephens, edited by Jimmy Grafton
Producer: Dennis Main Wilson

25: *No Title* *
First broadcast: 15/07/1952
Script: Spike Milligan and Larry
Stephens, edited by Jimmy Grafton
Producer: Dennis Main Wilson

Series 3

(Regular cast: Peter Sellers, Harry Secombe, Spike Milligan, The Ray Ellington Quartet, Max Geldray, Andrew Timothy as announcer and The BBC Dance Orchestra conducted by Wally Stott. Michael Bentine has now departed)

01: *Fred of the Islands* *
First broadcast: 11/11/1952
Script: Spike Milligan and Larry
Stephens, edited by Jimmy Grafton
Producer: Peter Eton

02: *The Egg of the Great Auk* *
First broadcast: 18/11/1952
Script: Spike Milligan and Larry
Stephens, edited by Jimmy Grafton
Producer: Peter Eton

03: *I Was a Male Fan Dancer* *
First broadcast: 25/11/1952
Script: Spike Milligan and Larry
Stephens, edited by Jimmy Grafton
Producer: Peter Eton

04: *The Saga of HMS Aldgate* *
First broadcast: 02/12/1952
Script: Spike Milligan and Larry
Stephens, edited by Jimmy Grafton
Producer: Peter Eton

05: *The Expedition for Toothpaste* *
First broadcast: 09/12/1952
Script: Spike Milligan and Larry
Stephens, edited by Jimmy Grafton
Producer: Peter Eton
(At this point Milligan went into
hospital suffering from a nervous
breakdown. This show and the next
had already been written. After a few

weeks, Milligan resumed writing the
shows in collaboration with Larry
Stephens)

06: *The Archers* *
First broadcast: 16/12/1952
Script: Spike Milligan and Larry
Stephens, edited by Jimmy Grafton
Producer: Peter Eton
(Without Spike Milligan)

07: *Robin Hood* *
First broadcast: 26/12/1952
Script: Spike Milligan and Larry
Stephens, edited by Jimmy Grafton
Producer: Peter Eton
(Without Spike Milligan, with Dick
Emery and Carole Carr)

08: *Where Does Santa Claus Go in the
Summer?* *
First broadcast: 30/12/1952
Script: Spike Milligan and Larry
Stephens, edited by Jimmy Grafton
Producer: Peter Eton
(Without Spike Milligan, with Ellis
Powell)

09: *The Navy, Army, and Air Force* *
First broadcast: 06/01/1953
Script: Spike Milligan and Larry
Stephens, edited by Jimmy Grafton
Producer: Peter Eton

(Without Spike Milligan, with Dick Emery)

10: The British Way of Life *
First broadcast: 13/01/1953
Script: Spike Milligan and Larry Stephens, edited by Jimmy Grafton
Producer: Peter Eton
(Without Spike Milligan, with Graham Stark)

11: A Survey of Britain *
First broadcast: 20/01/1953
Script: Spike Milligan and Larry Stephens, edited by Jimmy Grafton
Producer: Peter Eton
(Without Spike Milligan, with Dick Emery)

12: Flint of the Flying Squad *
First broadcast: 27/01/1953
Script: Spike Milligan and Larry Stephens, edited by Jimmy Grafton
Producer: Peter Eton
(Without Spike Milligan, with Graham Stark)

13: Seaside Resorts in Winter *
First broadcast: 03/02/1953
Script: Spike Milligan and Larry Stephens, edited by Jimmy Grafton
Producer: Peter Eton
(Without Spike Milligan, with Dick Emery)

14: The Tragedy of Oxley Towers *
First broadcast: 10/02/1953
Script: Spike Milligan and Larry Stephens, edited by Jimmy Grafton
Producer: Peter Eton
(Without Spike Milligan, with Graham Stark and Valentine Dyall)

15: The Story of Civilisation *
First broadcast: 17/02/1953
Script: Spike Milligan and Larry Stephens, edited by Jimmy Grafton
Producer: Peter Eton
(Without Spike Milligan, with Dick Emery).

16: The Search for the Bearded Vulture *
First broadcast: 24/02/1953
Script: Spike Milligan and Larry Stephens, edited by Jimmy Grafton
Producer: Peter Eton
(Without Spike Milligan, with Graham Stark)

17: The Mystery of the Monkey's Paw *
First broadcast: 03/03/1953
Script: Spike Milligan and Larry Stephens, edited by Jimmy Grafton
Producer: Peter Eton
(With Dick Emery)

18: The Mystery of the Cow on the Hill *
First broadcast: 10/03/1953
Script: Spike Milligan and Larry Stephens, edited by Jimmy Grafton
Producer: Charles Chilton

19: Where Do Socks Come From? *
First broadcast: 17/03/1953
Script: Spike Milligan and Larry Stephens, edited by Jimmy Grafton
Producer: Charles Chilton

20: The Man Who Never Was
First broadcast: 31/03/1953
Script: Spike Milligan and Larry Stephens, edited by Jimmy Grafton
Producer: Peter Eton

21: The Building of the Suez Canal *
First broadcast: 07/04/1953
Script: Spike Milligan and Larry Stephens, edited by Jimmy Grafton
Producer: Peter Eton

22: The De Goonlies *
First broadcast: 14/04/1953
Script: Spike Milligan and Larry Stephens, edited by Jimmy Grafton
Producer: Peter Eton

23: The Conquest of Space *
First broadcast: 21/04/1953
Script: Spike Milligan and Larry Stephens, edited by Jimmy Grafton
Producer: Peter Eton

24: The Ascent of Mount Everest
First broadcast: 28/04/1953
Script: Spike Milligan and Larry
Stephens, edited by Jimmy Grafton
Producer: Peter Eton

*25: The Story of the Plymouth Hoe
Armada* *
First broadcast: 05/05/1953
Script: Spike Milligan and Larry
Stephens, edited by Jimmy Grafton
Producer: Peter Eton

Special: Coronation edition *
First broadcast: 03/06/1953
Script: Spike Milligan and Larry
Stephens, edited by Jimmy Grafton
Producer: Peter Eton
(Without Max Geldray, with Graham
Stark)

Series 4

*(Regular cast: Peter Sellers, Harry Secombe, Spike Milligan, The Ray Ellington
Quartet and Max Geldray. Episodes 1-5 were announced by Andrew Timothy and
the rest by Wallace Greenslade)*

01: The Dreaded Piano Clubber
First broadcast: 02/10/1953
Script:: Spike Milligan and Larry
Stephens
Producer: Peter Eton

*02: The Man Who Tried to Destroy
London's Monuments*
First broadcast: 09/10/1953
Script: Spike Milligan and Larry
Stephens
Producer: Peter Eton

*03: The Ghastly Experiments of Dr.
Hans Eidelburger*
First broadcast: 16/10/1953
Script: Spike Milligan and Larry
Stephens
Producer: Peter Eton

*04: The Building of Britain's First
Atomic Cannon* *
First broadcast: 23/10/1953
Script: Spike Milligan and Larry
Stephens
Producer: Peter Eton

05: The Gibraltar Story *
First broadcast: 30/10/1953
Script: Spike Milligan and Larry
Stephens
Producer: Peter Eton

*06: Through the Sound Barrier in an
Airing Cupboard* *
First broadcast: 06/11/1953
Script: Spike Milligan and Larry
Stephens
Producer: Peter Eton

*07: The First Albert Memorial to the
Moon* *
First broadcast: 13/11/1953
Script: Spike Milligan and Larry
Stephens
Producer: Peter Eton

08: The Missing Bureaucrat *
First broadcast: 20/11/1953
Script: Spike Milligan and Larry
Stephens
Producer: Peter Eton

09: Operation Bagpipes *
First broadcast: 27/11/1953
Script: Spike Milligan and Larry
Stephens
Producer: Peter Eton

10: The Flying Saucer Mystery *
First broadcast: 04/12/1953
Script: Larry Stephens
Producer: Peter Eton

11: The Spanish Armada *
First broadcast: 11/12/1953

Script: Spike Milligan and Larry
Stephens
Producer: Peter Eton

12: The British Way *
First broadcast: 18/12/1953
Script: Spike Milligan and Larry
Stephens
Producer: Peter Eton

13: The Giant Bombardon
First broadcast: 26/12/1953
Script: Spike Milligan and Larry
Stephens
Producer: Peter Eton
(With Michael Bentine)

*14: Ten Thousand Fathoms Down in a
Wardrobe* *
First broadcast: 01/01/1954
Script: Spike Milligan and Larry
Stephens
Producer: Peter Eton

15: The Missing Prime Minister
First broadcast: 08/01/1954
Script: Spike Milligan and Larry
Stephens
Producer: Jacques Brown

16: Dr. Jekyll and Mr. Crun *
First broadcast: 15/01/1954
Script: Spike Milligan and Larry
Stephens
Producer: Peter Eton

17: The Mummified Priest
First broadcast: 22/01/1954
Script: Spike Milligan and Larry
Stephens
Producer: Peter Eton

18: The History of Communications
First broadcast: 29/01/1954
Script: Spike Milligan and Larry
Stephens
Producer: Peter Eton

19: The Kippered Herring Gang *
First broadcast: 05/02/1954

Script: Spike Milligan and Larry
Stephens
Producer: Peter Eton

20: The Toothpaste Expedition *
First broadcast: 12/02/1954
Script: Spike Milligan and Larry
Stephens
Producer: Peter Eton

21: The Case of the Vanishing Room
First broadcast: 15/02/1954
Script: Spike Milligan
Producer: Peter Eton

22: The Great Ink Drought of 1902 *
First broadcast: 22/02/1954
Script: Spike Milligan
Producer: Peter Eton

*23: The Greatest Mountain in the
World*
First broadcast: 01/03/1954
Script: Spike Milligan
Producer: Peter Eton

*24: The Collapse of the British
Railway Sandwich System*
First broadcast: 08/03/1954
Script: Spike Milligan
Producer: Peter Eton

25: The Silent Bugler
First broadcast: 15/03/1954
Script: Spike Milligan
Producer: Peter Eton

26: Western Story *
First broadcast: 22/03/1954
Script: Spike Milligan
Producer: Peter Eton

*27: The Saga of the Internal
Mountain*
First broadcast: 29/03/1954
Script: Spike Milligan
Producer: Peter Eton

28: The Invisible Acrobat *
First broadcast: 05/04/1954
Script: Spike Milligan
Producer: Peter Eton

29: *The Great Bank of England Robbery*
First broadcast: 12/04/1954
Script: Spike Milligan
Producer: Peter Eton

30: *The Siege of Fort Knight*
First broadcast: 19/04/1954
Script: Spike Milligan
Producer: Peter Eton

Special: The Starlings
First broadcast: 31/08/1954
Script: Spike Milligan
Producer: Peter Eton
(With Peter Sellers, Harry Secombe, Spike Milligan and Andrew Timothy.

Performed without musicians or audience)

Special: Short insert in 'Christmas Crackers'
First broadcast: 25/12/1953

Special: Archie in Goonland *
First broadcast: 11/06/1954
Script: Spike Milligan and Eric Sykes
Producer: Roy Speer
(With Peter Brough and Archie Andrews, Peter Sellers, Spike Milligan, Harry Secombe, Hattie Jacques and the BBC Variety Orchestra conducted by Paul Fenoulhet)

Series 5

(Regular cast: Peter Sellers, Harry Secombe, Spike Milligan, The Ray Ellington Quartet, Max Geldray and Wallace Greenslade as announcer)

01: *The Whistling Spy Enigma*
First broadcast: 28/09/1954
Script: Spike Milligan
Producer: Peter Eton

02: *The Lost Gold Mine of Charlotte*
First broadcast: 05/10/1954
Script: Spike Milligan
Producer: Peter Eton

03: *The Dreaded Batter-Pudding Hurler of Bexhill-on-Sea*
First broadcast: 12/10/1954
Script: Spike Milligan
Producer: Peter Eton

04: *The Phantom Head Shaver of Brighton*
First broadcast: 19/10/1954
Script: Spike Milligan
Producer: Peter Eton

05: *The Affair of the Lone Banana*
First broadcast: 26/10/1954
Script: Spike Milligan
Producer: Peter Eton

06: *The Canal*
First broadcast: 02/11/1954
Script: Spike Milligan
Producer: Peter Eton
(With Valentine Dyall)

07: *Lurgi Strikes Britain*
First broadcast: 09/11/1954
Script: Spike Milligan and Eric Sykes
Producer: Peter Eton

08: *The Mystery of the Marie Celeste (Solved)*
First broadcast: 16/11/1954
Script: Spike Milligan and Eric Sykes
Producer: Peter Eton

09: *The Last Tram (from Clapham)*
First broadcast: 23/11/1954
Script: Spike Milligan and Eric Sykes
Producer: Peter Eton

10: *The Booted Gorilla*
First broadcast: 30/11/1954
Script: Spike Milligan and Eric Sykes
Producer: Peter Eton

11: *The Spanish Suitcase*
First broadcast: 07/12/1954
Script: Spike Milligan and Eric Sykes
Producer: Peter Eton

12: *Dishonoured, or The Fall of Neddie Seagoon*
First broadcast: 14/12/1954
Script: Spike Milligan and Eric Sykes
Producer: Peter Eton

13: *Forog*
First broadcast: 21/12/1954
Script: Spike Milligan and Eric Sykes
Producer: Peter Eton

14: *Ye Bandit of Sherwood Forest*
First broadcast: 28/12/1954
Script: Spike Milligan and Eric Sykes
Producer: Peter Eton
(With Charlotte Mitchell)

15: *Nineteen-Eighty-Five*
First broadcast: 04/01/1955
Script: Spike Milligan and Eric Sykes
Producer: Peter Eton

16: *The Case of the Missing Heir*
First broadcast: 11/01/1955
Script: Spike Milligan and Eric Sykes
Producer: Peter Eton

17: *China Story*
First broadcast: 18/01/1955
Script: Spike Milligan and Eric Sykes
Producer: Peter Eton

18: *Under Two Floorboards – A Story of the Legion*
First broadcast: 25/01/1955
Script: Spike Milligan and Eric Sykes

Producer: Peter Eton

19: *The Missing Scroll* (a.k.a. *Lost Music*)
First broadcast: 01/02/1955
Script: Spike Milligan and Eric Sykes
Producer: Peter Eton

20: *Nineteen-Eighty-Five*
First broadcast: 08/02/1955
Script: Spike Milligan and Eric Sykes
Producer: Peter Eton

21: *The Sinking of Westminster Pier*
First broadcast: 15/02/1955
Script: Spike Milligan and Eric Sykes
Producer: Peter Eton

22: *The Fireball of Milton Street*
First broadcast: 22/02/1955
Script: Spike Milligan and Eric Sykes
Producer: Peter Eton

23: *The Six Ingots of Leadenhall Street*
First broadcast: 01/03/1955
Script: Spike Milligan and Eric Sykes
Producer: Peter Eton

24: *Yehti*
First broadcast: 08/03/1955
Script: Spike Milligan and Eric Sykes
Producer: Peter Eton

25: *The White Box of Great Bardfield*
First broadcast: 15/03/1955
Script: Spike Milligan and Eric Sykes
Producer: Peter Eton

26: *The End*
First broadcast: 22/03/1955
Script: Spike Milligan and Eric Sykes
Producer: Peter Eton

Series 6

(*Regular cast: Peter Sellers, Harry Secombe, Spike Milligan, The Ray Ellington Quartet, Max Geldray and Wallace Greenslade as announcer*)

01: *The Man Who Won the War*
First broadcast: 20/09/1955
Script: Spike Milligan and Eric Sykes
Producer: Peter Eton

02: *The Secret Escritoire*
First broadcast: 27/09/1955
Script: Spike Milligan and Eric Sykes
Producer: Peter Eton

03: The Lost Emperor
First broadcast: 04/10/1955
Script: Spike Milligan
Producer: Peter Eton

04: Napoleon's Piano
First broadcast: 11/10/1955
Script: Spike Milligan
Producer: Peter Eton

05: The Case of the Missing CD Plates
First broadcast: 18/10/1955
Script: Spike Milligan
Producer: Peter Eton

06: Rommel's Treasure
First broadcast: 25/10/1955
Script: Spike Milligan
Producer: Peter Eton

07: Foiled by President Fred
First broadcast: 01/11/1955
Script: Spike Milligan
Producer: Peter Eton

08: Shangri-La Again
First broadcast: 08/11/1955
Script: Spike Milligan
Producer: Peter Eton

09: The International Christmas Pudding
First broadcast: 15/11/1955
Script: Spike Milligan
Producer: Peter Eton

10: The Pevensey Bay Disaster
First broadcast: 03/04/1956
Script: Spike Milligan
Producer: Peter Eton

11: The Sale of Manhattan
First broadcast: 29/11/1955
Script: Spike Milligan
Producer: Peter Eton

12: The Terrible Revenge of Fred Fu-Manchu
First broadcast: 06/12/1955
Script: Spike Milligan
Producer: Peter Eton

13: The Lost Year
First broadcast: 13/12/1955
Script: Spike Milligan
Producer: Peter Eton

14: The Greenslade Story
First broadcast: 20/12/1955
Script: Spike Milligan
Producer: Peter Eton
(With John Snagge)

15: The Hastings Flyer – Robbed *
First broadcast: 27/12/1955
Script: Spike Milligan
Producer: Peter Eton

16: The Mighty Wurlitzer
First broadcast: 03/01/1956
Script: Spike Milligan
Producer: Peter Eton

17: The Raid of the International Christmas Pudding
First broadcast: 10/01/1956
Script: Spike Milligan
Producer: Peter Eton

18: Tales of Montmartre
First broadcast: 17/01/1956
Script: Spike Milligan and Eric Sykes
Producer: Peter Eton
(With Charlotte Mitchell)

19: The Jet-Propelled Guided NAAFI
First broadcast: 24/01/1956
Script: Spike Milligan
Producer: Peter Eton

20: The House of Teeth
First broadcast: 31/01/1956
Script: Spike Milligan
Producer: Peter Eton
(With Valentine Dyall)

21: Tales of Old Dartmoor
First broadcast: 07/02/1956
Script: Spike Milligan
Producer: Peter Eton

22: The Choking Horror
First broadcast: 14/02/1956
Script: Spike Milligan
Producer: Pat Dixon

23: *The Great Tuscan Salami Scandal*
First broadcast: 21/02/1956
Script: Spike Milligan
Producer: Pat Dixon
(With John Snaggc)

24: *The Treasure in the Lake*
First broadcast: 28/02/1956
Script: Spike Milligan
Producer: Pat Dixon

25: *The Fear of Wages*
First broadcast: 06/03/1956
Script: Spike Milligan and Larry Stephens
Producer: Pat Dixon

26: *Scradje*
First broadcast: 13/03/1956
Script: Spike Milligan and Larry Stephens
Producer: Pat Dixon
(With John Snagge)

27: *The Man Who Never Was*
First broadcast: 20/03/1956
Script: Spike Milligan and Larry Stephens
Producer: Pat Dixon

Special: China Story
First broadcast: 29/08/1956
Script: Spike Milligan and Eric Sykes
Producer: Dennis Main Wilson

Special: The Missing Christmas Parcel – Post Early for Christmas
First broadcast: 08/12/1955
Script: Eric Sykes
Producer: Peter Eton and John Lane
(A 15-minute broadcast in *Children's Hour*. Without musicians)

Special: The Goons Hit Wales
First broadcast: 01/03/1956
Script: Spike Milligan
(5½-minute insert in St David's Day programme)

Series 7

(Regular cast: Peter Sellers, Harry Secombe, Spike Milligan, The Ray Ellington Quartet, Max Geldray and Wallace Greenslade as announcer)

01: *The Nasty Affair at the Burami Oasis*
First broadcast: 04/10/1956
Script: Spike Milligan and Larry Stephens
Producer: Peter Eton

02: *Drums Along the Mersey*
First broadcast: 11/10/1956
Script: Spike Milligan
Producer: Peter Eton
(With Valentine Dyall)

03: *The Nadger Plague*
First broadcast: 18/10/1956
Script: Spike Milligan and Larry Stephens
Producer: Pat Dixon

04: *The MacReekie Rising of '74*
First broadcast: 25/10/1955
Script: Spike Milligan and Larry Stephens
Producer: Pat Dixon
(Without Spike Milligan, with George Chisholm)

05: *The Spectre of Tintagel*
First broadcast: 01/11/1956
Script: Spike Milligan and Larry Stephens
Producer: Pat Dixon
(With Valentine Dyall)

06: *The Sleeping Prince*
First broadcast: 14/02/1957
Script: Spike Milligan and Larry Stephens
Producer: Pat Dixon

07: The Great Bank Robbery
First broadcast: 15/11/1956
Script: Spike Milligan and Larry
Stephens
Producer: Pat Dixon

08: Personal Narrative
First broadcast: 22/11/1956
Script: Spike Milligan and Larry
Stephens
Producer: Pat Dixon

*09: The Mystery of the Fake Neddie
Seagoons*
First broadcast: 29/11/1956
Script: Spike Milligan and Larry
Stephens
Producer: Pat Dixon

10: What's My Line?
First broadcast: 05/12/1956
Script: Spike Milligan and Larry
Stephens
Producer: Pat Dixon

11: The Telephone
First broadcast: 13/12/1956
Script: Spike Milligan and Larry
Stephens
Producer: Pat Dixon

12: The Flea
First broadcast: 20/12/1956
Script: Spike Milligan and Larry
Stephens
Producer: Pat Dixon

*13: Six Charlies in Search of an
Author*
First broadcast: 26/12/1956
Script: Spike Milligan and Larry
Stephens
Producer: Pat Dixon

14: Emperor of the Universe
First broadcast: 03/01/1957
Script: Spike Milligan and Larry
Stephens
Producer: Pat Dixon

15: Wings Over Dagenham
First broadcast: 10/01/1957
Script: Spike Milligan and Larry
Stephens
Producer: Pat Dixon
(With George Chisholm)

16: The Rent Collectors
First broadcast: 17/01/1957
Script: Spike Milligan and Larry
Stephens
Producer: Pat Dixon
(With Bernard Miles)

17: Shifting Sands
First broadcast: 24/01/1957
Script: Spike Milligan and Larry
Stephens
Producer: Pat Dixon
(With Jack Train as his old ITMA
character Colonel Chinstrap)

18: The Moon Show
First broadcast: 31/01/1957
Script: Spike Milligan and Larry
Stephens
Producer: Pat Dixon

*19: The Mysterious Punch-up-the-
Conker*
First broadcast: 07/02/1957
Script: Spike Milligan and Larry
Stephens
Producer: Pat Dixon
(This episode contains the 'What time
is it Eccles?' sketch)

20: Round the World in EightyDays
First broadcast: 21/02/1957
Script: Spike Milligan and Larry
Stephens
Producer: Pat Dixon

21: Insurance, the White Man's Burden
First broadcast: 28/02/1957
Script: Spike Milligan and Larry
Stephens
Producer: Pat Dixon

22: *The Africa Ship Canal*
First broadcast: 07/03/1957
Script: Spike Milligan and Larry
Stephens
Producer: Pat Dixon

23: *Ill Met by Goonlight*
First broadcast: 14/03/1957
Script: Spike Milligan
Producer: Pat Dixon

24: *The Missing Boa Constrictor*
First broadcast: 21/03/1957
Script: Spike Milligan and Larry
Stephens
Producer: Pat Dixon

25: *The Histories of Pliny the Elder*
First broadcast: 28/03/1957
Script: Spike Milligan and Larry
Stephens
Producer: Pat Dixon

Special: The Reason Why
First broadcast: 22/08/1957
Script: Spike Milligan and Larry
Stephens
Producer: Jacques Brown
(With Valentine Dyall. Music pre-
recorded, no audience)

Special: Robin Hood
First broadcast: Not broadcast in UK
Script: Spike Milligan and Larry
Stephens
Producer: Pat Dixon
(With Valentine Dyall and Dennis
Price. Not broadcast in the UK)

Special: Operation Christmas Duff
First broadcast: 24/12/1956
Script: Spike Milligan and Larry
Stephens
Producer: Pat Dixon
(A BBC General Overseas Service-
only edition)

Series 8

(Regular cast: Peter Sellers, Harry Secombe, Spike Milligan, The Ray Ellington Quartet, Max Geldray and Wallace Greenslade as announcer)

01: *Spon*
First broadcast: 30/09/1957
Script: Spike Milligan
Producer: Charles Chilton
(Without Harry Secombe, with Dick
Emery)

02: *The Junk Affair*
First broadcast: 07/10/1957
Script: Spike Milligan and Larry
Stephens
Producer: Charles Chilton

03: *The Burning Embassy*
First broadcast: 14/10/1957
Script: Spike Milligan and Larry
Stephens
Producer: Charles Chilton

04: *The Great Regent's Park Swim*
First broadcast: 21/10/1957

Script: Spike Milligan and Larry
Stephens
Producer: Charles Chilton

05: *The Treasure in the Tower*
First broadcast: 28/10/1957
Script: Spike Milligan and Larry
Stephens
Producer: Charles Chilton

06: *The Space Age*
First broadcast: 04/11/1957
Script: Spike Milligan and Larry
Stephens
Producer: Roy Speer

07: *The Red Fort*
First broadcast: 11/11/1957
Script: Spike Milligan and Larry
Stephens
Producer: Roy Speer

08: The Missing Battleship
First broadcast: 18/11/1957
Script: Spike Milligan and Larry
Stephens
Producer: Roy Speer
(Without Max Geldray)

09: The Policy
First broadcast: 25/11/1957
Script: Spike Milligan and Larry
Stephens
Producer: Roy Speer

10: King Solomon's Mines
First broadcast: 02/12/1957
Script: Spike Milligan and Larry
Stephens
Producer: Roy Speer

11: The Stolen Postman
First broadcast: 09/12/1957
Script: Larry Stephens
Producer: Roy Speer

12: The Great British Revolution
First broadcast: 16/12/1957
Script: Spike Milligan and Larry
Stephens
Producer: Roy Speer

13: The Plasticine Man
First broadcast: 23/12/1957
Script: Spike Milligan and Larry
Stephens
Producer: Roy Speer
(Without Ray Ellington)

14: African Incident
First broadcast: 30/12/1957
Script: Spike Milligan and Larry
Stephens
Producer: Roy Speer
(With Cecile Chevreau)

15: The Thing on the Mountain
First broadcast: 06/01/1958
Script: Larry Stephens and Maurice
Wiltshire
Producer: Roy Speer

16: The String Robberies
First broadcast: 13/01/1958

Script: Spike Milligan
Producer: Roy Speer
(With George Chisholm)

17: The Moriarty Murder Mystery
First broadcast: 20/01/1958
Script: Larry Stephens and Maurice
Wiltshire
Producer: Charles Chilton

18: The Curse of Frankenstein
First broadcast: 27/01/1958
Script: Spike Milligan
Producer: Charles Chilton
(Without Ray Ellington, with George
Chisholm)

19: The White Neddie Trade
First broadcast: 03/02/1958
Script: Larry Stephens and Maurice
Wiltshire
Producer: Charles Chilton

*20: Ten Snowballs that Shook the
World*
First broadcast: 10/02/1958
Script: Spike Milligan
Producer: Charles Chilton

21: The Man Who Never Was
First broadcast: 17/02/1958
Script: Spike Milligan and Larry
Stephens
Producer: Charles Chilton

22: World War One
First broadcast: 24/02/1958
Script: Spike Milligan
Producer: Charles Chilton

23: The Spon Plague
First broadcast: 03/03/1958
Script: Spike Milligan and John
Antrobus
Producer: Charles Chilton
(With George Chisholm)

24: Tiddleywinks
First broadcast: 10/03/1958
Script: Spike Milligan
Producer: Charles Chilton

25: *The Evils of Bushey Spon*
First broadcast: 17/03/1958
Script: Spike Milligan
Producer: Charles Chilton
(With A. E. Matthews)

26: *The Great Statue Debate*
First broadcast: 24/03/1958
Script: Spike Milligan and John
Antrobus
Producer: Charles Chilton

VINTAGE GOONS

(Regular cast: Peter Sellers, Harry Secombe, Spike Milligan, The Ray Ellington Quartet, Max Geldray and Wallace Greenslade as announcer)

01: *The Mummified Priest*
First broadcast: 22/09/1958
Script: Spike Milligan
Producer: Charles Chilton

02: *The Greatest Mountain in the World*
First broadcast: 29/09/1958
Script: Spike Milligan
Producer: Charles Chilton

03: *The Missing Ten Downing Street*
First broadcast: Not broadcast in UK
Script: Spike Milligan and Larry
Stephens
Producer: Roy Speer

04: *The Giant Bombardon*
First broadcast: 06/10/1958
Script: Spike Milligan
Producer: Roy Speer
(With Valentine Dyall)

05: *The Kippered Herring Gang*
First broadcast: Not broadcast in UK
Script: Spike Milligan
Producer: Roy Speer

06: *The Vanishing Room*
First broadcast: 13/10/1958
Script: Spike Milligan
Producer: Roy Speer

07: *The Ink Shortage*
First broadcast: Not broadcast in UK
Script: Spike Milligan
Producer: Roy Speer

08: *The Mustard and Cress Shortage*
First broadcast: Not broadcast in UK
Script: Spike Milligan
Producer: Tom Ronald

09: *The Internal Mountain*
First broadcast: Not broadcast in UK
Script: Spike Milligan
Producer: Charles Chilton

10: *The Silent Bugler*
First broadcast: Not broadcast in UK
Script: Spike Milligan
Producer: Charles Chilton

11: *The Great Bank of England Robbery*
First broadcast: 20/10/1958
Script: Spike Milligan
Producer: Charles Chilton

12: *The Dreaded Piano Clubber*
First broadcast: Not broadcast in UK
Script: Spike Milligan
Producer: Charles Chilton

13: *The Siege of Fort Night*
First broadcast: Not broadcast in UK
Script: Spike Milligan
Producer: Charles Chilton

14: *The Albert Memorial*
First broadcast: 27/10/1958
Script: Spike Milligan
Producer: Charles Chilton

Series 9

(Regular cast: Peter Sellers, Harry Secombe, Spike Milligan, The Ray Ellington Quartet, Max Geldray and Wallace Greenslade as announcer)

01: The Sahara Desert Statue
First broadcast: 03/11/1958
Script: Spike Milligan
Producer: John Browell

02: I Was Monty's Treble
First broadcast: 10/11/1958
Script: Spikc Milligan
Producer: John Browell

03: The £1,000,000 Penny
First broadcast: 17/11/1958
Script: Spike Milligan
Producer: John Browell

04: The Pam's Paper Insurance Policy
First broadcast: 24/11/1958
Script: Spike Milligan
Producer: John Browell

05: The Mountain Eaters
First broadcast: 01/12/1958
Script: Spike Milligan
Producer: John Browell

06: The Childe Harolde Rewarde
First broadcast: 08/12/1958
Script: Spike Milligan
Producer: John Browell

07: The Seagoon Memoirs
First broadcast: 15/12/1958
Script: Larry Stephens and Maurice Wiltshire
Producer: John Browell

08: Queen Anne's Rain
First broadcast: 22/12/1958
Script: Spike Milligan
Producer: John Browell

09: The Battle of Spion Kop
First broadcast: 29/12/1958
Script: Spike Milligan
Producer: John Browell

10: Ned's Atomic Dustbin
First broadcast: 05/01/1959
Script: Spike Milligan
Producer: John Browell

11: Who Is Pink Oboe?
First broadcast: 12/01/1959
Script: Spike Milligan
Producer: John Browell
(Without Peter Sellers but with Kenneth Connor, Valentine Dyall, Graham Stark, Jack Train and John Snagge)

12: The Call of the West
First broadcast: 20/01/1959
Script: Spike Milligan
Producer: John Browell

13: Dishonoured – Again
First broadcast: 26/01/1959
Script: Spike Milligan
Producer: John Browell

14: The Scarlet Capsule
First broadcast: 02/02/1959
Script: Spike Milligan
Producer: John Browell

15: The Tay Bridge
First broadcast: 09/02/1959
Script: Spike Milligan
Producer: John Browell

16: The Gold Plate Robbery
First broadcast: 16/02/1959
Script: Spike Milligan
Producer: John Browell

17: The £50 Cure
First broadcast: 23/02/1959
Script: Spike Milligan
Producer: John Browell
(Without Harry Secombe, with Kenneth Connor)

Series 10

(Regular cast: Peter Sellers, Harry Secombe, Spike Milligan, The Ray Ellington Quartet, Max Geldray and Wallace Greenslade as announcer)

01: A Christmas Carol
First broadcast: 24/12/1959
Script: Spike Milligan
Producer: John Browell

02: The Tale of Men's Shirts
First broadcast: 31/12/1959
Script: Spike Milligan
Producer: John Browell

03: The Chinese Legs
First broadcast: 07/01/1960
Script: Spike Milligan
Producer: John Browell

04: Robin's Post
First broadcast: 14/01/1960
Script: Spike Milligan
Producer: John Browell

05: The Silver Dubloons
First broadcast: 21/01/1960
Script: Spike Milligan
Producer: John Browell

06: The Last Smoking Seagoon
First broadcast: 28/01/1960
Script: Spike Milligan
Producer: John Browell

SYKES AND A . . . (BBC1)

Series 1

(Script: Johnny Speight. Regular cast: Eric Sykes – Eric; Hattie Jacques – Hat; Richard Wattis – Charles Brown)

29.01.1960
Sykes And A Telephone *
Michael Balfour, Arthur Mullard,
Vivien Grant

05.02.1960
Sykes And A Burglary *
Percy Edwards, Edwin Brown,
Richard Greenford

12.02.1960
Sykes And A New Car *
Deryck Guyler

19.02.1960
Sykes And An Uncle *
Campbell Cotts, Sidney Vivian,
Peter Bathurst, Geoffrey Denton,
Henry Drew, Henry Kay, Frank
Littlewood, Peter Morny,
Gordon Phillott

26.02.1960
Sykes And A Lodger *

Series 2

(Script: Eric Sykes, with Spike Milligan and John Antrobus. Regular cast: Eric Sykes – Eric; Hattie Jacques – Hat; Richard Wattis – Charles Brown)

11.08.1960
Sykes And A Movie Camera *
Deryck Guyler, John Brooking,
Mario Fabrizi, Stella Tanner

18.08.1960
Sykes And A Library Book *
Deryck Guyler, Cameron Hall,
Bruce Seton, 'Rustler'

25.08.1960
Sykes And A Holiday
Jacques Cey, Keith Smith,
Andre Charise, Romany Campbell

01.09.1960
Sykes And An Egg *
Richard Waring, Hugh Lloyd,
Cecil Brock, Eleanor Darling

08.09.1960
Sykes And A Brave Deed *
Bernard Hunter, Arthur Mullard,
Gay Cameron, Alec Bregonzi

15.09.1960
Sykes And A Cheque Book *
Richard Caldicot, Hamlyn Benson,
Hugh Lloyd, Frank Henderson

Series 3

(Script: Eric Sykes. Regular cast: Eric Sykes – Eric; Hattie Jacques – Hat; Richard Wattis – Charles Brown)

04.01.1961
Sykes And A Window *
Charles Lloyd Pack, Frank Atkinson,
Murray Kash

11.01.1961
Sykes And A Salesman
Bruno Barnabe, Thomas Gallagher,
Eric Phillips

18.01.1961
Sykes And A Fancy Dress *
Robert Atkins, Deryck Guyler,
Hugh Lloyd

25.01.1961
Sykes And A Bath
Deryck Guyler, Frank Henderson,
Keith Smith, John Bluthal,
Bob Todd

01.02.1961
Sykes And A Marriage *
Gladys Henson, Stella Tanner,
Frank Littlewood

08.02.1961
Sykes And An Ankle

Series 4

(Script: Eric Sykes. Regular cast: Eric Sykes – Eric; Hattie Jacques – Hat)

14.04.1961
Sykes And A Mission *
John Bluthal, Stuart Saunders,
Arthur Mullard, Joe Gibbons

21.04.1961
Sykes And A Stranger
Leo McKern, Bernard Hunter,
Eric Phillips, Bob Todd

28.04.1961
Sykes And A Cat
Ivor Salter, Patricia Kerry,
Eric Phillips, Lionel Wheeler,

05.05.1961
Sykes And A Bandage *
Fabia Drake, Michael Brennan,
Tony Bateman

12.05.1961
Sykes And A Suspicion *
Hugh Lloyd, Bernard Hunter,
Arthur Mullard, Stuart Saunders

19.05.1961
Sykes And A Surprise *
David Horne, Wallas Eaton

Series 5

(Script: Eric Sykes. Regular cast: Eric Sykes – Eric; Hattie Jacques – Hat)

30.12.1961
Sykes And A Gamble
Bill Kerr, Stuart Saunders,
Rosamund Waring, Alan
Simpson

06.01.1962
Sykes And A Job
Dick Emery, Campbell Singer,
Arthur Mullard

13.01.1962
Sykes And A Boat
Charles Lloyd Pack

20.01.1962
Sykes And A Journey
Graham Stark, Arthur Brough,
Hugh Lloyd, Nancy Roberts,
Keith Smith, Annie Leake,
Bob Todd

27.01.1962
Sykes And An Elephant
Deryck Guyler, Joan Hickson,
Colin Douglas and Burma

06.02.1962
Sykes And A Rolls
Martita Hunt, Victor Platt,
Stella Turner, Billy Milton,
Charles Bird, Johnny Clayton,
Eunice Black, Eleanor Darling,
Gareth Tandy, Malcolm Knight,
Adrian Blount

13.02.1962
Sykes And A Haunting
Dick Emery, Tony Vale

20.02.1962
Sykes And A Dream
Moira Redmond, Richard Caldicot,
Patricia Hayes, Brian Rawlinson,
Sidney Keith, Leonard Grahame,
Louis Haslow

Sykes/Christmas Night With the
Stars*
*(Eric Sykes, Hattie Jacques, Deryck
Guyler)*

5.12.1962
Sykes And His Sister

Series 6

(Script: Eric Sykes. Eric Sykes – Eric; Hattie Jacques – Hat)

21.02.1963
Sykes And A Fog *
Cardew Robinson, Molly Weir,
Arthur Mullard, Alfred Maron

28.02.1963
Sykes And A Phobia *
Ronald Fraser, Patrick McAlinney,
Keith Smith, Maxwell Foster

07.03.1963
Sykes And A Camping *
Jack Smethurst, Bill Rhodes

14.03.1963
Sykes And A Picture
Martin Miller, Toke Townley,
Howard Douglas

21.03.1963
Sykes And A Mouse *
Martin Miller, Victor Platt,
Roger Avon

28.03.1963
Sykes And A Walk
Deryck Guyler, Eric Phillips,
Charles Bird

04.04.1963
Sykes And A Referee *
Martin Miller, Kenneth
Wolstenholme,
George Roderick

11.04.1963
Sykes And A Pub *
Norman Mitchell, Brian Rawlinson,
David Lander

Series 7

(Script: Eric Sykes. Regular cast: Eric Sykes – Eric; Hattie Jacques – Hat)

25.02.1964
Sykes And A Box
Ronald Adam, Donald Pickering

03.03.1964
Sykes And A Plank
Deryck Guyler, Richard Shaw,
Annie Leake, Teddy Green

10.03.1964
Sykes And A Search *
Sheila Steafel, Margot Boyd

17.03.1964
Sykes And A Following
Harry Locke, William Kendall

24.03.1964
Sykes And A Menace *
Melanie Parr, Geoffrey Hibbert

31.03.1964
Sykes And A Log Cabin
Ronnie Barker, Derek Nimmo

07.04.1964
Sykes And A Band *
Wensley Pithey, Howard Douglas

Series 8

(Script: Eric Sykes. Regular cast: Eric Sykes – Eric; Hattie Jacques – Hat)

30.10.1964
Sykes And Two Birthdays *
Jeremy Longhurst, Gerald Campion

06.11.1964
Sykes And A Hypnotist
Robert Dorning, Valentine Dyall

13.11.1964
Sykes And A Protest *
Arthur Mullard, Campbell Singer

20.11.1964
Sykes And A Bird *
Fabia Drake, John Arnatt

27.11.1964
Sykes And A Cold War
Dick Emery, Dandy Nichols

04.12.1964
Sykes And A Gold?
Peter West, Howard Douglas

Series 9

(Script: Eric Sykes. Regular cast: Eric Sykes – Eric; Hattie Jacques – Hat)

05.10.1965
Sykes And A Mountain *
Anthony Sharp, Arthur White,
John Bailey

12.10.1965
Sykes And A Deb *
J.G. Devlin, Sally Bazely,
Christopher Sandford

19.10.1965
Sykes And A Business *
Hugh Paddick, Jean Trend,
Bill Treacher

26.10.1965
Sykes And A Golfer

Peter Alliss, Bill Cox,
Douglas Blackwell

02.11.1965
Sykes And A Big Brother *
Kenneth J. Warren, Campbell Singer,
Maitland Moss

09.11.1965
Sykes And A Uniform
John Junkin, Sydney Bromley,
Bill Treacher

16.11.1965
Sykes And A Nest Egg *
Bill Nagy

HANCOCK'S HALF-HOUR (BBC Light Programme)

Series 1

(Regular cast: Tony Hancock, Sidney James, Bill Kerr, Moira Lister, Kenneth Williams, Alan Simpson)

02.11.1954
The First Night Party
Gerald Campion

09.11.1954
The Diamond Ring *

16.11.1954
The Idol

23.11.1954
The Boxing Champion
Paul Carpenter

30.11.1954
The Hancock Festival *

07.12.1954
The New Car

14.12.1954
The Department Store Santa *

21.12.1954
Christmas at Aldershot *

28.12.1954
The Christmas Eve Party *

04.01.1955
Cinderella Hancock
Dora Bryan, Paul Carpenter

11.01.1955
A Trip to France

18.01.1955
The Monte Carlo Rally
Brian Johnston, Raymond Baxter

25.01.1955
A House on the Cliff

01.02.1955
The Sheikh

08.02.1955
The Marriage Bureau *
Peter Sellers

15.02.1955
The End of the Series

Series 2

(*Regular cast:* Tony Hancock, Sidney James, Bill Kerr, Andrée Melly, Kenneth Williams, Alan Simpson)

19.04.1955
A Holiday in France *
Harry Secombe (replacing Hancock)

26.04.1955
The Crown Jewels *
Harry Secombe (replacing Hancock)

03.05.1955
The Racehorse *
Harry Secombe (replacing Hancock)

10.05.1955
A Visit to Swansea *
Harry Secombe

17.05.1955
The Holiday Camp
Dennis Wilson

24.05.1955
The Chef that Died of Shame

31.05.1955
Prime Minister Hancock *

07.06.1955
The Rail Strike

14.06.1955
The Television Set

21.06.1955
The Three Sons *

28.06.1955
The Marrow Contest

05.07.1955
The Matador

Series 3

(*Regular cast:* Tony Hancock, Sidney James, Bill Kerr, Andrée Melly, Kenneth Williams, Alan Simpson)

19.10.1955
The Pet Dog

26.10.1955
The Jewel Robbery

02.11.1955
The Bequest

09.11.1955
The New Neighbour *

16.11.1955
The Winter Holiday *

23.11.1955
The Blackboard Jungle

30.11.1955
The Red Planet *

07.12.1955
The Diet *

14.12.1955
A Visit to Russia *

21.12.1955
The Trial of Father Christmas *
Ray Galton, Graham Stark

28.12.1955
Cinderella Hancock
Dora Bryan

04.01.1956
The New Year Resolutions *

11.01.1956
Hancock's Hair

18.01.1956
The Student Prince

25.01.1956
The Breakfast Cereal *

01.02.1956
How Hancock Won the War *

08.02.1956
The Newspaper *

15.02.1956
The Greyhound Track

22.02.1956
The Conjurer

29.02.1956
The Test Match
John Arlott, Godfrey Evans,
Colin Cowdrey, Frank Tyson

Series 4

(Regular cast: Tony Hancock, Sidney James, Bill Kerr, Hattie Jacques, Kenneth Williams)

14.10.1956
Back From Holiday
Alan Simpson, Ray Galton

21.10.1956
The Bolshoi Ballet
Alan Simpson, Ray Galton

28.10.1956
Sid James's Dad
Alan Simpson

04.11.1956
The Income Tax Demand
Alan Simpson, Ray Galton

11.11.1956
The New Secretary
Alan Simpson

18.11.1956
Michelangelo 'Ancock
Alan Simpson, Ray Galton

25.11.1956
Anna and the King Of Siam
Alan Simpson, Ray Galton

02.12.1956
Cyrano de Hancock

09.12.1956
The Stolen Petrol
Alan Simpson, Ray Galton

16.12.1956
The Espresso Bar
Ray Galton

23.12.1956
Hancock's Happy Christmas
Michael Anderson, Dorothy
Marks, Galton and Simpson

30.12.1956
The Diary

06.01.1957
The 13th of the Series

13.01.1957
Almost a Gentleman

20.01.1957
The Old School Reunion

27.01.1957
The Wild Man of the Woods

03.02.1957
Agricultural 'Ancock

10.02.1957
Hancock in the Police

17.02.1957
The Emigrant

24.02.1957
The Last of the McHancocks
James Robertson Justice

Series 5

(Regular cast: Tony Hancock, Sidney James, Bill Kerr, Hattie Jacques, Kenneth Williams)

21.01.1958
The New Radio Series

28.01.1958
The Scandal Magazine
John Vere

04.02.1958
The Male Suffragettes

11.02.1958
The Insurance Policy

18.02.1958
The Publicity Photograph

25.02.1958
The Unexploded Bomb
Alan Simpson

04.03.1958
Hancock's School

11.03.1958
Around the World in Eighty Days

18.03.1958
The Americans Hit Town
Jerry Stovin

25.03.1958
The Election Candidate
Alan Simpson

01.04.1958
Hancock's Car
Alan Simpson

08.04.1958
The East Cheam Drama Festival
Kathleen O'Hagan

15.04.1958
The Foreign Legion

22.04.1958
Sunday Afternoon at Home

29.04.1958
The Grappling Game

06.05.1958
The Junk Man

13.05.1958
Hancock's War

20.05.1958
The Prize Money
Alan Simpson, Patricia Hayes,
Christina Horniman

27.05.1958
The Threatening Letters
Alan Simpson

03.06.1958
The Sleepless Night

CHRISTMAS SPECIAL
25.12.1958
Bill and Father Christmas
Warren Mitchell

Series 6

(Regular cast: Tony Hancock, Sidney James, Bill Kerr)

29.09.1959
The Smugglers
Kenneth Williams, Patricia Hayes,
Noel Dryden

06.10.1959
The Childhood Sweetheart
Kenneth Williams, Patricia Hayes

13.10.1959
The Last Bus Home
Warren Mitchell, Hugh Morton

20.10.1959
The Picnic
Wilfred Babbage, Patricia Hayes,
Anne Lancaster, Liz Frazer

27.10.1959
The Gourmet
Warren Mitchell, Hugh Morton,
Raymond Glendenning

03.11.1959
The Elopement
Lillian Grasson, Wilfred Babbage,
Fraser Kerr, Leigh Crutchley

10.11.1959
Fred's Pie Stall
Wilfred Babbage, Hugh Morton,
Harry Towb

17.11.1959
The Waxwork
Warren Mitchell

24.11.1959
Sid's Mystery Tours
Warren Mitchell, Errol McKinnon,
Mavis Villiers

01.12.1959
The Fete
Wilfred Babbage, Hugh Morton,
Jack Watson

08.12.1959
The Poetry Society
Fenella Fielding, Warren Mitchell,
Fraser Kerr

15.12.1959
Hancock in Hospital
Patricia Hayes, Joan Frank

22.12.1959
The Christmas Club
Wilfred Babbage, Hugh Morton,
Frank Partington

29.12.1959
The Impersonator
Anne Lancaster, Peter Goodwright,
Ronald Wilson, Jerry Stovin,
Wilfred Babbage, Jack Watson

HANCOCK'S HALF-HOUR (BBC TV)

(Regular cast: Tony Hancock, Sidney James)

Series 1

06.07.1956
First TV Show *
Harold Goodwin, Irene Handl,
Eddie Leslie, Chris Dreaper,
Margaret Flint, Peter Haigh,
Iain MacNaughton, Graham
Leaman

20.07.1956
The Artist *
Irene Handl, Valentine Dyall,
Warren Mitchell, Desmonde
Rayner, Ivor Raymonde,
James Bulloch, Eleanor Fazan,
Leslie Cooper

03.08.1956
The Dancer *
Hermione Baddeley, Lorrae
Desmonde, Warren Mitchell,

Frank Lonergan, Liz Fraser,
Eleanor Fazan, Jessica Dent,
Michael Boudot, Philip Casson,
Roslyn Ellis, Kay Rose, Alan Simpson

17.08.1956
The Bequest *
Irene Handl, Reginald Beckwith,
Rose Howlett, Claude Bonser,
Tottie Truman Taylor, Gordon
Phillott, Fraser White, Ivor
Raymonde, Elizabeth Fraser

31.08.1956
The Radio Show *
Warren Mitchell, Eric Sykes,
Manville Tarrant, Alan Simpson,
Ray Galton, Iain MacNaughton,
George Crowther, Roy Patrick,
Desmond Rayner, John Vyvyan,

Graham Stark, Fraser White,
Kim Corcoran, Mario Fabrizi,
Frank Lonergan, Peter Emms,
Liz Fraser

14.09.1956
The Chef that Died of Shame *
Warren Mitchell, Constance Wake,
Peter Haigh, Raymond Rollett,
Dennis Chinnery, John Vere

Series 2

01.04.1957
The Alpine Holiday
Richard Wattis, Kenneth Williams,
June Whitfield, John Vere, Peggy Ann
Clifford, Dennis Chinnery, Patrick
Milner, Victor Bryant, Manville
Tarrant, Rose Howlett, Liz Fraser

15.04.1957
Lady Chatterley's Revenge *
Kenneth Williams, Hattie Jacques,
Warren Mitchell, John Vere,
Paddy Edwards, John Vyvyan,
Dennis Chinnery, Desmond Rayner,
Raymond Rollett, Anne Lancaster,
Rose Howlett, Evelyn Lund,
Anne Reid, Alan Simpson,
Charles Julian, Manville
Tarrant, Claude Bonser

29.04.1957
The Russian Prince *
Kenneth Williams, Hattie Jacques,
Bill Fraser, Michael Balfour,
Mario Fabrizi, Leonard Sharp,
Harry Lane, Dennis Chinnery,
Raymond Rollett, Anne Lancaster,
Janet Barrow, Iain MacNaughton,

Roger Oatime, Fraser White,
Frank Pemberton, Gordon Phillott

13.05.1957
The New Neighbour *
Kenneth Williams, Hattie Jacques,
John Vere, Bill Fraser, Mario
Fabrizi

27.05.1957
The Pianist *
Kenneth Williams, Hattie Jacques,
John Vere, Mario Fabrizi, Dennis
Chinnery, Ivor Raymonde,
Raymond Rollett, Roger Oatime,
Manville Tarrant, Graham Leaman,
Claude Bonser, James Bulloch,
Harry Drew, Leonard Sharp,
Harry Lane, Angela Crow

10.06.1957
The Auction *
Gordon Phillott, Graham Leaman,
Dennis Chinnery, George Crowther,
Totti Truman Taylor, Rose Howlett,
Manville Tarrant, Harry Lane,
Mario Fabrizi

Series 3

30.09.1957
The Continental Holiday *
Anton Diffring, Mario Fabrizi,
Peter Allenby, Tutte Lemkow,
Eugenie Sivyer, Leslie Smith,
Richard Statman, Peter Elliott,
David Grahame, George Elliott,
Edouard Assaly, Alec Bregonzi,

Anthony Shirvell, Bruce Wightman,
Arthur Bennett, Manville Tarrant,
Thomas Symonds

07.10.1957
The Great Detective *
John Vere, Terence Alexander,
Cameron Hall, Paddy Edwards,
Peggy Ann Clifford, Graham

Leaman, Pat Coombs, Evelyn
Lund, Totti Truman Taylor,
Manville Tarrant, Gordon Phillott,
Anne Reid, James Bulloch,
Patrick Milner, Peter Emms,
Basil Beale, John Vyvyan

14.10.1957
Amusement Arcade *
Dick Emery, Bill Fraser,
John Vere, John Vyvyan,
Evelyn Lund, Rose Howlett,
Elizabeth Gott, Peggy Ann
Clifford, Claude Bonser,
Manville Tarrant, Con Courtney,
Leslie Smith, Patrick Milner,
Bruce Wightman, Alan Simpson,
Alec Bregonzi, Thomas Symonds,
Anthony Shirvell

21.10.1957
Holiday in Scotland *
Raymond Huntley,
Iain MacNaughton, John Vere,
Richard Statman, Ann Marryott,
Eileen Delamare, Charles Juilan,
John Vyvyan, George Crowther,
Manville Tarrant

28.10.1957
Air Steward Hancock
Bill Fraser, John Vere,
Dave Freeman, Peter Allenby,
John Vyvyan, Leslie Smith,
Richard Statman, Alec Bregonzi,
Philip Carr, Stuart Hillier,
Cameron Hall, James Bulloch,
Anne Marryott, Basil Beale,
Manville Tarrant

04.11.1957
Regimental Reunion *
Campbell Singer, Gary Middleton,
John Vere, Terence Alexander,
Cameron Hall, Raymond Rollett,
Graham Leaman, Stuart Hillier,
Mario Fabrizi, John Vyvyan,
Claude Bonser, Alec Bregonzi,
Con Courtney, Bruce Wightman,

Manville Tarrant, Peter Allenby,
George Crowther, Arthur Mullard,
Harry Robins, Harry Lane

11.11.1957
The Adopted Family *
John Vere, Ian Fleming,
Pamela Manson, Ann Marryott,
Stuart Hillier, Mario Fabrizi,
John Vyvyan, Manville Tarrant,
Anne Reid, Patrick Milner,
Hugh Lloyd

25.11.1957
The Elocution Teacher *
(postponed from 18/11) Jack Hawkins,
John Vere, Stuart Hillier, John Vyvyan,
Nora Nicholson, Mary Reynolds

02.12.1957
The Lawyer: The Crown v. James S.
John Le Mesurier, Bill Fraser,
John Vere, Raymond Rollett,
Arthur Mullard, John Vyvyan,
Hugh Lloyd, Claude Bonser,
Anthony Shirvell, Roger Oatime,
Manville Tarrant, John Foster,
Anne Marryott, Patrick Milner,
Alec Bregonzi, Richard Sullivan

09.12.1957
*How to Win Money and Influence
People*
Dick Emery, John Vere,
Campbell Singer, John Vyvyan,
Bruce Wightman, Basil Beale,
Alec Bregonzi, Philip Carr,
Leslie Smith, Anthony Shirvell,
Mario Fabrizi, Burt Kwouk,
Nelson Grostate, Hugh Lloyd,
Jimmy Raphael, Manville Tarrant

16.12.1957
*There's an Airfield at the Bottom of
My Garden*
Dick Emery, John Vere, John Vyvyan,
Esther MacPherson, Cameron Hall,
Nancy Roberts, Gordon Phillott,
Paddy Edwards, Leslie Smith,

Claude Bonser, Vera Elmore,
Anne Reid, Brenda Duncan,
Elizabeth Gott, Alec Bregonzi,
Evelyn Lund

23.12.1957
Hancock's Forty-Three Minutes
'The East Cheam Repertory
Company': John Gregson,

Max Geldray, Alf Silvestri,
The Glamazons, The Keynotes,
Dido the Chimp, John Vere,
John Vyvyan, Dennis Chinnery,
Mario Fabrizi, Arthur Bennett,
Tommy Eytle, John McRay,
James Avon, Richard Wharton,
Michael Ely

Series 4

26.12.1958
Ericson the Viking
Pat Coombs, John Vere, Laurie
Webb, Ivor Raymonde, John
Vyvyan, Mario Fabrizi, Arthur
Mullard, Manville Tarrant,
Anthony Shirvell, Alec Bregonzi,
Philip Carr, Louis Adam,
Herbert Nelson, Pat O'Meara,
Rufus Cruickshank, George
Crowther, Richard Statman

02.01.1959
The Set That Failed
John Vere, Hugh Lloyd, Patricia
Hayes, Robert Dorning, Sidney
Vivian, Margaret Flint, John
Vyvyan, Ivor Raymonde,
Mario Fabrizi, Leslie Smith,
Anthony Shirvell, Rose Howlett,
Claude Bonser, Evelyn Lund,
Harry Robins, Stella Kemball,
Anne Marryott

09.01.1959
Underpaid! or, Grandad's SOS *
Warren Mitchell, Andrew Faulds,
Mario Fabrizi, John Vyvyan,
Philip Carr, Arthur Mullard,
Rolf Harris, Richard Statman,
Evelyn Lund, Harry Drew,
George Crowther, James Bulloch,
Con Courtney, Claude Bonser,
Anthony Shirvell, Len David

16.01.1959
The New Nose
John Le Mesurier, Arthur Mullard,
Liz Fraser, Roger Avon,
Annabelle Lee, Pamela Manson,
Barbara Archer, Mario Fabrizi,
Alec Bregonzi, Ivor Raymonde,
Anne Marryott

23.01.1959
The Flight of the Red Shadow *
Robert Dorning, John Vere,
Louis Howard, Rolf Harris,
Arthur Mullard, Mario Fabrizi,
Guy Mills, Manville Tarrant,
James Bulloch, Ivor Raymonde,
Harry Drew, George Crowther,
Louis Adam, Alan Simpson,
Ray Galton, Alec Bregonzi,
Con Courtney, Bert Simms,
Evelyn Lund, Ben Bowers,
Patrick Milner, Herbert Nelson,
Stanley Ayres, Frank Littlewood,
Anna Churcher, Ann Jay

30.01.1959
The Horror Serial *
John Le Mesurier, Arthur Mullard,
Dennis Chinnery, Alec Bregonzi,
John Vyvyan, Laurie Webb,
Anne Marryott, Hugh Lloyd,
Phyllis Norwood

06.02.1959
The Italian Maid *
Marla Landi, John Vere,
Frederick Schiller, Michael Stainton,

Elizabeth Gott, James Bulloch,
Jeanette Edwards, John Vyvyan,
Harry Lane, Betty Lloyd-Davies

13.02.1959
Matrimony – Almost *
Terence Alexander, John Vere,
Vivienne Martin, Philip Carr,
Cardew Robinson, Cameron Hall,
Arthur Mullard, Mario Fabrizi,
Ivor Raymonde, Gwen Ewen,
Paddy Edwards, Alec Bregonzi,
Edith Stevenson, James Bulloch,
Liz Fraser, Frank Littlewood,
Michael Greenwood, Lionel Wheeler,
Louis Adam, Patrick Milner,
Philip Howard, Evelyn Lund

20.02.1959
The Beauty Contest *
John Blyth, Robert Dorning,
John Vere, Roger Avon,
Harry Lane, Charles Julian,
Mario Fabrizi, Bert Simms,
Arthur Mullard, Herbert Nelson,
John Vyvyan, George Crowther,
James Bulloch, Frank Littlewood,
Joe Robinson, Richard Statman,
Con Courtney, Alan Simpson,
Patrick Milner, Ann Smith,
Phillipa Steward

06.03.1959
The Wrong Man *
(postponed from 27/2) Campbell
Singer, Roger Avon, John Vyvyan,

Gordon Phillott, James Bulloch,
Nancy Roberts, Alec Bregonzi, Arthur
Mullard, Laurie Webb, Alan Simpson

13.03.1959
The Oak Tree
John Vere, Reginald Beckwith,
Hugh Lloyd, Robert Dorning,
Mario Fabrizi, Laurie Webb,
Graham Leaman, Arthur Mullard,
Gwenda Ewan, Mary Fletcher,
Joyce Hemson, Margerie Mason,
Sonia Peters, Edwin Morton,
Albert Grant, James Langley,
John Caesar, Norman Taylor,
Robert Pitt, Bill Matthews, Victor
Charrington, Anthony Jennett

20.03.1959
The Knighthood
Richard Wattis, John Vere,
Robert Dorning, Andrew Faulds,
Mario Fabrizi, Ivor Raymonde,
Lynne Cole, John Vyvyan,
Jack Leonard, James Bulloch

27.03.1959
The Servants *
'The East Cheam Repertory
Company': John Le Mesurier,
Mary Hinton, John Vyvyan,
James Bulloch, Alec Bregonzi,
Hugh Lloyd, Nancy Roberts,
Charles Julian, Evelyn Lund,
Gordon Phillott, Patricia Hayes,
Con Courtney

Series 5

25.09.1959
The Economy Drive
Patricia Hayes, Liz Fraser,
Arthur Mullard, Laurie Webb,
Frank Pemberton, Herbert Nelson,
Alec Bregonzi, Mario Fabrizi,
Totti Truman Taylor, Peggyann
Clifford, Pamela Manson,
Ann Marryott, Beatrice Ormonde,

Joanna Douglas, Michael Ward,
Jeanette Edwards

02.10.1959
The Two Murderers
Patricia Hayes, Hugh Lloyd,
Arthur Mullard, Robert Dorning,
Mark Singleton, Ralph Nossek,
Tom Clegg, Albert Grant,

Betty Miller, John Vyvyan,
Louise Stafford

09.10.1959
Lord Byron Lived Here
John Le Mesurier, Hugh Lloyd,
Robert Dorning, William Mervyn,
Stan Simmons, Raymond Grahame,
Judy Rogers, John Vyvyan,
Marylyn Thomas, Robert Bryan,
Frances St Barbe-West, Dorothy
Watson, Susan Hunter, Michael
Wyatt

16.10.1959
Twelve Angry Men
Hugh Lloyd, Mario Fabrizi,
Ralph Nossek, Leonard Sachs,
Austin Trevor, Herbert Nelson,
William Kendall, Leslie Perrins,
Philip Ray, Kenneth Kove,
Betty Cardno, Lala Lloyd,
Alec Bregonzi, James Bulloch,
Marie Lightfoot

23.10.1959
The Train Journey
Raymond Huntley, Eve Patrick,
Hugh Lloyd, Cameron Hall,
Henry Longhurst, Robert Dorning,
Totti Truman Taylor, Philip Carr

30.10.1959
The Cruise
Gwenda Ewan, Philip Carr,
Ivor Raymonde, Patrick Milner,
Hattie Jacques, Harry Brunning,
Evelyn Lund, Dennis Chinnery,
John Le Mesurier, Brian Oulton,
Paddy Edwards, Richard Statman,
Frank Littlewood, Herbert Nelson,
Brian Tyler, Astor Sklair, Ricky
Felgate, Mario Fabrizi, Patricia
Shakesby, Una Trimming,
Laura Thurlow, James Bulloch,
Lionel Wheeler, Hugh Lloyd,
Laurie Webb

06.11.1959
The Big Night
Patricia Hayes, Sam Kydd,
Hugh Lloyd, Michael Balfour,
Robert Dorning, Anne Lancaster,
Mario Fabrizi, Tom Clegg,
Paddy Edwards, Annabelle Lee,
Ivor Raymonde, Joanna Douglas,
Beatrice Ormonde, Laura Thurlow,
Patricia Shakesby, James Bulloch,
Leonard Kingston

13.11.1959
The Tycoon
William Kendall, Robert Dorning,
Ralph Nossek, Mark Singleton,
James Bulloch, Hugh Lloyd,
Alec Bregonzi, Ivor Raymonde,
John Vyvyan, Una Trimming,
Rosamund Lesley, Anne Reid,
Anne Marryott, Bernice Swanson,
Harold Kasket, Bob Marshall,
Leonard Graham

20.11.1959
Spanish Interlude
Annabelle Lee, Paddy Edwards,
Lynne Cole, David Lander,
Brian Worth, John Vyvyan,
Ronnie Brody, Patrick Milner,
Herbert Nelson, Astor Sklair,
Pat O'Meara, Lionel Wheeler,
Tom McCall

27.11.1959
Football Pools
Hugh Lloyd, Sidney Vivian,
Robert Dorning, Laurie Webb,
Richard Statman, John Vyvyan,
Alec Bregonzi, Lionel Wheeler,
Patrick Milner, Herbert Nelson,
Philip Carr, Tom Clegg,
James Cliston, Edward Willis,
Ryan Jelfe, David Bell

Series 6

04.03.1960
The Cold
Hugh Lloyd, John Le Mesurier,
Patricia Hayes, Anne Marryott,
Richard Statman, Herbert Nelson,
Tom Clegg

11.03.1960
The Missing Page
Hugh Lloyd, George Coulouris,
Gordon Phillott, Kenneth Kove,
Totti Truman Taylor, Gibb
McLoughlin, James Bulloch,
Peggy Ann Clifford, Alec Bregonzi,
John Vyvyan, Frank Littlewood,
Ray Grover

18.03.1960
The Emigrant
Brian Oulton, David Lander,
Gordon Sterne, Hugh Lloyd,
Richard Statman, John Vyvyan,
Herbert Nelson, Harry Robins,
Johnnie Lee, Samuel Manseray,
Alec Bregonzi, John Bramley,
Joe Enrikie

25.03.1960
The Reunion Party
Hugh Lloyd, Cardew Robinson,
Clive Dunn, Eileen Way, Sidney
Vivian, Robert Dorning, Laurie
Webb

01.04.1960
Sid in Love
Joan Heal, Robert Dorning,
Vi Stevens, Hugh Lloyd,
Denny Dayviss, Peggy Ann
Clifford, James Bulloch,
Douglas Robinson, Anne
Marryatt, John Vyvyan,
John Bramley

08.04.1960
The Baby Sitters
Terence Alexander, Annabelle Lee,
Robert Dorning, Herbert Nelson,

Alec Bregonzi, Patrick Milner,
Michael Earl

15.04.1960
The Ladies' Man
Arthur Mullard, Liz Fraser
Brian Oulton, Robert Dorning,
Annabelle Lee, Laura Thurlow,
Honor Shepherd, Laurie Webb,
Barbara Evans, Gwenda Evans,
George Crowther, Herbert Nelson,
Harry Robins, Stan Simmons,
John Vyvyan, Bert Waller,
Eleanor Fazan

22.04.1960
The Photographer
William Kendall, Herbert Hare,
Robert Dorning, Hugh Lloyd, Totti
Truman Taylor, Laura Thurlow, Joanna
Douglas, Edward Malin, Murray Kash,
Laurie Webb, Anthony Shirvell,
Michael Earl, Philip Howard, John
Vyvyan, Ann Bassett

29.04.1960
The East Cheam Centenary
Robert Dorning, Hugh Lloyd,
Cameron Hall, Edward Malin,
James Bulloch, Lala Lloyd, Evelyn
Lund, Brian Oulton, Leslie Perrins,
Anne Marryott, Sidney Vivian, John
Snagge, Astor Sklair, Sylvia Osbourn,
Frank Littlewood, George Crowther,
Herbert Nelson, Michael Earl, John
Bramley, John Vyvyan, James Langley,
Michael Phillips, John Bosch

06.05.1960
The Poison Pen Letters
Patricia Hayes, John Welsh,
Anna Churcher, Andrew Lieven,
Totti Truman Taylor

Series 7

26.05.1961
The Bed-sitter
Michael Aspel

02.06.1961
The Bowmans
Patrick Cargill, Hugh Lloyd, Brian
Oulton, Peter Glaze, Constance
Coulton, Meadows White, Alec
Bregonzi, Gwenda Ewan, Ralph
Wilson, Victor Platt, William
Sherwood, Bruno Barnabe, Dennis
Chinnery

09.06.1961
The Radio Ham
Bernard Peake, Annie Leake,
Edwin Richfield, Bernard Hunter,
Andrew Faulds, John Bluthal,
Geoffrey Matthews, Honor
Shepherd, Geoffrey Lewis

16.06.1961
The Lift
Hugh Lloyd, John Le Mesurier,
Jack Watling, Diana King,
Charles Lloyd Pack, Jose Reed,
Colin Gordon, William Sherwood,
James Fitzgerald, Ralph Wilson

23.06.1961
The Blood Donor
June Whitfield, Frank Thornton,
Patrick Cargill, Hugh Lloyd,
Peggy Ann Clifford, Jean Marlow,
Ann Marryott, James Ottaway

30.06.1961
Succession – Son and Heir
Gwenda Ewan, Myrtle Reed,
June Whitfield

COMEDY PLAYHOUSE (BBC1)

Series 1

15.12.1961
Clicquot et Fils
Eric Sykes, Warren Mitchell

22.12.1961
Lunch in the Park
Stanley Baxter, Daphne Anderson

29.12.1961
The Private Lives of Edward Whiteley
Tony Britton, Raymond Huntley

05.01.1962
The Offer
Wilfrid Brambell, Harold H. Corbett

12.01.1962
The Reunion
Lee Montagu, J.G. Devlin, Dick
Emery

19.01.1962
The Telephone Call
Peter Jones, June Whitfield

26.01.1962
The Status Symbol
Alfred Marks, Graham Stark

02.02.1962
Visiting Day
Bernard Cribbins, Betty Marsden,
Wilfrid Brambell

09.02.1962
Sealed With a Loving Kiss
Ronald Fraser, Avril Elgar

16.02.1962
The Channel Swimmer
Sydney Tafler, Warren Mitchell

Series 2

01.03.1963 *Our Man in Moscow* Robert Morley	29.03.1963 *Have You Read This Notice?* Frankie Howerd
08.03.1963 *And Here, All the Way From . . .* Eric Barker	05.04.1963 *A Clerical Error* John Le Mesurier
15.03.1963 *Impasse* Bernard Cribbins, Yootha Joyce	12.04.1963 *The Handyman* Alfred Marks, Anthony Sharp

STEPTOE AND SON (BBC1)

(*Regular cast: Wilfrid Brambell – Albert; Harry H. Corbett – Harold*)

PILOT
05.01.1962
The Offer

Series 1

14.06.1962 *The Bird* Valerie Bell	28.06.1962 *The Economist* Frank Thornton
21.06.1962 *The Piano* Brian Oulton, Roger Avon	5.07.1962 *The Diploma*
	12.07.1962 *The Holiday* Colin Gordon

Short Special (part of *Christmas Night with the Stars*) 25.12.1962

Series 2

03.01.1963 *Wallah, Wallah Catsmeat* John Laurie, Leslie Dwyer, George Betton, George Tovey	17.01.1963 *The Stepmother* Joan Newell
10.01.1963 *The Bath* Yootha Joyce, Marjorie Lawrence	24.01.1963 *Sixty-Five Today* Frank Thornton, Richard Caldicot, Michael Bird, Anthony Chinn, Peter Ching, Myo Toon, Aman Tokyo

31.01.1963
A Musical Evening

07.02.1963
Full House
Dudley Foster, Jack Rodney,
Anthony Sagar

14.02.1963
Is That Your Horse Outside?
Patricia Haines, Richard Shaw,
Jo Rowbottom

Series 3

07.01.1964
Homes Fit for Heroes
Peggy Thorpe-Bates, Marie Makino

14.01.1964
The Wooden Overcoats

21.01.1964
The Lead Man Cometh
Leonard Rossiter, Billy Maxam

28.01.1964
Steptoe à la Cart
Gwendolyn Watts, Frank Thornton,
Lala Lloyd

04.02.1964
Sunday for Seven Days
Michael Brennan, Michael Stainton,
Mark Singleton, Damaris Hayman,
George Betton, Alec Bregonzi,
Billy Maxam, Betty Cardno,
Kathleen Heath, Katie Cashfield

11.02.1964
The Bond That Binds Us
June Whitfield

18.02.1964
The Lodger
Walter Swash

Series 4

04.10.1965
And Afterwards At . . .
George A. Cooper, Rose Hill,
Joan Newell, Mollie Sugden,
Robert Webber, Karol Hagar,
Rita Webb, Gretchen Franklin,
Fred Hugh, Leslie Sarony, George
Tovey, George Hirste, Betty Cardno,
Margaret Flint, Gerald Rowland,
James Bulloch, Tony Lambden

11.10.1965
Crossed Swords
Derek Nimmo, Basil Dignam,
Mark Singleton, Ralph Nossek,
Tim Buckland, Philip Howard,
Frank Littlewood, William Raynor,
Peter Thompson

18.10.1965
*Those Magnificent Men and Their
Heating Machines*

25.10.1965
The Siege of Steptoe Street
Robert Dorning, Lane Meddick,
Edwin Brown, Bill Maxam,
Charles Bird, Stan Simmons

01.11.1965
A Box in Town
Yootha Joyce, Freda Bamford, Annie
Leake, Philip Howard, Marjorie
Rhodes, Kathleen Heath, Audrey
Binham, Hilda Barry, Marie Makino,
Eileen Matthews, Ann Jay

08.11.1965
My Old Man's a Tory
Dudley Foster, Damaris Hayman,
Howard Douglas, Evelyn Lund,
Peter Thompson

15.11.1965
Pilgrim's Progress
Alan Gifford, Frank Thornton,

Sidonie Bond, Frederick Schiller,
Catharina Ferraz, Tim Buckland

Short Special (part of *Christmas Night with the Stars*)

Series 5

06.03.1970
A Death in the Family
Patrick Milner, Arthur Arnold

13.03.1970
A Winter's Tale

20.03.1970
Any Old Iron?
Richard Hurndall, Valerie Bell,
Roger Avon

27.03.1970
Steptoe and Son and Son
Ann Beach, Glynn Edwards

03.04.1970
The Colour Problem
Anthony Sharp, Geoffrey Adams,
Carmel Cryan

10.04.1970
TB Or Not TB!
Sidonie Bond, Lala Lloyd

17.04.1970
Men of Property
Norman Bird, Michael Balfour,
Hilda Fennemore, Jan Rossini,
Michael Earl, Peter J. Elliott,
Peter Thompson, Michael Stainton,
Stella Kemball, Ernest Arnley

Series 6

02.11.1970
Robbery with Violence
Dudley Foster, Edward Evans,
Graham Ashley, Michael Stainton,
James McManus

09.11.1970
Come Dancing
Tony Melody

16.11.1970
Two's Company
Jean Kent, Clinton Morris

23.11.1970
Tea for Two
Geoffrey Chater, Robert Raglan

30.11.1970
Without Prejudice
Gerald Flood, Norman Bird,
Ernest Arnley, Tim Buckland,
Philip Howard, Victor Harrington

07.12.1970
Pot Black
George Tovey, Alf Mangan,
Pat Milner, Bert Rogers

14.12.1970
The Three Feathers
John Arnatt, John Bailey

21.12.1970
Cuckoo in the Nest
Kenneth J. Warren, Edwin Brown

Series 7

21.02.1972
Men of Letters
Anthony Sharp, Bill Maxam

28.02.1972
A Star Is Born
Trevor Bannister, Margaret Nolan,
Betty Huntley-Wright, John Quayle,
Cy Town, John Anderson

06.03.1972
Oh, What a Beautiful Mourning
George A. Cooper, Mollie Sugden,
Rita Webb, Yvonne Antrobus,
Bartlett Mullins, Tommy Godfrey,
Queenie Watts, Stella Moray,
Margaret Flint, Simon Cord,
Gilly Flower

13.03.1972
Live Now, P.A.Y.E. Later
Colin Gordon, Edwin Apps,
Peter Madden, Carole Roberts

20.03.1972
Loathe Story
Joanna Lumley, Raymond Huntley,
Georgina Cookson

27.03.1972
Divided We Stand
Paul Lindley, Reginald Dodd

03.04.1972
The Desperate Hours
Leonard Rossiter, J.G. Devlin,
Corbert Woodall, Tommy Vance

Christmas Special 24.12.1973
Frank Thornton, Arnold Diamond, Mary Barclay

Series 8

04.09.1974
Back in Fashion
Madeline Smith, Roy Holder,
Peter Birrell, Michael Earl,
Ava Cadell, Christine Donna,
Sally Farmiloe, Claire Russell,
Hazel Wilson

11.09.1974
And So to Bed
Lynn Farleigh, Angus Mackay

18.09.1974
Porn Yesterday
Anthony Sharp, Dorothy Frere,
Joyce Windsor, Harry Fielder

25.09.1974
The Seven Steptoerai

Henry Woolf, Billy Horrigan,
Dougie Robinson, Marc Boyle,
Tim Condron, Vic Armstrong,
Bill Weston, Stuart Fell, Paddy
Ryan, Tony Smart, Audrey
Danvers-Walker, Ernest Jennings,
David J. Graham

03.10.1974
*Upstairs, Downstairs, Upstairs,
Downstairs*
Robert James

10.10.1974
Séance in a Wet Rag and Bone Yard
Patricia Routledge, Gwen Nelson,
Gilly Flower, David J. Graham

Christmas Special 26.12.1974
Leon Eagles

TILL DEATH US DO PART (BBC1)

PILOT
22.07.1965

Series 1

(Regular cast: Warren Mitchell – Alf Garnett; Dandy Nicholls – Else Garnett; Una Stubbs – Rita; Anthony Booth – Mike)

06.06.1966
Arguments, Arguments

13.06.1966
*Hair Raising! ***

20.06.1966
A House With Love In It

27.06.1966
Intolerance

04.07.1966
*Two Toilets? . . . That's Posh ***

18.07.1966
*From Liverpool With Love ***

01.08.1966
*Claustrophobia ***

Series 2

26.12.1966
Peace and Goodwill

02.01.1967
*Sex Before Marriage ***

09.01.1967
*I Can Give Up Any Time I Like ***

16.01.1967
*The Bulldog Breed ***

23.01.1967
*Caviar on the Dole ***

30.01.1967
*A Woman's Place is in the Home ***

06.02.1967
*A Wapping Mythology ***

13.02.1967
*In Sickness and In Health ***

20.02.1967
*State Visit ***

27.02.1967
Alf's Dilemma

SPECIAL
27.03.1967
Till Closing Time Do Us Part

Short Special (part of *Christmas Night with the Stars*) * 25.12.1967

Series 3

05.01.1968
The Phone

12.01.1968
The Blood Donor

19.01.1968
Monopoly *

26.01.1968
The Funeral *

02.02.1968
Football *

09.02.1968
The Puppy *

16.02.1968
Aunt Maud *

Special
18.06.1970
Up the Polls

Short Special (part of Christmas Night with the Stars) * 25.12.1971

Series 4

13.09.1972
To Garnett a Grandson

20.09.1972
Pigeon Racing

27.09.1972
Holiday in Bournemouth

11.10.1972
Dock Pilfering

18.10.1972
Alf Takes the Baby

25.10.1972
Alf's Broken Leg

Christmas Special 26.12.1972 *Jesus Christ Superstar*

Series 5

02.01.1974
TV Licence

09.01.1974
The Royal Wedding

23.01.1974
Strikes and Blackouts

30.01.1974
Party Night

05.02.1974
Elsie's Three-Day Week

12.02.1974
Gran's Watch

28.02.1974
Paki-Paddy'

Christmas Special 31.12.1974 *Outback Bound*

Series 6

08.01.1975	29.01.1975
Phone Australia	*Episode 4*
15.01.1975	05.02.1975
Marital Bliss	*Episode 5*
22.01.1975	12.02.1975
Episode 3	*The Letter*

Series 7

05.11.1975	26.11.1975
Moving in with Min	*Stuck in the Window*
12.11.1975	03.12.1975
Episode 2	*A Hole in One*
19.11.1975	17.12.1975
Episode 3	*Unemployed Alf*

FOREIGN ADAPTATIONS

Hancock's Half-Hour
Norway:
Fleksnes Fataliteter (1972–2002)

Germany:
Pfeifer (2000)

Steptoe and Son

Netherlands:
Stiefbeen en Zoon (NCRV, 1963)

United States:
Sanford and Son (NBC, 1972–77)

Sweden:
Albert & Herbert (Sveriges Radio, 1974)

Germany:
Zwei Mann um einen Herd (NDR,1979)

Portugal:
Camilo & Filho Lda (1995)

Till Death Us Do Part
Netherlands:
Tot de dood ons scheidt (KRO Televisie, 1969)

United States:
All in the Family (CBS, 1971–79)
[This show itself inspired a number of spin-offs:
Maude, 1972; *Good Times*, 1974; *The Jeffersons*, 1975; *Archie Bunker's Place*, 1979; *Checking In*, 1981; and *Gloria*, 1982.]

Germany:
Ein Herz und eine Seele (Westdeutscher Rundfunk, 1973)

Bibliography

Associated London Scripts

Adam, James, 'Two Very Practical Jokers', *TV Times*, 3 January 1958, pp.6–7

Anon., 'New Race of Humanizers of Popular Comedy', *The Times*, 21 July 1962, p.4

Anon., 'TV Groups Turn to Their Task', *The Times*, 13 June 1967, p.3

McCann, Graham, *Frankie Howerd: Stand-Up Comic* (London: Harper Perennial, 2005)

Took, Barry, *Laughter in the Air* (London: Robson, 1976)

Wilmut, Roger (ed.), *'No More Curried Eggs for Me'* (London: Methuen, 1982)
  Son of 'Curried Eggs' (London: Methuen, 1984)

ALS Writers

SPIKE MILLIGAN

Behan, Dominic, *Milligan: The Life and Times of Spike Milligan* (London: Methuen, 1988)

Bradbury, David and Joe McGrath, 'Spike Milligan', in *Now That's Funny!* (London: Methuen, 1998), pp.13–20

Carpenter, Humphrey, *Spike Milligan: The Biography* (London: Hodder & Stoughton, 2003)

Coniam, Matthew and Richard Larcombe, 'Catford on the Moon: Spike Milligan and the "Q" series', *Kettering*, No.2, November 2004, pp.27–46

Du Noyer, Paul, 'Blind Date! The Day Van Morrison Met . . . Spike Milligan?', *Q Magazine*, 35, August 1989, pp.44–50

Farnes, Norma, *Spike: An Intimate Memoir* (London: Fourth Estate, 2003)
  (ed.), *The Spike Milligan Letters* (London: M. & J. Hobbs, 1977)
  (ed.), *More Spike Milligan Letters* (London: M. & J. Hobbs, 1984)
  (ed.), *The Compulsive Spike Milligan* (London: Fourth Estate, 2004)

Games, Alexander (ed.), *The Essential Spike Milligan* (London: Fourth Estate, 2002)

Milligan, Spike, *Silly Verse for Kids* (London: Dennis Dobson, 1959)
  A Dustbin of Milligan (London: Louvain Landsborough, 1963)
  The Little Pot Boiler (London: Dennis Dobson, 1963)
  Puckoon (London: Anthony Blond, 1963)
  A Book of Bits, or A Bit of a Book (London: Dennis Dobson, 1965)

The Bedside Milligan (London: Tandem, 1971)

Small Dreams of a Scorpion (London: Hobbs/Michael Joseph, 1972)

Adolf Hitler: My Part in His Downfall (London: Michael Joseph, 1971)

Monty: His Part in My Victory (London: Michael Joseph, 1976)

Mussolini: His Part in My Downfall (London: Michael Joseph, 1978)

Indefinite Articles (London: Michael Joseph, 1981)

Where Have All the Bullets Gone? (Walton-on-Thames: Hobbs, 1986)

Goodbye Soldier (London: Michael Joseph, 1986)

Peace Work (London: Michael Joseph, 1991)

Spike Milligan: The Family Album: An Illustrated Autobiography (London: Virgin, 1999)

Milligan's War: The Selected War Memoirs of Spike Milligan (London: Michael Joseph, 1988)

with Anthony Clare, *Depression and How to Survive It* (London: Arrow, 1994)

Parkinson, Michael, 'Spike Milligan', in *Parkinson* (London: Pavilion, 1982)

Scudamore, Pauline, *Spike Milligan* (London: Granada, 1985)

(ed.), *Dear Robert, Dear Spike: The Graves–Milligan Correspondence* (London: Alan Sutton, 1991)

Ventham, Maxine, *Spike Milligan: His Part in Our Lives* (London: Robson, 2002)

ERIC SYKES

Adams, Bernard, 'Eric Sykes', *Radio Times*, 29 October 1964, p.61

Fox, Sue, 'A Life in the Day', *Sunday Times Magazine*, 2 October 2005, p.66

Langley, William, 'Eric Sykes: The Great Survivor', *SAGA Magazine*, October 2003, pp.30–1

Ross, Deborah, 'Eric Sykes – Mummy's Boy', *Independent*, 11 February 2002, p.7

Sykes, Eric, *The Great Crime of Grapplewick* (London: Macmillan/Virgin, 1984/1996)

UFOs Are Coming Wednesday (London: Virgin, 1995)

Smelling of Roses (London: Virgin, 1997)

Eric Sykes's Comedy Heroes (London: Virgin, 2003)

If I Don't Write It, Nobody Else Will (London: Fourth Estate, 2005)

GALTON & SIMPSON

Anon., 'Tony Hancock Team: Messrs Simpson and Galton on Writing Television Comedy', *The Times*, 2 March 1959, p.12

Bradbury, David and Joe McGrath, 'Ray Galton and Alan Simpson', in *Now That's Funny!* (London: Methuen, 1998), pp.29–39

Nathan, David, 'Three Writers', in *The Laughtermakers* (London: Peter Owen, 1971), pp.122–37

Scott, Caroline, 'Ray Galton: Best of Times, Worst of Times', *Sunday Times Magazine*, 19 March 2006, p.11

Walker, Lynn, 'Ragged Glory', *The Independent*, 20 October 2005, pp.46–7

JOHNNY SPEIGHT

Bradbury, David and Joe McGrath, 'Johnny Speight', in *Now That's Funny!* (London: Methuen, 1998), pp.21–8

McCann, Graham, 'Johnny Speight', *Dictionary of National Biography* (Oxford: Oxford University Press, 2004), vol.51, pp.780–1

Nathan, David, 'Three Writers', in *The Laughtermakers* (London: Peter Owen, 1971), pp.122–37

Speight, Johnny, *It Stands to Reason* (London: Hobbs/Michael Joseph, 1973)
For Richer, For Poorer (London: BBC, 1991)
Three Plays (London: Oberon Books, 1998)

TERRY NATION

Bignell, Jonathan and Andrew O'Day, *Terry Nation* (Manchester: Manchester University Press, 2004)

Nazarro, Joseph, 'Terry Nation', in *Doctor Who Magazine*, 145, 1989, pp.17–21

Pixley, A., 'Nation's Creations', in *Horizon Newsletter,* 36, 1997, pp.9–20

JOHN ANTROBUS

Antrobus, John, *Surviving Spike Milligan* (London: Robson, 2002)

ALS Shows

The Goons

Bennett, Richard, 'Danger! Goons at Play', *Radio Times,* 16 September 1955, p.9

Draper, Alfred, *The Story of The Goons* (London: Everest Books, 1976)

Farnes, Norma (ed.), *The Goons: The Story* (London: Virgin, 1997)

Fleming, Fergus, 'The Goons', in *British Comedy Greats*, ed. Annabel Merullo and Neil Wenborn (London: Cassell Illustrated, 2003), pp.90–4

Guy, John P., 'For TV Humour, A Goon Twist', *TV Mirror*, March 1956, pp.8–9.

Huson, Richard, 'Six Hours in "The Goonery"', *Radio Times*, 4 February 1955, p.9

Milligan, Spike, *The Goon Show Scripts* (London: Sphere, 1973)
More Goon Show Scripts (London: Sphere, 1974)
The Book of The Goons (London: Robson, 1974)
The Goon Cartoons, illustrated by Pete Clarke (London: M. & J. Hobbs, 1982)
'Still Goon-crazy, after all these years . . .', *The Listener*, 8 July 1982, p.11
The Lost Goon Shows (London: Robson, 1987)

Milligan, Spike et al., *The Book of The Goons* (London: Robson, 1984)

Nathan, David, 'The Goons' and 'The Goons Go On', in *The Laughtermakers* (London: Peter Owen, 1971), pp.41–77

Pedrick, Gale, 'The Goons – As Others See Them', *Radio Times,* 31 October 1958, p.7

Wilmut, Roger, with Jimmy Grafton, *The Goon Show Companion* (London: Robson, 1976/1998)

Hancock's Half-Hour

Anon., 'Tony Hancock Team: Messrs Simpson and Galton on Writing Television Comedy', *The Times*, 2 March 1959, p.12

Connolly, Joseph, 'Hancock's Half-Hour', in *British Comedy Greats,* ed. Annabel Merullo and Neil Wenborn (London: Cassell Illustrated, 2003), pp.99–102

Galton, Ray and Alan Simpson, compiled by Chris Bumstead, *Hancock's Half-Hour: Classic Years* (London: BBC, 1987)

Galton, Ray and Alan Simpson, *The Best of Hancock* (London: Robson, 1993)

Gould, Jack, 'TV: Comedy of Britain', *New York Times*, 31 March 1962, p.51

Hancock, Freddie and David Nathan, *Hancock* (London: Ariel, 1986)

Oakes, Phillip, *Tony Hancock* (London: Woburn-Futura, 1975)

Webber, Richard, *Fifty Years of Hancock's Half-Hour* (London: BBC, 2004)

Wilmut, Roger, *Tony Hancock 'Artiste'* (London: Eyre Methuen, 1978)
    The Illustrated Tony Hancock (London: Queen Anne Press, 1986)

Round the Horne

Took, Barry, *Round the Horne: The Complete and Utter History* (London: Boxtree, 1998)

Took, Barry with Mat Coward, *The Best of Round the Horne* (London: Boxtree, 2000)

Took, Barry and Marty Feldman, *Round the Horne* (London: Woburn Press, 1974)
    The Bona Book of Julian and Sandy: Leaves from their 'Round the Horne' Journal (London: Robson, 1976)

Steptoe and Son

Antrobus, John, 'My Favourite Londoner – Albert Steptoe', *Time Out*, 29 March, 2006, p.186

Brambell, Wilfrid, *All Above Board* (London: W. H. Allen, 1976)

Galton, Ray and Alan Simpson, *Steptoe and Son* (London: Longman, 1971)
    The Best of Steptoe and Son (London: Robson, 1988)

Galton, Ray and Alan Simpson, with Robert Ross, *Steptoe and Son* (London: BBC, 2002)

McCann, Graham, 'Steptoe and Son', in *British Comedy Greats,* ed. Annabel Merullo and Neil Wenborn (London: Cassell Illustrated, 2003), pp.157–161

Pedrick, Gale, *Steptoe and Son* (London: Hodder, 1964)
    Steptoe and Son at the Palace (London: Hodder, 1966)

Walker, Lynn, 'Ragged Glory', *The Independent*, 20 October 2005, pp.46–7

Sykes And A . . .

Gould, Jack, 'TV: Comedy of Britain', *New York Times*, 31 March 1962, p.51

Reynolds, Stanley, 'Sykes', *The Times*, 11 September 1973, p. 13

Sykes, Eric, 'Dear BBC Viewers. . .', *Radio Times*, 5 August 1960, p.2
    Eric Sykes of Sebastopol Terrace (London: Hobbs/Michael Joseph, 1981)
    Sykes of Sebastopol Terrace (London: Virgin, 2000)

Till Death Us Do Part

Booth, Tony, 'Alf Garnett', in *British Comedy Greats,* ed. Annabel Merullo and Neil Wenborn (London: Cassell Illustrated, 2003), pp.12–16

Burke, John, *Till Death Us Do Part* (London: Pan, 1967)

Speight, Johnny, *Till Death Us Do Part* (London: Frank Cass, 1973)

    Till Death Us Do Part Scripts (London: Woburn Press, 1973)

    The Thoughts of Chairman Alf (London: Robson, 1973)

    The Garnett Chronicles (London: Futura, 1987)

General

Allen, Fred, *Treadmill to Oblivion* (Boston: Little, Brown, 1954)

Allen, Steve, *The Funny Men* (New York: Simon & Schuster, 1956)

Askey, Arthur, *Before Your Very Eyes* (London: London: Woburn Press, 1975)

Beaton, Cecil and Kenneth Tynan, *Persona Grata* (London: Wingate, 1953)

Benny, Jack and Joan Benny, *Sunday Nights at Seven* (New York: Warner, 1990)

Bentine, Michael, *The Reluctant Jester* (London: Bantam, 1992)

Bergan, Ronald, *Beyond the Fringe . . . And Beyond* (London: Virgin, 1989)

Billington, Michael, *One Night Stands* (London: Nick Hern Books, 1993)

Black, Cilla, *Through the Years* (London: Headline, 1993)

    What's It All About? (London: Ebury Press, 2003)

Black, Peter, *The Biggest Aspidistra in the World* (London: BBC, 1972)

    The Mirror in the Corner (London: Hutchinson, 1972)

Booth, Anthony, with Stephanie Booth, *What's Left?* (London: Phoenix, 2003)

Bradbury, David and Joe McGrath, *Now That's Funny!* (London: Methuen, 1998)

Brandreth, Gyles, *Brief Encounters* (London: Politico's, 2003)

Briggs, Asa, *The History of Broadcasting in the United Kingdom* (Oxford: Oxford University Press, 1961–1979):

    Vol.1: *The Birth of Broadcasting,* 1961

    Vol.2: *The Golden Age of Wireless,* 1965

    Vol.3: *The War of Words,* 1970

    Vol.4: *Sound and Vision,* 1979

Bygraves, Max, *Stars In My Eyes* (London: Robson, 2003)

Cardiff, David, 'Mass Middlebrow Laughter: The Origins of BBC Comedy', *Media, Culture & Society,* vol.10, no.1 (January 1988), pp.41–60

Cotton, Bill, *The BBC as an Entertainer* (London: BBC, 1977)

    Double Bill (London: Fourth Estate, 2000)

Coward, Mat, *Classic Radio Comedy* (Harpenden: Pocket Essentials, 2003)

Craig, Mike, *Look Back with Laughter*, vols 1, 2 and 3 (Manchester: Mike Craig Enterprises, 1996)

Croft, David, *You Have Been Watching . . .* (London: BBC, 2004)

Cryer, Barry, *You Won't Believe This But . . .* (London: Virgin, 1998)

    Pigs Can Fly (London: Orion, 2003)

Emerson, Ralph Waldo, *Essays and Poems* (London: J.M. Dent, 1995)

Farnes, Norma, *Spike: An Intimate Memoir* (London: Fourth Estate, 2003)

Fisher, John, *Funny Way to be a Hero* (London: Frederick Muller, 1973)

Foster, Andy and Steve Furst, *Radio Comedy 1938–1968* (London: Virgin, 1996)

Freeman, John, *Face to Face* (London: Jonathan Cape, 1964)

Frith, Simon, 'The Pleasures of the Hearth: The Making of BBC Light Entertainment', in Tony Bennett et al. (eds), *Popular Culture and Social Relations* (Milton Keynes: Open University, 1983)

Gambaccini, Paul and Rod Taylor, *Television's Greatest Hits* (London: Network Books, 1993)

Goodwin, Cliff, *Sid James* (London: Arrow, 1996)
   When the Wind Changed: The Life and Death of Tony Hancock (London: Century, 1999)

Grade, Lew, *Still Dancing* (London: Collins, 1987)

Grade, Michael, *It Seemed Like a Good Idea at the Time* (London: Macmillan, 1999)

Greene, Hugh Carleton, *The BBC as a Public Service* (London: BBC, 1960)

Hillier, Fay, with William Hall, *Ooh You Are Awful – But I Like You!* (London: Sidgwick & Jackson, 2001)

Housham, David and John Frank-Keyes, *Funny Business* (London: Boxtree, 1992)

Howerd, Frankie, *On the Way I Lost It* (London: W. H. Allen, 1976)

Hudd, Roy, *Roy Hudd's Book of Music-Hall, Variety and Showbiz Anecdotes* (London: Virgin, 1994)

Hughes, John Graven, *The Greasepaint War* (London: New English Library, 1976)

James, Clive, *Clive James on Television* (London: Picador, 1991)

Jeffries, Stuart, *Mrs Slocombe's Pussy* (London: Flamingo, 2000)

Josefsberg, Milt, *The Jack Benny Show* (New York: Arlington House, 1977)

Kavanagh, Ted, *Tommy Handley* (London: Hodder, 1949)
   The ITMA Years (London: Woburn Press, 1974)

Lewis, Roger, *The Life and Death of Peter Sellers* (London: Arrow, 2004)

Lewisohn, Mark, *Radio Times Guide to TV Comedy* (London: BBC, 1998)

McCann, Graham, *Cary Grant: A Class Apart* (London: Fourth Estate, 1996)
   'Why the Best Sitcoms Must Be a Class Act', London *Evening Standard*, 21 May 1997, p.9
   'An Offer We Can Refuse', London *Evening Standard*, 2 December 1998, p.8
   Morecambe & Wise (London: Fourth Estate, 1998)
   'Sit Back and Wait for the Comedy', *Financial Times*, 24 November 1999, p.22
   'Don't Bury Your Treasures', *Financial Times*, 28 June 2000, p.22
   Dad's Army: The Story of a Classic Television Show (London: Fourth Estate, 2001)
   'You Never Had It So Good or So Funny', *Financial Times*, 13 November 2002, p.17
   'How to Define the Indefinable', *Financial Times*, 20 March 2003, p.14
   'Bob Hope: The Master of Special Delivery Bows Out', *Financial Times*, 29 July 2003, p.15
   'Steptoe and Son', *British Comedy Greats,* ed. Annabel Merullo and Neil Wenborn (London: Cassell Illustrated, 2003), pp.157–161
   'Johnny Speight', *Dictionary of National Biography* (Oxford: Oxford University Press, 2004)
   Frankie Howerd: Stand-Up Comic (London: Fourth Estate, 2004)
   (ed.), *The Essential Dave Allen*, (London: Hodder, 2005)

McFarlane, Brian, *An Autobiography of British Cinema* (London: Methuen, 1997)

Mellor, G. J., *The Northern Music Hall* (Newcastle upon Tyne: Frank Graham, 1970)

They Made Us Laugh (Littleborough: George Kelsell, 1982)

Miall, Leonard, *Inside the BBC* (London: Weidenfeld & Nicolson, 1994)

Midwinter, Eric, *Make 'Em Laugh* (London: Allen & Unwin, 1979)

Monkhouse, Bob, *Crying With Laughter* (London: Arrow, 1994)

    Over the Limit (London: Century, 1998)

Muir, Frank, *Comedy in Television* (London: BBC, 1966)

    A Kentish Lad (London: Bantam Press, 1997)

Nathan, David, *The Laughtermakers* (London: Peter Owen, 1971)

Nietzsche, Friedrich, *Twilight of the Idols*, translated by R.J. Hollingdale (London: Penguin, 2003)

Parkinson, Michael, *The Best of Parkinson* (London: Pavilion, 1982)

Perret, Gene and Martha Bolton, *Talk About Hope* (Carmel, CA: Jester Press, 1998)

Pertwee, Bill, *Promenades and Pierrots* (Devon: Westbridge, 1979)

    By Royal Command (Newton Abbott: David & Charles, 1981)

    A Funny Way to Make a Living! (London: Sunburst, 1996)

Plomley, Roy, *Desert Island Lists* (London: Hutchinson, 1984)

Poirer, Richard (ed.), *Ralph Waldo Emerson* (Oxford: Oxford University Press, 1990)

Priestley, J. B., *London End* (London: Heinemann, 1968)

Particular Pleasures (London: Heinemann, 1975)

Richards, Jeffrey, *Visions of Yesteryear* (London: Routledge, 1973)

    Films and British National Identity (Manchester: Manchester University Press, 1997)

Silvey, Roger, *Who's Listening? The Story of BBC Audience Research* (London: Allen & Unwin, 1974)

Sloan, Tom, *Television Light Entertainment* (London: BBC, 1969)

Smith, Ronald L., *Who's Who in Comedy* (New York: Facts on File, 1992)

    Comedy Stars at 78 RPM (London: McFarland, 1998)

Stone, Richard, *You Should Have Been in Last Night* (Sussex: The Book Guild, 2000)

Sykes, Eric, *Eric Sykes's Comedy Heroes* (London: Virgin, 2003)

Thompson, Ben, *Sunshine on Putty: The Golden Age of British Comedy from 'Vic Reeves' to 'The Office'* (London: Harper Perennial, 2004)

Took, Barry, *Laughter in the Air* (London: Robson/BBC, 1976)

    'Whatever Happened to TV Comedy?' *The Listener*, 5 January 1984, pp.7–8, and 12 January 1984, pp.8–9

Tynan, Kenneth, *Profiles* (London: Nick Hern Books, 1989)

Uglow, Jenny, 'Friends reunited', *The Guardian Review*, 30 April 2005, pp.34–5

Walker, Alexander, *Peter Sellers* (London: Macmillan, 1982)

Watt, John (ed.), *Radio Variety* (London: J. M. Dent, 1939)

Wheldon, Huw, *British Traditions in a World-Wide Medium* (London: BBC, 1973)

    The Achievement of Television (London: BBC, 1975)

The British Experience in Television (London: BBC, 1976)

Whitfield, June, *. . . and June Whitfield* (London: Corgi, 2001)

Wilde, Larry, *The Great Comedians* (Secaucus, New Jersey: Citadel Press, 1973)

Williams, Kenneth, *The Kenneth Williams Diaries*, ed. Russell Davies (London: HarperCollins, 1993)

Wilmut, Roger, *From Fringe to Flying Circus* (London: Eyre Methuen, 1980)
Kindly Leave the Stage: The Story of Variety, 1918–60 (London: Methuen, 1985)

Windsor, Barbara, *All of Me* (London: Headline, 2001)

Wyndham Goldie, Grace, *Facing the Nation: Broadcasting and Politics 1936–1976* (London: Bodley Head, 1977)

Notes

1. THE FRONT DOOR

Opening epigraph: *'It's a small world, but I wouldn't want to have to paint it'* – Steven Wright.

Opening epigraph: *The Goon Show*: 'Six Charlies in Search of an Author' first broadcast on 25 December 1956, BBC Home Service

1   John Lennon, reviewing *The Goon Show Scripts*, *New York Times*, 30 September 1973, p.446.

2. RECEPTION

Opening epigraph: *The Goon Show*: 'The Whistling Spy Enigma', written by Spike Milligan, first broadcast on 28 September 1954, BBC Home Service.

The Origins of Associated London Scripts

Opening epigraph: *'Tis hard to mesmerize ourselves . . .'*: Ralph Waldo Emerson, 'Society and Solitude', in Richard Poirer (ed.), *Ralph Waldo Emerson* (Oxford: Oxford University Press, 1990), p.422.

1   See my *Frankie Howerd: Stand-Up Comic* (London: Fourth Estate, 2004), pp.89–105.
2   The BBC began lobbying the GPO informally about speeding up the installation of telephones for its most highly prized employees from the end of 1951. On 20 March 1952, Sidney R. Campion, Principal Information Officer of the GPO's Public Relations Department (Press and Broadcast Division), wrote to the BBC's current Head of Variety, Michael Standing, in response to a specific request to get an early telephone service installed for Eric Sykes: 'As you probably know, we are "right up against it" in meeting the needs of the Defence programme. But I can assure you that there will be no unavoidable delay.' On 31 March, Campion wrote again, assuring Standing that he expected to have the service set up shortly. Another example of Sykes's relative importance within the Corporation was Peter Brough's attempt (in a letter to Michael Standing dated 10 June 1952) to set up an unprecedented 'golden handcuffs'-style arrangement to ensure that Sykes could 'not be called upon to write for anyone else during the run [of

Educating Archie]'. Source: BBC Written Archives (BBC WAC): Eric Sykes Ltd, Copyright File 1: 1949–1962.

3 Eric Sykes, *Eric Sykes's Comedy Heroes* (London: Virgin, 2003), p.134.

4 *Ibid.*

5 *Ibid.*, p.138.

6 Pat Dixon, in a memo dated 16 November 1953, noted that both writers were keen on the project. On 18 November, G. F. Meehan proposed that one pilot script be commissioned, but no written response is contained in the BBC archives, nor is there any further mention of the aborted idea (BBC WAC: Spike Milligan, File 1, 1951–1962).

7 The BBC Written Archives contain a number of missives from Dale during this period. The first, dated 19 December 1944, invited the Corporation's David Manderson to witness a production of 'The RAF Happy Show' at RAF Station Lissett, overseen by Flying Officer 'Scruffy' Dale (who also performed his own stand-up routine) and featuring Ronald Chesney, Alex Munro, Miles Manning, Percy Dixon, Jack Gillespie, Bunny Harvey and Ronnie Taylor and his RAF Band. Dale also sent in a script he had written for the popular radio sitcom *Much Binding in the Marsh*. Manderson wrote back to say that he was unable to come, and he also rejected the script. Undeterred, Dale made contact with Manderson again on 11 January 1945 and invited him to another 'Happy Show' extravaganza (this one promising not only several keen solo performers but also, Dale underlined, 'my own rep company'): 'How about giving me a date to compère a show? I won't let you down in material even if you must read through a hundred gags to find twenty suitable or clean enough for broadcasting.' Manderson replied on 2 February, pointing out that he did not use 'any males to compère my shows'. Dale did go on to contribute, fleetingly, to the odd edition of such radio Variety shows as *Bringing Home the Bacon, Old Town Hall* and *They're Out!* during the spring of 1946, before admitting defeat and joining the Jack Payne Organisation as a booker and trainee agent in August that same year. (Source: BBC WAC: Stanley Dale Artist's File, 1944–1959.)

8 Spike Milligan, quoted by Pauline Scudamore, *Spike Milligan* (London: Granada, 1985), pp.162–3.

9 'I don't remember Spike launching into it *quite* like that,' Eric Sykes told me. 'It wasn't that sudden. It was more a case of, you know: "What could we do with this . . .?" And we chatted. And the basic idea grew out of that conversation.' Interview with the author, 19 February 2004.

10 Alan Simpson, interviewed by Kevin Saddington on BBC Radio Northampton on 15 September 1996.

11 One of the reasons for Monkhouse and Goodwin's departure had been the fact that Hancock had taken such a strong dislike to their material – so strong that he had ended up using it as toilet paper (see Bob Monkhouse, *Crying With Laughter* [London: Arrow, 1994], p.97).

12 See Norma Farnes, *Spike: An Intimate Memoir* (London: Fourth Estate, 2003), p.54.

13 Eric Sykes, interview with the author, 19 February 2004.

14 Alan Simpson, interview with the author, 15 March 2004.

15 *Ibid.*

16 Eric Sykes, interview with the author, 19 February 2004.

17 Spike Milligan, quoted by Pauline Scudamore, *Spike Milligan op. cit.*, p.164.

18 Beryl Vertue, interview with the author, 14 June 2005.

19 *Ibid.*

20 Alan Simpson, interview with the author, 15 March 2004.

21 *Ibid.*

22 Beryl Vertue, interview with the author, 14 June 2005.

23 *Ibid.*

24 *Ibid.*

25 Recalled by Eric Sykes, interview with the author, 19 February 2004.

26 See John Antrobus, *Surviving Spike Milligan* (London: Robson, 2003), p.111.

27 Eric Sykes, interview with the author, 19 February 2004.

28 Galton and Simpson, quoted by David Bradbury and Joe McGrath, *Now That's Funny!*(London: Methuen, 1998), p.38.

29 Beryl Vertue, quoted by Barry Took, *Laughter in the Air* (London: Robson/BBC, 1976), p.135.

30 Recalled by Ray Galton, interview with the author, 15 March 2004.

31 Recalled by Eric Sykes, interview with the author, 19 February 2004.

32 Beryl Vertue, interview with the author, 14 June 2005.

33 Eric Sykes, *Eric Sykes's Comedy Heroes, op. cit.*, pp.139–41.

34 *Ibid.*

35 Speight, quotes by David Nathan, *The Laughtermakers* (London: Peter Owen, 1971), p.125.

36 Alan Simpson, speaking in the first part of the two-part documentary, *Associated London Scripts*, BBC Radio 4, 14 January 2003.

37 John Antrobus, quoted by Steve Bennett, *Chortle*, 9 November 2004.

38 John Antrobus, speaking on the BBC Radio 4 documentary, *Associated London Scripts*, BBC Radio 4, 14–21 January 2003.

39 John Antrobus, quoted by Steve Bennett, *Chortle*, 9 November 2004.

40 John Junkin, interview with the author, 1 June 2005.

41 Ray Galton, quoted by Barry Took, *Laughter in the Air, op. cit.*, p.174.

42 Terry Nation, quoted by Joe Nazzaro, 'Terry Nation', *Doctor Who Magazine*, 145, 1989, p. 17.

43 John Junkin, interview with the author, 1 June 2005. *Floggit's* ran on the BBC's Light Programme for two series, from 17 August to 30 November 1956 and from 8 April to 5 August 1957.

44 John Junkin, interview with the author, 1 June 2005.

45 *Ibid.*

46 Brad Ashton, interview with the author, 14 November 2000.

47 John Junkin recalled (*op. cit.*):
'I remember we were all supposed to contribute to *Idiot Weekly, Price 2d*, and I, obviously, used to go along – because there they all were: Peter and Spike, Graham Stark, Kenneth Connor and all sorts of wonderful people. And one day, the director [Richard Lester] came over to me and said, "John, you're going to have to play the second man in the duelling sketches." So I said,

"Why?" He said, "Because Eric's not well, you're the nearest one to his size and we've already ordered the costume." So I said, "Well, OK." And I duly did it, and – this is the strange coincidence – the other actor in the sketch was a man called Alun Owen, who I got to know over that week and who would go on to write those wonderful plays, and that was how I drifted into acting.'

48 Beryl Vertue, interview with the author, 14 June 2005.

49 *Ibid.*

50 *Ibid.*

51 *Ibid.*

52 John Antrobus, *Surviving Spike Milligan, op. cit.*, p.28. (Some of the inhabitants of Cumberland House were more positive. Marty Feldman, for example, even recorded a song – 'Kensington High Street' – in which he reminisced fondly about his old workplace: 'Kensington High Street/Is my street for good/It's a luvverly neighbourhood' [written by Bill Solly, published by Westminster Music Limited; released on the album *The Crazy World of Marty Feldman*, Decca 1969]).

53 John Junkin, interview with the author, 1 June 2005.

54 John Antrobus, *Surviving Spike Milligan, op. cit.*, p.24.

55 *Ibid.*, p.27.

56 Beryl Vertue, interview with the author, 14 June 2005.

57 Eric Sykes, interview with the author, 19 February 2004.

58 Dick Vosburgh, speaking on the BBC Radio 4 documentary, *Associated London Scripts*, BBC Radio 4, 14–21 January 2003.

59 Beryl Vertue, interview with the author, 14 June 2005.

60 James Adam, 'Two Very Practical Jokers', *TV Times*, 3 January 1958, p.6–7.

61 The first letter bearing this letterhead that has been preserved in the BBC archives was sent by Beryl Vertue and dated 6 November 1956 (BBC WAC: Eric Sykes Ltd, Copyright File no.1: 1949–1962).

62 Beryl Vertue, interview with the author, 14 June 2005.

63 Ray Galton, speaking on the BBC Radio 4 documentary, *Associated London Scripts, op. cit.*

64 *Ibid.*

65 Scruffy Dale's departure was first reported to an outside organisation when Beryl Vertue wrote a letter (dated 13 January 1962) to the BBC announcing that Dale 'has left this Company and therefore his name must be struck off all your records' (BBC WAC: Eric Sykes TV Artist's File no.1: 1952–1962). See Chapter 11, and also my *Frankie Howerd: Stand-Up Comic, op. cit.*, pp.168-70, for further information.

66 Source: BBC WAC: Eric Sykes TV Artist's File no.1: 1952–1962.

3. THE OFFICES

Room 1: Spike Milligan

1 Spike Milligan, quoted by David Nathan in *The Laughtermakers, op. cit.* p.42.

2   Spike Milligan, quoted in 'Blind Date! The Day Van Morrison Met . . . Spike Milligan?', Paul Du Noyer, *Q Magazine*, 35, August 1989, p.50.

3   Spike Milligan, in *The Laughtermakers, op. cit.*, p.59.

4   See Peter Sellers's account in his *Parkinson* interview on BBC1, first broadcast 28 October 1972, and released subsequently on vinyl as *Michael Parkinson Meets The Goons* (BBC REB 165M) and then as the first half of the double cassette as *Parkinson Interviews The Goons & Peter Sellers* (BBC Collection ISBN 0563388285).

5   Leo Milligan, quoted by Norma Farnes, *Spike: An Intimate Memoir* (London: Fourth Estate, 2003), p.46.

6   Spike Milligan, quoted by David Nathan, *The Laughtermakers, op. cit.*, p.45.

7   Spike Milligan, quoted by Alfred Draper, *The Story of The Goons* (London: Everest Books, 1976), p.44.

8   See Pauline Scudamore, *Spike Milligan, op. cit.*, p.2.

9   *Ibid.*, p.38.

10 Spike Milligan, quoted in the *Daily Telegraph*, 16 August 1998, p.10.

11 Spike Milligan, quoted by Scudamore, *Spike Milligan, op.cit.*, p.25.

12 Spike Milligan, quoted by David Nathan, *The Laughtermakers, op. cit.*, p.45.

13 Leo Milligan, quoted by Scudamore, *Spike Milligan, op. cit.*, p.54.

14 Spike Milligan, quoted by Norma Farnes (editor) in *The Goons: The Story* (London: Virgin, 1997), p.54.

15 Spike Milligan, interviewed by Michael Parkinson in 1980, reproduced in *Parkinson* (London: Pavilion, 1982), p.109.

16 *Ibid.*

17 *Ibid.*

18 *Ibid.*

19 Spike Milligan, quoted in 'Blind Date! The Day Van Morrison Met . . . Spike Milligan?', *op. cit.*, p.50.

20 Spike Milligan, interviewed by David Bradbury and Joe McGrath for their book, *Now That's Funny!, op. cit*, p.20.

21 Spike Milligan, quoted in 'Blind Date! The Day Van Morrison Met . . . Spike Milligan?', *op. cit.*, p.47.

22 Desmond Milligan, quoted by Humphrey Carpenter in *Spike Milligan: The Biography* (London: Hodder, 2003), p.30.

23 Spike Milligan, quoted by Scudamore, *Spike Milligan, op. cit.*, pp.10 and 11–12.

24 *Ibid.*, p.81.

25 Spike Milligan, quoted by Draper, *The Story of The Goons, op. cit.*, p.44.

26 Bob 'Dipper' Dye, as recalled in a handwritten note inside his own copy of Milligan's war memoir, *Monty: His Part in My Victory* (London: Michael Joseph, 1976).

27 Spike Milligan, in Spike Milligan and Anthony Clare, *Depression and How to Survive It* (London: Arrow, 1994), p.110.

28 The Central Pool of Artistes – and *Stars in Battledress* (SIB) as its touring productions were known – was instigated by Lieutenant-Colonel Basil Brown early in 1942. Unlike the civilian company ENSA, SIB was considered a more 'organic' form of military entertainment – by servicemen for servicemen – as well as more integral – it had access to areas prohibited to civilian performers.

In addition to Milligan, among the many other future stars who took part at some stage were Terry-Thomas, Benny Hill, Reg Varney, Charlie Chester, Ken Platt, Harry Secombe and Norman Vaughan. See John Graven Hughes's *The Greasepaint War*, (London: New English Library, 1976), and Bill Pertwee's entertaining anecdotal history, *Stars in Battledress* (London: Hodder, 1992).

29　The members were: Bill Hall (violin), Johnny Mulgrew (double bass) and Spike Milligan (trumpet and guitar).

30　Spike Milligan, quoted by Bill Pertwee in *Stars in Battledress, op. cit.*, pp.73–4.

31　*Ibid.*, p.73.

32　*Ibid.*

33　Spike Milligan, quoted by Scudamore, *Spike Milligan, op. cit.*, pp.10 and 11–12.

34　Spike Milligan, interviewed by Bradbury and McGrath, *Now That's Funny!*, *op. cit.*, p.15.

35　Spike Milligan, quoted by Bill Pertwee in *Stars in Battledress, op. cit.*, p.75.

36　Spike Milligan, quoted by Nathan, *The Laughtermakers, op. cit.*, p.48.

37　Spike Milligan, quoted by Scudamore, *Spike Milligan, op. cit.*, p.163.

38　Dialogue taken from the movie *The Cocoanuts* (1929), adapted by Morrie Ryskind from the stage play by George S. Kaufman.

39　Taken from the movie *The Bank Dick* (1940), written by W.C. Fields.

40　W.C. Fields, quoted in the *Saturday Evening Post* (US), 6 August 1938.

41　Spike Milligan, interviewed by Bradbury and McGrath, *Now That's Funny!*, *op.cit.*, p.14.

42　Stephen Leacock, 'Gertrude the Governess', in his *Nonsense Novels* (New York: NYRB, 2005), p.47.

43　Leacock's short story, 'Maddened by Mystery: or, The Defective Detective', which was included in his *Nonsense Novels* collection of 1911, continues to be regarded highly as an elegant 'meta-fiction'. Leacock's so-called 'Great Detective' – Sherlock Holmes is never mentioned by name and Dr Watson is referred to only as 'the Secretary' – is all exaggeration. His task – at the express request of the Archbishop of Canterbury, the Prime Minister of Great Britain and the Prefect of Paris – is to solve the mystery of the Prince of Württemberg's abduction on the eve of an important public function in France. It transpires, after a certain amount of investigation, that the abducted 'prince' is actually a thoroughbred dachshund, bred by 'the most beautiful woman in England', the Countess of Dashleigh, and has since been mutilated by its evil captors. In order, therefore, to save the honour of England and the finances of the fragrant Countess, the 'Great Detective' disguises himself as a dog and wins first prize at the Paris International Dog Show. Unfortunately, however, he is captured, without tags, by a dog-catcher and is subsequently destroyed.

44　Acknowledged by Milligan in a BBC press handout, dated January 1968, released to coincide with the launch on BBC2 of *The World of Beachcomber* – two series, starring Milligan, Frank Thornton, Leon Thau and Patricia Hayes that ran from 22 January 1968 to 27 October 1969. (The handout is preserved in the BBC WAC.)

45　Spike Milligan, quoted by Farnes in *The Goons, op. cit.*, p.10.

46　Spike Milligan, quoted by Nathan, *The Laughtermakers, op. cit.*, p.47.

47 Spike Milligan, *The Family Album* (London: Virgin, 1999), p.117.
48 Unsigned BBC audition report, dated 10 March 1949, BBC WAC: Spike Milligan Television Artist's File 1: 1947–1962.
49 Spike Milligan, interviewed by Bradbury and McGrath for *Now That's Funny!*, op. cit., p.15.
50 *Ibid.*
51 John Junkin, interview with the author, 1 June 2005.
52 John Antrobus, in *Surviving Spike Milligan*, op. cit., p.28.
53 Spike Milligan, 'New Members Welcome', in *Small Dreams of a Scorpion* (London: Hobbs/Michael Joseph, 1972), p.68.
54 Spike Milligan, in a letter to Robert Graves, dated 18 January 1969, reproduced by Pauline Scudamore in *Dear Robert, Dear Spike: The Graves–Milligan Correspondence* (Stroud: Alan Sutton, 1991), p.96.
55 Spike Milligan, quoted by Scudamore, *Spike Milligan*, op. cit., p.207.
56 Spike Milligan, *Depression and How to Survive It*, op. cit., p.17.
57 Spike Milligan, quoted by Farnes, *The Goons*, op. cit., p.116.
58 Spike Milligan, 'Manic Depression', in *Small Dreams of a Scorpion*, op. cit., p.22.
59 John Antrobus, *Surviving Spike Milligan*, op. cit., p.111.
60 Spike Milligan, *Depression and How to Survive It*, op. cit., p.29.
61 Spike Milligan, in a letter to Ronnie Waldman at the BBC, dated 22 August 1956: BBC WAC: Spike Milligan Television Artist's File 1: 1947–1962.
61 Recounted by Eric Sykes, conversation with the author, 11 December 2004.
63 Recounted by Farnes, *Spike*, op. cit., p.65.
64 Beryl Vertue, interview with the author, 14 June 2005.
65 Spike Milligan, *Depression and How to Survive It*, op. cit., pp.16 and 18.
66 *Ibid.*, p.15.
67 Spike Milligan, speaking in the mental health video, *Me Depressed? Don't Make Me Laugh* (Australia: Monkey See Productions, 1990).
68 Eric Sykes, speaking in the documentary *The Unseen Spike Milligan*, first broadcast by Channel 4 on 24 December 2005.
69 Farnes, *Spike*, op. cit., p.350.
70 *Ibid.*, pp.79 and 81.
71 Farnes, speaking in *The Unseen Spike Milligan*, first broadcast by Channel 4 on 24 December 2005.
72 Spike Milligan, speaking on *Face Your Image*, first broadcast on BBC1 on 14 March 1975.
73 Spike Milligan, in a letter to V. K. Harpwood at the BBC Variety Booking Office, dated 22 September 1955: BBC WAC: Spike Milligan: Artist's File 1: 1949–1956.
74 Spike Milligan, in a letter to the BBC's Jim Davidson, dated 16 July 1958: BBC WAC: Spike Milligan: File 1: 1951–1962.
75 *Daily Mail*, 5 March 1958.
76 See the cuttings in BBC WAC: Spike Milligan: File 1: 1951–1962.
77 Kenneth Adam, in a memo dated 7 May 1958, BBC WAC: Spike Milligan: File 1: 1951–1962.
78 Dennis Main Wilson, memo dated 12 October 1959, *ibid.*

79 Spike Milligan, quoted by Ronald L. Smith, *Who's Who in Comedy* (New York: Facts on File, 1992), p.328.

80 Friedrich Nietzsche, *Twilight of the Idols*, translated by R. J. Hollingdale (London: Penguin, 2003), p.48.

81 Eric Sykes, speaking at a tribute to Spike Milligan, *I Told You I Was Ill*, staged at the Guildhall, London, on 15 September 2002.

Room 2: Eric Sykes

1 Eric Sykes, quoted by Nathan, *The Laughtermakers, op. cit.*, p.75.

2 Eric Sykes, interview with the author, 19 February 2004.

3 Eric Sykes, *If I Don't Write It, Nobody Else Will* (London: Fourth Estate, 2005), p.6.

4 Eric Sykes, quoted by Deborah Ross, 'Eric Sykes – Mummy's Boy', *The Independent*, 11 February 2002, p.7.

5 Sykes, *If I Don't Write It*, p.5.

6 *Ibid.*, p.14.

7 *Ibid.*, p.58.

8 *Ibid.*, p.36.

9 *Ibid.*, p.57.

10 *Ibid.*, p.179.

11 Eric Sykes, quoted by David Nathan, *The Laughtermakers, op. cit.*, p.75.

12 Source: www.metoffice.gov.uk.

13 Eric Sykes, interview with the author, 19 February 2004.

14 Eric Sykes, *Eric Sykes's Comedy Heroes, op. cit.*, p.92.

15 Eric Sykes, interview with the author, 19 February 2004.

16 Frankie Howerd, quoted by David Nathan, *The Laughtermakers, op. cit.*, p.194.

17 Eric Sykes, interview with the author, 19 February 2004.

18 The phrase comes from the lion tamer routine, written by Eric Sykes for Frankie Howerd in *Variety Bandbox*, 16 October 1949; the recording was included subsequently on the LP *50 Years of Radio Comedy* (BBC, REC 138M).

19 Script excerpt transcribed from a recording of *Variety Bandbox*, circa 1948, reproduced here by kind permission of Eric Sykes.

20 Frankie Howerd, *On the Way I Lost It* (London: W. H. Allen, 1976), p.69.

21 Eric Sykes, interview with the author, 19 February 2004.

22 Source: BBC WAC: Daily Viewing Barometers for Sundays during 1948 (e.g. 5 December 1948).

23 Source: Post Office/National Television Licence Records Office.

24 Eric Sykes, interview with the author, 19 February 2004. (Also see Frankie Howerd, *On the Way I Lost It, op. cit.*, p.82.)

25 Sykes, speaking on the BBC Radio 2 documentary, *There'll Never Be Another*, first broadcast 1 August, 2000.

26 *Ibid.*

27 Eric Sykes, interview with the author, 19 February 2004.

28 The award was given by the *Daily Mail*.

29 Eric Sykes, interview with the author, 19 February 2004.

30 *Ibid.*

31 *Archie in Goonland* was broadcast on the BBC's Home Service on 11 June 1954. Neither the script nor the recording appears to have survived.

32 Sykes worked with Sellers on *The Idiot Weekly, Price 2d* in 1956 (Sykes edited the series as well as acting in it), and then appeared with him again on 5 and 12 January 1957 on the two ATV specials, *Eric Sykes Presents Peter Sellers*.

33 Spike Milligan, quoted by Farnes, *Spike, op. cit.*, p.352.

34 Eric Sykes, quoted by Freddie Hancock and David Nathan in *Hancock* (London: Ariel, 1986), p.48.

35 Eric Sykes, quoted by Cliff Goodwin, *When the Wind Changed: The Life and Death of Tony Hancock* (London: Century, 1999), p.133.

36 John Browell, quoted by Barry Took, *Laughter in the Air, op. cit.*, p.65.

37 Eric Sykes, quoted John P. Guy in 'For TV Humour, A Goon Twist', *TV Mirror*, March 1956, pp.8–9.

38 Eric Sykes, quoted by Nathan, *The Laughtermakers, op. cit.*, p.77.

39 The 'Aladdin' low-vision reading machine is an easy-to-use closed circuit unit that enables the reader to place a book, magazine, or sheet of paper on an adjustable tray. A camera then projects the print information on to a TV-style monitor. The reader can adjust the size and clarity of the print that they see on the screen, or reverse the contrast from black letters on a white background to white letters on a black background (or use some other combination of colours – Sykes would use blue and yellow), since one or the other may be preferable for a specific visual disability.

40 Eric Sykes, quoted by Nathan, *The Laughtermakers, op. cit.*, p.75.

41 Johnny Speight, *For Richer, For Poorer* (London: BBC, 1991), p.166.

42 Bill Lyon-Shaw was one of the first generation of television directors in the field of Light Entertainment, alongside the likes of Michael Mills, Duncan Wood and Bill Ward. Among the early shows he oversaw on BBC TV were *Hi There!, The Harry Secombe Show, Richard Hearne, Jimmy Logan, Vic's Grill, The Howerd Crowd* (see my *Frankie Howerd, op. cit.*, pp.116–17).

43 Both Muir and Sykes would later recall the year as being 1960, but, as a subsequent report in *The Times* – dated 9 March 1959 – confirms, it was definitely 1959. The appointment of Muir and Norden became official at the start of April 1959.

44 See Chapter 11 of Frank Muir's autobiography, *A Kentish Lad* (London: Bantam Press, 1997), for a first-hand account of his and Norden's time as comedy consultants.

45 See Eric Sykes, *If I Don't Write It, Nobody Else Will, op. cit.*, pp.330–1, and my *Frankie Howerd, op. cit.*, p.160.

46 See Chapter 7 for an in-depth discussion of the series and its cast.

47 John Junkin, interview with the author, 1 June 2005.

48 Michael Mills, then Head of Comedy at BBC TV, offered Sykes the role in 1967; the first series of the sitcom was broadcast the following year with Derek Nimmo as Brother Dominic (see Sykes, *If I Don't Write It, Nobody Else Will, op. cit.*, pp.385–6).

49 Eric Sykes, *If I Don't Write It, Nobody Else Will, op. cit.*, p.375.

50 John Russell Taylor, *The Times*, 27 July 1967, p.6.
51 Eric Sykes, *Eric Sykes's Comedy Heroes, op. cit.*, p.165.

Room 3: Galton & Simpson

1   Denis Norden, speaking on the BBC Radio 4 documentary, *Associated London Scripts*, BBC Radio 4, 14–21 January 2003.

2   Ray Galton, quoted by Caroline Scott, 'Ray Galton: Best of Times, Worst of Times', *Sunday Times Magazine*, 19 March 2006, p.11.

3   Tuberculosis is an infectious disease caused by the bacillus *Mycobacterium tuberculosis*. It most often affects the lungs (pulmonary tuberculosis), but may also involve the bones and joints, skin, lymph nodes, intestines and kidneys. Encouraged by poverty, poor ventilation and overcrowding, it claimed more victims in nineteenth-century Britain than all other infectious diseases put together. Until the Second World War, the main cures were prolonged rest, sunlight, fresh air and a well-balanced diet. Provision for sufferers was funded by The National Insurance Act of 1911, which invested £1.5m in sanatoria and treatment; by 1930 there were 500 institutions with 25,000 beds. The incidence of the infection was reduced eventually by pasteurisation of milk (which killed the bacillus) and the introduction of the BCG vaccine after 1945.

4   See *The Times*, 21 October 1949, p.5.

5   Ray Galton, quoted by Caroline Scott, 'Ray Galton', *op. cit.*, p.11.

6   *Ibid.*

7   Alan Simpson, quoted by David Nathan, *The Laughtermakers, op. cit.*, p.131.

8   *Ibid.*

9   Alan Simpson, interview with the author, 15 March 2004.

10 Alan Simpson, speaking on the BBC Radio 4 documentary, *Associated London Scripts*, BBC Radio 4, 14–21 January 2003.

11 Ray Galton, interviewed by Paul Merton, 29 September 2002, at the British Film Institute.

12 Alan Simpson, quoted by Richard Webber, *Fifty Years of Hancock's Half-Hour* (London: BBC, 2004), p.11.

13 Ray Galton, interview with the author, 15 March 2004.

14 Alan Simpson, *ibid.*

15 *Ibid.*

16 Ray Galton, quoted by David Nathan, *The Laughtermakers, op. cit.*, p.130.

17 Alan Simpson, interview with the author, 15 March 2004.

18 A radio serial, *Afloat with Henry Morgan*, had been broadcast, and much repeated, during the 1930s.

19 Alan Simpson, quoted by David Nathan, *The Laughtermakers, op. cit.*, p.132.

20 Ray Galton, interviewed by Paul Merton, 29 September 2002, at the British Film Institute.

21 Alan Simpson, interview with the author, 15 March 2004.

22 *Ibid.*

23 Alan Simpson, quoted by Richard Webber, *Fifty Years of Hancock's Half-Hour, op. cit.*, p.19.

24 Alan Simpson, interview with the author, 15 March 2004.
25 Ray Galton, interview with the author, 15 March 2004.
26 Alan Simpson, interview with the author, 15 March 2004.
27 BBC WAC: Alan Simpson Copyright File 1: 1954–1962.
28 The sixth season of *Take It From Here*, which started on 12 November 1953, introduced 'The Glums' as a new section of the show. The working-class Glums were an antidote to the kind of cosy and clean-living middle-class families that radio, up until that point, had tended to promote. Mr Glum, the head of the family (played by Jimmy Edwards), was boozy, brusque and brash; his wife (played by Alma Cogan) was invariably heard merely as an indistinguishable noise emanating from 'upstairs'. The family was completed by the dim-witted son, Ron (Dick Bentley), and his girlfriend, Eth (June Whitfield).
29 Anon., 'Comedians Find Television Can Be No Joke', *The Times*, 5 November 1958, p.13.
30 Jack Gould, 'TV: Comedy of Britain', *New York Times, op. cit.*, p.51.
31 John Antrobus, *Surviving Spike Milligan, op. cit.*, p.10.
32 Galton and Simpson, 'Who's Who' notes in the programme for the 1966–7 stage revue, *Way Out in Piccadilly*, p.19.
33 Alan Simpson, interview with the author, 15 March 2004.
34 Anon., 'Tony Hancock Team: Messrs Simpson and Galton on Writing Television Comedy', *The Times*, 2 March 1959, p.12.
35 See Nathan, *The Laughtermakers, op. cit.*, p.33, and also Frank Muir's BBC lunchtime lecture, delivered on 14 December 1966 and published subsequently in pamphlet form as *Comedy in Television* (London: BBC, 1966), pp.11–13.
36 *Citizen James* ran for three series on the BBC between 1960 and 1963. It starred Sid James as 'Sidney Balmoral James' – a variation on his crafty, fast-talking, street-smart *Hancock's Half-Hour* character – with support from another former member of the Hancock rep, Bill Kerr (as his eager henchman), Liz Fraser (as James's frustrated, marriage-craving fiancée) and Sydney Tafler (as his friend and bookie). After creating the first series, Galton and Simpson passed on their scriptwriting responsibilities to Dick Hills and Sid Green. The comment from Ray Galton was quoted by Cliff Goodwin in *Sid James* (London: Arrow, 1996), p.132.
37 Ray Galton, interview with the author, 15 March 2004.
38 Anon., *The Times*, 24 October 1958, p.15.
39 Ray Galton, interview with the author, 15 March 2004.
40 *Ibid.*
41 Frank Muir, quoted by Nathan, *The Laughtermakers, op. cit.*, p.32.
42 Transcribed from the recording *Frankie Howerd At The Establishment* (Decca 4556, 1963).
43 BBC WAC: Audience Research Report on *The Frankie Howerd Show*, 11 December 1964 (VR/64/663 4 January 1965).
44 Frankie Howerd, *On the Way I Lost It, op. cit.*, p.209.
45 The first edition of the first series, on 11 December 1964, was watched by an estimated 20.6 per cent of the then total population of the UK (in other

words, 11,196,100 – the biggest BBC audience of the night), and received a
Reaction Index of 66 per cent. The final edition, on 15 January 1965,
attracted 19.7 per cent of the total population (10,706,950), with an RI of 59.
The first edition of the second series, on 22 February 1966, drew in 25.1 per
cent of the total population (13,641,850), with an RI of 67; the final edition,
shown on 29 March 1966, attracted 20 per cent of the population
(10,870,000), with an RI of 65.

46 Excerpt from a script by Galton and Simpson, *The Frankie Howerd Show*,
first broadcast on BBC1 on 22 February 1966 (reproduced with the permission of the authors).

47 Ray Galton, interview with the author, 15 March 2004.

48 The influential critic Bosley Crowther, for example, seemed to over-react in
spectacular fashion to what he called this 'presumptuous' movie. Writing in
The New York Times (17 October 1961, p.47), he snorted: 'Norman Wisdom
can move over. The British have found a low comedian who is every bit as low
as he is and even less comical.'

49 For the full story of this troubled production, see my *Frankie Howerd, op.
cit.*, pp.228–37.

50 See Chapter 11.

51 Alan Simpson, interview with the author, 15 March 2004.

52 Ray Galton, *ibid*.

Room 4: Johnny Speight

1 See my 'Johnny Speight', *Dictionary of National Biography* (Oxford: Oxford
University Press, 2004), vol.51, pp.780–1.

2 Johnny Speight, quoted by Nathan, *The Laughtermakers, op. cit.*, p.124.

3 Johnny Speight, *For Richer, For Poorer* (*op. cit.*, p.12.

4 *Ibid.*

5 *Ibid.*, p.14.

6 *Ibid.*, p.63.

7 Johnny Speight, quoted by Nathan, *The Laughtermakers, op. cit.*, p.124.

8 *Ibid.*

9 Johnny Speight, *For Richer, For Poorer, op. cit.*, pp.11 and 13.

10 *Ibid.*, pp.13–14.

11 *Ibid.*, p.20.

12 Johnny Speight, quoted by Nathan, *The Laughtermakers, op. cit.*, p.124.

13 Johnny Speight, *For Richer, For Poorer, op. cit.*, p.29.

14 *Ibid.*, p.32.

15 *Ibid.*, p.99.

16 *Ibid.*, p.47.

17 *Ibid.*, p.50.

18 *Ibid.*, p.52.

19 *Ibid.*, p.69.

20 *Ibid.*, p.98.

21 *Ibid.*, p.76.

22 *Ibid.*, p.76.

23 Johnny Speight, quoted by Nathan, *The Laughtermakers, op. cit.*, p.125.
24 Johnny Speight, *For Richer, For Poorer, op. cit.*, p.76.
25 *Ibid.*, p.77.
26 Johnny Speight, quoted by Nathan, *The Laughtermakers, op. cit.*, p.125.
27 Johnny Speight, *For Richer, For Poorer, op. cit.*, p.129.
28 *Ibid.*, p.98.
29 See my 'Johnny Speight', *Dictionary of National Biography, op. cit*, pp.780–1.
30 Quoted by Frankie Howerd, *On the Way I Lost It, op. cit.*, p.113.
31 Eric Sykes, *Eric Sykes's Comedy Heroes, op. cit.*, p.157.
32 Johnny Speight, *For Richer, For Poorer, op. cit.*, p.29.
33 *Ibid.*, p.126.
34 Johnny Speight, *It Stands To Reason* (London: Hobbs/Michael Joseph, 1973), p.225.
35 Speight, speaking in the documentary *Howerd's Way, op. cit.*
36 Speight, in a script for *The Frankie Howerd Show*, series three, BBC Light Programme, 2 October 1955 – 22 January 1956.
37 Johnny Speight, speaking in the BBC Radio 2 documentary *Howerd's Way*, 29 August 1992.
38 Johnny Speight, quoted by Nathan, *The Laughtermakers, op. cit.*, p.126.
39 *The Times*, 18 May 1963, p.5.
40 Quoted by John Fisher, *Funny Way to be a Hero* (London: Frederick Muller, 1973), p.308.
41 Johnny Speight, *For Richer, For Poorer, op. cit.*, p.141.
42 Michael Caine, *What's It All About?* (London: Century, 1992), p.131.
43 *The Times*, 21 July 1962, p.4.
44 Johnny Speight, *For Richer, For Poorer, op. cit.*, p.139.
45 See George Bernard Shaw, Prefaces to *Man and Superman* and *On the Rocks* in *Complete Prefaces* (London: Paul Hamlyn, 1965), pp.158–9, 162, 176, 187, 353–4.
46 Johnny Speight, *For Richer, For Poorer, op. cit.*, p.129.
47 Denis Norden, speaking on the BBC Radio 4 documentary, *Associated London Scripts*, BBC Radio 4, 14–21 January 2003.
48 Johnny Speight, *For Richer, For Poorer, op. cit.*, p.153.
49 John Antrobus, *Surviving Spike, op. cit.*, p.41.
50 Johnny Speight, quoted by Nathan, *The Laughtermakers, op. cit.*, p.127.
51 Transcribed from the recording *Frankie Howerd at The Establishment* (Decca 4556, 1963).
52 Transcribed from a tape of *That Was The Week That Was*, broadcast on BBC TV on 6 April 1963.
53 Johnny Speight, *For Richer, For Poorer, op. cit.*, p.136.
54 Nicholas Parsons, *The Straight Man: My Life in Comedy* (London: Orion, 1994), pp.148–9.
55 Johnny Speight, quoted by Nathan, *The Laughtermakers, op. cit.*, p.126.
56 Beryl Vertue, interview with the author, 14 June 2005.
57 Johnny Speight, *For Richer, For Poorer, op. cit.*, p.139.
58 See my 'Broadcast Watchdog Cries Foul', *Financial Times*, 23 April 2003.
59 Hugh Carleton Greene, *The Third Floor Front* (London: Bodley Head, 1969), pp.13–14.

60 *The Times*, 6 May 1964, p.12.
61 *The Times*, 17 November 1965, p.12.
62 *The Times*, 29 April 1965, p.8.
63 Johnny Speight, quoted by Nathan, *The Laughtermakers, op. cit.*, p.111.
64 Transcribed from the *Till Death* sequence included in the *Royal Variety Performance*, broadcast on BBC1 on 5 November 1972.
65 Peter Cook, quoted by Nathan, *The Laughtermakers, op. cit.*, pp.113–14.
66 *Ibid.*
67 Eric Sykes, interview with the author, 19 February 2004.
68 John Antrobus, interviewed by Steve Bennett, 9 November 2004, for the website *Chortle*: http://www.chortle.co.uk/features/antrobus.htm.
69 *The Times*, 5 February 1965, p.15.
70 Johnny Speight, *Three Plays* (London: Oberon Books, 1998), p.56.
71 Haldane Duncan, 'A Life on the Floor', published on the 'TV Heroes' website: http://www.transdiffusion.org/emc/tvheroes/haldaneduncan/haldane2.php.
72 Michael Billington, *The Times*, 30 June 1967, p.8.
73 Johnny Speight, speaking in a special edition of *Late Night Line-Up*, first broadcast on BBC2 on 15 September 1972.
74 Johnny Speight, *For Richer, For Poorer, op. cit.*, p.143.
75 *Ibid.*

Room 5: A.N. Other's

1   Spike Milligan, quoted by Hancock and Nathan, *Hancock, op. cit.*, p.41.
2   BBC WAC: memorandum (entitled 'Programme Suggestion') from Peter Eton to the BBC's Head of Radio Variety, Michael Standing, dated 8 July 1952.
3   Beryl Vertue, quoted by Humphrey Carpenter, *Spike Milligan, op. cit.*, p.161.
4   Eric Sykes, interview with the author, 19 February 2004.
5   Alan Simpson, *ibid.*, p.161.
6   *Ibid.*
7   Spike Milligan, recalled by Eric Sykes, interview with the author, 19 February 2004.
8   BBC WAC: Frankie Howerd TV Artist's File 1: 1947–1962: letter sent by Stanley Dale/Frankie Howerd Scripts Ltd, 29 August 1955, to a number of people within the BBC Light Entertainment Department; and BBC WAC: Stanley Dale Artist's File: 1944–1959: letter written by Peter Charlesworth on Stanley Dale's behalf to Charlie Drake and Alistair Scott-Johnson at the BBC, 26 November 1957.
9   Brad Ashton, interview with the author, 14 November 2000.
10 *Ibid.*, p.160.
11 Memo from John Simmonds to the BBC's Assistant Head of Variety, 19 April 1957; quoted by Barry Took, *Star Turns,* (London: Weidenfeld & Nicolson, 1992) p.62.
12 Eric Sykes, interview with the author, 19 February 2004.
13 Barry Took, interview with the author, 17 May 2000, and *Star Turns, op. cit.*, p. 97.
14 Brad Ashton, interview with the author, 14 November 2000.

15 George Martin, *All You Need Is Ears* (New York: St Martin's Press, 1994), p.100.

16 Eric Sykes, interview with the author, 19 February 2004.

17 BBC WAC: Eric Sykes TV Artist's File no. 1: 1952–1962: letter, dated 13 January 1960, from Beryl Vertue to Myra Fleming in the Bookings Department at the BBC.

18 John Antrobus, *Surviving Spike Milligan, op. cit.*, p.69.

19 *Ibid.*

20 *Ibid.*, p.29.

21 *Ibid.*, p.69.

22 *Ibid.*, p.70.

23 Bernard Miles, quoted by Pauline Scudamore, *Spike Milligan, op. cit.*, p.217.

24 *The Times*, 21 March 1963, p.5.

25 John Antrobus, *Surviving Spike Milligan, op. cit.*, p.69.

26 *Ibid.*

27 *Ibid.*, p.15.

28 *Ibid.*, p.84.

29 Norma Farnes, *Spike, op. cit.*, p.63.

30 John Antrobus, *Surviving Spike Milligan, op. cit.*, p.15.

31 *Ibid.*, p.84.

32 *The Times*, 29 October 1964, p.16.

33 John Antrobus, *Surviving Spike Milligan, op. cit.*, p.86.

34 *Ibid.*, p.86.

35 *Ibid.*, p.87.

36 Barry Took, *Laughter in the Air, op. cit.*, p.138.

37 Barry Took, *Round the Horne: The Complete and Utter History* (London: Boxtree, 1998), p.112.

38 *Ibid.*

39 *Ibid.*, p.117.

40 Terry Nation, quoted by David Nathan, *Hancock, op. cit.*, p.132.

41 Terry Nation, *Radio Times*, 3 December 1964, p.9.

42 Peter Yeldham, interviewed for the website Memorable TV: http://www.memorabletv.com/interviewspeteryeldham.htm.

43 *Ibid.*

44 Brad Ashton, interview with the author, 14 November 2000.

4. THE OUTPUT

The Goons

1 The theatre critic David Lewin, writing in the *Daily Express* of 24 October 1947, described Bentine as 'a promising British comedian'.

2 Michael Bentine, quoted by Nathan, *The Laughtermakers, op. cit.*, p.70.

3 Harry Secombe, *Arias and Raspberries* (London: Pan, 1997), p.190.

4 Jimmy Grafton, writing in his and Roger Wilmut's invaluable *The Goon Show Companion* (London: Robson, 1976), p.18.

5   Since 1932, the Windmill Theatre had been permitted by the Lord Chamberlain's Office (the Government's guardian of public morality from 1660 until the abolition of this role in 1968) to present nude female tableaux on condition that all of the women involved remained absolutely stationary (and thus 'artistic' rather than 'sexual') for the duration of each performance, the stage lighting was kept 'subdued' and 'binoculars, minoculars, telescopes and no other artificial aids to vision' were permitted in the auditorium (a senior official from the Lord Chamberlain's Office – the aptly-named George Titman – used to visit the theatre on a regular basis to ensure that these rules were not being broken). The ostensible job of the theatre's resident comedians – who, at various times, included the likes of Eric Barker, Arthur English, Tony Hancock, Benny Hill, Alfred Marks, Bruce Forsyth, Jimmy Edwards and, very briefly, Morecambe and Wise – was to keep the mostly male audience entertained while the next nude routine was being set up, although many of the customers preferred merely to open their newspapers and read, or doze, until it was time for more women to disrobe. See my *Morecambe & Wise* (London: Fourth Estate, 1998), pp.72–76, for more information on The Windmill in this era.

6   Harry Secombe, *Arias and Raspberries, op. cit.,* p.119.

7   Grafton and Wilmut, *The Goon Show Companion, op.cit.,* p.17.

8   See Draper, *The Story of The Goons,* p.24; Grafton and Wilmut, *The Goon Show Companion, op cit.,* p.26; and Secombe, *Arias and Raspberries, op cit.,* pp.97–8.

9   Harry Secombe, *Arias and Raspberries, op. cit.,* pp.122–3.

10 Harry Secombe, quoted by Nathan, *The Laughtermakers, op. cit.,* p.62.

11 Devised originally by the song-writer and choreographer Ralph Reader as an annual fund-raising event for the British Scout and Guide movements, the Gang Show began in London in 1932 under the title of 'The Gang's All Here'. When the 1939 Gang Show was cancelled in mid-rehearsal as the nation began to mobilise, Reader's future seemed set for a new direction. When he joined the RAF, however, his counter-intelligence duties saw him pose as an entertainments officer, so he organised a series of Gang Shows for the RAF. These productions spread eventually to twenty-five different units, and consisted mainly of RAF recruits considered unsuitable for normal combat duties.

12 Peter Sellers, speaking on *Parkinson,* first broadcast on BBC1 on 9 November 1974, and in Nathan, *The Laughtermakers, op. cit.,* p.72.

13 Grafton and Wilmut, *The Goon Show Companion, op. cit.,* pp.30–31.

14 Harry Secombe, *Arias and Raspberries, op. cit.,* p.187.

15 The scripts for this series are preserved in the Frank Muir and Denis Norden Archive at the University of Sussex Library.

16 Spike Milligan, quoted by Nathan, *The Laughtermakers, op. cit.,* p.49.

17 See Harry Secombe, *Arias and Raspberries, op. cit.,* p.197.

18 Harry Secombe, *ibid.,* p.187.

19 Grafton and Wilmut, *The Goon Show Companion, op. cit.,* pp. 32–33.

20 *Ibid.,* p.34.

21 Jimmy Grafton, interviewed by David Dimbleby for a BBC1 profile of Milligan called *Face Your Image,* first broadcast on 14 March 1975.

22 Dennis Main Wilson, interviewed by Alan Lawson with Norman Swallow in 1991 for the BECTU History Project.

23 Harry Secombe, *Arias and Raspberries, op. cit.*, p.197.

24 The Crazy Gang consisted of three experienced comedy double-acts: Jimmy Nervo and Teddy Knox; Bud Flanagan and Chesney Allen, and Charlie Naughton and Jimmy Gold. The team was sometimes supplemented by the unpredictable solo comic 'Monsewer' Eddie Gray. Appearing in their own stage shows from the early 1930s, as well as on several special Variety bills, and in movies and television shows, they stayed together until 1962.

25 In a memo of 13 August 1951, for example, the show was called 'Crazy People'; in a memo of 2 October 1951, it was called 'Crazy Show'; in a memo of 7 January 1952, it was called 'Crazy People' again (BBC WAC: *The Goon Show*: R19/446 – 1950–1954).

26 *Radio Times*, 27 May – 2 June 1951, p.9

27 Spike Milligan, quoted by Nathan, *The Laughtermakers, op. cit.*, p.48.

28 There has always been some disagreement concerning the true reasons for Bentine's departure from The Goons. According to Jimmy Grafton (who was certainly in a good position to witness the sequence of events leading up to the exit), Bentine simply 'had other fish to fry': 'There was no acrimony, and the early friendships [were] steadily maintained' (*The Goon Show Companion, op. cit.*, p.39). Harry Secombe, while acknowledging that Bentine left of his own volition and on cordial terms, provided a rather more nuanced account, suggesting that, by the end of the second series, the struggle for creative control had begun to grow more intense: 'After the performance there would be a post-mortem, and that was when the difference of opinion between Spike and Mike would sometimes surface. There were never big rows, it was usually the interpretation of a character, or coming in too soon, or someone else's lines that was the cause of contention' (*Arias and Raspberries, op. cit.*, p.208). Spike Milligan's recollection, on the other hand, grew more sour as the years went by, claiming in 1998 that what trust had existed between Bentine and himself had broken during the second series: 'Michael . . . said to Peter Sellers – and Peter recounted exactly what he said – he said: "Look, we don't need Spike. He's not funny." And that has stuck in my mind ever since' (interviewed by Bradbury and McGrath, *Now That's Funny!, op. cit.*, p.16). Michael Bentine's own explanation, however, was as follows: 'I was with *The Goon Show* till 1952, so the six years from 1946 till then represents a large chunk of my life. I remember we suffered enormous tensions in putting the shows together, but there was also the joyous side and the memories all four of us have' (quoted by Draper, *The Story of The Goons, op. cit.*, p.30.

29 The majority of the descriptions of the characters are taken from Spike Milligan's summaries in *The Goon Show Scripts* (London: Sphere, 1973), n.p., and *More Goon Show Scripts* (London: Sphere, 1974), pp.6–7.

30 Spike Milligan, quoted by Farnes, *The Goons, op. cit.*, p.120.

31 Peter Sellers, speaking in the BBC1 programme *Michael Parkinson Meets The Goons, op. cit.*

32 See *The Sunday Times*, 9 November 1958, quoted in *The Goon Show Scripts op cit.*, p.8

33 Spike Milligan, quoted by Bradbury and McGrath, *Now That's Funny!, op. cit.*, p.17.

34 See Michael Sellers, speaking in Cathy Henkel's documentary *I Told You I Was Ill: The Life and Legacy of Spike Milligan* (Australia: Film Finance Corporation/South Australian Film Corporation/Adelaide Film Festival/Hatchling Productions, 2005).

35 Jimmy Grafton, *The Goon Show Companion, op. cit.*, p. 27.

36 Spike Milligan, speaking on *Face Your Image, op. cit.*

37 Spike Milligan, quoted by Roger Lewis, *The Life and Death of Peter Sellers* (London: Arrow, 2004), p.176.

38 Spike Milligan, quoted by Bradbury and McGrath, *Now That's Funny!, op. cit.*, p.17.

39 Peter Eton, 'Introduction', in Spike Milligan et al., *The Book of The Goons* (London: Robson, 1974), p.10.

40 *The Observer*, 23 December 1956; reproduced in *The Observer Book of Profiles*, edited by Robert Low (London: Virgin, 1991), pp.322–25.

41 'Shifting Sands', 24 January 1957.

42 'The Mysterious Punch-up-the-Conker', 7 February 1957.

43 Quoted by David Nathan, *The Laughtermakers, op. cit.*, pp.42–3.

44 'The Internal Mountain', 29 March 1954.

45 'The End' (sometimes known as 'The Confessions of a Secret Senna-Pod Drinker'), 22 March 1955.

46 'The Phantom Head-Shaver of Brighton', 19 October 1954.

47 See Peter Eton, in *The Book of The Goons, op. cit.*, pp.10–11. (Apparently, when Ben Lyon, one of the stars of the radio sitcom *Life with the Lyons*, heard this laughter as it was being edited down, he asked what Eton was doing. 'Throwing away laughter,' Eton replied. 'Don't do that,' Lyons exclaimed. 'We're short of laughter this week. Give it to me' – and the 'spare' laughter ended up spliced into *Life with the Lyons*.)

48 'The Terrible Revenge of Fred Fu-Manchu', 6 December 1955.

49 The formal title of the 'private and confidential' internal guide – an informal version of which had already been brought to the attention of programme-makers – was *BBC Variety Programmes Policy Guide for Writers & Producers* (London: BBC, 1948). It was nicknamed 'The Green Book' simply because of the colour of its cloth.

50 *Ibid.*, p.4.

51 *Ibid.*, p.5.

52 *Ibid.*, p.13. The decision to ban impersonations of Churchill (and certain other elder statesmen) came from the upper echelons of the BBC. As for Lynn and Fields, the decision was forced upon the BBC by either the performers themselves or their management.

53 Another play on words was the name of Willium 'Mate' Cobblers (cobblers – cobbler's awls – balls).

54 The joke – of which there have been innumerable variations – goes roughly like this: In a poor little town in the middle of nowhere, a stranger walks into a bar, sits down, buys a drink and remarks on the fact that no women are to been seen anywhere. 'That's because there's none in town,' explains the bartender. The stranger is amazed: 'How on earth, then, do all of you men cope?' The bartender smiles: 'It ain't too bad. When we get lonesome we go

out the back where there's a barrel with a knothole in it. It don't sound appealing at first, but, once you've tried it, you're hooked.' The stranger raises an eyebrow, downs a few more drinks, and then, feeling curious, he sets off out the back and inserts himself through the knothole. A few minutes later, he returns to the bar, and exclaims: 'Man, that was something special! What do I owe you?' The bartender just grins and says: 'Nothin' – but now it's your turn to get in the barrel.'

55 See Peter Eton, quoted by Nathan, *The Laughtermakers, op. cit.*, pp.50–1.
56 See Spike Milligan, *More Goon Show Scripts, op. cit.*, pp.12–13.
57 'The Scarlet Capsule', 2 February 1959.
58 'Nineteen-Eighty-Five', 8 February 1955.
59 Peter Eton, *The Book of The Goons, op. cit.*, p.10.
60 'The Scarlet Capsule', 2 February 1959.
61 See Farnes, *The Goons, op. cit.*, p.118.
62 See *Michael Parkinson Meets The Goons, op. cit.*
63 In 1958, a small group of BBC producers and studio managers (the leading lights were Daphne Oram, Desmond Briscoe and Norman Bain) began using what they termed 'radiophonic' techniques to create new and unconventional sounds for music and drama programmes. The process consisted of recording real sounds – such as those created by the human voice, bottles, bells, musical instruments, percussion devices or even boxes of gravel or pebbles – and then manipulating them to produce entirely new material. The latest tape machines provided reverse playback, speed and pitch changes, or were used to create sound loops, whilst reverberation and equalisation helped modify the sound quality. Various elements of the work were then edited together (often note by note) using tape-splicing techniques. These processes (similar to Pierre Schaeffer's *musique concrète* and the experiments pioneered by Luciano Berio and Karlheinz Stockhausen) created or enhanced the atmosphere in a programme, but were not considered an 'art in itself'. The BBC, however, having seen the potential of this new aspect of broadcasting, decided in 1956 to establish an Electronics Effects Committee – which in turn agreed the following year to set up a Radiophonic Workshop (using outdated equipment from the BBC's Redundant Plant, as well as £2,000 for additional requirements). The Workshop was based initially in a large area created within Rooms 13 and 14 of the BBC's studio complex in London at Maida Vale. From the early 1960s, its influence was evident in a wide range of mainstream and avant-garde projects, and it acquired a higher public profile for the music and special effects that it supplied to such cult classics as *Doctor Who*, *Blake's Seven* and *The Hitchhiker's Guide to the Galaxy*. It remained functional until 1995 when, owing to budget cuts, it was no longer able to survive.
64 BBC WAC: Listener Research Reports, *The Goon Show*: R19/446 – 1950–1954 and Spike Milligan: Artist's File 1, 1949–1956.
65 Gale Pedrick, 'The Goons – as Others See Them', *Radio Times*, 31 October 1958, p.7.
66 Mimi Smith, quoted by Ray Coleman, *John Winston Lennon, vol.1: 1940–1966* (London: Sidgwick & Jackson, 1984), p.26.

67 HRH The Prince of Wales, 'Foreword', in Spike Milligan, *More Goon Show Scripts*, *op. cit.*, p.10.

68 Michael Foot was quoted by Gale Pedrick, 'The Goons – as Others See Them', *Radio Times*, 31 October 1958, p.7; Bernard Levin was writing in the *Manchester Guardian*, and was quoted subsequently by Philip Oakes in *Books and Authors*, December 1957.

69 See *The Times*, 2 March 1958, p.16, and 3 March, p.7.

70 John Antrobus, in *Surviving Spike Milligan*, *op. cit.*, p.41.

71 Spike Milligan, quoted by Philip Oakes, *Books and Authors*, December 1957.

72 Contrary to many accounts (encouraged by Spike Milligan's exaggerated complaints about the Corporation), the BBC had been keen to retain the services of The Goons when they turned their attention to television. On 23 April 1956, while *A Show Called Fred* was still in the process of being planned, Ronnie Waldman, the then Head of Light Entertainment, wrote to Milligan telling him that he would be 'delighted to have such a show on BBC Television'. Milligan replied (on 30 April) with the complaint that the team's previous television effort on BBC TV, the one-off *Goon Reel*, 'would now be bearing great fruit for you if it had been afforded a longer run'. Waldman did not give up, and, on 17 May (midway through the run of *A Show Called Fred*), he took Milligan for lunch and assured him that the BBC would match Associated-Rediffusion's offer of £450 per programme for the next series. Milligan appears to have been tempted by this, but, in a letter sent the following day, he claimed that it would be difficult to persuade his director, Richard Lester, to change channels unless the BBC bettered, rather than merely matched, the commercial company's offer. Waldman immediately sent a cable to Cecil McGivern, the Controller of Television, to request permission to increase the offer; somewhat oddly, McGivern, who was abroad at the time, replied that he could not understand the cable, and the chance was lost. This was not the end of the story, however, because Milligan contacted Waldman again on 10 January 1958 to ask what the chances were of making a BBC television series in the same mould as *Fred*. Waldman replied on 24 January, and said that the chances were 'very high indeed' – although he could not resist adding sardonically: 'if only you and I can agree on how much you think I and anyone else in the BBC knows about Television!' (BBC WAC: Spike Milligan, Television Artist's File 1: 1947–1962).

73 Spike Milligan, quoted by Farnes, *The Goons*, *op. cit.*, p.6.

Sykes And A . . .

1 Ronnie Waldman, 'The Toughest Job', *Radio Times*, 4 December 1953, pp.5–6.

2 Eric Sykes, *If I Don't Write It, Nobody Else Will*, *op. cit.*, p.231.

3 John Le Mesurier, *A Jobbing Actor* (London: Elm Tree, 1984), p.64.

4 *Ibid.*, p.65.

5 Hattie Jacques would appear in fourteen *Carry On* movies in total.

6 Eric Sykes, quoted by William Langley, 'Eric Sykes: The Great Survivor', *SAGA Magazine*, October 2003, pp.10–12.

7 The BBC's Radio Drama Company (RDC), or 'The Rep' as it was known informally, was founded in 1940 – partly in response to the increasing demands of a popular radio drama service but also because of the desire to keep all of the BBC's fifty or so regular actors safe and 'on call' (in the Concert Hall at Broadcasting House) during wartime in London. The Company continues to exist today.

8 Eric Sykes, *If I Don't Write It, Nobody Else Will, op. cit.*, p.339.

9 *Ibid.*, p.338.

10 *The Times*, 30 January 1960, p.11.

11 In a memorandum preserved in the BBC archives (BBC WAC: Eric Sykes, TV Artist's File 1: 1952–1962), the producer/director Dennis Main Wilson said of the writing for the second series: 'All the Antrobus and Milligan scripts, of course, were largely rewritten by Eric Sykes, who nonetheless refuses to take a credit.' Other documents in the archive indicate that, for the third series, Sykes had planned to write some of the episodes himself, write some jointly with John Antrobus, and have some written by Antrobus alone. The BBC, however, made it clear that it wanted all of the scripts from now on to be written exclusively by Eric Sykes. He agreed, and this was the arrangement that would continue for the rest of the run.

12 Jack Gould, 'TV: Comedy of Britain', *The New York Times*, 31 March 1962, p.51.

13 See *The Times*, 9 August 1967, p.6.

14 Donald Baverstock, memorandum dated 24 August 1962 (BBC WAC: Eric Sykes, TV Artist's File 1: 1952–1962).

15 It is often claimed, inaccurately, that Sloan took over from Eric Maschwitz as Head of Light Entertainment at the start of the 1960s, but, in truth, Maschwitz remained in the post until 1963; however, for the last four years of his tenure, he left the day-to-day duties to his deputy while he concentrated on special projects.

16 Eric Sykes, *If I Don't Write It, Nobody Else Will, op. cit.*, p.339.

17 Excerpt taken from *Sykes And A Stranger*, first broadcast on 21 April 1961 (remade for *Sykes* and broadcast on 19 October 1972).

18 Eric Sykes, interview with the author, 19 February 2004.

19 Eric Sykes, *Eric Sykes's Comedy Heroes, op. cit.*, p.103.

20 *Ibid.*

21 A sign of how highly Eric Sykes rated Lotterby is the number of laudatory letters he sent to the assistant director's superiors at the BBC. On 3 April 1963, for example, Sykes wrote to BBC1's Controller, Stuart Hood, thanking the BBC for its support during his last series and praising the contribution of Lotterby – 'who, in my opinion, should be in the top rank of producers' (BBC WAC: Eric Sykes, TV Artist's File 3).

22 Dennis Main Wilson, quoted by David Nathan, *The Laughtermakers, op. cit.*, p.120.

23 *Ibid.*, p.121.

24 Eric Sykes, interviewed in 2003 for an extra feature on the second of the three-disc DVD set of *Sykes: The Complete 1972 Series* (BBC Worldwide 2004: Network 7952179).

25 Eric Sykes, interview with the author, 19 February 2004.
26 It should be acknowledged that not everyone found it funny. Roger Lewis, in his *The Life and Death of Peter Sellers, op. cit.* (pp. 498–9), judged it 'one of Sellers' worst performances' in a 'dragged-out sketch' that is shown (quite incorrectly, as it happens) 'in a single thirty-minute take [with] no change of camera angle', and he criticises the actor for 'mocking [Hattie Jacques'] unattractiveness', signalling his own enjoyment in a manner that is 'amateur and boring', and failing to hide his supposed 'contempt for being on TV'. While there is much in Lewis's remarkable book with which I agree and admire, we will have to agree to disagree on this particular issue.
27 Excerpt taken from *Sykes And A Stranger*, first broadcast on 21 April 1961 (remade for *Sykes* and broadcast on 19 October 1972).
28 Kenneth Adam, telegram to Eric Sykes, 26 February 1964 (BBC WAC: Eric Sykes, TV Artist's File 3).
29 Tom Sloan, telegram to Eric Sykes, 9 November 1964, commemorating the fiftieth episode, 'Sykes And A Protest', broadcast on 13 November.
30 Eric Sykes, *If I Don't Write It, Nobody Else Will, op. cit.*, p.453.
31 See, for example, Tom Sloan's own BBC 'lunchtime lecture', *Television Light Entertainment* (London: BBC, 1969), for a sense of his attitudes and achievements.
32 Eric Sykes, *If I Don't Write It, Nobody Else Will, op. cit.*, pp.337–8.
33 *Ibid.*, p.386.
34 Eric Sykes, letter to Kenneth Adam, 1 December 1964: BBC WAC: Eric Sykes, TV Artist's File 3.
35 Donald Baverstock, memo to Kenneth Adam, 10 December 1964: *Ibid.*
36 Kenneth Adam, letter to Eric Sykes, 10 December 1964: *Ibid.*
37 Eric Sykes, letter to Kenneth Adam, 14 December 1964: *Ibid.*
38 See 'BBC Comedies Challenge ITV Serials', *The Times*, 20 September 1965, p.5.
39 Michael Bentine's *All Square* ran for two series on ATV at peak-time on Saturday evenings during 1966 and 1967.
40 Eric Sykes, letter to Kenneth Adam, 3 December 1965: BBC WAC: Eric Sykes, TV Artist's File 3.

Hancock & Steptoe

1 Alan Simpson, interview with the author, 15 March 2004.
2 Galton and Simpson, excerpt from *All Star Bill*, first broadcast 6 January 1953 on the BBC's Light Programme.
3 Ray Galton, speaking in the BBC2 *Arena* documentary *Written by Ray Galton & Alan Simpson*, first broadcast on 25 December 2005.
4 Alan Simpson, speaking in Paul Jackson's *In Conversation with . . . Galton and Simpson, op. cit.*
5 Dennis Main Wilson, in a memo to the Assistant Head of BBC Radio Variety, 1 May 1953 (BBC WAC: Alan Simpson Copyright File 1: 1951–1962).
6 Dennis Main Wilson, memo dated 12 February 1954 (BBC WAC: Dennis Main Wilson: 1).

7   Galton and Simpson, quoted by Richard Webber, *Fifty Years of Hancock's Half Hour, op. cit.,* pp.41–2.

8   Ray Galton, speaking in Paul Jackson's *In Conversation with . . . Galton and Simpson,* first broadcast on BBC Radio 4, 29 March 2001.

9   Alan Simpson, speaking in Paul Jackson's *In Conversation with . . . Galton and Simpson, op. cit.*

10   Hancock and Nathan, *Hancock, op. cit.,* p.74.

11   Ray Galton, speaking in Paul Jackson's *In Conversation with . . . Galton and Simpson, op. cit.*

12   *The Phil Harris & Alice Faye Show,* which starred the real-life husband and wife team of the musician and comedian Harris and the comic actor and singer Faye, ran from 1946 to 1954. Harris's character invariably found himself bemused, rattled and generally in trouble because of his sardonic buddy-guitarist Frank Remley (played with relish by Elliot Lewis in a manner reminiscent of Harris's similar role in *The Jack Benny Show*). Eventually, after Harris ceased to be Jack Benny's musical director, the Remley character was changed in name only – to Elliot.

13   Ray Galton, interviewed by Paul Merton, *op. cit.*

14   Ray Galton, quoted by Richard Webber, *Fifty Years of Hancock's Half Hour, op. cit.,* p. 44.

15   Dennis Main Wilson, quoted by Roger Wilmut in *Tony Hancock 'Artiste'* (London: Methuen, 1978), p.46.

16   Alan Simpson, interviewed by George Murphy, *op. cit.*

17   Alan Simpson, interviewed by Paul Merton, *op. cit.*

18   Alan Simpson, interview with the author, 15 March 2004.

19   BBC Audience Research Report, quoted by Nathan, *Hancock, op. cit.,* p.59.

20   *Ibid.*

21   Peter Eton, memorandum dated 7 December 1954 (BBC WAC: *The Goon Show*: File R19/446: 1950–1954).

22   See Nathan, *Hancock, op. cit.,* p.68.

23   Nathan, *op. cit.,* p.67.

24   Harry Secombe, *Strawberries and Cheam* (London: Pan, 1997), p.23.

25   Dennis Main Wilson, quoted by Hancock and Nathan, *Hancock, op. cit.,* p.67.

26   Tony Hancock, quoted by Anthony Carthew, 'Why A Star Cracked Up', *Daily Herald,* 7 May 1955, p.5.

27   Bill Kerr, quoted by Richard Webber, *Fifty Years of Hancock's Half Hour, op. cit.,* p.36.

28   Ray Galton, *ibid.,* p.112.

29   Alan Simpson, interviewed by George Murphy for the website Cult TV: http://www.cultv.co.uk/galtonandsimpson.htm.

30   Ray Galton, quoted by Richard Webber, *Fifty Years of Hancock's Half Hour, op. cit.,* p.36.

31   Ray Galton, interview with the author, 15 March 2004.

32   Alan Simpson, quoted by Nathan, *The Laughtermakers, op. cit.,* p.136.

33   John Cleese, speaking in the first of the three-part BBC1 *Omnibus* documentary, *Laughter in the House,* first broadcast 24 March 1999.

34   Clive Dunn, *ibid.*

35   Eric Maschwitz wrote to Galton and Simpson on 20 May 1960 to inform them of James's change of mind (BBC WAC: Galton and Simpson: File T48/272/1).

36   Ray Galton, quoted by Richard Webber, *Fifty Years of Hancock's Half Hour, op. cit.*, p.162.

37   Alan Simpson, *ibid.*, p.161.

38   Galton and Simpson, quoted by Hancock and Nathan, *Hancock, op. cit.*, pp.101–2.

39   Beryl Vertue, interview with the author, 14 June 2005.

40   Alan Simpson, *Written by Ray Galton & Alan Simpson, op. cit.*

41   The show was first 'tele-recorded' during the late 1950s on a BBC-designed device known as VERA (Vision Electronic Recording Apparatus) by sending tape through it at a speed of nearly seventy feet per second (giving a recording time of only fifteen minutes from a 21-inch-diameter reel of tape), and then on a slightly more sophisticated – or at least less primitive – US-made machine called Ampex (which used only a 10-inch wide spool of film for an hour's film).

42   The BBC, it seems, deemed Duncan Wood's editing methods to be 'costly and expensive', but Tony Hancock defended his producer/director to the extent of refusing to sign another contract unless the methods were tolerated (see Oakes, *Tony Hancock* [London: Woburn-Futura, 1975] p.45).

43   Spike Milligan, quoted by Nathan, *The Laughtermakers, op. cit.*, p.116.

44   Duncan Wood, *ibid.*, p.118.

45   J.B. Priestley, 'Tony Hancock', *Particular Pleasures* (New York: Stein & Day, 1975), p.170.

46   Denis Norden, quoted by Hancock and Nathan in *Hancock, op. cit.*, p.80.

47   Tony Hancock's five-year contract with the Kavanagh theatrical agency expired at the end of 1958. He then signed to Associated London Scripts, where his friend Stanley Dale advised him (as he had advised Frankie Howerd) to form his own ancillary companies as a hedge against taxation – so his television fees were paid to Tony Hancock (Television) Limited and his radio fees to Tony Hancock (Radio) Limited.

48   Beryl Vertue, quoted by Hancock and Nathan in *Hancock, op. cit.*, p.111.

49   Galton and Simpson, speaking in the documentary *Tony Hancock*, first broadcast on BBC2 on 26 December 2005.

50   *Ibid.*

51   *Ibid.*

52   See Oakes, *Tony Hancock, op. cit.*, p.19.

53   Spike Milligan, quoted by Alan Simpson, interview with the author, 15 March 2004.

54   Alan Simpson, speaking on BBC 7's *Comedy Controller* sequence, 26 February 2006.

55   Ray Galton, *Radio Times*, 28 December 1961, p.50.

56   Duncan Wood, quoted by Nathan, *The Laughtermakers, op. cit.*, p.117.

57   Ray Galton, quoted by Caroline Scott, 'Ray Galton', *op.cit.*, p.11.

58   Alan Simpson, speaking on BBC 7's *Comedy Controller* sequence, *op. cit.*

59   Alan Simpson, *Written by Ray Galton & Alan Simpson, op. cit.*

60 Alan Simpson, interview with the author, 15 March 2004.

61 Ray Galton, in Ray Galton and Alan Simpson, with Robert Ross, *Steptoe and Son* (London: BBC, 2002), p.23.

62 Alan Simpson, speaking in the documentary *When Steptoe Met Son*, first broadcast on Channel 4 on 20 August 2002.

63 Harry H. Corbett, speaking in an archive excerpt (dating from 1967) included in *Written by Ray Galton & Alan Simpson, op. cit.*

64 Ray Galton, interviewed by Paul Merton, *op. cit.*

65 Alan Simpson, speaking on BBC 7's *Comedy Controller* sequence, *op. cit.*

66 Ray Galton, interview with the author, 15 March 2004.

67 See Wilfrid Brambell, *All Above Board* (London: W. H. Allen, 1976) and Galton and Simpson with Ross, *Steptoe and Son, op. cit.*, pp.37–8.

68 *Desert Island Discs*, 30 March 1964.

69 Galton and Simpson with Ross, *Steptoe and Son, op. cit.*, pp.39–40. ('Oil Drum Lane' was actually used before by Galton and Simpson, in an episode of *Hancock* called 'The Missing Page', as the address of one of the minor characters.)

70 Galton and Simpson with Ross, *Steptoe and Son, op. cit.*, p.54.

71 See Nathan, *Hancock, op. cit.*, p.132.

72 *The Times*, 4 January 1964, p.4.

73 Galton and Simpson with Ross, *Steptoe and Son, op. cit.*, p.62.

74 Source: BBC WAC Viewing Barometers.

75 Gale Pedrick, in the sleeve notes for the record *Steptoe and Son* (Pye: NPL 18081, 1962).

76 Duncan Wood, quoted by Galton and Simpson with Ross, *Steptoe and Son, op. cit.*, p.53.

77 'Special Correspondent,' *The Times*, 21 July 1962, p.4.

78 Alan Simpson, interviewed by Kevin Saddington on BBC Radio Northampton, 15 September 1996.

79 *Ibid.*

80 Harry H. Corbett, quoted by Galton and Simpson with Ross, *Steptoe and Son, op. cit.*, p.117.

81 See Chapter 11.

82 Alan Simpson would say of the General Election 'incident': 'Wilson really did ask the BBC outright to put *Steptoe and Son* back to a later slot. It was ridiculous when you think about it, but in a way it was a very real backhanded compliment. Wilson's reckoning was that if *Steptoe* was on at its usual time, all the Labour voters wouldn't go out to vote: a cheeky generalisation that, that only Labour voters watched it, and a very snobbish attitude. But anyway, Wilson thought all the Labour voters would stay at home and watch *Steptoe* and not vote. His idea was for the programme to be on at half past nine, after the polling stations had closed. [. . .] Anyway, the BBC told him to get stuffed – in the nicest possible way, of course – but that's why I think Harold Wilson never liked the BBC from that point on.'

83 Harry H. Corbett, quoted by Galton and Simpson with Ross, *Steptoe and Son, op. cit.*, p.40.

84 Harry H. Corbett, *Written by Ray Galton & Alan Simpson, op. cit.*

85 Alan Simpson, quoted by Nathan, *The Laughtermakers, op. cit.,* pp.135–6.
86 Frank Muir, in a BBC 'Lunch-Time Lecture' delivered on 14 December 1966 and published subsequently in pamphlet form as *Comedy in Television* (London: BBC, 1966), pp.9–10 and 17.
87 Tom Sloan, in a BBC 'Lunch-Time Lecture' delivered on 11 December 1969 and published subsequently in pamphlet form as *Television Light Entertainment* (London: BBC, 1969), pp.10–11.
88 Alan Simpson, quoted by Nathan, *The Laughtermakers, op. cit.,* p.137.
89 Galton and Simpson with Ross, *Steptoe and Son, op. cit.,* p.231.

Till Death Us Do Part

1 Tom Sloan, *Television Light Entertainment, op. cit.,* p.11.
2 Frank Muir, *A Kentish Lad, op. cit.,* p.263.
3 Frank Muir and Denis Norden, 'The Engagement', transcribed in *The Glums* (Harmondsworth: Penguin, 1980), pp.64–65.
4 Johnny Speight, quoted by Nathan, *The Laughtermakers, op. cit.,* p.127.
5 Dennis Main Wilson, interviewed by Alan Lawson with Norman Swallow in 1991 for the BECTU History Project.
6 Johnny Speight, quoted by Nathan, *The Laughtermakers, op. cit.,* p.127.
7 He changed his surname to 'Mitchell' when standing in for Pete Murray as a DJ on Radio Luxembourg because the station controller felt that listeners would find 'Misell' too difficult to spell.
8 Anthony Booth, quoted by Robert Chalmers, 'Confessions of a Loose Cannon', *The Independent,* 4 December 2005, pp.13–19.
9 Anthony Booth, with Stephanie Booth, *What's Left?* (London: Phoenix, 2003), p.54.
10 *Ibid.,* p.102.
11 Dennis Main Wilson, interviewed by Alan Lawson with Norman Swallow for BECTU, *op. cit.*
12 *Ibid.*
13 Frank Muir, *A Kentish Lad, op. cit.,* pp.261–2.
14 Dennis Main Wilson, interviewed by Alan Lawson with Norman Swallow for BECTU, *op. cit.*
15 *Ibid.*
16 *Ibid.*
17 Frank Muir, *A Kentish Lad, op. cit.,* pp.262–3.
18 Script by Johnny Speight, transcribed from 'Arguments, Arguments', first broadcast on BBC1 on 6 June 1966.
19 *The Times,* 7 June 1966, p.14.
20 See *The Times,* 9 June 1966, p.14 and 10 June 1966, p.11.
21 *The Times,* 10 June 1966, p.11.
22 Script by Johnny Speight, transcribed from 'The Blood Donor', first broadcast on BBC1 on 12 January 1968.
23 Script by Johnny Speight, transcribed from 'Sex Before Marriage', first broadcast on BBC1 on 2 January 1967.
24 Script by Johnny Speight, transcribed from 'The Blood Donor', *op. cit.*

25 Script by Johnny Speight, transcribed from 'The Blood Donor', *op. cit.*
26 Script by Johnny Speight, transcribed from 'Sex Before Marriage', *op. cit.*
27 Script by Johnny Speight, transcribed from 'A Woman's Place is in the Home', first broadcast on BBC1 on 30 January 1967.
28 Script by Johnny Speight, transcribed from 'Two Toilets? . . . That's Posh', first broadcast on BBC1 on 4 July 1966.
29 T.C. Worsley, *Financial Times*, reproduced in Johnny Speight, *Till Death Us Do Part Scripts* (London: The Woburn Press, 1973), p.14.
30 Johnny Speight, interviewed by Bradbury and McGrath, *Now That's Funny!*, *op. cit.*, p.26.
31 Prince Philip, quoted by Johnny Speight, *For Richer, For Poorer, op. cit.*, p.145. (According to Speight [p.144], the Queen Mother told him that she regarded those who criticised the show as 'cranks'.)
32 See *The Times*, 28 July 1967, p.13.
33 Warren Mitchell, speaking on *Parkinson* in 1979 on BBC1; transcribed in Michael Parkinson, *The Best of Parkinson* (London: Pavilion, 1982), p.71.
34 Warren Mitchell, quoted by Golda Zafer-Smith, 'Warren Mitchell and Friends', *Jewish Renaissance*, Autumn 2003, pp.6–8.
35 Frank Muir, *A Kentish Lad, op. cit.*, p.264.
36 Warren Mitchell, in Johnny Speight, *Till Death Us Do Part Scripts, op. cit*, p.17.
37 Warren Mitchell, speaking on *Parkinson, op. cit.*, p.72.
38 Anthony Booth, with Stephanie Booth, *What's Left?, op. cit.*, p.133.
39 Tom Sloan, *Television Light Entertainment, op. cit.*, p.11.
40 See *The Times*, 16 February 1968, p.1.
41 *The Times*, 17 February 1968, p.9.
42 London *Evening Standard*, 21 February 1968; reproduced in Johnny Speight, *Till Death Us Do Part Scripts, op. cit.*, pp.14–15.
43 *The Stage*, 22 February 1968; *ibid.*
44 *The Observer*, 25 February 1968; *ibid.*
45 *Daily Mirror*, 8 August 1968; *ibid.*
46 See my 'Johnny Speight', *Dictionary of National Biography, op. cit.*, pp.780–1.
47 Johnny Speight, quoted by Nathan, *The Laughtermakers, op. cit.*, p.127.

Soldiers, Satire and Sci-Fi

1   The so-called 'Profumo Affair' was a political scandal named after the then Secretary of State for War, John Profumo. The scandal stemmed from his brief relationship with a showgirl named Christine Keeler. Profumo had met her at a party at Cliveden in 1961 organised by the London osteopath, Stephen Ward. Their relationship had lasted for only a few weeks, but rumours about the affair became public in 1962, as, more damagingly, did the fact that Keeler had also had a relationship with Yevgeny Ivanov, the senior naval attaché at the Soviet Embassy in London. Profumo's main error of judgement was to lie in the House of Commons: in March 1963, he claimed that there was 'no impropriety whatever' in his relationship with Keeler. In

June, however, he confessed that he had misled the House. He promptly resigned as a Cabinet minister, an MP and a Privy Councillor, and withdrew from public life. The Government received an official report on the incident from Lord Denning on 25 September 1963. A month later, the Conservative Prime Minister, Harold Macmillan, resigned, his ill-health exacerbated by the scandal; he was replaced by Sir Alec Douglas-Home. Stephen Ward was prosecuted for living on immoral earnings and committed suicide in August of the same year. Christine Keeler was found guilty on unrelated perjury charges and sentenced to nine months in prison.

2   Anon, 'Satire in the Age of Television', *The Times*, 15 December 1962, p.4.

3   Hugh Carleton Greene, 'Apologia Pro Vita Mea', *The Third Floor Front, op. cit.*, pp.133–4.

4   *Ibid.*, p.134.

5   Grace Wyndham Goldie, *Facing the Nation* (London: Bodley Head, 1977), p.231.

6   Greene, *The Third Floor Front, op. cit.*, pp.135.

7   Transcribed from *A Last Word on the Election*, written by Johnny Speight, Galton and Simpson et al., first broadcast on BBC1 on 18 October 1964.

8   Kenneth Williams, diary entry for 29 September 1964, *The Kenneth Williams Diaries* (London: HarperCollins, 1993), p.241.

9   Barry Took, interview with the author, 17 May 2000.

10 Barry Took and Marty Feldman, transcribed from *Round the Horne*, first broadcast on 20 February 1967 on the BBC's Light Programme (the soon-to-be renamed Radio 2).

11 Barry Took and Marty Feldman, transcribed from *Round the Horne*, first broadcast on 28 April 1968 on BBC Radio 2.

12 Barry Took and Marty Feldman, quoted by Took, *Round the Horne, op. cit.*, pp.18–19.

13 BBC WAC: *Daily Viewing Barometer*, 23 November 1963.

14 *Ibid.*, 30 November 1963.

15 Raymond P. Cusick, interviewed by Laurence Marcus and Stephen R. Hulse in 2001 for the website Television Heaven (http://www.televisionheaven.co.uk): 'The four Daleks,' he said, 'were made for something like £250.'

16 See *Daily Mail*, 12 December 1964, p.10.

17 Raymond P. Cusick, interviewed by Laurence Marcus and Stephen R. Hulse, *op. cit.*

18 *Radio Times*, 3 December 1964, p.9.

19 See *Daily Mail*, 12 December 1964, p.10.

20 *The Times*, 22 December 1965, p.11.

5. THE EXIT

Frontispiece dialogue: *The Life of Brian* (Handmade Films, 1979), screenplay by Graham Chapman, John Cleese, Terry Gilliam, Eric Idle, Terry Jones and Michael Palin.

The Legacy of ALS

1 Anon., 'New Race of Humanisers of Popular Comedy', *The Times*, 21 July 1962, p.4.

2 *Ibid.*

3 *Ibid.*

4 Beryl Vertue, interview with the author, 14 June 2005.

5 *Ibid.*

6 *Ibid.*

7 *Ibid.*

8 *Ibid.*

9 *Ibid.*

10 *Ibid.*

11 *Ibid.*

12 Galton and Simpson with Ross, *Steptoe and Son, op. cit.*, p.188.

13 See my *Dad's Army: The Story of a Classic Television Show* (London: Fourth Estate, 2001), pp.201–3.

14 Beryl Vertue, interview with the author, 14 June 2005.

15 See 'TV Groups Turn to Their Tasks', *The Times*, 13 June 1967, p.3.

16 Beryl Vertue, interview with the author, 14 June 2005.

17 *Ibid.*

18 *Ibid.*

19 *Ibid.*

20 *Ibid.*

21 Associated London Theatre was formed after the merger between ALS and RSO. One of the first productions it backed was the West End version of the musical *Hair*. See 'Business Diary', *The Times*, 21 August 1968, p.21.

22 Beryl Vertue, interview with the author, 14 June 2005.

23 For an excellent 'insider's' account of NEMS during this period, see Tony Bramwell, with Rosemary Kingsland, *Magical Mystery Tours: My Life with The Beatles* (London: Robson, 2005).

24 In a report in *The Times* on 1 February 1966 (page 10), David Shaw was said to have acknowledged that Davivil, a firm of which he was a director, had been connected with bond-washing. He had, as a consequence, resigned as a director from the City finance house Jessel Securities as well as from the board of all those companies associated with Jessel Securities.

25 Paul McCartney, quoted in Debbie Geller and Anthony Wall's *In My Life: The Brian Epstein Story* (New York: St Martin's Griffin, 2002), pp.153–4. Similarly, the Beatles' former press officer, Tony Barrow, would recall in his memoir *John, Paul, George, Ringo & Me* (London: André Deutsch, 2005: p.87), that Brian Epstein's decision to bring in Robert Stigwood as his co-managing director had not been well received: 'We were appalled by this move because neither The Beatles, nor Cilla Black, nor the NEMS staff had much time for Stigwood's business strategies.'

26 Beryl Vertue, interview with the author, 14 June 2005.

27 See *The Times*, 31 October 1967, p. 24. A statement from NEMS said that,

following Epstein's death, various policy agreements between him and Stigwood were 'not now practically possible' and so the board had agreed 'on the most amicable basis' to allow Stigwood and his associates to go their separate ways.

28 Beryl Vertue, interview with the author, 14 June 2005.
29 *Ibid.*
30 *Ibid.*
31 See *The Times*, 27 February 1968, p.8.
32 Farnes, *Spike, op. cit.*, p.66.
33 Eric Sykes, *If I Don't Write It, Nobody Else Will, op. cit.*, p.381.
34 *Ibid.*
35 *Ibid.*
36 Farnes, *Spike, op. cit.*, p.68.
37 *Ibid.*, p.217.
38 W. H. Auden, 'In Memory of Sigmund Freud', *Collected Poems*, ed. Edward Mendelson (London: Faber and Faber, 1976), p.275.
39 *When Comedy Changed Forever* was a stunningly obtuse documentary, first broadcast in Britain on BBC 3 on 7 March 2006, purporting to tell the story of British comedy from the seemingly arbitrary starting-point of the 1970s to the present day, showing how the work of Vic Reeves and Bob Mortimer, from the seminal first broadcast of *Vic Reeves' Big Night Out*, 'made possible' the journey from old-style acts such as Bernard Manning to contemporary phenomena like *Little Britain*.
40 Eddie Izzard, 'Foreword', in *The Essential Spike Milligan*, compiled by Alexander Games (London: Fourth Estate, 2002), pp.vii–viii.
41 John Cleese, quoted by Marshall Sella, *The New York Times Magazine*, 29 December 2002.
42 Sir Peter Hall, quoted on the website Guardian Unlimited: http://books.guardian.co.uk/reviews/artsandentertainment/0,, 1675607,00.html. The House of Commons tribute was made by the MP Nigel Evans in June 2004.
43 BBC Press Office release, December 2005: http://www.bbc.co.uk/pressoffice/pressreleases/stories/2005/11_november/22/christmas.pdf.
44 Paul Jackson, quoted in the *Daily Mirror*, 7 June 1998, p.9.
45 Beryl Vertue, interview with the author, 14 June 2005.

Index

Index